The Spirit of the Sixties

AMERICAN RADICALS
A SERIES EDITED BY HARVEY J. KAYE
AND ELLIOTT J. GORN

Also available in this Routledge series:

WILLIAM APPLEMAN WILLIAMS
The Tragedy of Empire
BY PAUL M. BUHLE AND EDWARD RICE-MAXIMIN

MICHAEL HARRINGTON
Speaking American
BY ROBERT A. GORMAN

THE SPIRIT OF THE SIXTIES

Making Postwar Radicalism

JAMES J. FARRELL

ROUTLEDGE
NEW YORK AND LONDON

Published in 1997 by

Routledge
29 West 35th Street
New York, NY 10001

Published in Great Britain by

Routledge
11 New Fetter Lane
London EC4P 4EE

Portions of Chapter Two appeared originally in "Thomas Merton and the Bomb" *Religion and American Culture* (January 1995): 77–98 and are reprinted with permission.

Library of Congress Cataloging-in-Publication Data is available upon request.

CONTENTS

PREFACE

THE SIXTIES ARE A COLLECTION OF STORIES, and some of the stories are mine. In May of 1967, I gave a commencement address at my small high school. The theme was "courage and commitment." I expressed my admiration for John Fitzgerald Kennedy and Pope John XXIII, two figures who seemed to personify new frontiers in politics and religion.

A little over two years later, I was different. I still believed in courage and commitment, and in politics and morality. But in the fall of 1969, I thought, courage and commitment required protest against the establishments of politics and religion. I wrote home to tell my parents that I would be participating in one of the Moratorium marches in Washington. My father replied that he would disown me if I did. I wrote back to explain why I was going, and I went.

Although he did not disown me, we never agreed on Vietnam. I had declared my conscientious objection. A veteran of D-Day and the Battle of the Bulge, my father said I was a chicken. I probably was. But I was also my father's son, and he had taught me to take religion seriously. I did. I took it both personally *and* politically, and that was the difference between us.

When my father died eight years later, I discovered my second letter in his bureau drawer. It was the only letter of mine that he had kept. I like to think that for him, as for me, it was a sign of my coming of age.

Among the stories of the Sixties were millions of encounters like mine, between fathers and sons, mothers and daughters, husbands and wives, politicians and citizens. Like my father and me, these people had the courage of their commitments. Like us, they fought over how to live responsibly in the world. *The Spirit of the Sixties* tells a few of those stories.

History is an essential part of "the call of stories." Robert Coles, who used the phrase as the title of a book, learned from his mentor William Carlos Williams that "an important part of our lives [is] spent listening to people tell you their stories; and in return, they will want to hear *your* story of what *their* story means." In the past few years, I have read many stories of the Sixties; this book is my story of what their stories mean to me. It is the story of the letter in the bureau drawer, the story of an almost forgotten tradition called personalist politics.[1]

Like Coles, I believe that "the whole point of stories is not 'solutions' or 'resolutions' but a broadening and even a heightening of our struggles— with new protagonists or antagonists introduced, with new sources of concern or apprehension or hope, as one's mental life accommodates itself to a series of arrivals, guests who have a way of staying, but not necessarily staying put."[2] The guests in this book are a particular set of protagonists of the Sixties, and the historians who have imaginatively interpreted their lives. All of their voices—both Sixties activists and historians of the Sixties—are essential to this book, which has become, in the process, a convocation of people making history.

Although I am exhausted, this book is by no means exhaustive. I have not tried to write about all of the Sixties; I have only unraveled the thread of personalist politics. The Sixties comprised a complex web of people and purposes, ideas and institutions, and I have dealt with a fairly small selection of them. Nor have I attempted any archival research; instead I have tried to read the published accounts of Sixties radicalism in a new light. I am certain that I have made many mistakes; I wish that I knew where they were. I do not see this book as the final word on the Sixties, or even the last word on political personalism. But I offer it as my contribution to a cultural conversation, and I welcome the corrections and encouragement that come in the community of citizens and scholars.

It is a personalist precept that persons are made in community. The same is true for books. This book represents a conversation of many communities, embodied in words and actions. For me, the conversation began a long time ago, when my parents introduced me to the community of readers. I grew up in overlapping communities of family and church and school, and I came, in the Sixties, to see how they connected to other communities in American culture. At the University of Illinois, Fred Jaher and Waldo Heinrichs welcomed me personally to the community of scholars. In the intervening years, I have benefited immensely, as I hope this book will show, from the community of scholars whose work has enriched mine.

At St. Olaf College, the community of scholars is also a community of friends. Both the Department of History and the Paracollege have put up with me and my ideas for years. The faculty and staff of the St. Olaf Library have been an invaluable resource for a reader and researcher. My students have been a constant source of energy and creativity. This year especially I have been guided by research assistants Sam Graber, Colette Cloutier, Siri Macgregor, and Erika Peterman. Finally, a generous grant to the college from O.C. and Patricia Boldt has given me time—that most precious of academic commodities—to reflect on what the Sixties teach us about what it means to be human in America.

But the sustaining community in my life is my family—Barb, my best friend for a quarter of a century, and my sons John and Paul. Barb encouraged me to consider college teaching at a time when I was doubtful, and she has provided constant support for me and my work. John and Paul have been patient with an old man they consider a relic of the Sixties, especially when I have monopolized the computer that we share. To the three of them, but to Barb especially, I wish to dedicate this book.

DISCOVERING SPIRIT IN THE SIXTIES

ONE OF THE MOST IMPORTANT DEVELOPMENTS of the American 1960s was the understanding that the personal is political. Activists in the civil rights, antiwar, and women's movements taught Americans that everyday life was an arena of politics and that everyday choices had political implications. They showed Americans how political participation changed not only policy, but also the participants.

But the personal became political in the 1960s because persons in preceding decades had created a philosophical and practical foundation for such activism. Among the spiritual progenitors of Sixties activism were Peter Maurin, Dorothy Day, Ammon Hennacy, Thomas Merton, Martin Luther King Jr., Bayard Rustin, Kenneth Rexroth, Allen Ginsberg, Lawrence Ferlinghetti, Gary Snyder, A.J. Muste, Paul Goodman, Barbara Deming, and David Dellinger. These people practiced a politics of personalism that became the defining spirit of the Sixties.

Especially in the civil rights and ban-the-bomb movements, activists practiced a personalist politics that flourished in America between 1955 and 1965 and furnished an important but ignored foundation for Sixties protest. Challenging the dominant "ideology of liberal consensus," they popularized a new style of dissent, and created a "usable past" for younger activists of the 1960s. While the New Left and the counterculture generally rejected identification with the Old Left, they adopted a great deal of the personalist politics of the late Fifties and early Sixties.[1]

The Spirit of the Sixties tells how the personal became political and vice versa.

Political Personalism

Political personalism was an eclectic integration of radical traditions in American history. The personalism of the 1960s was a combination of Catholic social thought, communitarian anarchism, radical pacifism, and humanistic psychology. It was a way of looking at, and looking out for, the world. Too unorganized to be a philosophy or an ideology, political personalism was more a creed than a catechism, more a perspective than a particular position.

Although there were extraordinary variations, personalist politics generally operated on the following assumptions:

1) Political personalism stressed the inviolable dignity of persons, which was not the same as the rights of individuals. For some personalists, the dignity of human beings was God-given; for others, it was just a given. But if people were created in God's image, as religious personalists believed, then other people were obligated to treat them well. In many ways, then, the genesis of Sixties protest was Genesis.[2]

2) Personalism focused especially on poor and marginal persons, using their condition as an index of the health and justice of society. In a personalist perspective, poor people were a sure sign of an impoverished society. "An edifice that produces beggars," said Martin Luther King Jr., "needs restructuring." Political personalists fought for equality, for the full inclusion of the despised and dispossessed into society.[3]

3) Political personalism was suspicious of systems, including the market economy and the state, because they were not ultimately focused on the dignity of persons. Personalists were suspicious of the market economy because they did not believe in *homo economicus*, who feels no obligation to others. They decried the depersonalization of people in the impersonal factories and bureaucracies of the modern economy. And they refused to countenance the injustices that the market accepted as normal. Personalists were suspicious of the state in part because they feared the corruptions of power, and in part because the habit of looking to the state for solutions to social problems excused

individuals who could be doing something here and now. Therefore, they questioned the statist voice of postwar political discourse, and spoke instead in what Robert Karl Manoff calls the "civil voice."[4]

4) Personalists believed in "the revolution of the heart" and "the here and now revolution" that came from the personal practice of moral beliefs. Political personalists did not think that the revolution was optional; instead they saw it as an essential obligation of vocation and of citizenship. They believed, as the Greeks did, that the purely private life is deprived. Rejecting important assumptions of liberal individualism, they thought that people were created for and constituted in community, and were morally responsible for each other. Religious personalists understood vocation, not just as a job, but as a call to help create the Kingdom of God on Earth. And they understood citizenship not just as residency in a country, but as an active collaboration for the common good.

5) Personalists believed that changes in consciousness and changes in "conscience-ness" could bring social change. They hoped to convert moribund individuals to moral action. They hoped to make Americans more "person-able"—not more friendly, but able to perceive and preserve the personhood of their neighbors. Because they believed in "the revolution of the heart" and the personal practice of moral beliefs, they did not depend on specific groups in society—the proletariat, for example—in their theory of social change. They were able to identify many possible agents of change—racial or religious minorities, young people, workers, women, intellectuals—because they believed that an appeal to the heart could be efficacious.

6) Personalists did not stop, as many American reform movements have, with an emphasis on the conversion of the individual: they understood the importance of institutions, and they acted politically for social and structural changes. Assuming that the institutions of a community created and converted individuals, they took political action to affect law and policy and to create structures of justice, which they saw as love in action. As Bayard Rustin said after serving a prison term for draft refusal, "I came out of prison realizing that talking to individuals about being good is a pile of crap. You've got to have social organization which helps people bring out the goodness in them, not one that brutalizes them."[5]

7) Political personalists believed that people in community could govern themselves and their needs to reduce the conflicts caused by competitive individualism, laissez-faire capitalism, and corporate liberalism. As believers in literal self-government, they were often anarchists advocating not disorder, but less coercive and competitive forms of

order. Preferring the voluntarism of free people to the coercions of the state, they wanted to strengthen local institutions more than the national government. They believed that conscientious individuals could create a new world in the shell of the old, a world in which it would be easier to be good. Throughout the 1960s, therefore, personalists created parallel institutions to serve whole persons better than the established institutions could. The prefigurative politics of this "here and now revolution" was a hallmark of American personalism.[6]

8) Assuming the essential harmony of personal and political life, political personalists assumed that everyday values—especially religious and household values like compassion and cooperation—could and should be applied to politics. Rejecting the "Christian realism" that created "separate spheres" of ethics for individuals and corporate entities, they embraced the values which women had nurtured in the "separate spheres" of the American cult of domesticity. In many ways, the political personalism of the postwar era was a lot like the "domestic feminism" of the turn of the century in its attempts to apply "women's values" to the public sphere.

9) Political personalists believed in the harmony of rhetoric and reality. They believed that language was communal, and that the purpose of words was to tell the truth. Hypocrisy, in the Sixties, was one of the cardinal sins, and political personalists regularly called the American authorities to account for their rhetoric. The "credibility gap" which developed during the decade was, to political personalists, a violation of the linguistic social contract that bound people to each other, and a violation of democratic theory, which assumes that citizens need to be informed to act wisely.

10) Political personalists also believed in the harmony of means and ends. "The more violence," they said, "the less revolution." They believed that the beloved community would be the product of a process of love. Consequently, in their organizations and actions, they tried to practice the cooperative virtues that they hoped would characterize a future society.

Francis Sicius suggests that personalism flourished in the United States because it embraced "the heart of the American intellectual tradition." While many American activists viewed "individuals pessimistically, history materialistically, and political action collectively," personalists drew on an American intellectual tradition that was more optimistic, spiritual, and personal. Personalists often worked with American liberals and Leftists, but they worked from different premises.[7]

While postwar American liberalism accepted American individualism, focusing on freeing individuals from constraints, personalists believed that people were freed from community and social obligations. Postwar liberals presumed the benefits of capitalism and promoted economic growth as the path to prosperity and social justice, but personalists often thought that capitalism capitalized on the poor, and that consumerism was a false god. Postwar liberals accepted representative democracy and procedural equality; by contrast, personalists tended more toward participatory democracy and substantive equality. Liberals in the Democratic Party generally accepted the racism and segregation of the South, but personalists condemned this degradation of persons. While liberals promoted ideas of pluralism and the broker state, personalists thought that some groups were not well represented by the moneyed interest groups with access to power. In keeping with scientific and business trends of the twentieth century, liberals accepted managerial models of expertise and hierarchy. Personalists, on the other hand, wanted people to have resources to solve their own problems. New Deal liberals accepted the centralization and power of the state; personalists preferred decentralized forms of communitarian anarchism. Liberals were fully committed to the Cold War, and to the militarism needed to protect the Free World from Communism; personalists were often pacifists, and sometimes anti-anti-communists.

But if personalists were not liberals, neither were they conventional Leftists. Although many of the first generation of personalists had connections to the Old Left (Dorothy Day and David Dellinger were socialists; A.J. Muste had been a Trotskyist; Bayard Rustin a Communist), they had severed their connections before World War II. The Old Left built on the rock of scientific materialism, but postwar personalists preferred the sands of spiritual idealism. Because of the Depression, the Old Left focused on economic issues; postwar affluence permitted a personalist concern for cultural issues and for quality of life. While the Old Left organized for collective action, personalists often dis-organized for voluntary action. The socialist tradition emphasized national ownership and administrative centralization, but the personalists preferred decentralized sharing. The Old Left placed its faith in labor and the industrial proletariat; personalists placed their faith in persons, whatever their place. While the Old Left was relentlessly secular, personalist radicalism was often rooted in religion.

Few American activists of the postwar world used the word personalism, but many of them used the language of political personalism. Dorothy Day, Peter Maurin, A.J. Muste, David Dellinger, Staughton Lynd, Paul Goodman, Barbara Deming, Kenneth Rexroth, Martin Luther King Jr., Bayard Rustin, and Abbie Hoffman all had firsthand experience with personalism. But other activists like SNCC's (Student Nonviolent Coordinating Committee) Robert Moses, SDS's (Students for a Democratic Society)

Tom and Casey Hayden, FSM's (Free Speech Movement) Mario Savio and CALCAV's (Clergy and Laity Concerned About Vietnam) Robert McAfee Brown also spoke in the civil voice of personalism.

In this book, personalism serves as a conceptual tool for understanding clusters of ideas and actions that recurred in many radical movements of the postwar period. It is a concept that collects and connects the various movements of the Sixties, making *The Spirit of the Sixties*, I hope, a spirited study of people who had "virtually nothing in common save one thing: a desire, in post-World War II America, to posit newly imagined notions of personhood as alternatives to an increasingly immense and totally rationalized technology of cultural depersonalization."[8]

Paths to Personalism

The paths to political personalism proceeded, in part, through philosophy. Although the word was first used by Walt Whitman in 1868, it received its greatest development in several parallel philosophical traditions.[9]

Two branches of philosophical personalism influenced American radicals in the twentieth century. The first, realistic personalism, was a variation of traditional metaphysical realism, and was most attractive to theists who understood ultimate reality as a spiritual, supernatural being. Emmanuel Mounier, editor of the journal *Esprit* from 1932 until his death in 1950, served as synthesizer for the movement, which originated in conversations among such intellectuals as Jacques Maritain, Gabriel Marcel, Nicolai Berdyaev, Jean Danielou, and Jacques Madaule.

According to John Hellman, this French version of personalism started in the early 1930s as "a movement of defence against two antithetical threats: individualism and its manifestation, liberal capitalism, and communalism and its manifestation, communism. It mirrored the desperate efforts of intellectuals in the 1930s to navigate a 'third way' between capitalism and communism." Emphasizing spiritual and communitarian dimensions of human personhood, it countered the more secular and economic ideologies of the era. Deeply rooted in religion, personalism considered Christianity "the most radical of counter-cultures" and tried to bring the spirit of radical Christianity into contemporary politics and society.[10]

Theistic personalists believed that people were created in the image of God, and endowed by their creator with purposes in the process of creation. Persons were not subservient to the political community; they were ends in themselves, and the preservation and growth of whole persons was the central purpose of the political community. Created and called by God, persons acted for God in the world. Understanding themselves and others as parts of a common creation coordinated by the natural law, they felt responsible for the larger community. Although Mounier and others trusted deeply in the transformative power of God's love, they also worked for political transformations.[11]

Personalists distinguished between the socially constituted person and the atomistic individual. While individuals might be satisfied with the material goods of capitalism or communism, the person could be fulfilled only by the combination of material security with spiritual and communitarian life. Opposed to modern liberalism, the French personalists espoused an organic collectivism that Mounier expressed often in terms of the Mystical Body of Christ, with its implication that contemporary communities could embody and enact the spirit of Christianity.[12]

This communitarian spirituality was one of the most distinctive aspects of personalism. Contending that persons could only be fulfilled in communities—communities that were threatened by capitalism and communism—the personalists emphasized "the collective vocation of the Christian." The person, said Mounier, "finds himself in forgetting, in giving himself," not just to a transcendent God, but to the people of God's creation. Following Jesus, who said that what you do to the least of these, you do to me, the personalists expected to find God in both mystical and ministering experiences.[13]

Personalism offered a modern anti-modernism against the "established disorder" of rationalism, scientism, and dehumanizing industrialism. Mounier's journal *Esprit*'s prospectus counterpoised the strength of the spirit "against the usurpations of matter and the dissolution of the person." Berdyaev had argued, in 1927, for a "New Middle Ages," in which religion would transcend the private sphere, and become a catalyst for social action and cohesion. And French personalists agreed that religious renewal would be the base of political reform.[14]

Emmanuel Mounier was a devout Catholic devoted to overcoming the antipathy between the Church and left-wing activists. He wanted "to marry black France with red France, the priests with the Jacobins, and create a transcendent synthesis." Personalism provided Mounier's proposal for the marriage. Personalism would reinvigorate religion by bringing a sterile bourgeois spirituality into contact with rebellions against the structural injustice of the modern world: Mounier claimed that "one cannot be totally Christian, today . . . without being a rebel." Personalism would reinvigorate activism by providing a spiritual foundation for its social concerns, by curbing its impersonal collectivism, and by providing—in its emphasis on multidimensional persons—a criterion for evaluation. Mounier thought that revolutions "should be made for people, and not for abstractions and parties." Personalism would reinvigorate a spiritually dead middle class by its emphasis on asceticism, aesthetics, and ethics.[15]

Although Mounier was never a Marxist—he considered the atheism and collective discipline of communism a threat to the person—he appreciated the young Marx, and attacked the dehumanization and alienations of capitalism. And he admired many aspects of Marxism: "If you think that the human personality is something sacred," Mounier argued, "you shall begin by destroying what oppresses that personality. Marxism can be summarized this way."[16]

Esprit attracted solid intellectual support during the Thirties for its synthesis of Bergsonian spirituality, Nietzchean heroism, and Catholic anti-individualism and anti-liberalism. Banned by the Vichy government between 1941 and 1944, *Esprit* was even more influential after World War II, when it served as part of a broadening of the Left in French Catholicism that included worker priests, Christian progressives, and people attracted to Pierre Teilhard de Chardin's teleological prophecies.[17]

French personalism was never a programmatic movement, unless the program were inconsistency or paradox. Moreover, there were many changes in the politics of personalism—from religious renewal to Vichy to the Resistance to postwar Leftism. Although personalism was deeply rooted in the spiritual traditions of Western religion, and especially Catholicism, Mounier eventually claimed that it derived from humanist socialism, and Left-Catholic precursors like Le Sillon and Marc Sangnier. Still, the main tenets of the personalist perspective remained identifiable. And the paradoxes and peregrinations of personalism offered plenty of material for American activists, who appropriated the term in a drastically different political and cultural context.[18]

French personalism came to America with the French-born Peter Maurin, one of the founders of the Catholic Worker movement. Rooted in the same religious and social traditions that inspired Mounier, Peter Maurin was practicing and preaching ideas that Mounier would later call personalist. Maurin deepened his own practice by contact with French personalism and, with Dorothy Day, he imported the language and ideas of French personalism into American radicalism. Maurin arranged for the first English publication of Mounier's *Personalist Manifesto*, and for continuing contacts with personalists like Jacques Maritain. "In Europe," according to Francis Sicius, "personalism has become an abstraction, relegated to philosophical journals and conferences; in America it flourishes on the streets in the form of Catholic activism."[19]

The second strain of philosophical personalism, personal idealism, developed more in America. According to John H. Lavely, "it is idealistic: all reality is personal. It is pluralistic: reality is a society of persons. It is theistic: God is the ultimate person and, as such, is the ground of all being and the creator of finite persons." This philosophy of personal idealism was developed by Borden Parker Bowne and several generations of Methodists at Boston University. In response to "the failure of impersonalism," Bowne argued for a philosophy that held that truth is of, by, and for persons.[20]

Bowne's student Edgar Brightman developed a comprehensive personalist philosophy, which was one of the main attractions of Boston University for Martin Luther King Jr. Brightman and his Boston colleagues argued that "the person is the ontological ultimate" and that "personality is the fundamental explanatory principle." They believed that people are, by nature, social, and that they grow as persons-in-community. Personalists believed in both human freedom and human purpose, and they used the discipline of ethics to negotiate the relationship between the two. Early in the century, Bowne contended that "abstract ethics is good as far as it goes." But he insisted that "morals must be vitalized by being brought into connection with our everyday human life in the world that now is."[21]

In that spirit, Brightman's *Moral Laws* (1933) tried to develop a social ethics of personalism, articulating eleven "laws." Eight of the laws were logical and axiological; the last three were "personalistic laws." The Law of Individualism suggested that "each person ought to realize in his or her own experience the maximum value of which he or she is capable in harmony with moral law." According to the Law of Altruism, "each person ought to treat all other persons as ends in themselves and, as far as possible, cooperate with others in the production and enjoyment of shared values." And the Law of the Ideal of Personality required that "all persons ought to judge and guide all of their acts by their ideal conception (in harmony with the other Laws) of what the whole personality ought to become both individually and socially."[22]

Brightman—a democratic socialist who supported conscientious objection during World War II—died shortly after Martin Luther King Jr. arrived at Boston University, and King completed most of his work with Brightman's student and successor Harold DeWolf, who added a set of communitarian laws to Brightman's formulation. These laws, which DeWolf thought were implicit in Brightman's, were the Law of Cooperation, the Law of Social Devotion, and the Law of the Ideal of Community. The first called for human cooperation; the second said that people should "subordinate personal gain to social gain," and the third argued that people should choose values consistent with their ideals "of what the whole community ought to become," and should "participate responsibly in groups to help them similarly choose and form all their ideals and choices." DeWolf thought that these moral laws were consistent with both the natural law and the New Testament.[23]

These two traditions of philosophical personalism did not contain all of the personalist ideas and perspectives that influenced American radicalism.

There were also English personalists who influenced people like Kenneth Rexroth. Nor did American radicals derive all of their personalism from philosophy. Some of it was religious; some was anarchist; some was simply common sense. But philosophical personalism provides a context for a fuller understanding of the radical texts of the 1960s.

A Personalist Perspective and the Spirit of the Sixties

Between 1933 and the Sixties, but especially between 1955 and 1965, a diverse group of Americans applied personalist ideas and ideals to the politics of the civil rights and ban-the-bomb movements, and to early incarnations of the counterculture and the student movements. They extended their innovative activism into the 1960s, where it was imitated by a younger generation of American radicals. *The Spirit of the Sixties* examines postwar radicalism against this personalist backdrop.

Chapter Two, "Catholic Worker Personalism," discusses the development of personalist perspectives in the Catholic Worker movement and traces the roots of personalism in the biographies of founders Dorothy Day and Peter Maurin. It reveals how personalism unified spirituality and social action, and how the Catholic Workers institutionalized the precepts of personalism in their newspaper, in houses of hospitality, in conversational roundtables, and in rural communes. The chapter examines the development of personalist pacifism, both in the Catholic Worker movement and in the writings of Thomas Merton, whose popularity helped introduce personalist perspectives to a wider audience. It also begins an exploration of the communitarian anarchism that distinguished personalists from the liberals and socialists of the postwar United States.

Chapter Three, "The Beat of Personalism," focuses on the American development of a second strain of personalism in the Beat movement. It explores how poet and critic Kenneth Rexroth integrated French and English personalist perspectives with the anarcho-pacifism of the West Coast "little magazines," and it shows Rexroth's influence on the poets of the Beat movement. Focusing on the poetry of Allen Ginsberg, Gary Snyder, and Lawrence Ferlinghetti, the chapter emphasizes the religious and ethical aspects of the Beat movement, and the embodiment of personalist perspectives in their writing. It concludes with a brief discussion of Beat and personalist themes in the popular folk music revival of the late Fifties and early Sixties.

Chapter Four, "Civil Rights Personalism," stresses the personalist perspectives of Martin Luther King Jr., who studied with the philosophical personalists of Boston University. It shows how personalism reinforced the teachings of the African-American churches, and how King integrated these perspectives with Gandhian nonviolence in a catalytic American synthesis. The chapter also emphasizes King's pacifism and his connections—especially through Bayard Rustin—to the East Coast radical pacifists connected with *Liberation* magazine. Finally, the chapter examines the religious and existential personalism of the Student Nonviolent Coordinating Committee (SNCC), which influenced so many student activists of the early 1960s.

Until his death in 1967, the most important antiwar activist of the 1960s was A.J. Muste, who was 74 years old at the beginning of the decade. Chapter Five, "Liberated Personalism," examines the personalist perspectives of Muste and the people who published *Liberation* magazine and organized the ban-the-bomb protests of the late Fifties and early Sixties. It describes the beliefs and behavior of the intellectuals—Muste, David Dellinger, Paul Goodman, Staughton Lynd, Barbara Deming—who taught a younger generation the meanings and methods of social protest. It shows how these people practiced their personalism in the projects of the Committee for Nonviolent Action (CNVA). It also describes the personalism of a proto-feminist group, Women Strike for Peace (WSP), which—influenced by CNVA and the Committee for a Sane Nuclear Policy (SANE)—sought to liberate womanhood from the home and make it political, first in the antinuclear movement, and later in the antiwar movement of the 1960s.

Chapter Six examines the personalist presumptions of the student movements of the Sixties. "Student Personalism" examines the intellectual roots of Students for a Democratic Society (SDS), and shows how the students synthesized diverse influences into a perspective that was implicitly, if not explicitly, personalist. It explains how this personalist perspective affected SDS strategy, especially in the Economic Research and Action Projects (ERAP) of the mid-Sixties. The chapter also focuses on the personalist components of campus politics, from the Free Speech Movement of 1964 to the free universities of the later Sixties.

Chapter Seven, "The Vietnamization of Personalism," looks at the Vietnam wars, especially the war at home, from a personalist perspective. It shows the personalist roots of the early antiwar movement, and of the conscientious objections and draft resistance that followed. It also suggests the limitations of political personalism, and examines how and why the leaders of the antiwar movement substituted Marxist perspectives later in the decade. Although personalist politics still animated many protesters of the late Sixties, the leadership devolved into dogmatic struggles that destroyed SDS, if not the antiwar and student movements.

Chapter Eight, "Countercultural Personalism," suggests that the countercultural drop-outs of the late Sixties continued and developed the personalist politics that had been subsumed on the protest scene. Inspired by the personalist presumptions of humanistic psychology, countercultural activists criticized the depersonalized life of mainstream culture and offered alternatives that promised to create a new world in the shell of the old.

An "Epilogue" suggests that political personalism did not perish with SDS or the antiwar movement, but persisted in the women's movement, the environmental crusade, and antinuclear activism. The first history of the 1970s was called *It Seemed Like Nothing Happened*, but this study suggests that, in fact, something—and something lasting—did happen. While a "Reagan revolution" dominated the national agenda and national press of the 1980s, a personalist resolution continued to inspire dissent.

Personalism and the History of the Sixties

I have not tried to treat the Sixties in all of their complexity, but rather to explicate the decade with a personalist perspective. I have explored a single strand that wove diverse threads of the Sixties into a single fabric. While a personalist perspective on the Sixties cannot explain everything, it offers advantages that other explanations do not.

1) Most importantly, a personalist perspective defines and displays the common elements of many different movements within "the Movement." Most of the monographic studies of the Sixties have focused on specific movements or specific events. They give us remarkable depth and richness, but they obscure the ways in which both people and passions and ideas and practices, moved among movements. The concept of personalism helps us to remember that radical pacifists were not only pacifists, that civil rights workers were not simply interested in race, that student activists were not just involved at the universities. Personalism gave people in the Sixties a common language, which was intellectually deeper and more significant than even many activists knew. The Movement was built on a rich philosophical foundation, which sometimes got lost in the activity of the decade.

2) Because personalism roots Sixties radicalism in the Fifties, a personalist perspective permits consideration of continuities that are too often obscured by an emphasis on the Sixties as a "revolutionary" decade. It is important to remember that, at least chronologically, the Fifties and the Sixties were only a day apart. Even in the antiwar movement, the two most important leaders of the Sixties were not Abbie Hoffman and Jerry Rubin, but A.J. Muste and David Dellinger—veteran political personalists. Nor was the New Left really new in the early 1960s. Rather, the New Left formulated its ideas and actions on a complex

foundation of old ideas that had been preserved in the "free spaces" of the Catholic Worker, the Beat movement, the civil rights movement, little magazines like *Politics* and *Liberation*, and the activism of the Committee for Nonviolent Action and Women Strike for Peace.[24]

At the other end of the decade also, historians tend to conclude the Sixties without attending to continuities. It is relatively easy to choose some event (Kent State, Altamont, Watergate, and the fall of Saigon are favorites) as the end of the Sixties, and to see the Seventies and the Eighties as a period of reaction. While there is substantial truth to this interpretation, it depends largely on the identification of Sixties radicalism with mass movements of protest. The massive protests did end, but not the personalism that prompted them. A personalist perspective permits us to see how the spirit of the Sixties survived the death of its body politic in the "backyard revolutions" of the 1970s and 1980s.

3) A personalist perspective also permits a better understanding of postwar radicalism, especially the radicalism of the Fifties. For too long, the Fifties have been the "happy days" of popular culture and the "unhappy daze" of historians. The concept of personalism, however, clarifies the character of radicalism in what is usually seen as a quiescent decade. Personalism, for example, makes sense of traditions that don't fit on the usual Left/Right continuum. Highlighting communitarian anarchism, for example, a personalist perspective illuminates a rich tradition in American radicalism that was neither Right nor Left. More than other political perspectives, personalism elucidates recurrent radical complaints about alienation and apathy, about bureaucracies and corporate structure, and about the commodification of people in a conformist consumer society. It explains the small-scale counterinstitutions that responded to people's yearning for community. And it clarifies the ways in which anarcho-pacifist roots tangled with the Left-socialist tradition in the 1960s.

By emphasizing traditions like communitarian anarchism, a personalist approach also explains the *cultural* politics of the Sixties. While most American social movements have focused on changing policy, Sixties radicals wanted to change both the culture of politics and the politics of culture. They did not believe that purely political solutions—like legislation—were adequate for deeply rooted cultural problems. Their "here-and-now revolution," therefore, emphasized the prefigurative politics of personalism as much as—or more than—conventional electoral politics.

4) A personalist perspective also re-emphasizes the autonomy and importance of the early Sixties. Too often, we read the early Sixties only through the spectacles of the late Sixties. In part, of course, this is

what history is for. But history also asks us to respect the contingency of the times. The personalists of the early Sixties could not act, for example, in terms of 1968 or 1969; they were trying to shape the society of 1968 and 1969, but they didn't know how their work would turn out. Personalism helps us to see the Sixties—especially the early Sixties—the way that participants did at the time.

5) A personalist perspective also allows us to see the conservative—and especially the religious—roots of much postwar radicalism. Most historians of the decade have chosen interpretive frameworks which slight the role of religion as a motivator and mobilizer of activists. But in the Sixties, religion both affected and reflected the extraordinary activism of the decade. Faith, the preachers said, could move mountains; faith certainly moved many of the people who made the movements of the Sixties. Sometimes their faith was in God; sometimes radicals were "Christian atheists" or "Jewish agnostics"; sometimes they placed their faith in an American secular humanism derived from the major religious traditions. Whatever their religious commitments, however, the radicals of the Sixties affected what one scholar has called "the restructuring of American religion"; it was part of what another scholar labels "the Sixties spiritual awakening."[25]

Indeed, I would like to suggest that Sixties radicalism was substantially spiritual. When we think of the decade, we should focus not only on the Marxist radicalism of the late Sixties, but on the religious radicalism that preceded it; not on the newness of the New Left but on the old-ness of its cultural origins; not on revolution for the hell of it but on revolution for the heaven of it; not on the violent revolution that didn't happen but on the nonviolent revolution that did. To think about the Sixties not just as a political Movement but as many connected movements of the spirit, however, it is necessary to recall the original meaning of the word "religion." At its most radical—at its root—the word religion means connectedness. From the Latin verb "religare," it means "to bind together," and it is meant to bind people to God, to other people, and to God's creation.

Many of the movements for social justice in the Sixties drew support not because they were radically new, but because they were radically old, steeped in the rich "second languages" of American religion and republicanism. People didn't move left in the Sixties just because of compelling intellectual analysis of social problems; they moved left partly because people like Martin Luther King Jr. and Dorothy Day and A.J. Muste appropriated the religious language of the churches and the democratic language of the civil society—including language about the sacredness of persons—and articulated its radical implications.

6) Finally, a personalist perspective on the politics of the 1960s can illu-

minate our own times. Interpretations of the 1960s are an essential part of the politics of the 1990s. While I hope that *The Spirit of the Sixties* contributes to academic discourse, I also expect it to be a part of the contemporary cultural conversation about the decade. This personalist perspective on the uprisings of the 1960s challenges the neo-conservative popular orthodoxy of the Sixties. That orthodoxy insists that the Sixties were the cultural crossroads when America turned the wrong way. Inspired by the radical Left and the counterculture, the story goes, the country embraced Big Government, the welfare mess, the Vietnam syndrome, rock music, free love, psychedelic drugs, undisciplined education, affirmative action, multiculturalism, cultural relativism, secular humanism, feminism, homosexuality, and the Devil, all at once. Such an interpretation involves considerable deceit and distortion. But, reinforced by the simplistic images of the Sixties that appear in movies and on television, it colors our understanding of our cultural and political heritage.

The neoconservative orthodoxy asks us to see the Sixties as a revolt against American values. But, in fact, it was a revolt against some American values in the name of other American values. "The New Left's goals," noted Lyman Sargent, derived mainly "from the stated values of Western civilization—liberty, equality, justice, peace—which are everywhere dishonored." It was not, despite all the rhetoric of both critics and activists, an un-American activity. This study emphasizes many of the continuities of Sixties activism—with democratic and republican traditions, with Romantic reform and American anti-modernism, with the Social Gospel and Catholic social teaching, with Bohemian radicalism and the anarcho-pacifist tradition, and with some essential elements of the Old Left. Against the "first language" of American individualism, Sixties radicals often spoke a "second language" of communitarian subjectivism that called Americans not to negative protests, but to positive social change. The neoconservative orthodoxy has taken as truth Spiro Agnew's charge that protesters were "nattering nabobs of negativism." The politics of personalism did say "No" to many American values, but it was, as David Pichaske has suggested, an "affirmative no." Like the explicit "negativism" of Dwight Macdonald, the personalists said "No" to some things because they said "Yes" to others. As Macdonald said, "It is precisely because we believe in the possibility of large-scale progress that we react so violently to the imperfections of the present." And the utopianism, the counter-institutions, and the value structure of Sixties personalist politics all offered constructive alternatives to mainstream ideology and institutions. This book, then, unearths the personal and political roots of the "affirmative no" of Sixties radicalism.[26]

2

Catholic Worker Personalism

The Sixties arguably began not on the first of January, but on the 15th of June in 1955. On that day, a small group of activists protested the nationwide Operation Alert civil defense drill. A three-day exercise designed to test the ability of the United States to function under atomic attack, the drill began with "raids" on Washington and fifty-four other American cities that "killed" eight million people and "injured" seven million. President Eisenhower and other officials evacuated the capitol to perform essential governmental functions at relocation sites, while millions of other Americans also practiced their part in nuclear war: they hid in shelters. But in New York City, twenty-eight friends from the Catholic Worker movement, the Fellowship of Reconciliation, and the War Resisters League remained aboveground in City Hall Park protesting the policy that prepared people for nuclear holocaust.

Inspired by Ammon Hennacy, whose self-proclaimed "One-Man Revolution" was a precursor of Sixties activism, Dorothy Day and her Catholic Worker colleagues had decided to protest the civil defense drill as a penance for Hiroshima and the hydrogen bomb, as a demonstration of the futility of defense in the nuclear age, as a sign of noncooperation with the prevailing Cold War mentality, and as an example of Christian witness. As was customary, they notified the authorities and the press of their action; Hennacy even notified the FBI and added a personal note for J. Edgar Hoover: "We are, as you know, subversives, though no more than always."[1]

The response to the civil defense protest showed how pacifists were understood at a time when peace was an epithet often associated with communism. Twenty-eight activists were arrested and charged with violating the New York State Defense Emergency Act of 1951, which mandated participation in drills. Echoing the Rosenberg trial, the judge reproached the pacifists, calling them "murderers of the 3,000,000 people 'killed' by the hypothetical H-Bomb dropped on New York." But they were not jailed because he did not want to "make martyrs of them."[2]

The arrests and trial, however, did not deter recidivism, as the activists made the protest an annual event. In 1956, Hennacy, Day, and others refused to participate again, and were sentenced to five days in jail; in 1957, they got thirty days. In 1957, when the judge told Hennacy that he should "render therefore to Caesar the things that are Caesar's and unto God the things that are God's," Hennacy responded that too many modern people rendered too much to Caesar and not enough to God. When the judge called Hennacy an anarchist and bomb thrower, Hennacy (who *was* an anarchist) reminded him that the "government is the biggest bomb thrower of all." In 1960, Norman Mailer, Dwight Macdonald, and Nat Hentoff joined 1,000 protesters, singing the civil rights anthem "We Shall Overcome" as the police ordered them to take shelter. The following year, more than 2,000 gathered in City Hall Park. After that, there were no more drills. After that, there were the Sixties.[3]

The 1955 civil defense protests brought the pacifist politics of the Catholic Worker movement to public view, and inspired activists in the early Sixties. The pacifism derived from a more comprehensive personalism that had developed in the Catholic Worker movement, which was the first American community to integrate and institutionalize personalist assumptions, ethics, and political activism. Beginning in 1933 in the Catholic Worker movement, Peter Maurin and Dorothy Day had interpreted the Christian gospels, Catholic social thought, and European social philosophers for modern American life. Catholic Worker personalism asserted the absolute primacy of the human person, and decried violence to persons in modern institutions, including war, the nation-state, and both Marxist and capitalist economies.[4]

Against the "practical" reformism of the New Deal, and the "practical" radicalism of the secular Left, the Catholic Workers juxtaposed the sociology of St. Francis of Assisi. Acting like Third Order Franciscans, they offered a "third way" between capitalism and communism, between radical individualism and collectivist radicalism. Catholic Worker personalism emphasized the primacy of the person in social change. Although they were lay people, they assumed that their vocation was ministry. Inspired by the beatitudes of the Sermon on the Mount, they tried to follow Christ's example in ministering to the poor and the outcasts of American society. Responding to the prayer "thy kingdom come, thy will be done," they tried to embody the kingdom of God in New York. Commemorating the triumphant Christ of the cross, they celebrated the revolutionary potential of individual sacrifice. As Dwight Macdonald suggested, they were "religious in a way that is hard for most people to understand. . . . They practice their faith on Mondays, Tuesdays, Wednesdays, Thursdays, Fridays, and Saturdays, as well as on Sundays."[5]

By the 1960s, the Catholic Worker movement was an established facet of American radicalism, providing an example of social and political involvement for people who would challenge the dominant assumptions of their society. The story of the Catholic Worker movement, therefore, is a necessary prelude to any comprehensive analysis of the 1960s. After describing the religious and political pilgrimages of the Worker's founders, Dorothy Day and Peter Maurin, this chapter examines the Catholic Worker synthesis of personalist politics, and its expression in the postwar writings of Thomas Merton.

Dorothy Day

Dorothy Day converted to Catholicism in December 1927 and to personalism in the 1930s, but her personalist politics had strong connections to her earlier life in the radical Left. Born in 1897, Dorothy came of age in Chicago, where she encountered the destitution that came from the institutions of the new industrial capitalism. When she entered the University of Illinois in 1914, she also joined the Socialist Party; she stayed in Urbana just two years, but socialism stayed with her for a lifetime.[6]

Day moved to New York and worked as a reporter for the *Call*, a socialist paper; she eventually wrote for *The Masses*. Associating with Mike Gold, Max Eastman, Floyd Dell, and Eugene O'Neill, and reporting on the down-and-out workers of American industrialism, she absorbed the radical views of Bohemian New York. After the government closed *The Masses* during World War I, Dorothy Day drifted from place to place and job to job—New York, Europe, Chicago, New Orleans, as nurse, reporter, cashier, clerk, activist, organizer. She came into contact with a literary set including Allen Tate, Malcolm Cowley, Kenneth Burke, Hart Crane, and John Dos Passos, and through the Cowleys with Southern anarchist Forster Batterham, who became her common-law husband.[7]

Day was also attracted to religion, and read widely in religious literature. The birth of a daughter, Tamar Teresa, in 1926 dramatized the spiritual differences between Day and her husband, leading to their separation and to Day's conversion to Catholicism. She seemed to want the sort of spiritual home for her daughter that had eluded her in her wanderings. As a woman and a mother, Day looked for a philosophical foundation for care and nurturing. She seemed to long for the religious radicalism of some of the Catholic saints—John of the Cross, Teresa of Avila, Francis of Assisi. Despite the obvious shortcomings of the institutional church, Day wanted, said Daniel Berrigan, "to live as though the truth were true."[8]

Day's religious convictions, therefore, generally reinforced her radicalism. When Sacco and Vanzetti were executed, the sense of solidarity that she felt with workers and the poor helped her "gradually understand the doctrine of the Mystical Body of Christ whereby we are members of one another." She worked for the Anti-Imperialist League, a Communist affiliate, and then for the Fellowship of Reconciliation. She began to read the radical European philosophy that would influence her later work. Proudhon, Tolstoy, and Kropotkin proved congenial to Day, as did English distributists Eric Gill, G.K. Chesterton, Hilaire Belloc, and Vincent McNabb who advocated a rejection of machine technology and industrial capitalism for rural, handicraft societies. Day herself did not oppose modern technology; she simply expected machines to serve people and not vice-versa. In 1932, she went to Washington to cover the Hunger March for *Commonweal*. Feeling that her work was not integrated with her faith, she visited the National Shrine of the Immaculate Conception at Catholic University, and she prayed "that some way would open up for me to use what talents I possessed for my fellow workers, for the poor." Within a few days of her return to New York, Peter Maurin was at her door.[9]

Peter Maurin

French peasant intellectual Peter Maurin was the proximate cause of Catholic Worker personalism. Born in 1877, he had spent a lifetime in search of a vocation in service to the poor. Growing up in a small French mountain village, Maurin experienced the communal sharing that shaped his vision of life. The fifteen families of the village tended each other's flocks, baked together in the communal oven, and worshiped together at the church in a neighboring town. The families raised what they ate, and ate what they raised. Much of Maurin's life was devoted to bringing this "peasant wisdom" to the modern world.[10]

In 1895, inspired by the compassionate example of his teachers, Maurin took vows as a De la Salle brother, and served as a teacher, first in his native Languedoc, then in Paris. By 1903, Maurin left the De la Salle brotherhood for the informal brotherhood of Le Sillon. Inspired by Leo XIII's encyclical *Rerum Novarum*, Marc Sangnier and the Sillonists sought to renew the Catholic Church by reforming the social order. They worked with the poor of Paris, establishing rest homes and hospices; and they worked for the poor of France, using newspapers and magazines to spread the good news of the new Catholic social teachings, and organizing cooperatives and unions to implement those teachings. Although they failed to change the social and economic institutions of France, they succeeded in marrying the gospel to the gutter, and in teaching young Peter Maurin a form of personalist politics.[11]

A teacher of the poor, Maurin was a student of Leo Tolstoy and Peter Kropotkin. Reading *Fields, Factories, and Workshops* and *Mutual Aid*, Maurin was impressed by Kropotkin's critique of contemporary industrialism. Kropotkin thought that the progress of the nineteenth century had not brought progress for everybody. He decried the ways in which people were alienated and dehumanized in the factories and offices of the new economic institutions. Like the Arts and Crafts movement in England, Kropotkin promoted the usable and humanizing past of small-scale institutions, artisanal work, and cooperative living as an alternative to modern life. This decentralized anarchism was attractive to Maurin in an age of increasing urbanization, industrialization, nationalism, and militarism. Kropotkin's anarchism also fit with the principle of subsidiarity in Catholic social teaching, which suggested that social responsibility ought to be institutionalized as close to the people as possible.[12]

Maurin's personalism had European roots, and European parallels. His philosophy preceded and proceeded from the personalism and decentralism of Emmanuel Mounier and Nicolas Berdyaev. Although he anticipated many of the ideas of the French personalists, Maurin also brought their ideas to an American audience. He carried Mounier's *Personalist Manifesto* with him in his travels, and arranged for its English publication.[13]

Both his background and his reading made Maurin an antimodernist. He believed that, in the modern world, "the Christian values are being replaced by Benjamin Franklin's mottoes: 'Your dollar's your best friend. Business is business. A penny saved is a penny earned. Cash and carry.'" Because modernism threatened human dignity and sociability, Maurin hoped to see modernism succeeded by a new participatory peasant society. Asked once if it was possible to go back in time, he responded, "People are always telling me I can't go back in time. It's nonsense. They can't go ahead. They are in the blind alley of industrialism and can't go ahead."[14]

Perhaps because of his European peasant origins, Maurin never fully acclimated himself to American assumptions about human nature and individualism. He believed that people were conceived as social and cooperative creatures, that they were socially constituted, and that they should practice what Kropotkin called "mutual aid." As Mary Segers suggests, Maurin wanted "to replace 'rugged individualism' with 'gentle personalism,'" replacing a society of systematic selfishness with communities of systematic unselfishness. "I am not afraid of the word communism," Maurin proclaimed to an American audience that was.[15]

Maurin's Christian communism also conflicted with American assumptions about the sanctity of private property. While he was not opposed to "private property with responsibility," he wanted people to remember that private property was a trust. Since property and creation were gifts of God, people should act as God's stewards to use them for the community. In one of his "Easy Essays," he argued that

> The use of property
> to acquire more property
> is not the proper use
> of property.
> The right use of property
> is to enable the worker
> to do his work
> more effectively.
> The right use of property
> is not to compel the worker,
> under threat of unemployment,
> to be a cog in the wheel
> of mass production.[16]

Maurin believed in enacting the Thomistic doctrine of the common good. As Dorothy Day recalled, Maurin "thought in terms of our common humanity, or our life here today. He stressed the idea of building a new society within the shell of the old—that telling phrase from the preamble to the I.W.W. constitution, 'a society in which it is easier for people to be good,' he added with a touching simplicity, knowing that when people are good, they are happy."[17]

From Jacques Maritain, who worked with the French personalists, Maurin took the idea of "pure means," arguing that the means to social change should be consonant with the ends: "they must embody as far as possible the ends which are sought and thus be small incarnations of the desired social order." Instead of waiting for reformist legislation, or for proletarian revolution, Maurin preferred to enact utopia one day at a time.[18]

Maurin's assumptions about means and ends set him at odds with the dominant assumptions of the American political economy. While the world's economists wanted to increase the production of goods and services, Maurin wanted to increase the production of good people. For him, the primary economic indicator was not the wealth of nations, but the commonwealth of persons. While economists assumed that they could think about the economy without considering the culture it produced, Maurin contended that an economy based on competition and profits would produce a cutthroat culture of disconnected individualists.[19]

Responding to the Tolstoyan pacifism of his personalism, Maurin left France in 1909 for Canada and the United States, where he lived as an itinerant worker. In 1925, in New York City, he recommitted himself to the lay apostolate that he had begun in France and started to write the essays that would later be published as "Easy Essays." He read many Catholic publications, and became impressed with a Catholic writer named Dorothy Day. George Shuster, the editor of *Commonweal*, suggested that Maurin should meet her and he sought her out in December of 1932.[20]

The Catholic Worker

Together, Day and Maurin planned to publish a newspaper that would proclaim the personalist gospel to America's working people. Unlike most revolutionary publications, which attempted to convert readers to secular radicalism, the *Catholic Worker* aimed for a comprehensive radicalism that united spirit and society.[21]

Both Day and Maurin intended to build their utopia on a firm foundation of spirituality. Both of them believed in the primacy of the spiritual, but neither of them believed in a spirituality divorced from worldly concerns. According to one Catholic Worker, "It wasn't a spiritualism that was removed from day-to-day life or from a sense of radical Christian life." Dorothy Day, recalls another Worker, "didn't separate the natural and supernatural." She believed that "everything is sacramental." And the grace and holiness of creation justified her faith in the creative possibilities of personalism. For Day and for Maurin, piety and prayer, and the sacraments of communion and confession, were as much a part of their politics as were the newspaper or the strikes and picketing.[22]

Maurin wanted to call the paper the *Catholic Radical*, but Day preferred the *Catholic Worker*. "We used the word in its broadest sense," said Day, "meaning those who worked with hand or brain, those who did physical, mental or spiritual work. But we thought primarily of the poor, the dispossessed, the exploited." The "Worker" in the masthead connected the paper to Day's communism and to the *Daily Worker*, but it also committed Day and Maurin to a critique of work as a central social (and spiritual) problem.

The *Catholic Worker* decried the assumption of American capitalism (and of American labor) that work could be understood mainly as a commodity rather than as a means of fulfilling people's spiritual and material needs. They questioned a factory system in which, according to Pope Pius XI, "raw materials went into the factory and came out ennobled and man went in and came out degraded."[23]

In appropriating the IWW and Communist slogan "work not wages," Maurin suggested that people should shape work to humanize human beings. Dorothy Day described Peter's Christian philosophy of work: "God is our creator. God made us in His image and likeness. Therefore we are creators. He gave us a garden to till and cultivate. We become cocreators by our responsible acts, whether in bringing forth children, or producing food, furniture, or clothing. The joy of creativeness should be ours." Although neither Maurin nor Day expected the American economy to provide such work for every person, they hoped that more people might be able to work for the intrinsic satisfactions of shaping nature, expressing their own cocreative capablities, and serving the common good. A gift from God, work was also a gift to the community. In this spirit, the first Catholic Worker house of hospitality was named after Saint Joseph, the patron saint of work.[24]

Both Day and Maurin felt that Catholic social teaching offered a revolutionary alternative to American social conditions. Maurin said often that the Christian message was dynamite, but that Catholic clerics and scholars were afraid to use it. According to Marc Ellis, Maurin wanted to synthesize "the voluntary poverty of St. Francis, the charity of Saint Vincent de Paul, the intellectual approach of St. Dominic, and the manual labor of St. Benedict." Both Day and Maurin quoted and promoted papal encyclicals like Leo XIII's *Rerum Novarum* (1891) and Pius XI's *Quadragesimo Anno* (1931).[25]

Both of them read (and published) the work of Monsignor John Ryan, the director of the Social Action Department of the National Catholic Welfare Conference from 1919 to 1945. Ryan argued that the natural law tradition, as developed by Thomas Aquinas and updated in the popes' encyclicals, offered a foundation for Catholic social reform. That tradition argued that, since people were created in the image of God, they had rights based on their inherent human dignity. This tradition, unlike the tradition of Lockean individualism that dominated American social thought, saw people as social by nature, so that human rights and responsibilities both sprang from human nature, and not from a subsequent social contract. Human persons were, therefore, the measure and end of organized society. When Pope Pius XI updated *Rerum Novarum* with *Quadragesimo Anno*, he reinforced the natural law idea that human rights must be pursued within an organic society, and that individual rights were subordinate to the common good. Ryan and the American bishops understood the state as a necessary expression of human social obligations, and as a necessary force in promoting human rights and the common good. But Ryan and the bishops also insisted on the principle of subsidiarity, which would locate social change as close to the family and the local community as possible.[26]

The Catholic Workers drew on this tradition of Catholic social thought, but extended it as well. They were inspired not just by the natural law philosophy of human rights and responsibilities but by the social gospel of love, not just by the encyclicals but also by the radical Christianity of Jesus and the early church. They often saw the institutional church as a scandal, with "plenty of charity but too little justice." And they advocated not just the standard Left program of legislation and neighborhood organizing, but personalist action to solve social problems. As far as possible, they hoped to be the word made flesh, an embodiment of Christ's love.[27]

The News That's a Fight to Print

Dorothy Day and Peter Maurin propagated their personalist faith in the advocacy journalism of the *Catholic Worker*, which she edited from 1933 until her death in 1980. The *Catholic Worker* premiered on May Day 1933, and it synthesized the radical experience of its founders. The first issue explained the paper's purpose, and included articles on blacks and sharecroppers in the South, and on child labor, housing, and strikes in New York. The *Worker* offered a critique of both capitalism (for its individualism, materialism, and indifference to the poor) and communism (for its enforced collectivism, its secularism, and its emphasis on the inevitability of class struggle). It also printed articles that analyzed the ultimate philosophical questions posed by the "good news" of the gospels. And it offered an alternative program, rooted in Christian spirituality and aimed at distributive justice. "We are not giving you news such as you get in your daily paper," Day told readers. "We are giving you ideas as to Catholic Action."[28]

Day's editorial policy, recalled Jim Forest, was a positive one, "practical and personalist, . . . showing what individuals and small groups of people were doing to create a better place. [Dorothy] often said we should be 'proclaimers and acclaimers' rather than 'denouncers.' We shouldn't be writing against the government." Instead of frightening people into a revolution, Day hoped to inspire them to change by showing them how to do right in a world of wrongs.[29]

Dorothy Day edited most of the newspaper, while Peter Maurin contributed his "Easy Essays." One of them, "What the Catholic Worker Believes," synthesized the gospel they preached in the paper:

The Catholic Worker believes
in the gentle personalism
of traditional Catholicism.
The Catholic Worker believes
in the personal obligation
of looking after
the needs of our brother.
The Catholic Worker believes
in the daily practice
of the Works of Mercy.
The Catholic Worker believes
in Houses of Hospitality
for the immediate relief
of those who are in need.
The Catholic Worker believes
in the establishment
of Farming Communes
where each one works
according to his ability
and gets
according to his need.
The Catholic Worker believes
in creating a new society
within the shell of the old
with the philosophy of the new,
which is not a new philosophy
but a very old philosophy,
a philosophy so old
that it looks like new.

Maurin's blank verse wordplays took "the outrageous core of the Christian message and put it in a way that compelled attention and even retention."[30]

The newspaper was not objective or neutral. Stories focused not just on the political and economic leaders, but also on the people of the neighborhood. Dorothy Day encouraged workers themselves to write about their manual labor in a column signed by "Ben Joe Labray," a contemporary pseudonym of St. Benedict Joseph Labre, patron saint of the bread lines. "Nowhere," says Arthur Sheehan, "was there that 'objective' type of newspaper reporting that tells of a plane crash with a minute description of the disintegration of the machine and the added afterthought that the pilot was killed. The *Catholic Worker* was a personalist paper and the writing had the warm appealing quality of a good novel."[31]

The *Catholic Worker* challenged the conventions of American journalism and offered a civil voice in opposition to the statist voice of the mainstream press. "Whenever the *New York Times* refers to me," noted Day, "it's as a 'social worker.' Pacifism and anarchism are just dismissed." In the *Catholic Worker*, however, pacifism, personalism, and anarchism were front-page news, and the paper conscientiously promoted its revolution by ideas. The power of these ideas was almost palpable. The monthly sheet was an immediate success; within a few years, its circulation topped 100,000. By 1938, the print run had leaped to 190,000.[32]

As Peter Maurin's "Easy Essay" suggested, the *Catholic Worker* was not the only proclamation of the Worker gospel. The movement also included roundtable discussions to empower workers to educate themselves, "agronomic universities" to bring people back to fulfilling work on the land, and houses of hospitality to care for people who were not well served by America's economic institutions. Because they all emphasized learning Christianity by doing it, they constituted an educational program at odds with the education offered in American schools and the mainstream press.

The Friday night roundtable discussions at St. Joseph's House offered workers and the poor a voice in their own education, and introduced them to a variety of committed intellectuals: Jacques Maritain, Carleton J. Hayes and Harry Carman, Hannah Arendt, Michael Harrington, Daniel and Phillip Berrigan, Danilo Dolci, Evelyn Waugh, W.H. Auden, Julian Beck and Judith Malina, Noam Chomsky and Robert Coles. These roundtables embodied Maurin's ideal of intellect in the attainment of social justice:

> The scholar has told the bourgeois
> that a worker is a person for all that.
> But the bourgeois has told the scholar
> that a worker is a commodity
> for all that.
> Because the scholar has a vision
> the bourgeois calls him a visionary. . . .
> The scholars must tell the workers
> what is wrong
> with things as they are.
> The scholars must tell the workers
> how a path can be made
> from the things as they are
> to the things as they should be.
> The scholars must collaborate
> with the workers
> in making a path
> from the things as they are

to the things
as they should be.
The scholars must become workers
so the workers may be scholars.[33]

In roundtables, in theory, Workers and workers could engage in the "clarification of thought" that complemented practical love and social change.

Both Peter Maurin and Dorothy Day traveled widely, preaching the
gospel of the Catholic Worker. Maurin was an accomplished soapbox
speaker; when he was not engaged at New York's Union Square, he might
be found on Boston Common, at the National Catholic Rural Life Conference, at colleges and universities, or at Worker houses in other cities. Day
traveled to demonstrate her solidarity with the poor and oppressed throughout the country; she often described her trips in her column "On Pilgrimage." Both Day and Maurin were in great demand as speakers and they
considered this teaching an essential part of their vocation and ministry.[34]

Housing Hospitality

Day and Maurin and other Catholic Workers also practiced political personalism in Houses of Hospitality, where people who pursued voluntary
poverty fed and sheltered people whose poverty was involuntary. To Maurin, the poor were ambassadors of God, sent to give people the opportunity
to offer their gifts. Both Day and Maurin were familiar with "the old
I.W.W. technique of a flophouse and a pot of mulligan set on the stove,"
and they set out to create a spiritual equivalent. Like Gandhi, they believed
that "a good deed does not consist merely of feeding the hungry with
bread, but of loving both the hungry and the satisfied. For it is more
important to love than to feed, because one may feed and not love, but it is
impossible to love and not feed."[35]

The Catholic Worker houses institutionalized the virtue of hospitality.
Based on the hospices of early and medieval Christian communities, they
joined social service and spiritual function, as people worked for each other
and for God. Ultimately, Maurin hoped that every American home would
have a hospitality room, where families would welcome the less fortunate
members of their community.[36]

Peter Maurin insisted on voluntary poverty both as a sign of solidarity,
and as a method of cultural enrichment. The choice of Franciscan poverty
could liberate people from the fears of losing jobs or losing the possessions
that possessed them. The Catholic Workers could also help redistribute
wealth by liberating people from their surplus resources. "We need the
Houses of Hospitality," said Maurin, "in order to give the rich an opportu-

nity to serve the poor." The work of the volunteers would be healing for them as well as for the poor people they served.[37]

Catholic Worker personalists understood persons as body and soul, but, unlike the institutional church, they ministered more to the body than the soul. Although they believed in the redemptive quality of suffering, they still attempted to relieve the involuntary suffering of the poor. Instead of practicing random acts of kindness, they hoped to institutionalize disciplined communities of compassion. Practicing the corporal and spiritual works of mercy in their street missions, they embodied the love of Christ in their care for the bodies of others. The Catholic Workers emphasized this Catholic action because they saw action as an arena of conversion, a place where the offering of kindness could make a person kinder, where good intentions could be incarnated. They thought that, while people might *be* good, they might also *become* good by doing good.

Indeed, they thought that people create love by practicing love. Both Day and Maurin admired St. John of the Cross, who said, "Where there is no love, put in love and you will take out love." Peter Maurin loved the phrase "to make love," and the Catholic Workers made a lot of it. Everyday, they modeled the practical, down-to-earth ways that people could love one another. "If the love was not there in the beginning, but only the need" said Dorothy Day, "such gifts made love grow."[38]

The works of mercy of the Worker community are often seen as apolitical or prepolitical. But, as Walter Brueggeman suggests, "Compassion constitutes a radical form of criticism, for it announces that the hurt is to be taken seriously, that the hurt is not to be accepted as normal and natural but is an abnormal and unacceptable condition for humanness." Compassion militates against the systematic numbness of structural injustices. "Thus, compassion that might be seen merely as generous goodwill is in fact criticism of the system, forces, and ideologies that produce the hurt." The emphasis on action in the Catholic Worker movement created a kind of activism that linked the work of hospitality with the work of protest.[39]

Dorothy Day saw this connection between compassion and social criticism clearly. "When we were invited to help during a strike," she recalled, "we went to perform the works of mercy, which include not only feeding the hungry, visiting the imprisoned, but enlightening the ignorant and rebuking the unjust. We were willing to 'endure wrongs patiently' for ourselves (this is another of the spiritual works of mercy) but we were not going to be meek for others, enduring *their* wrongs patiently." Both Maurin and Day emphasized social action more than political action, because, they said, social action included a spiritual dimension that political action often lacked. But Day especially found that the spirit of social action led her to political protest.[40]

Implicit in the Houses of Hospitality was a critique of the professional-ization of social work, of expertise in government, and of the specialization of American society. In "Feeding the Poor," for example, Maurin contended that:

> In the first centuries
> of Christianity
> the hungry were fed
> at a personal sacrifice,
> the naked were clothed
> at a personal sacrifice,
> the homeless were sheltered
> at a personal sacrifice.
> And because the poor
> were fed, clothed and sheltered
> at a personal sacrifice,
> the pagans used to say
> about the Christians
> "See how they love one another."
> In our own day
> the poor are no longer
> fed, clothed and sheltered
> at a personal sacrifice
> but at the expense of taxpayers.
> And because the poor
> are no longer
> fed, clothed and sheltered
> at a personal sacrifice
> the pagans say about the
> Christians
> "See how they pass the buck."

The Catholic Workers didn't wait for a professional or a bureaucrat to identify social problems or solutions. Rejecting the systems of specialization that tended to make "sitizens" of citizens, they returned to republican ideals of poor relief in which local people cared for their own poor. By 1938, there were Catholic Worker houses in Boston, Chicago, Rochester, St. Louis, Baltimore, Washington, Pittsburgh, Milwaukee, Akron, Detroit, Cleveland, and Philadelphia. And, especially as Peter Maurin and Dorothy Day began to proselytize around the country, a national network of Catholic Workers began to develop, resisting "the taking over by the state of all those services which could be built up by mutual aid."[41]

This anti-statist anarchism was an essential part of their personalism.

Concerned as much with the notion of the state as with the state of the nation, they resisted the centralizing state-building tendencies of the twentieth century. Catholic Workers were not anarchists in the popular connotation of the word—lawless, bomb-throwing radicals craving a kind of crazed chaos—but in the more rooted and radical sense of people who preferred to govern themselves. Dorothy Day thought that "anarchism meant *increased* responsibility of one person to another, of the individual to the community along with a much lessened sense of obligation to or dependence on the 'distant and centralized state.'" Although she knew that the state could accomplish many things, "her purposes were different . . . her approach directed at people's attitudes, at their moral lives, at their overall ethical purpose as human beings. She wanted to affect not just the overall problem, but people's everyday lives—their manner of living with one another." Although she was an anarchist, Dorothy preferred the word "libertarian," because it was easier on the American ear. Peter Maurin acknowledged privately that he was an anarchist, but preferred to be known publically as a Christian communist. When that was also misconstrued, he called himself a "communitarian."[42]

As Catholic Worker Bob Ludlow explained, "Anarchists believe that the *whole* people composing a community should take care of what governing is to be done rather than have a distant and centralized state do it. . . . Anarchists advocate directive government (mutual aid) but reject coercive government." Christian anarchism, he said, recognized the limitation of human nature expressed in original sin. But it also recognized the "divine possibilities" of human nature expressed in the idea of grace.[43]

Agronomic Universities

The program of the Catholic Worker included the newspaper, roundtable conversations, and Houses of Hospitality, but it also included rural farms. Inspired by Gandhi, Kropotkin and the English Distributists, and by Maurin's peasant experience, Catholic Workers founded communitarian farms, where body and mind could be exercised for the glory of God. On the farms, committed idealists like Peter Maurin tried to integrate cultural and agricultural labor; they expected residents to work in the fields and to participate in conversational forums about the issues of the day. Unlike the work of the industrial assembly line, agricultural labor, Maurin believed, offered expression to people's capabilities as artists and craftsmen. And the "agronomic universities" would also model the anarchist alternative of decentralized communities where people voluntarily cooperated with each other, instead of being coerced by the state.

The Catholic Worker farms were a small part of a larger cultural emphasis on agrarian life in the 1930s, including the Southern Agrarians, Ralph Borsodi's School for Living, the Catholic Rural Life movement, and various New Deal programs to support rural resettlement and subsistence farming. These groups argued "that men and women should exert greater control over their livelihood and adopt a higher standard of worth than mere consumerism. Choosing how to live, they zealously demonstrated, is a moral undertaking, entailing the cultivation of certain values and the discouragement of others." At a 1940 School for Living seminar in New York, Peter Maurin christened this coalition "the green revolution."[44]

Like many of these groups, the Catholic Worker farms offered an anarchist interpretation of the relationship of nature and human nature that conflicted with the agricultural policy of American society. They attempted to follow Genesis 1:28 to "Be fruitful and multiply; replenish the earth and have dominion over it." American agriculture had long been infatuated by the language of subduing the earth, but the Catholic Workers were more interested in replenishing the earth, because replenishment described what the dominion must be like. People, they thought, must have a relationship with the earth that fills it up again, that makes it whole, that makes it healthy, that makes it holy, that keeps it, as God said at the Creation, very good. They understood the simple Biblical injunction—"Replenish the earth"—as an invitation to take part in the ongoing gift of God's harmonious creation, to be cocreators with God. The farms were also an attempt to wean people from the industrial food chain, and to teach them methods of sustaining and sustainable agriculture. In a slogan that presaged the bioregionalism of the 1970s, Maurin urged people to "eat what you raise and raise what you eat."[45]

Both the farms and the houses of hospitality exemplified a sort of Christian communism, in which committed workers established communes for social and economic cooperation. "My whole scheme," claimed Maurin, "is a Utopian, Christian communism." Rejecting the ontological individualism of American capitalism and the forced collectivism of communism, this Christian communitarianism offered the alternative of voluntary collectivism. The houses of hospitality provided a free space for the poor, but they also provided a free space for the social experimentation of the volunteers. Catholic Worker houses were essentially urban communes in which volunteers committed themselves to lives of care, prayer, and simplicity. Just as their religious orientation and their lay ministry were a challenge to core cultural values, so too the Worker communes offered an alternative to American institutions of privatized families. While most Americans found fulfillment in the single-family home, the Catholic Workers found grace in Christian community.[46]

Pacifist Personalism

Although it began with an emphasis on labor relations, the *Catholic Worker* came to focus more on pacifism, because war violated the dignity of persons, and because of the way that the modern warfare state consumed the resources that otherwise might contribute to social justice. As early as 1934, the *Worker* had featured a debate between Christ and a Patriot, noting that although Jesus lived in an occupied nation controlled by pagans, he had opposed violent and nationalist solutions to Roman control. During the Spanish Civil War, when almost all of the Catholic hierarchy supported Franco's forces because they were anticommunist, the *Catholic Worker* was expelled from the Catholic Press Association for maintaining its pacifism and neutrality.[47]

The Worker movement championed the individual conscience over both the institutional state and the institutional church. While the institutional church preached a just war doctrine that offered moral criteria for government decision makers, Dorothy Day's personalism focused her attention not on the state, but on the individual. She was especially appalled by conscription, the most dramatic instance of the state compelling citizens to serve its interests. And she was especially impressed by those individuals who refused or resisted the draft, and those who offered their conscientious objection to war. During World War II Dorothy Day helped found the Association of Catholic Conscientious Objectors to provide alternative service opportunities for conscientious Catholics. Worker ideals also circulated widely in the camps for conscientious objectors, which became incubators for postwar political personalism.[48]

World War II was a difficult time to preach the Christian doctrine of loving enemies, but Dorothy Day preached just such a gospel. In June 1940, she claimed in the *Worker* that the conditions for a just war could not be met in the modern age. *Catholic Worker* pacifism during World War II, and its opposition to conscription during the Cold War brought frequent charges of un-Americanism. Subscriptions to the newspaper plummeted from 120,000 to 50,000 during the war years, and only ten houses of hospitality remained.[49]

Using the just war theory, many Catholic publications opposed the obliteration bombing of World War II and the atomic bombing of Hiroshima and Nagasaki. The Workers were appalled at the violation of persons in these mass murders. The political personalism of the Catholic Worker also put it on a collision course with the new strategic thinking of the Atomic Age. "Mr. Truman was jubilant," reported Dorothy Day in the September 1945 *Catholic Worker*. "President Truman. True man. . . . Truman is a true man of his time in that he was jubilant. He was not a son of

God, brother of Christ, brother of the Japanese, jubilating as he did. . . . *Jubilate Deo.* We have killed 318,000 Japanese."[50]

During the early years of the Cold War, the era of McCarthyism and the hydrogen bomb, the *Catholic Worker* continued its critique of American militarism. Unlike the mainline churches, which gradually adapted to the ideology of the state, the Catholic Workers preached and practiced Christian pacifism. They found that religion gave them a critical distance from social and political institutions, and sustained resistance to injustice and violence. Unlike the popular 1950s evangelist Billy Graham who claimed that Christians could participate in war because they were not "personally responsible," Day thought that peace resulted from individual action in conformity to the gospels. And she and her Worker colleagues continued their emphasis on personal responsibility and public witness, affirming their faith that one person can change history. Worker Ammon Hennacy, for example, began to protest against the Atomic Energy Commission; each August 6, he would begin a fast and a picket line that lasted as many days as there were years since Hiroshima. Hennacy's eccentric witness was not intended to change other people; as he said, it was to make sure that other people didn't change him. Although he often picketed the Atomic Energy Commission, his protests were intended to shape conscience as much as to shape policy.

Hennacy's personalist pacifism was, by the 1950s, associated with the Catholic Worker, but it was rooted in native radicalism. He had been a Socialist early in the century, Dorothy Day recalled, and he had refused military induction during World War I. Jailed in the Atlanta Penitentiary, Hennacy was "won by the personalist approach" of his cellmate, anarchist Alexander Berkman, who was completing a sentence for his attack on Henry Clay Frick during the Homestead Strike. "Forced to rely on himself, [Hennacy] recognized the importance of beginning with himself, starting here and now, and not waiting for someone else to start the revolution."[51]

Hennacy's witness, and Day's journalism, also helped to make Hiroshima Day a day of public repentance for the American peace movement, a day which converted the triumphalism of American militarism to a feast of American pacifism. The eccentric witness of these personalist pacifists eventually generated a ritual day of reflection, if not repentance, for Americans who were neither personalist nor pacifist. During the Sixties, Hiroshima Day offered antiwar activists a regular occasion for contemplation of war and its effect on persons. In similar fashion, American personalists imitated the English Campaign for Nuclear Disarmament with their Easter marches, connecting the religious deliverance of Passover and the redemptive character of the crucifixion and resurrection with the movement against nuclear weapons.

But the personalist pacifism became even more public when in 1955 ten Catholic Workers and eighteen others refused to go underground during Operation Alert. Their commitment to civil disobedience of the civil defense law embodied their commitment to consistency in personal and political values. Although personalism did not *require* civil disobedience, it provided a structure of values in which people might break the law to uphold transcendent values. In such cases, the protesters thought, civil disobedience was what they owed the state as citizens. Rejecting the Fifties' identification of patriotism with statism, the personalist activists dissented and disobeyed when they thought the state had threatened a person's life, dignity, or pursuit of justice. Inspired by personalism's focus on the individual, its commitment to prophetic love (and consequently to justice), its private and public consistency, its communitarian anarchism, and its ethic of action, the Catholic Workers and their compatriots began to work for a cultural revolution by way of a revolution in the heart.

The success of the civil defense protests, while limited, showed the power of personalist protest. Although it represented a radical challenge to the social order, personalism stated the challenge in terms of conventional values like love and responsibility. Writing about her jail experience after the civil defense protest of 1957, Dorothy Day claimed that, despite failures, "we are all seeking love, seeking God, seeking the beatific vision." So was the Catholic Workers' kindred spirit, Thomas Merton.[52]

Thomas Merton: Catholic Worker

Born in 1915, raised in Europe and America, orphaned at 15, and a hellion in college, Thomas Merton converted to Catholicism in 1938 and entered the Trappist Monastery of Our Lady of Gethsemani in 1941. He renounced the world, but not the written word, and his writing—most notably the bestselling *The Seven Storey Mountain* of 1948—brought him fame as an exemplary Catholic. Eventually, during the 1950s, his contemplative life led him to contemplate the practice of peace and justice in the modern world. From 1941 to 1957, Merton had supported the ideal of isolation in order to preserve the purity of prayer life. But after 1957, he came to believe that "a monastery is not a snail's shell, nor is religious faith a kind of fallout shelter into which one can plunge to escape the criminal realities of an apocalyptic age."[53]

The criminal realities of an apocalyptic age included the impersonalisms of racism and consumer capitalism, but Merton focused especially on American acceptance of nuclear weapons. He agreed with journalist I.F. Stone's charge that "in a period when no general ever makes a speech anymore without giving God a plug, and self-righteous moralizings ooze from every political pore, real morality has been completely abandoned in our imbecile fascination with these new destructive toys. The atom is our totem; the bomb our Moloch; faith in overwhelming force is being made into our real national religion."[54]

American public faith in the overwhelming force of the atomic bomb had begun in 1945, and the Bomb's religious dimensions were accentuated by the development of the Cold War as a religious crusade. After the victory of World War II, the sins of the Soviet Empire replaced the Nazi threat to "civilization," and religious anticommunism condemned this "Red fascism." Richard Cardinal Cushing of Boston claimed that communism "threatens us Catholics and our institutions, [as] it threatens with equal violence and fatal purpose all others who love God or seek to serve Him." Whittaker Chambers, whose bestselling autobiography *Witness* testified to the religious dimension of anticommunism, argued that "the communist vision is the vision of Man without God. It is the vision of man's mind displacing God as the creative intelligence of the world." Because they supported the fight against "godless" communism, few religious leaders spoke out against American nuclear weapons policy. Ministers told activist A.J. Muste that they couldn't give sermons on peace, because the topic was considered communistic.[55]

In the revivals of the 1950s, religion served the polity almost as much as piety. It was an era of priestly civil religion, in which American mission became identified with God's mission. "If you would be a true patriot," advised evangelist Billy Graham, "then become a Christian. If you would be a loyal American, then become a loyal Christian." President Eisenhower encouraged this marriage of religion and realpolitik with a series of national prayer breakfasts. Congress added the phrase "under God" to the Pledge of Allegiance, so that schoolchildren could affirm the alliance of America and God in a world where "the prospect of atomic war" was so prominent. Congress also added a nonsectarian prayer room in 1955, and "In God We Trust" to coins a year later.[56]

At its extremes, this identification of religion with American nationalism could almost consecrate the atomic bomb. "We still believed that God was on our side," recalls Lawrence Wright. "We believed in the forces of light and the forces of darkness. My parents' generation had seen America rise out of the Depression to become the liberator of Europe and the dominant power in the world. The sins of the Nazi empire reinforced our own belief that we were the defender of the faith. We saved civilization. As our reward, God gave us the Bomb." In a 1950 debate over the peacetime draft, Senator Edward Martin argued that "Americans must move forward with the atomic bomb in one hand and the cross in the other."[57]

Although the Catholic Church was staunchly anti-communist, and American Catholics provided considerable support for McCarthyism, the church also had an important tradition of teaching about peace. Following the lead of Pope Pius XII, many Catholics used the traditional doctrine of the "just war" to justify weapons for deterrence. Both just war theory and Christian pacifism evaluated war from the standpoint of its actual or potential victims, and both "put violence on trial, placing the burden of proof on those who take up arms rather than on those who refuse." In contrast to pacifist claims, however, just war theory assumed that war could be an instrument of justice in the world, and established criteria for conscientious decisions. Just war theory taught that nations could enter a war if there were a just cause, if there were a competent authority, if it were an issue of comparative justice, if there were right intention, if the entry into war was a last resort, with a reasonable probability of success, and if the damage and costs of the war were likely to be proportional to the good expected by taking up arms. Once in the war, just war theory required that a nation abide by the principles of proportionality and discrimination; that is, the human costs of the war could not exceed the benefits, and the lives of innocent people could never be taken directly.[58]

Christian "realists" like Reinhold Niebuhr and John Courtney Murray also justified the nuclear deterrent. Assuming that sinful human nature and imperfect human institutions would always combine to produce injustice and aggression, "the realists taught that war was the norm, and peace the welcome deviation, in the human condition." And they concluded that Christians might do evil deeds (such as, go to war) with good intentions. For them, war was, however tragically, "a practical and unavoidable necessity."[59]

Both the just war theory and Christian realism were complex contributions to moral reasoning, admitting many different applications of moral principles to contemporary situations. But in the context of the 1950s, critics like Thomas Merton found them insufficient to prevent the coming of World War III. In Merton's life and writing after 1957, he combined personalism and the civil voice of nuclear discourse in a synthesis that would be increasingly influential in American culture.

Even in the isolation of Gethsemani, Thomas Merton experienced the "political intrusion" of nuclear weapons. Because of his cloistered life, Merton did not learn about Hiroshima until several months after the explosion. He did not begin to read seriously on nuclear issues until 1957, but in the next ten years he experienced nuclear weapons as a personal and a policy intrusion, as airplanes of the Strategic Air Command practiced bombing runs over the Kentucky hills. Merton recorded many of these awe-ful epiphanies in his journals: "3:15 p.m." he noted on February 2, 1964: "Right on time the SAC plane flies low over the blue hills slowly, ponderously, yet lightly like a shark in water making the wide turn in relative quiet, pretending we are God knows what city in Russia or whatever else it is they pretend." About a year later, after five bombers buzzed the hills, he noted that "only the first and the last went directly over me, but directly so I was looking right up at the bomb. This was quite fantastic. Of course, the mere concept of fear was utterly meaningless, out of the question. I felt only an intellectual and moral intuition, a sort of 'of course,' which seemed to be part of the whole day and its experience."[60]

Unlike most Americans, who ignored the intrusion of nuclear weapons into their everyday lives—in civil defense drills, in fallout shelters, in Conelrad and the Emergency Broadcast System, in fallout from the tests, in Atoms for Peace, in mutant movies and science fiction, in fears about an atomic apocalypse—Merton converted his intellectual and moral intuition into personalist protest. His personalism permeated his writing. "The basic thing in Christian ethics," he told Dorothy Day, "is to look at the *person* and not at the *nature*. . . . Because when we consider "nature" we consider the general, the theoretical, and forget the concrete, the individual, the personal reality of the one confronting us. Hence we see him not as our other self, not as Christ, but as our demon, our evil beast, our nightmare."[61]

Like most of the exponents of the civil voice in nuclear discourse, Merton empathized with the persons who were victims—past, present, and future—of nuclear weapons. In May 1964, for example, a group of Japanese *hibakusha* (survivors) visited Merton at the monastery. "They are men and women signed and marked with the cruelty of this age," he noted in his journal, "bearing in their flesh signs generated by the *thoughts* in the mind of other men. They are a significant indication of what Western 'civilized' thinking really means. When we speak of freedom, we are also apparently saying that others like these good charming, sweet, innocent people will be burned and annihilated, if and when we think we are menaced."[62]

Although Merton never formally discarded the Church's tradition of the just war, he could imagine no circumstances in which the use of nuclear weapons could be justified. "As you know," he explained to Catholic historian John Tracy Ellis in 1961, "one of the things that most bothers me is the attitude of so many Catholics to nuclear war. They make no distinction between out-and-out pacifism which refuses to serve even in a 'just war' and the Christian obligation, pointed out by the recent Popes, to avoid the criminal tragedy of nuclear annihilation of civilian centers, even for the best of causes. Apparently much popular thought in this country simply goes along with the immoral and secularist attitude that since communism is evil, we can do anything we like to wipe it out."[63]

Merton also took the bomb as "a sign, a revelation of what the rest of our civilization points to," and he composed prophetic protests against the "fetishism of power, machines, possessions, medicines, sports, clothes, etc., all kept going by greed for money and power." Like many personalists,

Merton understood nuclear weapons not just as a nuclear problem or a war problem, but as a cultural problem. Personalist holism allowed Merton to grieve not just the policies of his government, but the cultural practices of his fellow citizens, as they created a society that he sometimes called "post-Christian."[64]

Because he believed in the primacy of persons and in personal responsibility for institutionalized evil, Thomas Merton promoted a personalist approach to politics. "Now above all," he said, "it is time to embody Christian truth in action even more than in words." "This means," he added, "reducing the distance between our interior intentions and our exterior acts. Our social actions must conform to our deepest religious principles. Beliefs and politics can no longer be kept isolated from each other." Christian social action should be, he said, "action that discovers religion in politics, religion in work, religion in social programs for better wages, Social Security, etc." Understanding the religious character of everyday life meant that social action would be seen as "part of the redemptive work of Christ, liberating man from misery, squalor, subhuman living conditions, economic or political slavery, ignorance, alienation." And from the Bomb. For Merton and for other personalists, this approach to politics combined Christian concepts of vocation with American concepts of citizenship. A Christian calling consisted, for Merton, of a calling to do work for the community, or for the common good. His own calling as a monk meant that he was one of a group of "people who have adopted a way of life which is marginal with respect to the rest of society, [and] implicitly critical of that society."[65]

American citizenship also entailed aspects of personalism. Merton thought that, properly understood, democracy was personalist, because "this democratic respect for the person can be traced to the Christian concept that every man is to be regarded as Christ, and treated as Christ." And democracy, he felt, was "founded on a kind of faith: on the conviction that each citizen is capable of, and assumes, complete political responsibility. Each one not only understands the problems of government but is willing and ready to take part in their solution. In a word, democracy assumes that the citizen knows what is going on, understands the difficulty of the situation, and has worked out for himself an answer that can help him contribute, intelligently and constructively, to the common work (or 'liturgy') of running his society."[66]

Merton contended, therefore, that Christians and American citizens had a responsibility to inform themselves about the political issues of their times, and to speak and act on their convictions. An informed conscience required, in Merton's view, reading outside the statist voice of political discourse. "One who merely echoes the opinions in the newspaper," he warned, "is not taking an 'active' part in the life of his nation. . . . A falsely informed public with a distorted view of political reality and an oversimplified, negative attitude toward other races and peoples, cannot be expected to react in any other way than with irrational and violent responses." Since responsible action depended on the truth, and language and discourse were vehicles for truth, Merton considered them perverted when they became misdirected by militarism.[67]

Merton expected that an informed public would see the contradictions in American military policies. On the one hand, he noted, "we claim to possess the only effective and basically sincere formula for world peace because we alone are truly honest in our claim to respect the human person. For us, the person . . . comes absolutely first. Therefore the sincerity and truth of all our asserted aims, in defense and in civil affairs, is going to be judged by the *reality* of our respect for persons and their rights." On the other hand, Merton felt, "the plans we have devised for defending the human person and his freedom involve the destruction of millions of human persons in a few minutes, not because the great majority of those persons are themselves hostile to us, or a threat to us, but because by destroying them we hope to destroy a *system* which is hostile to us and which, in addition, is tyrannizing over them."[68]

"Unfortunately," mourned Merton, "mere words about peace, love, and civilization have completely lost all power to change anything." And so he proposed a language beyond words, a language of personalist commitment. He claimed that Gandhian nonviolence was, in fact, "a kind of language. The real dynamic of nonviolence can be considered as a purification of language, a restoration of true communication on a human level, when language has been emptied of meaning by misuse and corruption. Nonviolence is meant to communicate love not in word but in act. Above all, nonviolence is meant to convey and defend truth which has been obscured and defiled by political doublespeak."[69]

By 1961, Merton realized that he was "one of the few Catholic priests in the country who has come out unequivocally for a completely intransigent fight for the abolition of war and the use of nonviolent means to settle international conflicts. Hence by implication not only against the bomb, against nuclear testing, against Polaris submarines, but against all violence." In January of 1962, he publicly supported the General Strike for Peace and suggested that Catholics practicing personalism should not work in weapons industries. In February, he dedicated a Mass to antiwar strikers and peace workers of the world. And many of Merton's protests finally appeared in print in 1962. The powerful prose poem *Original Child Bomb* related the calculated inhumanity of the bombing of Hiroshima. *Breakthrough to Peace*, which Merton edited, included essays by Lewis Mumford, Norman Cousins, Erich Fromm, Gordon Zahn, Jerome Frank, and Merton himself, and it pointed the way to principles for a peaceable world.[70]

But even Merton faced religious resistance to the message of peace. As early as 1957, he knew that "the Cistercians of the Strict Observance are very much opposed to any voice with even a slightly radical sound being raised in their midst." In March 1962, his superiors prohibited the publication of his peace writings, because they considered war to be an inappropriate subject for a monk. Eventually, they ordered him not to publish on the subject of war and peace. "I wanted to act like a reasonable, civilized, responsible Christian of my time," Merton recorded in his journal. "I am not allowed to do this. I am told I have 'renounced this.' Fine! In favor of what? In favor of a silence which is deeply and completely in complicity with all the forces which carry out oppression, injustice, aggression, exploitation, war. In other words, silent complicity is presented as a greater good than honest, conscientious protest." For Merton, silent complicity made people guilty bystanders: he appealed to the Abbot General, but the prohibition was upheld.[71]

Merton's personal struggle with complicity and the culture of silence resonated, in the early 1960s, with the public trial of Adolf Eichmann. In "A Devout Meditation in Honor of Adolf Eichmann," Merton enunciated a new, and more personalist, understanding of the evils of Nazi Germany, an understanding that focused not so much on the evils of Nazi leaders as on the complicity of German followers. At the same time, he examined his own conscience and the conscience of his American compatriots.[72]

Merton's meditation on Adolf Eichmann was occasioned by Hannah Arendt's 1963 articles in the *New Yorker*, examining the 1961 trial of Eichmann for "crimes against the Jewish people," crimes against humanity, and other war crimes. Eichmann, born in Germany and raised in Austria, joined the Nazi Party and the S.S. in 1932. During the 1930s, he worked for the Nazis to promote Jewish emigration. After the outbreak of World War II in September 1939, he took on more and more tasks, first securing the shipment of Jews to concentration camps, then arranging the execution of enemies of the Third Reich in territories recently conquered by the armies, and finally organizing the transportation and genocide of the Jews in the extermination camps in Poland. He claimed, in his defense, that he was only following the orders of higher authorities. Eichmann was apprehended in Argentina in 1960, and the trial began in June 1961. Convicted in December, Eichmann was hanged in May of 1962.

The trial provoked much commentary, including the Arendt essays that eventuated in *Eichmann in Jerusalem*, and Kurt Vonnegut's *Mother Night*. In Eichmann, Arendt had expected to find "the demonic incarnation of evil," but, she concluded, he exemplified only "the banality of evil." The only notable characteristic of his behavior "was not stupidity but *thought-lessness* . . . It was this absence of thinking—which is so ordinary an experience in our everyday life,' that appalled Arendt. The bureaucracy of Nazi Germany—with its compartmentalization of tasks, separation of planning from execution, hierarchical structure, compensation for conformity, and technicized or euphemistic language—insulated people like Eichmann from responsibility for "the bureaucratization of homicide." Arendt felt that other nation-states, including the United States, had also institutionalized moral and political assumptions that made mass murder legal and acceptable.[73]

Merton agreed. In thinking about Eichmann, Merton found it difficult and disturbing to imagine "this calm, 'well-balanced,' unperturbed official conscientiously going about his desk work, his administrative job which happened to be the supervision of mass murder. He was thoughtful, orderly, unimaginative. He had a profound respect for system, for law and order. He was obedient, loyal, a faithful officer of a great state. He served his government very well. He was not much bothered by guilt. . . . Eichmann was devoted to duty, and proud of his job."[74]

Eichmann's sanity suggested that, in the modern world, "it is precisely the *sane* ones who are most dangerous," and Merton suggested that the sane ones of the 1960s were conscientiously going about the desk work of preparing a nuclear holocaust. "It is the sane ones, the well-adapted ones," Merton observed, "who can without qualms and without nausea aim the missiles and press the buttons that will initiate the great festival of destruction that they, *the sane ones*, have prepared." Many people worried about madmen firing nuclear weapons, but Merton knew that "the sane ones will have *perfectly good reasons*, well-adjusted reasons, for firing the shot. They will be obeying orders that have come down the chain of command. And because of their sanity, they will have no qualms at all. When the missiles take off, then, *it will be no mistake*." Disconnected from the civil voice, from the claims of moral conscience, even virtues like loyalty and obedience could be perverted.[75]

Merton's devout meditation was perhaps the best expression of his civil personalism, because Eichmann embodied everything that personalism was not. A government bureaucrat dutifully devoted to the mass murder of Jewish persons, Eichmann could not discern an obligation to do otherwise. He could not translate the cares and concerns of his personal life to the political sphere. He could not imagine an ethics independent of the state. But for Merton, as for other personalists, the Eichmann affair was not simply a matter of one man's evil choices; it was also an issue of the institutionalization of insanity, the day-to-day production and reproduction of institutions that made it easier to do evil. Merton feared that institutional support for ordinary insight, intelligence and morality was no longer strong enough to avert catastrophe, and he often compared the American situation to aspects of Nazi Germany. Bureaucracy, conformity, and the dominance of the statist voice in nuclear discourse, thought Merton, might also enable Americans to commit mass murder. Like Erich Fromm, Merton was concerned about *The Sane Society*, and about those "future Eichmanns, men of sanity and efficiency who will be in key positions during the great crises of the nuclear age." Like many other artists and intellectuals of the period 1955-65, Merton believed in the madness of sanity and the sanity of madness.[76]

Merton's personalist pacifism had a great influence on the American peace movement, but little immediate influence on the American Catholic Church or on the mainstream Protestant denominations. In his 1963 encyclical *Pacem in Terris*, however, Pope John XXIII opened the way for a revision of Church teaching on nuclear issues, and for a re-evaluation of the more "radical" ideas of Thomas Merton. "In this age of ours, which prides itself on its atomic power," the Pope claimed, "it is irrational to think that war is a proper way to obtain justice for violated rights." The encyclical called for a ban on nuclear weapons, for disarmament, and for a new world order more stable than the so-called balance of power. And it set the stage for Vatican II's *Pastoral Constitution on the Church in the Modern World*, which questioned the proportionality and discrimination of nuclear weapons, and which strongly affirmed nonviolence—and even pacifism and conscientious objection—as forms of Christian discipleship.[77]

Pacem in Terris also affirmed the right and responsibility of civil disobedience. "If civil authorities legislate for, or allow, anything that is contrary to [the moral] order and therefore contrary to the will of God, neither the laws made nor the authorizations granted can be binding on the consciences of the citizens, since *we must obey God rather than men* [emphasis in original]." For Pope John and for the Catholic Workers, conscience was an active agent of everyday life—including the social and political dimensions of everyday life—and not just an occasional interloper. Ideally, the politics of conscience *was* the politics of everyday life.[78]

Later that year, Merton was awarded the PAX Medal. In accepting the award, he sent a message affirming *Pacem in Terris*, claiming that the encyclical and other Church teachings (including the gospels) placed him "in the rather awkward position of receiving a prize for doing what is the only plain and obvious duty of a reasonable human being who also happens to be a Christian. It is like getting a medal for going to work in the morning, or stopping at traffic lights, or paying one's bills." His peace work, said Merton, "implies no heroism, no extraordinary insight, no special moral qualities, and no unusual intelligence." But this was the essence of personalism, that people embody Christianity every day as a biographical and as a public fact.[79]

In his own life, Thomas Merton helped to influence other actors in this personalist moral renaissance. James Forest claimed that "Thomas Merton was the parish priest of the Catholic Peace Movement." Although he remained at the commune of Gethsemani, he was a one-man committee of correspondence, encouraging others in their work of peace. His letters show Merton's personalist practice, and his civil voice, as he tried out a language for subverting the statist voice of nuclear discourse. The letters also helped create a community of consciousness which could support personalists in their nonviolent civil obedience to conscience.[80]

"I suppose it is my job," he told a friend in 1962, "to be at least remotely the Church's arm around [peace activists], as nobody else much (in the clergy) seems interested." A number of peace activists entered his embrace by making pilgrimages to the monastery. In November 1964, for example, shortly after the elections, Merton offered a retreat on "The Spiritual Roots of Protest" for the Fellowship of Reconciliation, which was attended by A.J. Muste, James Forest, Dan and Phil Berrigan, John Yoder, John Oliver Nelson, W.H. Ferry, Tom Cornell, and Tony Walsh. Just before he was assassinated, Martin Luther King Jr. told a friend that he planned to make a retreat with Merton before completing plans for the Poor People's Campaign. In addition, Merton lent the prestige of his name to the peace organizations PAX and the Catholic Peace Fellowship. And, because of his earlier fame as a spiritual voice of the Church, Merton was also responsible for winning personalist pacifism a wider hearing among American Catholics generally.[81]

The Radical Catholic Legacy

Although European and American philosophers had written abstractly about personalism early in the twentieth century, the Catholic Worker movement created its own brand of political personalism after 1933. By 1962, when a younger generation announced its intentions in the Port Huron Statement, the Catholic Worker movement had three decades of experience with the propagation and practice of personalism. They had confronted the Depression, chronic poverty, two wars, and the atomic bomb. They had grown from two people in a New York apartment to several hundred people in several dozen Houses of Hospitality. They had published a monthly newspaper that sold for a penny a copy and maintained a circulation of 60,000. And they had made the news themselves, with the practical personalism of the civil defense protests. When a New Left looked for a usable past, the Catholic Worker offered one example.

The spirit of the New York Catholic Workers and of Catholic workers like Thomas Merton inspired many people. Volunteers who worked in the houses of hospitality for a summer or a year left to serve elsewhere. In this way, as Dwight Macdonald said, the movement was "a kind of university, constantly taking in freshmen and graduating seniors." Daniel Berrigan said that "Peter [Maurin], dead, was a teacher of the sixties and seventies in a way very few among the living were."[82]

The politics of the Catholic Worker movement also offered examples for activists of the Sixties. In general, Catholic Workers avoided electoral politics and governmental policy, but they believed in a politics of example and a politics of witness. Peter Maurin assumed that social change came not so much from social movements mobilized for political power, but from the example of individuals in community. "Cultural transformations came from below, subverting the dominant culture through personal example and perseverance." Both Maurin and Day knew that people often wanted the security and direction of an organization, but, as anarchists, they preferred the difficulties of freedom and personal responsibility. Maurin and Day both worried that organization resulted only in organizations, and not in the transformations of the self that could sustain social change. "If everybody organized himself," Maurin said, preaching the gospel of personal responsibility, "everybody would be organized."[83]

Ultimately, the Catholic Workers believed, as Father Pacifique Roy told them at a retreat, that "love is the measure by which we shall be judged," and so they didn't worry much about measuring up to cultural criteria for success. Sometimes they appeared foolish, but Dorothy Day didn't care. "Let us be fools for Christ," she said. "Let us recklessly act out our vision, even if we shall almost surely fail, for what the world calls failure is often, from a Christian viewpoint, success." Day understood "the foolishness of love," but she understood also the foolishness of the alternatives. Long before the love generation, her vision of a "harsh and dreadful love" generated a movement that justified itself.[84]

"Politically," as Dwight Macdonald noted in 1952, "the Catholic Workers are hard to classify. They are for the poor and against the rich, so the capitalists call them Communists; they believe in private property and don't believe in class struggle, so the Communists call them capitalists; and they are hostile to war and the State, so both capitalists and Communists consider them crackpots." The politics of Catholic Worker personalism was a politics of witness, a politics of example, a politics of pastoralism (in both senses of the word), a politics of perfectionism.[85]

The deep spirituality of Catholic Worker personalism was one of its most important—and least understood—legacies. Unlike other radical movements, which accepted the increasing secularism of American society, the Catholic Worker movement pointed out connections between secularism and social problems. "The essence of the Catholic Worker movement," said Dwight Macdonald, was "the union of the everyday and the ultimate."[86]

The Movement was revolutionary in the root sense of the word "revolution": Catholic Workers expected the world to revolve back to the good and the true. While most Americans—including most American dissenters—saw the twentieth century as progress, the Catholic Workers were not so sure. While most Americans saw the past as "old fashioned," the Catholic Workers saw the past as a place of possibilities radically different from the present. To Catholic Workers like Dorothy Day and Peter Maurin, then, revolution meant the revolving and reversal of modernity, the repentance and return to traditions which enriched the lives of persons.

Catholic Workers identified the issues of the Sixties before the Sixties began, and they offered models of protest long before the protest decade. From the beginning, Catholic Workers called attention to the problems of the poor that would be addressed by Lyndon Johnson's War on Poverty, and Martin Luther King's Poor People's Campaign. They promoted pacifism, conscientious objection and nonviolent direct action long before the antiwar movement. They practiced personal service long before the Peace Corps. Because they confronted the world's indifference, they made a difference in the world.

THE BEAT OF PERSONALISM

Howl

A FEW MONTHS AFTER THE 1955 Operation Alert affair, at a now-famous October 13 reading at the Six Gallery in San Francisco, Beat poet Allen Ginsberg memorialized the personalist protesters in his own "Howl" of protest. In his poem, they appear (inaccurately) as the people "who distributed Supercommunist pamphlets in Union Square weeping and undressing while the sirens of Los Alamos wailed them down, and wailed down Wall, and the Staten Island ferry also wailed."[1]

Transforming Walt Whitman's "barbaric yawp" into his own wail of madness, Ginsberg lamented the personal destruction of American culture. "I saw the best minds of my generation destroyed by madness," Ginsberg began, and he catalogued the causes for madness in American culture. After describing the frantic and furious carousing of the "angelheaded hipsters," Ginsberg asked who had butchered "the absolute heart of the poem out of their bodies," who had "bashed open their skulls and ate up their brains and imagination." His metaphorical answer was Moloch, the false god of the Old Testament who demanded the sacrifice of children:

"Moloch whose fate is a cloud of sexless hydrogen! Moloch whose name is mind! . . . Moloch! Moloch! Robot apartments! invisible suburbs! skeleton treasuries! blind capitals! demonic industries! spectral nations! invincible madhouses! granite cocks! monstrous bombs!" Ginsberg's seething anger at the madness of American culture derived from a sense that the "Moloch" of contemporary culture was devouring America's children to feed its insatiable desires for comfort and security.[2]

The other poets who participated in the notorious poetry reading of October 1955 were Michael McClure, Gary Snyder, Philip Whalen, and Philip Lamantia. McClure recalled the context of their texts:

> We were locked in the Cold War and the first Asian debacle—the Korean War. . . . We hated the war and the inhumanity and the coldness. The country had a feel of martial law. An undeclared military state had leapt out of Daddy Warbucks' tanks and sprawled over the landscape. As artists we were oppressed and indeed the people of the nation were oppressed. . . . We knew that we were poets and had to speak out as poets. We knew that the art of poetry was essentially dead—killed by war, by academies, by neglect, by lack of love, and by disinterest. We knew we could bring it back to life. . . . We wanted voice and we wanted vision.

Ginsberg's Beat variation of the civil voice thrilled the crowd that night, because, as McClure said, they knew that "at the deepest human level a human voice and body had been hurled against the harsh wall of America and its supporting armies and navies and academies and institutions and ownership systems and power-support bases."[3]

Ginsberg's human voice and body were engaged in what might be called a personalist poetry. In a May 1956 letter to poet and critic Richard Eberhart, Ginsberg defended "Howl" against charges of nihilism. Eberhart, who was planning a *New York Times Book Review* article on West Coast poetry, had told Ginsberg that "you deal with the negative or horrible well but you have no positive program." Ginsberg explained that,

> The title notwithstanding, the poem itself is an act of sympathy, not rejection. In it I am leaping *out* of a preconceived notion of social "values," following my own heart's instincts—*allowing* myself to follow my own heart's instincts, overturning any notion of propriety, moral "value," superficial "maturity," Trilling-esque sense of "civilization," and exposing my true feelings—of sympathy and identification with the rejected, mystical, individual even "mad."

Ginsberg claimed that the poem called its readers to "the enlightenment of mystical experience," and consequently to empathy and a "'starry spangled shock of MERCY' and mercy is a real thing and if that is not a value I don't know what is." "Thus," said Ginsberg, "I fail to see why you characterize my work as destructive or negative. Only if you are thinking an outmoded dualistic academic theory ridden world of values can you fail to see I am talking about *realization* of LOVE."[4]

After explaining the structure and technique of the poem, Ginsberg summarized his intentions in terms that would have been familiar to Dorothy Day and Peter Maurin: "The criticism of society is that 'Society' is merciless. The alternative is private, individual acts of mercy. The poem is one such." Like Dorothy Day, Ginsberg's interest in works of mercy came from his mysticism. In 1948, when reading a William Blake poem, he experienced "this vision or this consciousness of being alive unto myself, alive myself unto the Creator. As the son of the Creator—who loved me." Like Day and Thomas Merton and Martin Luther King Jr., Ginsberg found that his "cosmic consciousness" led him to a life of "American tenderheartedness." Instead of the tough, cool hipsters that Norman Mailer admired, Ginsberg and the Beats were exploring a "warmhearted, open, Dostoevskian, Alyosha-Myshkin-Dimitri compassion."[5]

The tenderhearted compassion of the Beat poets made them attentive to society's victims, and to the social construction of victims. More than almost any other group of the 1950s, the Beats exposed the cultural contradictions of American life. Unlike the academic social criticism of mass culture that also flourished in the Fifties, the Beats provided a popular criticism rooted in a strong sense of the purposes of persons. To a great extent, the Beat movement was a howl against death—and the death in life—of the Atomic Age. The Beats railed against the threat of megadeath and against the anomie of people who had never really lived. Allen Ginsberg's obsession with "the disease of the age"—nuclear fallout and radiation sickness—reinforced his "idea of the transience of phenomena—the poignant Kewpie-doll dearness of personages vanishing in time." Faced with atomic and anomic death, Ginsberg and the Beat generation were especially attentive and appreciative of the everyday life around them, and they juxtaposed imminent doom with the immanent vitality of their poetry and prose.[6]

During the 1950s, Ginsberg and Kerouac and the Beat movement developed a second strain of personalism in America. After poet and critic Kenneth Rexroth integrated personalist perspectives with the anarchopacifism of the West Coast, Allen Ginsberg, Gary Snyder, William Everson, Lawrence Ferlinghetti, and Jack Kerouac brought these ideas from "little magazines" to the national media. They influenced the creation of a coffeehouse culture in which poetry, jazz, and folk music came together in a captivating critique of the "Social Lie" of Fifties America. By creating free spaces in print and performance, the Beat movement brought a personalist perspective to the young people who would take it elsewhere in the Sixties. Beat personalism did not derive from the same philosophical sources that influenced the Catholic Worker movement, but it shared elegiac and communitarian perspectives, and the popularity of Beat poetry extended its distinctive personalist ethic beyond the religious realm of Catholic Worker personalism.

The Rexroth Circle

The master of ceremonies at Ginsberg's 1955 reading was Kenneth Rexroth, a poet who promoted both the poetry and anarcho-pacifism of the early San Francisco Renaissance. Born in 1905 to an activist family, Rexroth, like Dorothy Day, had been a part of a circle of Bohemian radicals and avant-garde writers. Like Day, he had also looked for a spiritual center in religion, professing the Anglican faith in the mid-twenties, and spending time at a monastery where he confirmed his belief in "ethical activism." Throughout his life, he professed that "Literature is work. Art is work. And work, said St. Benedict, is prayer."[7]

Rexroth participated in the Federal Writers Project in the San Francisco Bay area during the 1930s, and he helped to organize writers and artists in the Communist John Reed clubs. He also belonged to several Communist front organizations during the decade. In 1938, however, he turned away from Communist connections ("I came into the Popular Front from the Left," he said, "and went out by the same door."), and became more active in anarcho-pacifist activities. He was influenced by anarchists as diverse as Peter Kropotkin, Alexander Berkman, and Pierre-Joseph Proudhon. As early as 1939, as he felt the United States drifting into war, he tried to coordinate a network of literary pacifists associated with organizations like the Fellowship of Reconciliation, the Women's International League for Peace and Freedom, the National Council for the Prevention of War, and the Keep America Out of War Committee. He filed for conscientious objection for personal and religious reasons. Like other conscientious objectors, Rexroth had a reason, early on, to believe that the personal was political, and vice versa.[8]

During World War II, Rexroth assisted Japanese Americans who opposed the forced evacuation to relocation camps. Working with the Fellowship of Reconciliation, he helped them escape the evacuation by arranging educational passes from the internment camps. He also attended meetings of the American Friends Service Committee, and acted as a local representative of the National Committee for Conscientious Objectors. Every other week, he hosted pacifist meetings in his home, naming them the Randolph Bourne Council, after the literary radical who had protested American involvement in World War I. During the war, too, he supported the artists and writers who served terms for conscientious objection at the Civilian Public Service Camp at Waldport, Oregon.[9]

And they supported him. William Everson recalled that "the whole San Francisco Renaissance had in some way a powerful inception at Waldport. First, the Interplayers, which was one of the leading theater groups in San Francisco in the postwar period, began at Waldport. And the rest of us who were writers gravitated down to where Rexroth was pulling it together." At Waldport, the conscientious objectors had published two resistance magazines, *Compass* and *The Illiterati*, the latter devoted to "creation, experiment, and revolution to build a warless, free society." And Waldport's Untide Press published Everson's *X War Elegies* and Kenneth Patchen's *An Astonished Eye Looks Out of the Air*.[10]

From 1945 to 1948, Rexroth institutionalized his anarcho-pacifism in the Libertarian Circle, a group of philosophical anarchists who met Wednesday nights to discuss radical readings and ideas. And on Fridays, in his own home, he hosted weekly poetry readings and a conversational community devoted to the art and politics of poetry. This radical artistic community was, according to Morgan Gibson, "anarchopacifistic in politics, mystical-personalist in religion, and experimental in esthetic theory and practice." At the Libertarian Circle and at the poetry readings, recalled poet Robert Duncan, "we were all brought up on Daddy Rexroth's reading list." The list included six books by anarchist theorist Peter Kropotkin, and three about French socialist and anarchist Pierre-Joseph Proudhon. Also included were readings from Michael Bakunin, Alexander Berkman, Emma Goldman, William Godwin, Wilhelm Reich, Engels, Lenin, Lao-Tsu, and Tolstoy. Discussions also encompassed religious and political figures like Martin Buber, Eric Gill, Nicolai Berdyaev, Thoreau, and Gandhi.[11]

Rexroth included British Personalists as well. During the Forties, he maintained contact between the San Francisco literati and English "New Romantics" like Alex Comfort, Herbert Read, Henry Treece, George Woodcock, and D.S. Savage. In introducing *The New British Poets* (1949), Rexroth praised "the religious personalism and political anarchism which provide the dominant ideology of the movement." He noted their similarities to Catholic anarchist Eric Gill in "the rejection of mechanistic civilization, sterile scientism, and top-heavy rationalism." He celebrated their "quest for the true integrality of the person" and their sacramental reverence for life. Finally, he applauded the shift from "the gospel of artistic impersonality" to "the person to person responsibility of artistic creation."[12]

Rexroth and his anarcho-pacifist circle helped establish "little magazines" like *Circle* and *Ark* and *Moby I* and *Moby II*. "Generally," Lawrence Ferlinghetti reported, "the contents of *Circle* expressed antiwar, anarchist or anti-authoritarian attitudes, coupled with a new experimentation in the arts." In an editorial preface to the first issue, *The Ark*'s editors evoked their own form of personalism: "In direct opposition to the debasement of human values made flauntingly evident by the war, there is rising among writers in America, as elsewhere, a social consciousness which recognizes the integrity of the personality as the most substantial and considerable of values." They acknowledged and opposed the increasing statism of the postwar world: "Because mutual aid and trust have been coldly, scientifically destroyed; because love, the well of being, has been methodically parched; because fear and greed have become the prime ethical movers, States and State-controlled societies continue to exist." They saw anarchism as the "polished mirror" in which the falsehoods of the American political economy could be seen. "Therefore," they said, "we are concerned with a thorough revaluation of the relations between the individual and society." Among the contributors to the *Ark* in 1947 were Rexroth, Kenneth Patchen, George Woodcock, Paul Goodman, and Ammon Hennacy.[13]

Rexroth saw the poet as "one who creates Sacramental relationships," and he used his poetry both to bear witness to the "Social Lie" and to the possibilities of social life. *The Dragon and the Unicorn* (1952), a book-length poem written during the years that the San Francisco Renaissance assembled at his apartment, was Rexroth's personalist manifesto. He contended that "All things, all entities of/ Whatsoever nature are/ Only perspectives on persons." He believed in personal responsibility for war, famine, pestilence, treason, and murder. He decried "the logical positivist/ The savage with an alarm clock," and celebrated instead the beauty of life's mysteries.[14]

Rexroth believed that "Ultimately the fulfillment/ Of reality demands that/ Each person in the universe/ Realize every one of the/ Others in the fullness of love." He understood persons essentially as lovers whose love took on many interpenetrating forms. Personal friendship (or "philia") extended to Christian love (or "agape"); sexual love (or "eros") grew from Christian love, and proceeded to universal compassion (or "caritas"); and compassion completed the circle as the foundation of friendship. For Rexroth, the beloved community included sexual love, which led people from the self to *an* other and to *all* others.[15]

Standing in the path of this personal and interpersonal fulfillment in community were the State and the capitalist system, both designed "to depersonalize and quantify persons." Persons became labor power for the factories, and firepower for the government:

> Every collectivity
> Is opposed to community.
> As capitalism and the

State have become identical,
All existence assumes the
Character of a vast
Conspiracy to quantify
The individual and
Convince him that all other
Seeming persons are actually
Already successfully
And happily quantified,
And that all human relations
Are quantitative, commodity
Relationships. This means murder.[16]

When poet Dylan Thomas died in November 1953, Rexroth described this murder of the innocents. In a memorial poem called "Thou Shalt Not Kill," which anticipated Allen Ginsberg's "Howl," Rexroth condemned a culture that maimed or murdered the best minds of a generation by its indifference and opposition. Comparing them to the Christian martyrs, he accused a culture that could not bear the truth. "You are the murderer," Rexroth charged:

You are killing the young men.
You are broiling Lawrence on his gridiron.
When you demanded he divulge
The hidden treasures of the spirit,
He showed you the poor.

The standard operating procedures of Western culture operated to kill the body and the soul of dissent:

He was found dead at a Liberal Weekly luncheon.
He was found dead on the cutting room floor.
He was found dead at a *Time* policy conference.
Henry Luce killed him with a telegram to the Pope.
Mademoiselle strangled him with a padded brassiere.

Poets and prophets were driven to drink, to therapy, to the busy-ness of business, to the "prefrontal lobotomies" of Communism, to the madhouse:

The first-born of a century
Slaughtered by Herod.
Three generations of infants
Stuffed down the maw of Moloch.

Against the slaughter of his time, Kenneth Rexroth offered a model of human development in which people progressed from personal freedom to erotic engagement, then to the sacramental mysticism of marriage, and finally to an ethics of universal responsibility. Synthesizing the sacred and the secular, the mundane and the mystical, Rexroth outlined the development of love and compassion in the "integral person," responsible for all. In *The Dragon and the Unicorn* (1952), Rexroth echoed Peter Maurin's vision:

> A community of love is
> A community of mutual
> Indwelling, in which each member
> Realizes his total
> Liability for the whole.[17]

The personalist politics of the Rexroth circle permeated Beat poetry. With others in the Bay community, Rexroth and his friends created a sensibility that connected aesthetic and political concerns, rejecting the academic impersonality of the New Criticism. They saw poetry both as personal expression and political statement, and they tried to bring prophetic poetry back into the public forum. "The only poetic tradition," claimed Ginsberg, "is the voice out of the burning bush." Their personalist poetry became their contribution to a politics of cultural change.[18]

To promote this social change, they performed their poetry in public places, including coffeehouses, bars, and jazz clubs. In addition, at one of the meetings of the Libertarian Circle, Lewis Hill, director of the Committee for Conscientious Objectors, proposed a radio station to disseminate dissident ideas even further; the result was KPFA/FM, Pacifica Radio, named not for the ocean but for the pacifism of its founders. According to Lawrence Ferlinghetti, Pacifica Radio was "left-liberal, anti-war, humanist, philosophical, individualistic, and, in the tradition of Thoreau, anarchist rather than Communist." Alan Watts and Kenneth Rexroth were among the regular contributors, and the station broadcast many important intellectuals and activists to listeners in the Bay Area.[19]

Beat Poetry

When Allen Ginsberg arrived in the Bay Area from New York in 1954, there was already a personalist sensibility present in San Francisco. The beginnings of a counterculture already existed in the writers' groups and poetry readings in Berkeley and the city; in coffee houses and clubs like the Black Cat, the Cellar, Cafe Trieste, and the Vesuvio Bar; and in little magazines like *City Lights*, *Goad*, *Inferno*, and *Golden Goose*. At Rexroth's, Ginsberg came into contact with the other poets of the Six, and with Lawrence Ferlinghetti, who would publish and publicize the Beats. At Rexroth's, too, poets Gary Snyder and William Everson encountered the political personalism that influenced their lives and poetry. Together, these artists created a "personalist poetics" that considered poetry an extension of the person. They created and performed confessional poems that connected the cultural and political. They crafted their prose and poetry for a person-to-person immediacy. Writing often about marginalized people in impersonal institutions, they marginalized themselves from the mainstream of American life and literature. And as Romantic artists, they tried to live the lives of their poetry.[20]

Gary Snyder had come to San Francisco in November 1953, and, influenced in part by a common anarcho-pacifism, immediately began a literary relationship with Kenneth Rexroth. At the Six Gallery reading, Snyder read "A Berry Feast," connecting his words to the world of nature, where he worked on the land as a logger, riprapper, and fire lookout. Jack Kerouac especially appreciated Snyder's anarchistic ideas about "how Americans don't know how to live." The next year Kerouac and Snyder shared a cabin; subsequently Kerouac used Snyder as the model for Japhy Ryder in *The Dharma Bums*.[21]

Twenty-five in 1955, Snyder began to study Oriental languages and Zen. From 1960-64 and 1965-68, he lived in Japan, the final year at the Banyan Ashram on a volcanic island. In his writings of the 1960s, Snyder established himself as a "bard-seer," a man whose work and thought and life were consistent and coherent. Often compared to Thoreau, he influenced a budding countercultural consciousness with *Myths and Texts* (1960), *Riprap and Cold Mountain Poems* (1965) and *Earth House Hold* (1969). Practicing a "poetry of compassion," he combined Buddhism with Native American spirituality, and the anarchism of the Industrial Workers of the World with the ecological values of the wilderness. While Peter Maurin hoped to reestablish agronomic communes based on Irish monasticism, Snyder looked to tribal traditions that preceded settled agriculture. Like Maurin, Snyder offered a vision of the past as prelude: "As poet I hold the most archaic values on earth. They go back to the late Paleolithic: the fertility of the soil, the magic of animals, the power-vision in solitude, the terrifying initiation and rebirth, the love and ecstasy of the dance, the common work of the tribe. I try to hold both history and wilderness in mind, that my poems may approach the true measure of things and stand against the unbalance and ignorance of our times."[22]

Poet William Everson had been a farmer before World War II. During the War, he helped establish the Arts Program at the conscientious objectors' camp at Waldport. In 1949, he converted to Catholicism and began a correspondence with Dorothy Day. In 1950, he worked eleven months at the Peter Maurin Catholic Worker House in Oakland, and left in 1951 to join the Dominicans. He continued to write poetry which he said,

"Thomistically speaking," attempted to reveal "the beatitude that obtains in all created things—the trace of the Creator left in them because they are His and of Him." To Rexroth, Everson was "the finest Catholic poet writing today," a representative not of "the stultifying monkey see monkey do Americanism of the slothful urban backwoods urban parish . . . but the Church of saints and philosophers—of the worker priest movement and the French Personalists." After he entered the Dominican order in 1951, Everson published mainly in the *Catholic Worker* as Brother Antoninus.[23]

At Rexroth's, Ginsberg had also encountered the man who would publish his poems and publicize his ideas. Poet, painter, publisher, and proprietor of the City Lights bookstore, Lawrence Ferlinghetti returned home after the reading at the Six Gallery and sent Ginsberg an Emersonian telegram: "I greet you at the beginning of a new career. When do I get the manuscript?" *Howl and Other Poems* became the fourth offering of the Pocket Poets series of Ferlinghetti's City Lights Press. A first edition appeared in October 1956, and a second printing was ordered.[24]

That printing brought the Beats to public attention, thanks to Chester McPhee, the Federal Government, and the city of San Francisco. When a shipment of *Howl and Other Poems* arrived from the printer in England in March of 1957, McPhee, the San Francisco Collector of Customs, declared it obscene and seized five hundred copies of the book. On May 19, Lawrence Ferlinghetti defended the poem in the *San Francisco Chronicle*, arguing that "it is not the poet but what he observes which is revealed as obscene. The great obscene wastes of *Howl* are the sad wastes of the mechanized world, lost among atom bombs and insane nationalisms. . . . Ginsberg chooses to walk on the wild side of this world, along with Nelson Algren, Henry Miller, Kenneth Rexroth, Kenneth Patchen, not to mention some great American dead, mostly in the tradition of philosophical anarchism." The Customs Service eventually released the book, but early in June the San Francisco police arrested Ferlinghetti and City Lights bookstore manager Shigeyoshi Murao for publishing and selling obscene materials. Poets and literary critics—including Kenneth Rexroth—testified at the late summer trial, which concluded with the court's judgment that the work was not obscene, and which brought the voice and vision of Beat poetry into the national limelight. By the end of the trial, in fact, 10,000 copies of *Howl and Other Poems* had been printed.[25]

Ginsberg's "America" was one of the "other poems" included in the collection, and it also called for personal resistance to American culture. Addressed to the nation, to America, it was a prophetic call for repentance, and a radical proposal for social change. Parodying the Fifties' obsession with national goals—in the statist voice—Ginsberg outlined the state of the nation, and calculated its national resources, including "the millions of underprivileged who live in my flowerpots under the light of five hundred suns." Like "Howl," "America" was both personal confession and cultural critique; it demanded commitment from the country, and from its citizens. Calling on the tradition of 1930s radicalism—a tradition denied during the 1950s "end of ideology"—Ginsberg asked,

> America, when will we end the human war?
> Go fuck yourself with your atom bomb. . . .
> America when will you be angelic?
> When will you take off your clothes?
> When will you be worthy of your million Trotskyites?
> When will you send your eggs to India? . . .
> When can I go into the supermarket and buy what I need
>   with my good looks?

But Ginsberg did not simply blame the System, or scapegoat society. "It occurs to me," says the poet, "that I am America," and, in a personalist fashion, he concludes by pledging his allegiance: "America I'm putting my queer shoulder to the wheel."[26]

With Ginsberg and Snyder and Everson, Lawrence Ferlinghetti also practiced a personalist poetics. Unlike the younger Beat poets, Lawrence Ferlinghetti had, in fact, seen the devastation of nuclear war. After serving during World War II as the commander of a submarine chaser in the North Atlantic, he finished his tour of duty in the Pacific. In mid-September 1945, he visited the ruins of Nagasaki; he recalled that "you'd see the hands sticking up out of the mud—all kinds of broken teacups—hair sticking out of the road—a quagmire—people don't realize how total the destruction was." Like Jacob Bronowski, who also saw Nagasaki in the fall of 1945, Ferlinghetti found "civilization face to face with its own consequences." And he recoiled from war, beginning to develop his anarchist and anti-nuclear leanings. During the early Fifties, he regularly participated in the Friday evening discussions at Kenneth Rexroth's.[27]

His own poetry reflected and affected the conundrums of American culture of the 1950s. "I Am Waiting" appeared in Ferlinghetti's second book, *A Coney Island of the Mind* (1958), which sold 15,000 copies by the end of the decade (and 700,000 by 1989). Like Ginsberg's "America," this poem expressed both the perils and the promises of American society. Ferlinghetti juxtaposed some of the foremost cultural icons of American society with many of the most pressing social problems of the 1950s. Like Joseph Heller's *Catch-22*, the poem also transmuted the clichés of American culture so that they comically conveyed a counter-cultural message: "I am waiting," Ferlinghetti said, "for the war to be fought/ which will make the world safe/ for anarchy." Using the language of everyday life, Ferlinghetti questioned the quality of American life. Waiting for the atomic tests to end, for Ike to act, for the Salvation Army to take over, and "for the meek to be blessed/ and inherit the earth/ without taxes," Ferlinghetti looked for a world without nationalisms in which forests and animals could reclaim the earth as theirs. But most of all, as the refrain suggested, Ferlinghetti was waiting for "a renaissance of wonder." Seeing life as full of wonder, Ferlinghetti and the Beats wondered why the American way of life seemed so unimaginative.[28]

Many of Ferlinghetti's most popular poems resembled Peter Maurin's "Easy Essays." Both men combined a poetic line with a vernacular voice, political commentary with literary imagery, irony with satire, and world-view with wordplay in their attempts to essay political themes that would reach a wider audience. Like Maurin, Ferlinghetti delighted in puns and their double meanings, and in the transformation and transvaluation of clichés. Like Ginsberg's work, the poetic prosody of Maurin and Ferlinghetti used short phrases arranged in lines that emphasized breath rhythms more than rhyme.[29]

In May 1958, still waiting for Ike to act, Ferlinghetti composed and performed his "Tentative Description of a Dinner to Promote the Impeachment of President Eisenhower." A witty political satire, the poem charged the President and the Atomic Energy Commission with death-dealing deceit. After indicting the President, Ferlinghetti imagined a banquet where "the natives of the Republic began assembling in the driving rain from which there was no escape—except Peace." At his banquet of the imagination, so many citizens aroused themselves from apathy to attend that, as they sat down "waiting for the symbolic mushroom soup to be served,"

> The President himself came in
> Took one look around and said
> We Resign."

The poem did not, in fact, cause the President to resign, but FBI director J. Edgar Hoover was asked what he thought about this un-American activity. "It appears that Ferlinghetti may possibly be a mental case," Hoover suggested with unconscious irony.[30]

With the City Lights Press and bookstore, and public readings in bars and coffeehouses, Ferlinghetti and the Beats began to change the way people related to poetry. They tried to make their populist poetry popular by bringing it out of the academy and into the streets. Observing this "revolution of the word" in 1957, Kenneth Rexroth noted that "poetry has become an actual social force."[31]

The Social Force of Literature

The social force of Beat literature came from its social criticism, its elegiac qualities, and its enabling fictions of action and community. Young people of the Fifties responded to Beat critiques of rationality, control and Victorian sexuality; they resonated with the Beat sense that something important had been lost when progress became America's most important product; and they were attracted to the communitarian promise of Beat literature.

Beat social criticism involved an attack on what Kenneth Rexroth called "the Social Lie," the untruths and half-truths embodied in the whole process of socialization. In societies that systematically exploited and alienated people, Rexroth claimed, people were "governed ideologically by a system of fraud." From Pennsylvania Avenue to Madison Avenue to their own local schools, Americans were taught social fictions to maintain their compliance to the system. Learning these lies, they learned to believe in the American Way of Life, in the progress of Western civilization, in the perpetual improvement of products, in the increasing freedom of the Free World. They believed in the democracy of politics and the democracy of goods.[32]

The Beats countered this "Social Lie" with a process of desocialization, both cultural and personal. Culturally, they criticized the institutions—the State, state-supported education, free enterprise, advertising, churches and families—which produced and reproduced stunted lives justified by social lies. Personally, the Beats tried to strip themselves of their socialization, to search out the "nakedness of mind, ultimately of soul" at "the bedrock of consciousness." Working from that foundation of personal consciousness, and from their consciousness of what a person should be, the Beats questioned the character of the affluent society. Like Thoreau and Whitman, they saw their personal lives in cultural terms, and they tried to shape the fate of American culture with the facts of their own poetic lines and lives.[33]

The Beats assaulted the rationality that supported the "Social Lie." While Lewis Mumford and other Fifties critics worried about the "irrational elements in art and politics," the Beats worried about the rational elements, and tried to provide the nation a shock treatment for its pathological sanity. As John Clellon Holmes said in *Nothing to Declare*, "the burden of my generation was the knowledge that something rational had caused all this . . . and that nothing rational could end it. The bombs had gotten bigger but the politics had stayed the same." Drugs like marijuana, peyote, mescaline (and eventually LSD) offered a chance to transcend the limitations of a scientific worldview. The Beats felt that Americans had emphasized calculation and rationality far too much, and that a more spontaneous, free-feeling personal existence would get people back in har-

THE BEAT OF PERSONALISM

63

mony with both nature and human nature. Like Emmanuel Mounier, who had claimed that modern individuals were "completely devoid . . . of all madness, of all mystery, of the sense of being and the sense of love, of suffering and of joy," the Beats felt that too few Americans had ever really experienced the fullness of life.[34]

More specifically, they wondered about Americans' sparing sense of sexual ecstasy. Unlike many of their compatriots, the Beats were interested in the sensuous body beneath the grey flannel suit. They asked, "What, then, is the American, this nude man?" and they exposed themselves to America in more ways than one. They claimed that the privatization of the body was political, and they transformed their own bodies into a body politic. Claiming that the body was holy, they flaunted their bodily functions before an American audience that had a million euphemisms for "bedroom and bathroom behavior," for sex and for shit. The Beat interest in the body as a sensual reality, and not just as a vehicle for the brain, meant that, unlike the nuclear strategists, they would not forget the physicality of nuclear war. They would re-member "the incontestable reality of the body—the body in pain, the body maimed, the body dead and hard to dispose of"—in ways that were obscured by the orthodox abstractions of defense and deterrence.[35]

The avowed homosexuality of some of the Beats added to their critique of American ideological orthodoxies. Throughout the Cold War, Americans across the political spectrum had connected sexual and political "perversion." Liberals like Arthur Schlesinger and John Kennedy called for a new virility in American life. And conservatives like Senator Kenneth Wherry contended that "you can't . . . separate homosexuals from subversives. . . . I don't say every homosexual is a subversive, and I don't say every subversive is a homosexual. But a man of low morality is a menace in the government, whatever he is, and they are tied up together."[36]

Ginsberg's homosexuality, observed critic Morris Dickstein, "contributed to his political consciousness, by making him sensitive to the element of hyper-masculinity and aggressiveness in the American mentality. He revived Whitman's vision of a society where communal ties are based on a renewal of personal tenderness. And of course he was delighted at 'the reappearance in the form of long hair and joyful dress of the affectionate feminine in the natural Adamic man, the whole man, the man of many parts.'" In a *Paris Review* article, Ginsberg contended that "the Cold War is the imposition of a vast mental barrier on everybody, a vast anti-natural psyche. A hardening, a shutting off of the perception of desire and tenderness which everybody *knows*." And at the end of his poem "Who Be Kind To," Ginsberg dreamed

That a new kind of man has come to his bliss
to end the cold war he has borne
against his own kind flesh
since the days of the snake.[37]

This sensual side of Beat personalism was very different from Catholic Worker asceticism. While the Catholic workers thought that American society ignored the bodily needs of its members, the Beats thought that society repressed bodily needs. Beats disdained the sacraments of the church, but saw sex as sacramental: instead of practicing corporal works of mercy, the Beats practiced corporal works of indulgence—in sex (often homosexual), in drugs, and in alcohol. Although "work" was a sacred word for the Catholic Workers, "work" was a Beat synonym for sexual intercourse. While Catholic Workers were most concerned with justice, the Beats were more concerned with freedom, especially the personal freedom that seemed anathema to the citizens of the Free World.[38]

Although Allen Ginsberg read his poetry at the Catholic Worker House of Hospitality in New York, Dorothy Day did not approve of the hedonistic side of Beat behavior. In her autobiography of 1952, Day had noted that "the very sexual act itself was used again and again in Scripture as a figure of the beatific vision." But her attitude toward Beat sexual beatitude was decidedly downbeat. Indeed, when she discovered in 1962 that an underground newspaper called *Fuck You: A Magazine of the Arts* was being printed on Catholic Worker presses, the result was the widely celebrated "Dorothy Day stomp." Incensed by the sexual license of her young Workers, she summarily threw them all out.[39]

In response to the Social Lie, the Beats presented a vision of community poised between elegy and utopia. Like the Catholic Workers, the Beats mourned the loss of communitarian societies that came with the gains of consumer capitalism. They saw people—even the privileged—alienated by the institutions of modern life. Like the Workers, therefore, they used a sense of loss and nostalgia to propose a sort of postmodern primitivism. Unlike Americans caught up in the Fifties paeans to progress, the Beats remembered that human beings had lived well with each other without the statist and commercial structures of modern society. In their own lives, they sought to recover the more primitive community of voluntary association.[40]

Jack Kerouac's novels added social force to the poetry of Allen Ginsberg and Lawrence Ferlinghetti, offering images of alternative communities and commitments. Loosely based on the exploits of the legendary Neal Cassady, Kerouac's 1957 *On the Road* celebrated the transcontinental community of the Beats. As the novel raced up the bestseller lists, it offered a vision of vitality and intensity that made everyday life seem empty. "The only people for me," said Kerouac, "are the mad ones . . . the ones who are mad to live, mad to talk, mad to be saved . . . the ones who never yawn or save a commonplace thing, but burn, burn, burn like fabulous roman candles exploding like spiders across the stars." For Kerouac, the cocked thumb and the cock itself were tickets to a life of wild abandon barely imagined in the age of Eisenhower. Tom Hayden, who graduated from high school in 1957, recalled that "Kerouac aroused a deep desire 'to prowl in the wilderness' among young readers like myself."[41]

In *The Dharma Bums*, Kerouac celebrated "a great rucksack revolution, thousands or even millions of young Americans wandering around with rucksacks, going up mountains to pray, making children laugh . . . wild gangs of holymen getting together to drink and talk and pray." Kerouac predicted a revolution of "Zen lunatics who go about writing poems that happen to appear in their heads for no reason and also by being kind and also by strange unexpected acts giving visions of eternal freedom to everybody and all living creatures."[42]

The Beats' spontaneous, free-wheeling writing publicized their personal existence, and made it political. According to Michael McClure, they "had come to believe that the way to the universal was by means of the most intensely personal." Beat literature was more descriptive than prescriptive, but it included a libertarian personalist ethic that challenged the status quo. Everyday life in Fifties America was intensely political, and Beat deviance was one exception that proved the rule of conformity. The Beat movement distinguished itself from mainstream literature and life by its commitment to open forms, to personal engagement, to spontaneity, to immediacy, to nakedness, and to a seething sound and fury. Their confessional style and their deviance from social norms called into question both the forms of poetry and the structures of society.[43]

But there was no attraction to the ballot box or the party system. Beat literature often essayed explicitly political themes, but Beat culture did not encourage formal political engagement. Even though there was a Beat candidate for President in 1960, many Beats preferred the politics of personal life to the life of partisan politics. "I renounce the notion of all social responsibility," announced poet Phillip Whalen. "In the wildest hipster" added John Clellon Holmes, "there is no desire to shatter the 'square' society in which he lives, only to elude it. To get on a soapbox or write a manifesto would seem to him absurd." Instead, by exposing what Rexroth called "the Social Lie"— the materialism, mechanization, militarism, and conformity of the culture, the Beats expressed their anger at the insanity of institutions that depersonalized people. And, in their lives, they tried to create "sane asylums" where people might cope with and confront the cultural madness.[44]

In the process, the Beats were among the people of the American 1950s who tried to "make the world safe for anarchism," an anarchism which offered a secular route to personalist politics.

"Disaffiliation from the inhuman," claimed Kenneth Rexroth, "means affiliation with the truly human." Such affiliation, he thought, did not involve political power or programs; "what matters is the immediate realization of humane content, here, there, everywhere in every fact and relationship of society. . . . The only way to realize it is directly, personally, in the immediate context. . . . This means personal moral action. I suppose, if you want to call it that, it means a spiritual revolution."[45]

The Beatific Vision

The Beat spiritual revolution challenged American religion, rejecting the private pieties, positive thinking, and public hypocrisies of the 1950s. But the Beats were not irreligious: Kerouac and Ginsberg, for example, "had come to the realization that rebellion took many forms, but religious rebellion was perhaps the profoundest gesture of the artist." Crafting political criticism in religious terms, they hoped to bring spiritual regeneration through poetry. "I suppose," said Kenneth Rexroth, writing in 1957, "in a religious age, it would be called religious poetry, all of it. Today we have to call it anarchism. . . . [Albert Schweitzer] calls it reverence for life." Whatever it was, it was countercultural spirituality.[46]

In his 1952 *New York Times* article, "This Is the Beat Generation," John Clellon Holmes had claimed that "the problem of modern life is essentially a spiritual one." Ginsberg told Richard Eberhart that his poems were "religious and I meant them to be and the effect on audience is (surprising to me at first) a validation of this." In the tradition of Peter Maurin's "Easy Essays," Ferlinghetti's 1958 poem "Christ Climbed Down" used the image of the crucified Christ to criticize the shortcomings of an affluent American Christmas, and a domesticated American Christianity. Like the Catholic Workers, Ferlinghetti considered the Christ of the Beatitudes more important than the socially safe churches of contemporary Christianity. Several of the Beat generation claimed that "beat" was an abbreviation of "beatific"; like the Catholic Workers, some of them preached the "beatitudes"; in 1959, several of the Beats published a magazine called *Beatitude* "designed to extol beauty and promote the beatific life among the various mendicants, neo-existentialists, christs, poets, painters, musicians, and other inhabitants of North Beach." Ginsberg's "Footnote to Howl" asserted the holiness of the world and the goodness of creation, even while it rejected the conventional dualisms of contemporary Judaism and Christianity. And Gary Snyder began a "Note on the Religious Tendencies" of the Beats by suggesting that "this religiosity is primarily one of practice and personal experience, rather than theory."[47]

According to Snyder, the Beats were striving for contemplation, morality, and wisdom, corresponding roughly to the Buddhist *dhyana*, *sila*, and *prajna*. His description of the sources of Beat morality paralleled, in many particulars, the ethic of Catholic Worker personalism: "Love, respect for life, abandon, Whitman, pacifism, anarchism, etc. This comes out of various traditions including Quakers, Shinshu Buddhism, Sufism. And from a loving and open heart. At its best this state of mind has led people to actively resist war, to start communities, and to try to love one another."[48]

More catholic than the *Catholic Worker*, Ginsberg, Kerouac, Snyder, and the Beats were among the people who brought Eastern ideas—especially Zen Buddhism—to the attention of the American public in the postwar world. To many of the Beats, Zen was especially attractive because it seemed to transcend the world of war and violence, consumption and alienation. Zen invited people to consider the exploration of inner space as important as the national fetish with outer space. Buddhism and Zen also gave the Beats models of compassion. The *bodhisattva*—the wandering Buddha—gave them a model of the artist as pilgrim, illuminating the emptiness of social forms and bringing light into the darkness.[49]

The eclecticism of Beat religion led to an eclectic ethics of action as well. Beat "pads" served as houses of hospitality for like-minded hipsters who practiced an ethic of sharing. Both the Catholic Workers and the Beats emphasized personal integrity and risk-taking. They preached variant versions of the personalist gospel, but they both accentuated the importance of practicing what they preached, and the centrality of a consistent personal and public ethic. Both found the Bomb and American culture threatening to human life and human dignity, and they used newspapers and poetry to take their protests to the American people. The Catholic Workers chose poverty, while the Beats worked for it, but both of them decried the material comforts that were secured by American national security policy. According to Lawrence Lipton, the Beats had chosen "the New Poverty" instead of "the New Prosperity," and "voluntary self-alienation from the family cult, from Moneytheism and all its works and ways." Catholic workers practiced civil disobedience, the Beats the deviant disobedience of social and sexual outlaws.[50]

In 1961, Lawrence Ferlinghetti joined with David Meltzer and Michael McClure to publish *The Journal for the Protection of All Beings*. The opening editorial of this "Love-Shot Issue" offered "an open place where normally apolitical men may speak uncensored on any subject they feel most hotly and coolly about in a world which politics has made." As anarchists, they expressed no interest "in protecting beings from themselves," but an interest—like the *Catholic Worker*—in "the lives they do not allow themselves to live and the deaths other people would give us, both of the body and the spirit." And reflecting the atomic insecurities of 1961, the copyright page offered the disclaimer: "Due to the transitory nature of life on earth, this Journal is not sold on a subscription basis." Contributors included Thomas Merton, Bertrand Russell, Norman Mailer, Gregory Corso, Gary Snyder, Robert Duncan, Allen Ginsberg, Peter Orlovsky, and William Burroughs. According to Theodore Roszak, these writers practiced "the politics of the Loony Left." For example, in the journal William Burroughs proposed the unthinkable thought that the United States form an alliance with Red China. Ginsberg suggested that "Socialist-Co-Op Anarchism"—plus peyote— could cure the Cold War. More broadly, they believed that "what passes for political policy and controversy in our world is largely the rationalization of pathological processes. To recognize this is not an excuse to stop thinking; but it is the beginning of wisdom."[51]

Beat Politics

Because they complicated the symbols of faith of the American middle class, the Beats were not wildly welcomed into American Cold War culture. Critics called them "beatniks," with a suffix suggesting Communist complicity, just as the term "peacenik" implied that peace was an un-American activity. The Beats were decried as "The Cult of Unthink," the "Know Nothing Bohemians," and they were condemned for their drugs, dissent, dress, and hygiene. At colleges, too, professors panned the subjects, lyrics, and language of the Beats. Even Irving Howe, an avowed leftist teaching at Brandeis, put down Beat poetry.[52]

They were also criticized by activists in the collectivist tradition, who mistook their political personalism for eccentric individualism. Even some people in the New Left misunderstood Beat cultural politics. In *A Prophetic Minority*, for example, SDS activist Jack Newfield suggested that "the closest the Beats came to politics was to write bad poetry against the Bomb." Casey Hayden of the Student Nonviolent Coordinating Committee contended that "the beatniks were—and are—just the Movement without altruism and energy. They are alienated by exactly the same things we are, but they just can't act on their discontent in an effective political way."[53]

Such criticism did not generally dampen the enthusiasm of disaffected young people for the Beats. Often, criticism by authority figures gave more authority to the Beats, making them an "oppositional sign." Even critics admitted the allure of the Beat generation. Near the end of a long article lambasting the Beats as "undisciplined and slovenly amateurs who have deluded themselves that their lugubrious absurdities are art," *Life* staff writer

Paul O'Neil noted that many people shared their uneasiness with the materialism and conformity of contemporary American society. But only the Beats had voiced their rejection, making them "the only rebellion around."[54]

The critics' definition of the Beat movement as apolitical helps to define the bounds of thinkable thought in the era of the liberal consensus. To most people, politics meant the pursuit of power or policy via the party system and electoral politics. Looking back to the political engagement in the Party politics of the 1930s, critics complained about a Beat politics of disengagement that "stressed individual conscience over group action, personal testimony over ideology, anarchism over collectivism." The most political (or meta-political) act of the Beats, therefore, was to challenge society's definition of politics, and to assert the importance of a politics of culture. Even the elusiveness of the Beats was an act of political personalism, a manifesto that suggested to more conventionally political people the activist possibilities of personal transformation. David McReynolds of the War Resisters League, for example, felt that the "beat generation, by its very existence, serves notice on all of us who are political that if we want to involve youth in politics we must develop a politics of action. The beat generation can understand Gandhi much better than they understand Roosevelt. They can understand Martin Luther King better than they can understand Hubert Humphrey."[55]

The Folk Beat

More than the conventional poetry of the academy, Beat poetry was a performance art. In the bars and coffeehouses of San Francisco—The Cellar, The Place, the Coffee Gallery, The Coexistence Bagel Shop—people who shared Beat perspectives created a vibrant subculture of caffeine, jazz, poetry, and politics. Poets like Kenneth Rexroth and Lawrence Ferlinghetti experimented with fusions of poetry and jazz. In the process, they brought poetry and the politics of personalism to a wider public audience.[56]

On the East Coast, New York's Greenwich Village maintained its tradition as an American arts center with clusters of cafes, cinemas, bookstores and theaters. Included among them were Le Metro Cafe, Cafe Wha?, the Gaslight Poetry Cafe, Gerde's Folk City, Cafe Reggio, the San Remo, and the Bitter End. These cafes and coffeehouses attracted poets, writers, painters, actors, and activists. The San Remo served as a hangout for Dorothy Day, Paul Goodman, Merce Cunningham, Miles Davis, Julian Beck, and Judith Malina. In the East Village, Stanley's attracted younger artists like Diane Wakoski, Diane DiPrima, Ted Berrigan, and Jerome Rothenberg. All of these institutions offered space for socializing, swapping stories and ideas, and performing.[57]

Coffeehouses also flourished in college towns and other places. In Cambridge, Tulla's Coffee Grinder and Club 47 Mount Auburn offered coffee, poetry readings, film series, jazz, and folk music. At Berkeley, it was the Club Cabale. At the University of Minnesota, the Ten O'Clock Scholar introduced students to Beat poetry and local singers like Bob Dylan. In Joliet, Illinois folksingers gathered at the Know Where; in Omaha, both The Third Man and The Crooked Ear catered to a Midwestern avant-garde.[58]

These campus bohemians set the tone for serious discussions of politics, poetry and personal responsibility. Young people who had grown up in the shadow of the Bomb, they resonated with the "thanatological consciousness" of European existentialism, which impressed them with the importance of making their own meanings in life. They dressed in black—as if in mourning for a fragile world—and countered the fatuous optimism of the "Fabulous Fifties" with a darker, more critical spirit. As Kenneth Rexroth explained, "You cannot expect/ To terrify children with/ Atom bomb drills and quiet them/ With Coca-Cola." At the University of Michigan, SDS president Al Haber explained in 1960, "the term 'beat' has come to characterize all those who have deviated from the traditional college patterns. They are variously professional students, bohemians, political types, and nonstudents who still seem to be around." They were not widely popular, but "in time of dissension and irresolution," their action was "the first step toward radicalism," because "participation crystallizes commitment."[59]

Starting in the late Fifties, folk music joined jazz and Beat poetry on the coffeehouse stages, creating a new blend of political and personalist themes. Like Catholic Worker roundtables, the coffeehouses created an open forum for conversations about the character of American culture. And folk music provided "perspective by incongruity" on that culture. During the late Fifties and early Sixties, folk music brought Beat themes to the American people, harmonizing folk's Old Left heritage with Beat anarcho-pacifism and the freedom songs of the spreading civil rights movement.[60]

While Beat poetry came to the coffeehouses from the anarcho-pacifist personalism of San Francisco, folk music came from the Old Left. From the time of the songbooks of the Industrial Workers of the World (IWW), but especially during the Thirties and Forties, folk music served the Left both as a popular attraction and as a form of propaganda. Idealizing the proletariat and personalizing political party programs, folk musicians used music as a political weapon. Singers like Woody Guthrie sang traditional songs and his own compositions, many of which focused on deprived and marginalized people. Pete Seeger also exemplified this political activism. He first encountered folk music in the Thirties, when he accompanied his musicologist father on a ballad-collecting trip to North Carolina. In 1940, he traversed the country with Woody Guthrie. A year later, with Lee Hays and Mill Lampell, he started the Almanac Singers (because, they said, "a farmhouse would have two books in the house, a Bible and an Almanac. One helped us to the next world, the other helped us to make it through this one."). They sang mainly for Popular Front and union audiences. In the fall of 1941, they settled together in New York in a cooperative apartment called Almanac House, where they held Sunday "Hootenannies" to help pay the rent. By the late Forties and early Fifties, the folk singers' radical repertoire gave them a reputation (generally well-deserved) as Communist sympathizers. The 1948 Progressive Party presidential campaign of Henry Wallace featured folk music instead of the conventional campaign band. And, in 1949, the Weavers' song "If I Had a Hammer" premiered on the folk circuit as a protest of the Smith Act prosecutions of Communist Party leaders. To both its adherents and detractors, "folk music in the postwar era often seemed like left-wing politics in cultural disguise."[61]

Even with its political associations, folk music was increasingly popular until its performers were blacklisted. From 1949 to 1952, the Weavers brought the folk sound (without its radical message) to enthusiastic audiences; they sold more than 4,000,000 records in 1952. But their radical past caused them to be blacklisted, assuring Americans that folk messages would not contaminate the American public by radio or television. Pete Seeger, the most famous of the Weavers, did not appear on network television until 1967, when his performance was still censored by CBS.[62]

Deprived of national media audiences, the more political performers like Pete Seeger were relegated to left-wing summer camps, selected colleges and coffeehouses, and civil rights rallies and meetings. Still, as the number of college students rose from three million in 1960 to five million in 1965 to ten million in 1973, the number of venues featuring folk music also increased, and the number of guitar- and banjo-pickers increased too. Young people frequented the coffeehouses and clubs, and sought out folk music on college radio stations and in the back racks of big record stores. For many, the cultural politics of the coffeehouses seemed more important than the party politics of the Eisenhower years. Elinor Langer recalled that at Swarthmore in the late Fifties "there was almost no political activity. There was a folk festival, a tradition, a sort of bohemian remnant, organized in part by many of us who became radical later. We had some idea, I think, that folk singers were 'real': Reds or Blacks, prisoners or miners, or Elizabethan minstrels still uneasy in the New World. Inviting them to campus seemed slightly dangerous."[63]

Between 1957 and 1962, the politics of folk music were mainly in its associations, both political and proletarian. By acquainting college students and urban beatniks with the struggles of African Americans, workers, and other victims of society, the "Bohemian populism" of jazz, blues, and folk music introduced them to traditions of empathy and protest. In fact, according to Todd Gitlin, Fifties folk music "was an embattled minority's way of conjuring up an ideal folk." By 1961, the conjuring was complete; *Newsweek* reported that "basically the schools and students that support causes support folk music. Find a campus that breeds Freedom Riders, anti-Birch demonstrators, and anti-bomb societies, and you'll find a folk group. The connection is not fortuitous."[64]

The very idea of a folk was a challenge to a society committed to modernization, an implicit association with decentralized and communitarian visions. Like the Catholic Worker conception of an organic society, the concept of a folk involved an oral, small-scale traditional culture, instead of the mechanical modernism of the Atomic Age. Unlike the electrified sound of rock 'n' roll, folk implied a respect for the past and a commitment to simplicity that seemed threatened by the technological futurism of the Fifties. Echoing the elegiac themes of Beat poetry, folk music recalled the organic communities of the past and prefigured a more humane future society.[65]

Just as Beat poetry challenged American academic poetry, so folk music challenged the apparently apolitical American music of Tin Pan Alley. Pop music of the Fifties consisted largely of boy-meets-girl romantic ballads. Pete Seeger contended that even these ostensibly apolitical songs had political implications. "Wrap Your Troubles in Dreams and Dream Your Troubles Away," he said, was "one of the most political songs I know." Pop's pervasive privatism reinforced the idea of separate private and public spheres. Its songs offered little challenge to a culture of consumption, but they implicitly supported the "postwar charter" in which Americans sacrificed political involvement for the satisfactions of affluence. For many college students, the folk music of the coffeehouses provided a parallel institution for the pop music of the Hit Parade.[66]

Like pop music, many folk tunes focused on romantic love. But unlike pop, folk songs also focused on justice. As Bob Dylan said, "There's other things in this world besides love and sex that're important." Especially after the infusion of civil rights songs in the early Sixties, folk music preached an agapic love that transcended the romantic conventions of pop music. Like Social Gospel revivalists, folk singers "depicted a sinful society and exhorted the individual to redeem his community rather than himself." There was also an implicit politics of folk performance. Unlike the slick productions of the hit parade, folk music featured its simplicity, its gritty realism, its down-home sound. Simple guitar chords and a voice of authenticity made folk music accessible to musicians like Bob Dylan, whose vocal skills were hardly marketable in the harmonious world of popular song.[67]

A national folk music revival began in 1957, the year of Senator McCarthy's death, when the Kingston Trio recorded the hit song "Tom Dooley," which sold 2.6 million copies in its first five years. Commercial promoters preferred less political performers like the Trio, the Limeliters, the Brothers Four, and the New Christy Minstrels, whose success in the late Fifties eventually assisted the revival of more critical folk voices. In the early Sixties, the cult became a culture, as folk music enjoyed a remarkable revival.[68]

Joan Baez was the first folk phenomenon of the Sixties. Born in 1941, the daughter of a Quaker physicist who founded the Peninsula Committee for the Abolition of Nuclear Tests, Baez grew up with pacifist and personalist perspectives. As a junior in high school, she attended a three-day conference of world issues sponsored by the American Friends Service Committee. The main speaker was 27-year-old Martin Luther King Jr., who transfixed Baez with his talk of a nonviolent revolution with weapons of love. The following year, she met Gandhi scholar Ira Sandperl, who became her spiritual and political advisor. Like the Catholic Workers, she refused to take part in a civil defense drill at her high school. Baez enrolled at Boston University, but found that she learned more in the coffee houses of Harvard Square. She sang her first sets at the age of 18 in coffeehouses like Tulla's Coffee Grinder and Club Mt. Auburn 47. She appeared at the 1959 Newport Folk Festival and in concert with Pete Seeger. Her first album, Joan Baez, came out for Christmas 1960, and reached number three on the charts, selling more copies than any other female folksinger in record history.[69]

During the early Sixties, Baez extended her repertoire, adding civil rights songs and other topical material to the traditional ballads that had brought her fame. She began to sing "Amazing Grace," "Swing Low," "Oh, Freedom," and "We Shall Overcome." She added Malvina Reynolds' antinuclear "What Have They Done to the Rain?" and the traditional labor song "Joe Hill," along with a variety of Bob Dylan's compositions. *Time* featured her on a November 1962 cover, but the article called her an "otherworldly beatnik," and focused as much on her personal style as on her political message, suggesting that there was, in fact, a politics of personal style. Her direct simplicity offered a model of American womanhood that challenged the conventions of *Seventeen* and *Cosmopolitan*, suggesting that politics and performance were—like the home—appropriate places for young women.[70]

In 1963, Baez contributed $2000 for the March on Washington. In 1964, appearing before President Lyndon Johnson at a gala originally intended for John F. Kennedy, she criticized American involvement in Vietnam and sang "The Times They Are A-Changin'." The same year,

Baez renounced her personal complicity in the Vietnam War, withholding sixty percent of her income taxes. During the 1964-65 school year, she sang several times for the Free Speech Movement at Berkeley. In 1965, she and Ira Sandperl established the Institute for the Study of Nonviolence at Carmel, California. In 1966, she marched with Martin Luther King Jr. in Grenada, Mississippi. In 1966, in order to raise more money for antiwar causes, she posed with her sisters Pauline and Mimi Farina for the poster which read "Girls Say Yes to Boys Who Say No." In 1967, she and Sandperl visited Thomas Merton at Gethsemani. That same year, she was arrested for blocking the Oakland induction center and served ten days in jail. Two months later she did it again and served thirty days. In 1968, she married Resistance activist David Harris, and began a series of concerts to raise money for draft resistance.[71]

The second phenomenon of the Sixties was Bob Dylan. Inspired by Woody Guthrie, the young Minnesota musician sang traditional folk and bluegrass songs in coffeehouses like the Ten O'Clock Scholar near the University of Minnesota. There, he first encountered Beat poetry and began to set Beat themes and images to music. As Dylan said, "It was Ginsberg and Jack Kerouac who inspired me first." In December 1960, he moved to New York, where his girlfriend Suze Retolo—a secretary for CORE—steered him toward protest songs. At the Gaslight Cafe, the Cafe Wha?, and Gerde's Folk City, audiences soon heard songs that voiced many of the concerns of political personalists. Dylan sympathized with the downtrodden members of society, and he felt compelled to speak out. "The idea came to me that you were betrayed by your silence," Dylan told some friends.[72]

Bob Dylan revolutionized the topical song, creating a personalist poetry that he recited with guitar and harmonica. Dylan's jeremiads like "Blowin' in the Wind," "A Hard Rain's A-Gonna Fall," "Masters of War," "Talkin' World War Three Blues," and "Let Me Die in My Footsteps," brought political themes into the mainstream of popular music. Like the Beats, Dylan espoused an aesthetic of expressive spontaneity, and an ethic of personal disaffiliation from the conventional structures of social and political authority. "Bobby Dylan says what a lot of people my age feel but cannot say," said Joan Baez. In fact, folk music set many student perceptions to music, confirming an intuitive analysis of American culture. "We don't give a damn about Moses Herzog's angst or Norman Mailer's private fantasies," claimed an Ivy League senior. "We're concerned with things like the threat of nuclear war, the civil rights movements, and the spreading blight of dishonesty, conformism, and hypocrisy in the United States, especially in Washington. And Bob Dylan is the only American dealing with these subjects in a way that makes sense to us."[73]

Dylan's first album, which included only two of his own songs, sold just 5,000 copies after its release in early 1962. But *The Freewheelin' Bob Dylan* came out in May 1963, and sold 200,000 records by July. In August, Peter, Paul, and Mary released a version of Dylan's "Blowin' in the Wind" which reached the hit parade by selling 300,000 copies in a month. "The music that had been suppressed all too hysterically by the blacklisting of the 1950s was now," according to Susan Douglas, "a commercial gusher." By 1966, Dylan had sold 10 million records, and 150 other musicians had also recorded his works. In the process, folk music created a folk consciousness that resonated with the personalisms of the decade.[74]

Like the *Catholic Worker* and like Allen Ginsberg's *Planet News*, the topical songs of folk music were a form of advocacy journalism, interpreting the events of the day within an explicitly ethical framework. At a time when the nation's news media offered a constrained, conventional interpretation of the news, folk music offered young people *All the News That's Fit to Sing*, as Phil Ochs' 1964 album suggested. Explaining the title of his 1965 album, *Ain't That News*, Tom Paxton observed that "when the poor (again, with the help of the students), are making the first hesitant steps toward organization; when Negroes, disfranchised for years, are lining up to vote; when mass demonstrations and teach-ins protest this government's foreign policy; when after the long sleep of the Eisenhower years, you find heated dialogues and demonstrations throughout the country—that's news." Even before the proliferation of the alternative press, companies like Elektra were pressing alternative albums, and the folk sheet *Broadside* was circulating the new(s) lyrics to topical songs as quickly as possible.[75]

The headline news of the early Sixties was the civil rights movement, and folksingers quickly incorporated the movement's "freedom songs" into their repertory. From the beginning, the civil rights movement adapted songs from the gospel tradition. In Montgomery, for example, during the bus boycott, African Americans voiced their protests in hymns and spirituals, songs that had been charged with struggle from the time of slavery. Montgomery resident Hannah Johnston told Pete Seeger that the popular hymns included "Leaning on the Everlasting Arms," "What a Friend We Have in Jesus," "Onward Christian Soldiers," "Pass Me Not," and "O, Gentle Savior." Spirituals included "Steal Away," "Old Time Religion," "Shine on Me," "Study War No More," "Swing Low," "I Got a Home in That Rock," and "Poor Man Dives." Other popular songs included "This Little Light of Mine" and "We Are Soldiers in the Army." After the bus boycott, the Montgomery Gospel Trio carried the musical legacy of the struggle into voter registration drives in Alabama.[76]

Songs also served to express the solidarity of the student sit-in movement of 1960. Although the sit-ins themselves were usually conducted in silence, the workshops and rallies that supported the students usually rang with songs. The Vanderbilt University students invited Guy Carawan, the music director of the Highlander Folk School, to lead the songs surrounding their sit-ins. Highlander had assisted civil rights activists for most of the Fifties—Rosa Parks had attended Highlander shortly before her famous bus sit-in—and had instituted Easter weekend workshops on the politics of race for college students. At those workshops, Carawan tried to teach students the union songs of Woody Guthrie and Pete Seeger, but found that African American students resonated more with songs like "We Shall Overcome." In 1960, Carawan taught the Vanderbilt students "Keep Your Eyes on the Prize, Hold On," but the theme song of the Nashville Movement was "Freedom," an adaptation of the traditional sacred chant, "Amen." Later that same year, Carawan led songs at the founding meetings of the Student Nonviolent Coordinating Committee.[77]

By 1961, with Carawan's help, "We Shall Overcome" had become the anthem of the civil rights movement and the Sixties. Zilphia Horton of the Highlander Folk School had heard Black members of a tobacco workers' union singing the old religious song "I Will Overcome" with the pronoun "we." She added some verses and taught it to Pete Seeger, who changed the "will" to "shall" and added verses like "We'll walk hand in hand." Writing from jail in 1964, pacifist Barbara Deming tried to explain the popularity of the song. She especially liked the fact that it was "stubborn on the one hand, reassuring on the other. The words go 'We shall overcome . . . We are not afraid'; and in the same breath, 'Black and white together, we shall live in peace someday.'" Deming knew that the song didn't speak for everybody—she knew that many white people were deaf to it, and many black people saw nonviolence as simply tactical. But she also noted that "those in the revolt with a vision of the 'beloved community' have put a stamp on the movement—as the song reveals."[78]

The organizers and songleaders of the Student Nonviolent Coordinating Committee took the freedom songs of the Nashville Movement all across the South. Hymns and spirituals and folksongs accompanied the Freedom Rides of 1961, and the organizing of 1961-65. Music was such an essential element of the 1961–62 Albany [Georgia] Movement that six black college students formed the Freedom Singers. They premiered in concert with Pete Seeger in November 1962 and toured churches and colleges—both North and South—to spread the news of freedom and to raise money for SNCC. Invited to the Newport Folk Festival in 1963, they also sang for the August 1963 March on Washington.[79]

By 1962, white students and folksingers had responded to the power of the songs of black folk. At the Port Huron conference of Students for a Democratic Society, for example, Casey Hayden (a white SNCC staffer who had been arrested with her husband Tom in Albany) led freedom songs to reinforce the college students' solidarity with the civil rights movement and with each other. By 1962, also, folksingers had started to compose songs concerning civil rights, and to bring their repertory to civil rights rallies. Bob Dylan's "Oxford Town" and "The Lonesome Death of Hattie Carroll" brought news of civil rights to student audiences. In 1963, Dylan joined Pete Seeger, Theodore Bikel, and others for a 1963 voter-registration drive in Greenwood, Mississippi, where activists sang "We Shall Overcome," "Everybody Wants Freedom," "Ain't Goin' to Let Segregation Turn Me Around," "Eyes on the Prize, Hold On," "Oh, Freedom," "We Shall Not Be Moved," and "Wade in the Water." The most popular song, however, was "This Little Light of Mine—I'm Going to Let It Shine," with its message of personal witness and commitment.[80]

By Freedom Summer in 1964, the Mississippi Caravan of Music brought hundreds of musicians to the state to provide music for short programs known as Freedom Workshops that provided basic instruction in history, geography, mathematics, languages, and voter-registration procedures. Some musicians like Pete Seeger wondered what they were accomplishing. He knew that he was "just one more grain of sand in the world," but in personalist fashion, he concluded, "I'd rather throw my weight, however small, on the side of what I think is right than selfishly look after my own fortunes and have to live with a bad conscience."[81]

After 1962, the infusion of topical songs and political involvement energized folk music. Although Dylan's songs pushed the bounds of politics, Dylan himself generally stayed away from the politics of protest. He appeared at a few events in 1963, but soon renounced the role of prophet. Folk music was an ideal organizing tool, drawing aggrieved individuals into the collective activity of singing. In meetings, on the streets, in the jails, political personalists practiced community with songs that came from the African American and folk tradition. Folk musicians like Pete Seeger, Joan Baez, Judy Collins, Phil Ochs, Tom Paxton, and Arlo Guthrie often appeared at the political demonstrations of the decade. Seeger, Baez, Dylan, Odetta, and Peter, Paul, and Mary participated in the August 1963 March on Washington, where Baez led the anthem "We Shall Overcome." Folk music, said critic Morris Dickstein, "was the perfect expression of the green years of the early sixties, the years of integration, interracial solidarity, 'I have a dream,' and 'We shall overcome': the years of the Port Huron Statement and the early New Left; the years of the lunch-counter sit-ins and ban-the-bomb demonstrations. Folk music was the living bridge between the protest culture of the New Left and the genuinely populist elements of the Old Left of the 1930s and after."[82]

Like Beat poetry, folk music validated many people's developing perceptions of American society. Folksinger Malvina Reynolds told Pete Seeger that when people listened to folk songs, or bought folk records, they "might well be saying, 'Thank God, here's somebody who's saying what has been eating me since my first air-raid drill. I'm not alone.' And that is the beginning of action." For students from the suburban diaspora, folk music provided a connection to a committed community of memory. Sung in urban coffeehouses or on college campuses, folk music constituted a practice of commitment. Even for young people who didn't participate in the politics of the period, and especially for students too young to be involved in demonstrations, folk music offered a kind of proxy politics. Folk music provided a way for young people to participate, if only vicariously, in struggles of the civil rights movement. The music legitimized and publicized the social concerns of disaffected American youths.[83]

The 1963 Newport Folk Festival marked the height of the folk revival. It featured the Freedom Singers, Bob Dylan, Pete Seeger, Jim Garland, Joan Baez, and Peter, Paul, and Mary, and introduced new topical talent like Phil Ochs and Tom Paxton. 37,000 people attended. Popularity enmeshed folk music in the star system and the "American success syndrome," but it also provided impetus and an audience for music that contested the culture's values. Folk music, therefore, remained a part of the political scene throughout the Sixties. Dylan himself dropped out of political minstrelsy, but his early songs continued to resonate with young people. Especially at the local level, young women and men learned the folk classics and sang them to, and with, their friends and compatriots. Learning the songs at a time when music really mattered, they also learned something about a personalist perspective on politics.[84]

Conclusion

The Beat movements of the Fifties offered Americans of the Sixties a second path to the personalist perspectives of the Sixties. During the 1940s and 1950s, poet and critic Kenneth Rexroth integrated the perspectives of European anarchists and personalists with the anarcho-pacifism of the Waldport circle of conscientious objectors. He influenced Allen Ginsberg, Gary Snyder, William Everson, Lawrence Ferlinghetti, and Jack Kerouac, who, with the help of Chester McPhee, introduced these ideas to the American public. Complemented by the caustic comedy of Mort Sahl and Lenny Bruce, and with the social satires of *Mad* magazine and *The Realist*, the Beats began to tell the truth about the empire's new clothes. Folk music intersected this Beat community and also proved attractive to many people who suffered the alienations of American life. With the topical folksingers of the late Fifties and early Sixties, the Beats created a community constituted by literature, social criticism, personalist compassion, and cultural politics.

Although mainstream Americans interpreted the Beats as atheistic hedonists, Beat personalism was rooted in religion and ethics, both Western and Eastern. Like the Catholic Workers, the Beats drew on the experience of conscientious objectors to World War II and on the American anarcho-pacifist tradition. Both the Beats and the Catholic Workers decried the depersonalization of people in modern American society. They questioned the priorities of a civilization devoted to boodle and the Bomb. And both believed in the integration of spirituality and politics, as did civil rights activists like Martin Luther King Jr.

CIVIL RIGHTS PERSONALISM

JUST FIVE MONTHS AFTER THE Operation Alert civil defense protest and two months after Allen Ginsberg's apocalyptic "Howl," in December of 1955, Martin Luther King Jr. and the African American community of Montgomery, Alabama, began to practice a Gandhian politics of action that would reinforce the pacifist personalism of Dorothy Day and the anarchist personalism of the Beats. The early civil rights movement was almost inevitably personalist, because the strictures of Southern segregation structured life so much that everyday activities like riding a bus or sitting at a lunch counter would be interpreted as political.

But when Martin Luther King Jr. and other civil rights leaders interpreted these personal acts in terms of a personalist philosophy, they took on broader meaning and significance. Like Peter Maurin, King preached a new philosophy which was not really new. Like Maurin, he believed that radicalism came from going back to the roots of Christianity. King's first sermon was called "Rediscovering Lost Values," but he sometimes gave it under the title "Going Forward by Going Backwards."[1]

While Maurin preached Catholic social thought, King offered the African American social gospel. Martin Luther King Jr. and other African

American activists in the civil rights movement drew on the religious traditions of the black folk church, the Social Gospel, Gandhian nonviolence and American personalism to enunciate a vision of justice and activism that would become increasingly popular in the 1960s. With King's "voice merging" of these traditions, the flesh of African American activists became word, and the words of King's language shaped American radicalism and American culture in the Sixties and afterward. Although local people made the civil rights movement, it was King's vocation to be its public voice, a convocation of African American and liberal religious traditions in American history.[2]

Personalist Philosophy

King's personalism had philosophical roots. He first studied personalism under George Davis at Crozer Theological Seminary. Taking almost one-third of his courses from Davis, King learned about *agape*, altruism, and activism. According to Davis, personalism required acknowledgment of "the dignity, the beauty, and the love discernible in human personality, both non-Christian and Christian." Davis interpreted history as progress from the impersonal to the personal, as concern for people replaced inhuman ideas and institutions. For example, he celebrated shifts from the subjugation to the acknowledgment of women, from the rights of property to the rights of people, from slavery to freedom, from starvation to a living wage, and from the cruelties of unbridled competition to the cooperative commonwealth of the welfare state. Davis taught that *agape*, which obligated altruism, was the dominant principle of God's universe, and he emphasized the tradition of evangelical reformers in abolitionism, prison reform, insane asylums, and child welfare. For him, the personalist purpose of reform was human "solidarity" in which individuals mutually realized their dignity and destiny.[3]

King chose to pursue graduate work at Boston University because it was the center of American personalism, a particular tradition of Protestantism engaged with ethical issues and social causes. At Boston, he studied personalism with philosophers Edgar Brightman and L. Harold DeWolf; DeWolf taught six courses to King and he directed the young minister's dissertation. Brightman defined Personalism as "a system of philosophy that regards the universe as an interacting system of persons (or selves). According to it, everything that exists is either a person, or some experience, process, or aspect of a person or persons in relation with one another. Reality is social or interpersonal. A person is taken to be a complex unity of consciousness that is able to develop rational thought and ideal values."[4]

The young student especially appreciated the ethical implications of personalism, writing in *Stride Toward Freedom* that personalism "gave me metaphysical and philosophical grounding for the idea of a personal God, and it gave me a metaphysical basis for the dignity and worth of all human personality." King believed, like the poet Kenneth Rexroth, that "God is lover and beloved—a Person—or he is nothing Important." Rooted in a religious tradition that professed the personal intervention of a providential God, King objected to abstract, philosophical conceptions of God. "In God," he said, "there is feeling and will, responsive to the deepest yearnings of the human heart; this God both evokes and answers prayer."[5]

King's metaphysical foundation for the intrinsic value of persons led him to judge the state, its laws, and other institutions in terms of their effects on individual persons. "Segregation," said King, "stands diametrically opposed to the sacredness of human personality. It debases personality." Segregation was sinful because "it scars the soul of both the segregator and the segregated," and because "it ends up depersonalizing the segregated." King opposed racism and militarism because they treated people as things, violating their existence and/or dignity as persons. "When machines and computers, profit motives and property rights are considered more important than people," he claimed in *Where Do We Go From Here?* that "the giant triplets of racism, materialism, and militarism are incapable of being conquered."[6]

Personalism also reaffirmed the young King's notions about the moral law of the cosmos. For King and other personalists, moral law was not a mere abstraction of human thought, but a revelation of a personal God. Metaphysics and ethics were inextricably interrelated; because humans were created in God's image, they were obligated to respect the personhood of others. As Brightman said in his Law of the Ideal of Personality, "All persons ought to judge and guide all of their acts by their ideal conception . . . of what the whole personality ought to become both individually and socially." Furthermore, belief in moral law made it possible for King to believe in the redemptive suffering of nonviolence because, while "the arc of the moral universe is long, it bends toward justice."[7]

King's graduate studies also reaffirmed his sense of the social nature of human life, and the importance of person-in-community. "Life under the reign of God," DeWolf taught, "is not an individualistic affair. Since love is its dominant principle, it is communal to the very core." DeWolf's ethical doctrine included the Law of Social Devotion, which contended that "all persons ought to devote themselves to serving the best interests of the group and to subordinate personal gain to social gain." Because people fulfilled themselves in lives of service, personal growth, and community growth were dialectically related. Brightman's Law of Altruism argued that "each person ought to respect all other persons as ends in themselves, and, as far as possible, to cooperate with others in the production and enjoyment of shared values." Altruism involved not selflessness, but the development of the social self.[8]

King's academic studies, which immediately preceded his ministry at the Dexter Avenue Baptist Church in Montgomery, provided a rich foundation for political protest. With his undergraduate major in sociology and his seminary and graduate studies in theology and philosophy, King was well prepared to offer a personalist perspective on people and society. It was King's genius that his academic studies didn't remain merely academic; instead, he applied them in his ministry to his congregation and America. From 1955 to 1968, Martin Luther King Jr. offered attentive Americans a course in applied personalism.

African American Personalism

The personalist philosophy of the university was less important to King's development than the political personalism of the black churches. The personalist perspective was not new to King as a graduate student. Indeed, as Keith Miller suggests, "Personalism proved attractive to King not because its ideas were stimulating and provocative, but for the opposite reason. He appreciated personalist ideas because they were reassuringly familiar," an integral part of the traditional religion of the black churches. King's special mission was to bring the personalist liberation theology of African American religion into the mainstream of American political discourse. In the course of the Sixties, the faith of the black experience would move mountains, including the faith of white America.[9]

Martin Luther King Jr. grew up in the black Baptist Church, which had been established to protest the racism of the white churches. For this reason, notes James Cone, "the word 'black' was more important in defining his faith than the word 'Baptist.'" The black church offered an understanding of God, and of God's work in history, that made sense of slavery and segregation, and of black people's striving for freedom and justice. In African American churches like Martin Luther King Sr.'s Ebenezer Baptist Church, the gospel of personalism began in Genesis, when a personal God created people—and not just some of them—in the divine image. This act of creation gave each person human dignity and human rights, and suggested that people were made for community with each other. Exodus, and the journey to freedom, complemented the gospel of personalism, and inspired African American churches and activists. From the time of slavery, the story of the escape from oppression—of Moses and the Promised Land—resonated with the hopes of African American peoples. Exodus also reinforced the collectivism of personalism; it was not the story of individual freedom, but of the freedom of a people.[10]

Churches like Ebenezer taught African Americans that Christ's act of redemption created a community in which there was neither Jew nor Greek, neither slave nor free, neither male nor female, neither black nor white. "No matter what whites said about blacks or what wicked laws were enacted against their humanity," says James Cone, "the people of Ebenezer believed that God had bestowed upon them a somebodyness which had been signed and sealed by Jesus' death and resurrection."[11]

The idea of "somebodyness" was an assertion of a religious personalism with political implications. "Somebodyness" was an ideal of self-respect; it was knowing that you had been created in the image of God, and rejecting the culture's negative images of you. To be somebody was not to be better than everybody else; to be somebody was to know that you had value not for what you did, but for who you were. "We must have the spiritual audacity to assert our somebodyness." said King, because "he who feels he is somebody, even though humiliated by external servitude, achieves a sense of selfhood and dignity that nothing in all the world can take away." According to King, somebodyness would be a psychological cause and consequence of the civil rights movement.[12]

The African American churches emphasized a gospel of justice, love, obedience, and hope, which translated into a politics of protest, accommodation, self-help, and optimism. The Old Testament theme of justice, expressed especially in Exodus and the prophets, dominated the sermons and songs of the African American congregations. Justice was how love acted in the world: as King said in his dissertation, "Love is the ontological concept. . . . Justice is dependent on love. It is a part of love's activity." Like the Catholic Worker, the black churches made the condition of the poor the criterion of faith. To be Christian in the black church tradition was to do justice for the poor.[13]

The African American churches saw race and religion as inseparable. Martin Luther King Sr., who schooled his son in the social gospel of the black Baptist church, said that "in the act of faith, every minister becomes an advocate for justice." Unlike mainstream white churches, black churches understood the politics of the gospel, especially in regard to race. When racism affronted their human dignity, African Americans used religion to affirm the obligation of justice and the right to be treated as whole persons.[14]

But the call to justice was combined with an ethic of love, enunciated most clearly in the Sermon on the Mount. The ethic of love meant that, however much people hated you, you must love them. The commandment to love—even your enemies—promised a multiracial community of love. Expressing the harmony of ends and means, the black churches taught Martin Luther King Jr. that the public practice of love was the way to the beloved community.[15]

Christian vocation demanded obedience to God's will, and to the activist assumption that "God helps those who help themselves." Obedience to God's will, including God's call for justice, demanded protest; the call for love sometimes required accommodation, but it always demanded nonviolence; and hope entailed optimism that protest and personal virtue would, in God's time and with God's help, lead to a better world. Called to justice and love, the members of the black churches knew that they had to walk the talk, to make the word flesh in their own lives and actions.[16]

And hope required that, however difficult the journey, African Americans must remember that they were conspiring with God for God's purposes. Exodus taught African Americans that God was an active agent of social change, delivering his people from slavery and injustice. "God is able," Martin Luther King Jr. often reminded his listeners, "to make a way out of no way, . . . to transform dark yesterdays into bright tomorrows." The theme of deliverance echoed in the civil rights movement, and in the movements of the Sixties.[17]

Sometimes black preachers located the bright tomorrows in the afterlife. Sometimes heaven was the only place where African Americans could imagine their somebodyness. "During slavery," said James Cone, "heaven served as that element in the slaves' religion which enabled them to believe that they were somebody even though there was nothing in this world that recognized their humanity. It was a spirituality that affirmed their personhood in a society which denied it." Often, though, African American churches combined the salvation of heaven and earth. It was Martin Luther King's contribution to the black churches to clarify and amplify that vision of an immanent God working with them for a heaven on earth.[18]

The black churches knew that the way to heaven could be hell. But their theology of the cross taught members like King that Christ's crucifixion had brought salvation, and that unmerited suffering could be redemptive. "The cross," notes James Cone, "was the suffering that Christians freely assumed in their fight for the political freedom of the poor." Activists might be crucified, but God could bring life from death.[19]

Social Gospel Personalism

At Crozer Seminary and at Boston University, King learned and loved the liberal Social Gospel tradition of American Protestantism. Like Personalism, this tradition reinforced the theology he had learned in his father's mansions, both domestic and religious. With personalism, the Social Gospel gave King a language for communicating with white Americans who had not shared the African American experience of slavery and segregation.[20]

King's first and most influential encounters with the Social Gospel came in the African American community. Both his father and his grandfather had preached against the evils of segregation. Other Ebenezer homilists such as William Holmes Borders, Benjamin Mays, and Vernon Johns reinforced the social message of the black gospel. Unlike neo-orthodoxy, theological liberalism offered a theology of human possibility, combining individual conversion and social transformation. In Davis's classes at Crozier, King encountered Rauschenbusch's *A Theology for the Social Gospel*, which grounded activism in the life of Christ: "Since Christ revealed the divine worth of life and personality, and since his salvation seeks the restoration and fulfillment of even the least, it follows that the Kingdom of God, at every stage of development, tends toward a social order which will best guarantee to all personalities their freest and highest development." King also enjoyed Rauschenbusch's *Christianity and the Social Crisis*, which focused on the prophetic tradition and "the social aims of Jesus." Like Rauschenbusch, King believed that "a religion that ends with the individual ends."[21]

When he took his first pastorate at Dexter Avenue Baptist Church in Montgomery, the young minister established an organizational structure that included a Social and Political Action Committee "since the gospel of Jesus is a social gospel as well as a personal gospel seeking to save the whole man." This Social Gospel allowed King to connect the liberation movements of the postwar world with the philosophy of progress in Western civilization. The struggle for justice, he said, was part of the struggle to create the beloved community, the Kingdom of God on earth. An immanent God conspired with his people to achieve progress toward moral perfection and a just society.[22]

King's own experience of the pervasive social sins of racism, his reading of Reinhold Niebuhr, and his embrace of the liberal preachers' idea of "optimism despite tragedy" kept him from the fatuous optimism of some Social Gospelers and philosophical personalists. Progress came, according to King, from a dialectic set in motion by people dissatisfied with the sins of the social order. In an era of adjustment psychology, King refused to adjust to segregation or sectarianism, to poverty or violence. Instead, he thought that progress came from the calls of the "creatively maladjusted."[23]

King appreciated Niebuhr's realism and his critique of simplistic perfectionism, but he was never a pessimistic imperfectionist in the Niebuhrian tradition, because he understood the realistic power of love against evil, and because he rejected the ethical dualism of Niebuhr's position. King believed that *agape*—and nonviolent discipline—provided possibilities for preparing moral men for a moral society and vice versa. And, because he believed in the indivisibility of the moral universe, he argued that "there cannot be two consciences, one in civil and another in political life." People grounded in religious and household values could and should apply them to politics. King's synthesis of the Social Gospel and personalist philosophy convinced him that justice was possible, and reinforced the hope—if not the optimism—that he had learned at Ebenezer.[24]

The Social Gospel also offered King a language that gave his rhetoric a resonance in the white liberal community. As Keith Miller convincingly shows, King borrowed liberally from the sermons of white liberal preachers like Harry Emerson Fosdick, Phillips Brooks, J. Wallace Hamilton, and black liberals like Benjamin Mays, Howard Thurman, and Gardner Taylor. And he cited white theologians like Rauschenbusch, Niebuhr, and Tillich to complement the gospel of the black church. The use of traditional values to protest contemporary practices made King a "conservative militant," able to transform the African American demand for equality into "something it had never been before—a mainstream American idea."[25]

In the same way, King used the image of the American Dream to communicate the social gospel to white Americans. Throughout the late 1950s and early 1960s, he began to articulate his personalist vision of American society in terms of its own best political traditions. In his speeches, for example, King emphasized the universalism of the Declaration of Independence—all men, not just white men, were equal—and the divine origins of human rights. In this way, he connected the genesis of the United States with Genesis, and with the personalist emphasis on the dignity and worth of individuals. Using the rhetoric of the civil religion, he called on Christians and Americans to live up to their original ideals. In doing so, King made the civil rights movement "an *American* movement."[26]

The Americanization of Gandhi

During the Fifties, King also brought the nonviolent philosophy of Mahatma Gandhi into his religious synthesis. Mahatma Gandhi was an Indian social reformer instrumental to the independence of India. Like many European and American personalists, he focused his attention on the dignity and worth of human beings—even India's Untouchables. Like personalists, he decried distinctions between the personal and the public, the political and the religious, and the sacred and the secular. "I do not know of any religion apart from human activity," said Gandhi. "Religion which takes no account of practical affairs and does not help to solve them is no religion." Inspired by the civil disobedience of Henry David Thoreau, he led a massive campaign of nonviolent direct action. Like Peter Maurin and the Catholic Workers, he preached and practiced a gospel of voluntary poverty and a cult of cultivation and culture. Suspicious of modernization, he recalled his followers to the communal practices of the past.[27]

King appropriated Gandhi in his own religious and personalist terms. "Gandhi," King contended, "was probably the first person in history to lift the love ethic of Jesus above mere interaction between individuals to a powerful and effective social force on a large scale." From Gandhi, King learned how to connect the social force of nonviolence to the love ethic of African American spirituality. As Lerone Bennett says, "King's genius was not in the application of Gandhism to the Negro struggle but in the transmuting of Gandhism by grafting it onto the only thing that could give it relevance and force in the Negro community, the Negro religious community." Influenced by his parents' peaceable example, and by the writing of African American students of Gandhi such as Howard Thurman, Mordecai Johnson, Benjamin Mays, and William Stuart Nelson, King helped shape a civil rights movement based on nonviolent resistance to injustice. In the process, he—like all of the American pacifists who drew on Gandhi's work—Americanized the Indian leader, appropriating those aspects of Gandhi's message that fit best with the situations and strategies of American peace and justice movements.[28]

The African American community of the United States had enjoyed extensive contacts with Gandhi for thirty years preceding the Montgomery bus boycott. African Americans like Johnson and Thurman and Mays and William Stuart Nelson visited India in the 1930s and 1940s to learn from Gandhi, and Indian nationalists influenced by Gandhi regularly visited African American communities. In 1935, Gandhi told Thurman that "it may be through the Negroes that the unadulterated message of nonviolence will be delivered to the world." King himself visited India in 1959. For these intellectuals, Gandhi offered a method of overcoming oppression that was consonant with the teachings of the black church. The Gandhian ideal of *satyagraha*, based on a foundation of *ahimsa* (noninjury or nonkilling) and *satya* (truth), resonated with the emphasis in African American religion on love and redemptive suffering. The Gandhian faculty of Howard University inspired such activists as Harris Wofford and James Farmer, who founded the Congress of Racial Equality (CORE) in 1942. William Stuart Nelson taught the first college course on "The Philosophy and Methods of Nonviolence" at Howard University in 1960. And their writings in the African American press prepared black people for the coming of an American Gandhi.[29]

King's introduction to Gandhi came in 1949-50 at Crozer Seminary, when he heard both A.J. Muste and Mordecai Johnson (president of Howard University) speak about the Indian activist. Unconverted by

Muste's radical pacifism, King still recalled that he was "deeply moved by Mr. Muste's talk," and he read more of Muste's writings as he began to think about Gandhian nonviolence. Johnson impressed the young seminarian even more, and he later wrote that "his message was so profound and electrifying that I left the meeting and bought a half-dozen books on Gandhi's life and works."[30]

King's Gandhian approach to nonviolence also drew on the pacifist tradition of the white American Social Gospel preachers like Fosdick and Hamilton. Especially during the interwar period, "the peace-minded pulpit became a fixture in American life, and many thousands of Americans became pacifists or near-pacifists." Like these predecessors, King understood Gandhian nonviolence as a non-Christian expression of Christian beliefs. "God worked through Gandhi, and the spirit of Jesus Christ saturated his life," King told the *Christian Century* in 1962. "It is ironic, but inescapably true that the greatest Christian of the modern world was a man [Gandhi] who never embraced Christianity." By wrapping Gandhi in the Christian gospel, King and other American pacifists made him understandable to an American audience.[31]

King knew about Gandhian nonviolence before he became a public figure. But the Montgomery bus boycott brought him into contact with a group of pacifists from the War Resisters League and the Fellowship of Reconciliation. The most important of these contacts was Bayard Rustin, a Quaker organizer who had participated in the 1955 civil defense protests in New York's City Hall Park. Rustin and others led King to adopt nonviolence as a politics of action. Rustin came to Montgomery while King was out of town, just at a point when the city had issued an ultimatum: immediate settlement on unfavorable terms, or mass arrests. Rustin offered a Gandhian response to organizer E.D. Nixon; instead of waiting to be arrested, the leaders should voluntarily surrender. While crowds of people cheered them, they turned their arrests into a cause for celebration. Rustin also suggested that the Montgomery Improvement Association change its mass meetings into prayer meetings to provide the spiritual strength that would be needed for a protracted nonviolent bus boycott. He helped raise bail and plan strategy before he left Montgomery, and he recruited liberal allies, raised money, and publicized the boycott upon his return North. From New York, Rustin consulted King by telephone and maintained King's connections with pacifists like A.J. Muste and David Dellinger. Eventually, Rustin became such a trusted advisor that King added him to the staff of the Southern Christian Leadership Conference.[32]

Rustin linked the postwar radical pacifists and the civil rights movement. Born in 1910 and raised by Quaker grandparents, Rustin joined the Young Communist League during the Depression, but resigned in 1939. He converted from communism to socialism, and served as assistant to A. Philip Randolph of the Brotherhood of Sleeping Car Porters and to A.J. Muste of the Fellowship for Reconciliation. During World War II, Rustin declared his conscientious objection. Refusing to work in a Civilian Public Service Camp, he was imprisoned for 28 months. After the war, he became secretary of the War Resisters' League and participated in anti-nuclear demonstrations.[33]

In 1947, Rustin and George Houser organized a "Journey of Reconciliation" that presaged the "Freedom Rides" of the early Sixties. In "one of the very first attempts to apply Gandhian methods of nonviolent resistance to the field of civil rights," an interracial group of sixteen people rode buses throughout the South. Although they were supported by the Fellowship of Reconciliation, the Congress of Racial Equality, and the National Association for the Advancement of Colored People, the pilgrims met threats, violence, and imprisonment on the trip. Rustin served 22 days on a chain gang for his impertinence.[34]

By the time he arrived in Montgomery in 1956, Rustin had been arrested twenty-two times for his opposition to war and racism. He had worked with the Fellowship of Reconciliation, the Congress of Racial Equality, and the War Resisters League. Drawing on his Quaker background and on Gandhian nonviolence, Rustin worked with the Free India Committee after the war, with disarmament activists in England, and with West African independence leaders. At the invitation of Gandhi's Congress Party, he spent six months in India. But he also practiced nonviolence at home. In a 1951 New York protest against the Korean War, an outraged spectator seized a picket sign and rushed toward Rustin with the stick. Rustin handed the man his own stick, and invited him to use both of them. The man threw both his weapons down, although he later attacked another marcher with his fists.[35]

While Rustin worked for King, he also helped to organize the American antinuclear movement. Norman Cousins and A.J. Muste consulted him about the formation of the Committee for a Sane Nuclear Policy in 1957. In 1958, he helped with the first Aldermaston March in England. He planned the 1960-61 San Francisco-to-Moscow peace walk for the Committee for Nonviolent Action, as well as the 1963 March on Washington. Like Nobel Peace Prize winner Linus Pauling, Rustin fought for the "triple revolution" of peace, civil rights, and industrial relations. "I'm prepared to lie down in front of a truck to get work for Negroes," Rustin said, "but also for white people to get work because if there isn't work for one there is not work for the other. This is tied to peace because the billions spent on defense ought to be spent on a war on poverty."[36]

Both civil rights activists and nuclear pacifists of the 1950s were involved in "the Americanization of Gandhi," the process by which Gandhian principles of nonviolence became practices of protest in the United States. They were, as Keith Miller suggests, remarkably successful. "King's oratorical genius and his choreography of massive, nonviolent protests explained Gandhi to the entire nation, so successfully that King's Gandhi became America's Gandhi." Gandhi reinforced King's own idea about the power of truth and love, the courage of active nonviolence, and the redemptive power of unearned suffering.[37]

Montgomery

As Warren Steinkraus says, Martin Luther King's "contribution to personalism was largely of a practical nature—how one implements ideals amidst real social exigencies." The Montgomery, Alabama bus boycott was just such an exigency. On December 1, 1955, Mrs. Rosa Parks refused to give her seat on a bus to a white man, as Southern custom demanded. A seamstress at a Montgomery department store, Parks had been secretary to E.D. Nixon, a Montgomery leader who had been head of the state NAACP. During the summer of 1955, she had attended the Highlander Folk School where she had discussed the idea of civil disobedience.[38]

Because of his education and his commitments to equality, King was asked to serve as spokesman for the bus boycott that followed the arrest. He was impressed with the spirituality that moved people to protest, with their sense that God condemned the abuses on the buses. "Blacks believed," as James Cone says, "in the dignity and worth of their personhood, even though whites, with few exceptions, refused to treat blacks as human beings." King responded immediately to this personalist perspective. In his first speech during the Montgomery bus boycott, for example, delivered spontaneously on the night that Rosa Parks had been arrested, King called for justice, for the equal protection of the laws and for the equal treatment of persons.[39]

During the course of the Montgomery boycott, King began to emphasize the nonviolent love of African Americans more than the justice of white society. In the early days of the bus controversy, King was protected by armed guards; he even applied for a permit to carry a gun. But a conversion experience that assured him of God's grace, and ongoing conversations with Gandhian pacifists like Bayard Rustin, changed King's outlook. The conversion experience took place on January 27. After a telephone threat "to blow your brains out and blow up your house," King tried to assess the reasons for his commitment. He failed. But giving himself up to God, he heard a voice telling him to stand up for righteousness and justice and truth, and promising that "lo, I will be with you, even until the end of the world." Releasing the fear of death to faith, King could reassure people, when his house was bombed three days later, that "if I am stopped, this movement will not stop, because God is with the movement."[40]

The conversations about pacifism took place a few weeks later and convinced King that nonviolent means were as important as integrationist ends. In Montgomery, Glenn Smiley of the Fellowship of Reconciliation joined with Bayard Rustin to help King to see the connections between the bus boycott and the philosophy and practice of Gandhian nonviolence. Nonviolence did not mean passivism or inactivity; instead it involved pacifist direct action. Like Catholic Worker personalism, King's nonviolent personalism was embodied, but instead of ministering to the hurt bodies of society's victims, King encouraged society's victims to use their own bodies for social change. Like Mahatma Gandhi, he encouraged people to use their bodies to defy and dramatize injustice. Like Gandhi, he basically said to people, "Look, your bodies are just taking up space. If you would just move them from those private spaces to public spaces, they could have a political meaning." And so millions of people in the civil rights movement took their bodies off of buses, sat their bodies down at lunch counters, and marched their bodies on the street in order to demonstrate the evils of segregation. King's associate Ralph Abernathy captured the same idea years later in Selma, Alabama when he told marchers that "We come to present our bodies as a living sacrifice. We don't have much, but we do have our bodies, and we lay them on the altar today."[41]

Gandhi's example influenced King, but Gandhian nonviolence was perfectly consonant with his church upbringing: "Christ furnished the spirit and motivation," he said, "while Gandhi furnished the method." Nonviolence also fit with his philosophical personalism: he protested racism because it violated the worth of black persons, but he protested nonviolently to avoid violating the dignity of racist white persons. "While abhorring segregation," he said, "we shall love the segregationist. This is the only way to create the beloved community." Nonviolence allowed King to oppose evil and oppression without violating the persons who did evil. It allowed him to respect all individuals, depending on conversion more than coercion for his success.[42]

Nonviolent direct action offered a personalist theory of social change that animated the civil rights movement for at least a decade. First, nonviolent direct action transformed the persons who participated and the communities they inhabited. Second, nonviolent direct action could change the persons whose policy was protested. Because people who did evil could be good, appeals to their better selves might effect personal conversions that would lead to social change. Third, nonviolent direct action dramatized injustice in America and implicitly asked other Americans to support the civil rights movement vocally, financially, and legislatively. Nonviolent direct action couched in the language of the Christian faith and the American Dream aimed to expand the base of support for radical action. Similarly, because all people could potentially respond to personalist appeals, King felt free to form coalitions with people who did not accept all of his assumptions. Fourth, nonviolent direct action maintained the harmony of means and ends; it offered an example of peaceable conflict resolution, a model for the beloved community of the future. Nonviolent direct action was a way of "living the revolution now." Finally, in the Exodus and prophetic tradition, nonviolent direct action involved God as an agent of personal and social change: "God is with the movement."

In a February 1956 sermon, King revealed the personal and personalist roots of the campaign, telling his congregation that even without success in the boycott, they had won a victory "because the Negro has achieved from this a new dignity." Continuing, he outlined his personalist social theory:

> We are concerned not merely to win justice in the buses but rather to behave in a new and different way—to be nonviolent so that we may remove injustice itself, both from society and from ourselves. This is a struggle which we cannot lose, no matter what the apparent outcome, if we succeed ourselves in becoming better and more loving people.

King and most personalists agreed with Gandhi that, "as human beings, our greatness lies not so much in being able to remake the world—that is the myth of the 'Atomic Age'—as in being able to remake ourselves."[43]

Still, in fact, the political personalists of the civil rights movement did intend to remake the world—not by themselves, but in community with other people who would advance the cause in different ways. The personalist protests of Martin Luther King were only one part of an interrelated political strategy to achieve equality for African Americans. King saw his emphasis on education, religion, persuasion, and personal witness as necessary but not sufficient. Because "it is an immoral act to compel a man to accept injustice until another man's heart is straight," legislation was also needed. King knew that "direct action and legal action complement one another; when skillfully employed, each becomes more effective." The NAACP, for example, provided legal and financial support for King's campaigns, and he spoke often to NAACP chapters and conventions.[44]

Unlike the anarchists of the Catholic Worker and the Beat movement, Martin Luther King and most civil rights activists espoused a more positive view of government. King's "philosophical and theological training especially in personalism had endowed him with a deep sense of community," and a sense that "government as a moral agency could utilize its vast resources to provide the framework necessary for all individuals to develop as persons." While he occasionally applauded the self-sufficiency of the local community, King more often worked with the federal government, which was working against the constitutional violations of local Southern governments.[45]

Anti-Nuclear Personalism

King's personalist voice was not just concerned with civil rights. When he was attacked in 1959 for being "inconsistent in my struggle against war and too weak-kneed to protest nuclear war," King responded that

> repeatedly, in public addresses and my writings, I have unequivocally declared my hatred for this most colossal of all evils and I have condemned any organizer of war, regardless of his rank or nationality. I have signed numerous statements along with other Americans condemning nuclear testing and have authorized publication of my name in advertisements appearing in the largest circulation newspapers in the country, without concern that it was then "unpopular" to so speak out.[46]

Indeed, during the later 1950s, Martin Luther King Jr. used political personalism to connect civil rights and nuclear protest. King became a member of the pacifist Fellowship of Reconciliation in 1957, and late in the decade, he joined an interdenominational group of ministers calling for a nuclear test moratorium. He enthusiastically supported the Committee for a Sane Nuclear Policy, and signed several of their ads. In doing so, he found that it was indeed unpopular to so speak out, as *Time* asked of him and his co-signers, "How Sane the SANE?"[47]

King emphasized the connections of civil rights and the civil voice in nuclear discourse, saying "It is very nice to drink milk at an unsegregated lunch counter—but not when there is strontium 90 in it. . . . When sputniks dash through outer space and guided ballistic missiles are carving highways of death in the stratosphere," King warned in the Spring of 1960, the anti-communist slogan "Better Dead Than Red" was simply a prescription for suicide. "The choice today is no longer between violence and nonviolence," King claimed in the same article. "It is either nonviolence or non-existence." Coretta Scott King also became involved in antinuclear politics as a sponsor of Women Strike for Peace in 1961–62. Both Martin and Coretta refused to be issue specialists. As personalists, they confronted both racism and militarism with a consistent social ethics based on the worth of persons.[48]

SNCC Personalism

On February 1, 1960, four freshmen at the all-black North Carolina Agricultural and Technical College took political personalism to a new level when they decided to protest the quotidian dehumanization and humiliation of segregation. They had spent weeks talking about racism and the apathetic powerlessness that permitted it, and about the implications of Christian love and Gandhian *satyagraha* for an ethics of action. At the Woolworth's lunch counter in Greensboro, they sat down and ordered four cups of coffee. When they were not served, they sat-in until the store closed. Afterward, in the street, they formed a tight circle and recited the Lord's prayer.[49]

By not moving from their chairs, the four students sparked a student movement throughout the South, and catalyzed the subsequent student movements of the Sixties. In Nashville, a 21-year-old Fisk University student named Diane Nash chaired the Student Central Committee that applied the pressure of persons and purses to Nashville businesses. Nash saw the sit-ins as "applied religion," designed "to bring about a climate in which there is appreciation of the dignity of man and in which each individual is free to grow and produce to his fullest capacity." She had been inspired by weekly workshops on nonviolence started by Methodist minister James Lawson in September of 1959. A conscientious objector during the Korean War, Lawson had immersed himself in Gandhian philosophy during a sojourn in India. In 1960, he was a Vanderbilt divinity student and southern secretary of the Fellowship of Reconciliation. With Marion Berry and John Lewis, Nash and Lawson led a disciplined campaign of nonviolent direct action that succeeded in desegregating Nashville's lunch counters by summer 1960.[50]

Although the Greensboro sit-in was spontaneous, subsequent sit-ins drew on personalist principles well-established in the Congress of Racial Equality (CORE) and the Southern Christian Leadership Conference (SCLC). CORE had been established as a "Gandhi-type movement of nonviolent direct action against segregation" in 1942 with the assistance of A.J. Muste, James Farmer and the Fellowship for Reconciliation; George Houser of FOR served as CORE's executive secretary. In May 1942, CORE members Bayard Rustin and Jim Peck premiered the civil rights sit-in technique at Stoner's restaurant in Chicago. As Jack Newfield acknowledged, "Behind the sit-in technique was the pacifist ethic of placing one's body in moral nonviolent confrontation with an existing evil." Sit-ins, like the subsequent teach-ins and sing-ins, converted the spaces of everyday life to political protest through personalist practice. The sit-ins, said Newfield, were "a moral rather than economic or political protest. . . . They required no ideology, no politics, and no scholarship—just one's body and a certain set of ethical values."[51]

The sit-ins of 1960 inspired other social protests. According to Kenneth Rexroth, the Greensboro four had "picked up the massive chain of the

Social Lie and snapped it at its weakest point. Everything broke loose." By mid-April, an estimated 50,000 students had exercised their rights of sit-in-ship. Even Northern students like Tom Hayden and Al Haber at the University of Michigan took inspiration. To Hayden, the sit-ins brought morality to political life. "To Haber, the message of the sit-ins was simple: 'Act *now*.'" Students protested race relations, the arms race, compulsory ROTC, civil liberties, capital punishment—"all in the final analysis moral issues. In no case were they concerned with politics in the ordinary sense of the word." But in no case were they unconcerned with politics.[52]

By October, under the watchful eye of SCLC's incomparable Ella Baker and the Gandhian inspiration of Lawson, the sit-in students had established the Student Nonviolent Coordinating Committee (SNCC), and proclaimed:

> We affirm the philosophical or religious ideal of nonviolence as the foundation of our purpose, the presupposition of our faith, and the manner of our action.

> Nonviolence as it grows from the Judaic-Christian tradition seeks a social order of justice permeated by love. Integration of human endeavor represents the crucial first step towards such a society.

> Through nonviolence, courage displaces fear. Love transcends hate. Acceptance dissipates prejudice; hope ends despair. Faith reconciles doubt. Peace dominates war. Mutual regards cancel enmity. Justice for all overthrows injustice. The redemptive community supersedes immoral social systems.

> By appealing to conscience and standing on the moral nature of human existence, nonviolence nurtures the atmosphere in which reconciliation and justice become actual possibilities.

> Although each group in this movement must diligently work out the clear meaning of this statement of purpose, each act or phase of our corporate effort must reflect a genuine spirit of love and goodwill.

This manifesto drew on the peace and justice traditions of the Christian churches, and on CORE, the Fellowship of Reconciliation (FOR), and SCLC. Although many SNCC members accepted nonviolence only as a tactical measure, they acted within a framework of values that reinforced the personalist rhetoric of Martin Luther King Jr.[53]

SNCC added an increasingly activist dimension to African American personalism. Rejecting the political caution of the NAACP and SCLC, SNCC pushed for an immediate end to segregation. Suspicious of the established groups' emphasis on national leadership—they derisively referred to Martin Luther King Jr. as "De Lawd"—the students began to stir up the grassroots in a strategy of community organizing. Attempting to change people's consciousness, they set out to combat the learned helplessness of African Americans in the South by empowering local people in their communities, and by militantly standing up to the powers that be. Instead of dressing up to impress the authorities, SNCC organizers dressed down, making overalls and workclothes the uniform of Sixties activism. Like other personalist practitioners, they acted on their faith and left the results to fate. "For an ethic of success," said Godfrey Hodgson, "they substituted an ethic of honesty and courage." Even more than Martin Luther King Jr. and his adult followers, the students of SNCC put their bodies on the line, risking arrest, imprisonment, beatings, and death. Jailed for the practice of their beliefs, and often refusing the bail that would let their oppressors off the hook, they converted jails to a place for political education and the practice of the "beloved community." They exchanged ideas and information, hopes and dreams, and they sang the freedom songs that made them a community of memory.[54]

SNCC's own organization followed a communitarian anarchist model. Although SNCC established a coordinating committee, the group functioned like an "un-organization." Unlike most other civil rights organizations, SNCC adopted a policy of "group-centered leadership," emphasizing the development of numerous leaders more than single established leaders like King. SNCC's meetings were known as "soul sessions." As in other personalist organizations, "SNCC staff meetings and workshops became . . . not merely means to an end (voter registration or direct action) but ends in themselves as well. . . . These get-togethers were not only strategy sessions, but also models of the redemptive community."[55]

In May 1961, the Congress of Racial Equality matched SNCC's activism, as a group of black and white Freedom Riders recapitulated the 1947 "Journey of Reconciliation," desegregating buses and bus terminals throughout the South. Organized by CORE's James Farmer, the Freedom Rides were designed to test the enforcement of the recent Supreme Court decision against discrimination in bus terminals used for interstate travel. The travelers paid the price of political personalism; they were attacked by mobs and brutally beaten in Anniston and Birmingham, Alabama. One of the victims was Jim Peck, who had traveled with Bayard Rustin in the 1947 Journey of Reconciliation, and who had walked with Rustin and the others in City Hall Park. Another was Albert Bigelow, who had sailed the *Golden Rule* into the atomic test zones of the Pacific. "This is too much," exclaimed an exasperated Robert Kennedy at a tense point in the crisis. "I wonder whether they have the best interest of the country at heart. Do you know that one of them is against the atom bomb?"[56]

The brutality, along with hundreds of arrests, pricked the conscience of Northern liberals. The Freedom Rides brought support from Martin Luther King Jr. and from SNCC—whose members continued the interrupted trek from Birmingham to New Orleans—and finally caused the Kennedys to offer federal support for the personalist passengers. The Justice Department pressured the Interstate Commerce Commission to issue a ruling banning segregated bus and train facilities, and the commission did so in September.[57]

During the summer of 1961, SNCC also began to direct its work from direct action to community organizing and voter registration. Although there was considerable support for this strategy from liberals in the Kennedy administration and from private foundations, the primary catalyst was Robert Moses. Born in 1935, raised in New York, educated at Hamilton College, Bob Moses was a philosophy student deeply influenced by the activist existentialism of Albert Camus. Camus's writing on political morality projected a social order consisting of persons each refusing to permit the dehumanization of human beings, and refusing the temptation to turn resistance into a quest for power. Resolved to avoid acting as victim or executioner, Moses worked tirelessly, like the protagonists of Camus' *The Plague*, to cure the evils he found in the world, emphasizing humanist values more than political power.[58]

Moses had worked at summer camps of the American Friends Service Committee, and in 1959 helped Bayard Rustin organize a Youth March for Integrated Schools. In 1960, he filed for conscientious objector status. During the summer of 1960, at Rustin's request, he traveled to Atlanta to work in the offices of the Southern Christian Leadership Conference. There he met Ella Baker and began to work, unofficially, for SNCC. The next summer, in order to establish a voice for persons who had been muted, he started a Sisyphean project of voter registration in McComb, Mississippi. Moses' quiet courage, and his consistent insistence that SNCC's job was to identify and empower local leaders, made him a leading voice of the philosophy and praxis of SNCC, even though he never held any of the leadership positions. In fact, as SDS founder Tom Hayden recalled, "he created the pattern of non-leadership that affected many of us for years."[59]

Moses and SNCC focused on voter registration because African American disfranchisement was such a clear violation of Constitutional guarantees, and because the vote was a form of personal and political empowerment for people who had been systematically disempowered in the South. Moses also stressed the vote as an economic necessity, since automation was replacing many of the jobs—like cotton cultivation—that African Americans depended on for their livelihood. Although he often took part in national politics and protests, Moses believed in the importance of decentralization and community decision-making.[60]

Within months, Moses and the SNCC workers discovered, as many Sixties activists would, that people who put their bodies on the line would get them kicked, beaten, shot, tear-gassed, and billy-clubbed. SNCC volunteers were harassed, battered, arrested, and jailed. Local activist Herbert Lee was murdered. White juries in Southern courts acquitted the perpetrators and convicted the SNCC workers of inciting to riot. The FBI and the Justice Department took no dramatic action. Students began to doubt the inherent goodness of their enemies, the good faith of the government, and the Christian idealism of Gandhian nonviolence. They also began to cloak their political organizing with a revolutionary rhetoric that would spread later in the decade.[61]

Marching for Personalism

One of the most dramatic interpretations of personalist practice came in April 1963 in Birmingham, Alabama. King and his advisors structured another in a series of "morality plays" that would dramatize the evils of segregation and the goodness of Christian solidarity. When the police beat peaceful protesters, jolted them with cattle prods, and blasted them with fire hoses, people saw ethics in action. In this case, the personalist practice of the protesters proved persuasive. Carried on national TV, these dramatic performances convinced many Americans, including John Fitzgerald Kennedy, of the justice of the civil rights cause.[62]

King's "Letter from Birmingham Jail," written Easter weekend and published widely, brought the movement's personalist ideas to the American public in a literary masterpiece. In that letter, King described racism and segregation as an assault on personality forcing "a degenerating sense of 'nobodiness'" on Negroes. He condemned the Jim Crow laws of Birmingham as unjust laws because they violated the law of God. "To put it in the terms of St. Thomas Aquinas, an unjust law is a human law that is not rooted in eternal and natural law. Any law that uplifts human personality is just. Any law that degrades human personality is unjust. All segregation statutes are unjust because segregation distorts the soul and damages the personality. . . . To use the words of Martin Buber, the great Jewish philosopher, segregation substitutes an 'I-it' relationship for the 'I-thou' relationship,' and ends up relegating persons to the status of things."[63]

King claimed that socially constituted persons had a moral obligation to fight unjust laws. People were not atomistic individuals: "We are caught," he said, "in an inescapable network of mutuality, tied in a single garment of destiny. Whatever affects one directly, affects all indirectly." Consequently, "injustice anywhere is a threat to justice anywhere." And even the white Christians of the South should support integration "because integration is morally *right* and the Negro is your brother."[64]

King's letter advocated civil disobedience as a way of bending people toward justice. Because African Americans had no access to the levers of political power, but even more because King believed in the consistency of ends and means, King recommended a personalist form of protest. "We would present our very bodies," he said, "as a means of laying our case before the conscience of the local and national community." The black population, said Bayard Rustin, had decided "that the future lies in casting not just a ballot, what Thoreau called 'a piece of paper merely,' but the *total* vote—the human person against injustice."[65]

Like Thomas Merton and other personalists, King confronted the violence of American passivism, the apparent moral numbness of the affluent and comfortable. And he decried not only "the vitriolic words and actions of the bad people," but "the appalling silence of the good people." Countering "the myth of time" that promised progress in due time, King claimed that "human progress never rolls in on wheels of inevitability; it comes through the tireless efforts and persistent work of men willing to be co-workers with God." Like C. Wright Mills' "Pagan Sermon to the Christian Clergy," King indicted the nation's churches for their inactivity in the face of evil. He had expected the white church to support Christian claims of justice and love, and he was amazed by its hypocrisy. Assuming the complicity of complacency, he challenged them to answer the question that Adolf Eichmann ignored, "How responsible am I for the well-being of my fellows?" Like his mentor George Davis, King saw the tension in the South as a part of "social progress . . . from an obnoxious negative peace, where the Negro passively accepted his unjust plight, to a substance-filled positive peace, where all men will respect the dignity and worth of human personality."[66]

King's open letter appealed to the conscience of America. The American Friends Service Committee quickly printed 50,000 copies for distribution; it was reprinted in *Liberation*, the *Christian Century*, and the *New Leader;* it became a central chapter in King's 1964 book, *Why We Can't Wait*. More than a million copies circulated, mainly in the nation's Northern churches. Its personalist plea helped to create what King later called "a coalition of conscience" in America. John F. Kennedy joined the coalition of conscience on June 11, accepting King's personalist definition of the race issue with a nationally televised speech entitled "A Moral Imperative." Kennedy began with the claim of the Declaration of Independence that "all men are created equal." Then, echoing King's contention that injustice anywhere was a threat to justice everywhere, Kennedy said that "the rights of every man are diminished when the rights of one man are threatened." "We are confronted primarily with a moral issue," said the President, having been taught by America's personalists. Eight days later, after two years of deliberate delay, Kennedy decided to submit a civil rights bill to Congress.[67]

In August, King's "I Have A Dream" speech was the highlight of a dramatic "March on Washington for Jobs and Freedom" coordinated by Bayard Rustin. The March "provided a fleeting glimpse, perhaps, of what the 1960s might have been, before the assassination of Kennedy, the burning of Watts, and the Vietnam War, filled those years with despair. It offered a vision of the melting pot realized, of the injustice of three centuries remedied by nonviolence and decency, of the two societies fused into one. And then it ended, leaving a warm memory." Like Woodstock, later in the decade, it seemed to prefigure the beloved community.[68]

Throughout his career, King had framed the American Dream in personalist terms. For him, the dream was not a dream of individual achievement and material advancement. Instead, as he had said a year earlier in Washington, it was "a dream of equality of opportunity, of privilege and property wisely distributed; a dream of a land where men no longer argue that the color of a man's skin determines the content of his character; the dream of a land where every man will respect the dignity and worth of human personality—this is the dream."[69]

Freedom Summer

In 1964, SNCC decided to take advantage of the election year. Demanding that democracy's professed respect for the person be practiced, they campaigned for "one man, one vote" in the state of Mississippi. And they raised the stakes by inviting white college students to come to Mississippi for "Freedom Summer." They hoped to create a confrontation that would force the Federal government from its fence-sitting, and bring the power of the nation-state to bear on the states of the South. Over a thousand white volunteers came to Mississippi to help create alternative institutions like community centers, schools, and a political party.[70]

During Freedom Summer, SNCC created parallel institutions to build the new society in the shell of the old. Responding to the second-class education of Mississippi's segregated schools, SNCC formed freedom schools where African American youth could study traditional academic subjects, as well as contemporary issues, cultural expression, and leadership skills. Professor Staughton Lynd of Spelman College headed the project, which enrolled over 2,000 students in forty-one different schools.[71]

The freedom schools derived from a tradition of citizenship schools promoted by the Highlander Folk School and the Southern Christian

Leadership Conference and from the voter registration schools of SNCC's Mississippi Project. They also owed a debt to the students of Burglund High School in McComb, who had boycotted the public school and established "Nonviolent High" in October of 1961 when students who had participated in a SNCC-sponsored protest were suspended. The curriculum of the Freedom Schools emphasized self-respect, black history, and citizenship. The planners devised a citizenship curriculum that integrated education and politics, as had been SNCC's practice since its inception. The last section, written by Jane Stembridge, emphasized the importance and the efficacy of the nonviolent civil rights movement. "Nonviolence really changes society," the Citizenship Curriculum said, "because nonviolence changes people. Nonviolence is based on a simple truth: that every human being deserves to be treated as a human being just because he is one and that there is something sacred about humanity."[72]

The pedagogical practice of the Freedom Schools was, in part, personalist. Staughton Lynd suggested that by avoiding "the conventional paraphernalia of education," the Freedom Schools reminded people "that education is above all a meeting between people." Since one of the goals of the schools was to help African Americans express themselves as persons in ways that were taboo in Mississippi, teachers usually depended on more personal and more active learning than was standard in the schools of 1964. Discussions, role playing, stories, drama, student poetry, and Freedom School student newspapers all taught students that they could speak the truths and the hopes of their own lives in the "free spaces" of a Freedom School.[73]

The white volunteers who taught the citizenship curriculum knew a great deal abstractly, but their students often knew more experientially. Class sessions, therefore, often focused on bringing to consciousness what was already known, "naming" the experience and the system. This process included considerably more mutuality than standard pedagogical practice. The staff and students of Freedom Schools soon learned that teaching is learning and vice versa. Freedom Schools taught African Americans, but they also taught white SNCC summer volunteers the ways in which education was woven into the web of American racism. Freedom Schools provided a model of education that influenced white students when they returned to their universities. From the orientation on, Freedom Summer and Freedom Schools taught that experience and learning were inextricable. Anticipating Paolo Freire, they suggested that students and teachers might work together "not through the artificial sieve of certification and examination but on the basis of their common attraction to an exciting social goal."[74]

The voter registration project culminated in another important parallel institution, the Mississippi Freedom Democratic Party (MFDP). Based on the November 1963 "Freedom Vote," in which 75,000 African Americans cast ballots in a parallel election, the MFDP planned to challenge the state's exclusionary politics. Encouraged by Northern liberals like Allard Lowenstein and Joseph Rauh, activists united in the Council of Federated Organizations (COFO) registered 80,000 African Americans in the Mississippi Freedom Democratic Party. The party nominated candidates for Federal, state, and local offices, and held a convention in Jackson attended by 800 delegates.[75]

The convention elected 68 delegates, including four white people, to challenge the regular Mississippi delegation at the Democratic National Convention in Atlantic City. President Johnson was not pleased by their potential participation; eventually he and his liberal allies offered to seat two MFDP delegates-at-large, and promised that the 1968 convention would seat no delegations that were racially discriminatory. It was not enough. "We have been treated like beasts in Mississippi," argued delegate Annie Devine. "They have shot us down like animals." Devine and the other delegates wanted the Democrats to treat them like persons by refusing to seat the persons who had countenanced the racism and violence.[76]

The MFDP delegation refused the compromise, because the compromise refused to do justice for the 80,000 voices of the poor and disenfranchised in Mississippi. After almost a decade of protest, they could not countenance the hypocrisy of a liberalism that preached freedom and practiced discrimination. As Robert Moses said, "We're not here to bring politics into our morality but to bring morality into our politics." In conventional political terms, they snatched defeat from the jaws of victory by their uncompromising stance. But in terms of personalist politics, they had insisted on ethical consistency.[77]

After the debacle of the Democratic National Convention, it was difficult for activists to muster much enthusiasm for working within the system. Ninety percent of black voters cast ballots for Lyndon Johnson in 1964, but civil rights activists in the South increasingly decried the complicity of the federal government with the reactionary violence of the Southern resistance. Instead of attempting to compromise with American liberals, they began to celebrate their own intransigence against liberalism.[78]

Acts from Activism

Meanwhile, however, political liberalism was delivering some of the legislative goals of the civil rights movement. The civil rights personalism of Martin Luther King Jr. and Ella Baker and the Southern Christian Leadership Conference, of Bayard Rustin and the March on Washington, of Robert Moses and the Student Nonviolent Coordinating Committee, of

James Farmer and the Congress of Racial Equality, of Fannie Lou Hamer and the Mississippi Freedom Democratic Party, combined with the legal leadership of the National Association for the Advancement of Colored People and the labor/liberal wing of the Democratic Party, finally brought forth national legislation in 1964 and 1965. The 1964 Civil Rights Act undermined the legal structure of segregation in the South, while the 1965 Voting Rights Act guaranteed that African Americans could finally exercise their citizenship in the nation's polling places. The Twenty-Third Amendment outlawed the poll tax in all elections. As a result, between 1964 and 1968, the percentage of black registered voters increased from seven to fifty-nine percent.[79]

In the ten short years since Montgomery, the personalist politics of the civil rights movement had accomplished an impossible task. Civil rights personalism succeeded, in large part, because King and others had maintained connections to people who practiced not-so-personalist politics. Personalism provided the impetus, but politicians and judges provided the legal framework for the desegregation of the South. Although the personalist project was more radical than American liberalism, personalists like Martin Luther King counted on liberals to support the extension of rights and a fairer distribution of goods. But, as in the 346 years since Jamestown, the result was neither justice nor love.

For King and other civil rights activists, the legislative agenda of the civil rights movement preceded a social and religious transformation of American culture. At the 1957 Prayer Pilgrimage in Washington, D.C., King had asked for the ballot so that people might elect legislators who were men of goodwill," judges "who will 'do justice and love mercy,'" and governors "who have felt not only the tang of the human but the glow of the divine." In Selma, Alabama in 1965, as he began a concerted effort for the vote, he encouraged his followers "to march on ballot boxes until brotherhood becomes more than a meaningless word in an opening prayer, but the order of the day on every legislative agenda." The laws of Congress, therefore, were necessary but not sufficient for the radical social change that King envisioned. With other social activists, especially the students of SNCC, King realized that desegregation and voting rights were not enough to redress the poverty and powerlessness of African Americans. These acts transformed the South, but they did not create the beloved community.[80]

In many ways, however, the process of personalist politics was as important for African Americans as the legislative outcome. During the late 1950s and early 1960s, thousands of African Americans acted on the personalism represented by Martin Luther King Jr., Bayard Rustin, and the civil rights movement. They found that nonviolent civil disobedience and other forms of political mobilization paid political dividends in the form of legislation and judicial decisions, but they also found that "putting their bodies on the line" enhanced their own worth as persons; seeing themselves as historical actors, they overcame the feeling of fatalism that the culture encouraged in them. In their activism, they also recovered the rich tradition of citizenship, civil voices, and civic action. And consequently, they exemplified for later activists the possibilities of personalism. The success of the Montgomery boycott, for example, inspired the personalist politics of the anti-nuclear and antiwar movements. SNCC inspired SDS and the student movement. When King and Robert Moses and other black leaders later opposed the Vietnam War, many Americans could see the potential power of a personalist response.[81]

African American activism in the civil rights movement also altered white Americans' opinions of black people. "In a matter of weeks, in thousands of white brains" after the sit-ins, Kenneth Rexroth claimed, "the old stereotypes exploded." When people like Martin Luther King embodied the best traditions of America and American Christianity, it was harder to accept racist assumptions about African Americans. As Rexroth said, King was "the best possible demonstration of the untapped potential of humanity that the white South has thrown away all these years."[82]

The White Negro

Even after SNCC shifted from its religious roots to more purely political activity like voter registration, this personalist ethic proved attractive to young white people as well. During the 1950s, both Christian liberalism and Christian existentialism brought white students into the civil rights movement. Most Protestant denominations sponsored campus groups like the Methodist Student Movement (MSM) which wrestled with social questions. As Sara Evans reports, "in the late fifties throughout the South, the MSM harbored the most radical groups on most campuses." In their 1958 *Theses for Study and Debate*, the Study Committee of the United Student Christian Council claimed that "the Christian group on campus which does not promote involvement in political affairs denies [God's] authority in that area of life."[83]

At the University of Texas, for example, the University Y (YMCA/ YWCA) promoted discussion of the relation of religion and social life in the Social Gospel tradition. "In the Y," said executive secretary Frank Wright, "we start with the issues of life—no holds barred—and work toward the issues of faith." Such inquiry often led to concern about America's hypocrisy—religious, social and political. The University Y taught, as did the Catholic Worker, "that Christianity isn't just something for Sunday exercise, that Christianity is something that has to do with living seven days a week if it's worth a hoot, that it has something to do with your treatment of people." Like Martin Luther King Jr., these students found in Christian liberalism and the Social Gospel a politics of meaning and an ethic of action.[84]

The Texas Y's Christian Faith-and-Life Community was even more explicit in its focus on personal and personalist concerns, trying to promote the "possibility of personhood" in an "authentic, self-consciously disciplined community." Under the leadership of Joe Mathews, the group studied the social and political implications of the theology of such Christian existentialists as Rudolf Bultmann, Paul Tillich, and—most significantly—Dietrich Bonhoeffer. Mathews hoped to bring his followers to "a personal breakthrough, which, if duplicated enough times, could produce a social breakthrough." And he succeeded in bringing white Texas students to a breakthrough on race, as many members of the CFLC planned and participated in Austin's civil rights protests of 1960-61. From there, many—like Sandra "Casey" Cason—moved to SNCC and SDS. Cason graduated from Texas in the late Fifties, attended the 1960 NSA conference in Minneapolis, married an SDS member named Tom Hayden, and moved to Atlanta to work with Ella Baker. Cason was no exception; almost all the white Southern women active in the civil rights movement came to it by way of religion.[85]

Freedom Summer taught white students how the personal was political. Most of them came to Mississippi, not for political or ideological reasons, but inspired instead by personal beliefs of religion, idealism and optimism to right the wrongs of their country. "What the volunteers had discovered in Mississippi," said Doug McAdam, "was nothing less than the political significance of the personal. Encoded in this discovery was an ideology and rhetoric of personal liberation that, when fused with the earlier emphasis on political change, were to give the Sixties their distinctive cast." Freedom Summer taught white students about the possibilities of community as well. They admired "the strength of the [African American] Baptist Church with its embracing of the values of both the Sermon on the Mount and the Ten Commandments." They appreciated the communal symbols of the freedom movement, the "we-ness" of the anthem "We Shall Overcome," and the exhilaration that came from community action. And they began to use the black community's "brother" and "sister" to define their own familial sense of solidarity.[86]

They admired the courage and commitment of the SNCC volunteers: the engagement of the SNCC activists exemplified both a political creed and a way of life. One volunteer even noted an ambivalence about the work, fearing "that I am only helping to integrate some beautiful people into modern white society with all of its depersonalization. . . . It isn't nine-teenth-century romantic pastoralism which I feel, but a genuine respect and admiration for a culture which, for all the trouble, still isn't as commercial-ized and depersonalized as our Northern mass culture." Freedom Summer, in fact, freed white students by giving them "perspective by incongruity" on their own cultural presumptions.[87]

The white volunteers prized the black women whose "self-reliance and assertiveness stood at odds with the feminine mystique." In the communi-ties of the South, women often led the resistance to racism, and they usu-ally fed and sheltered the SNCC workers. "There is always a 'mama,'" said Charles Sherrod. "She is usually a militant woman in the community, out-spoken, understanding and willing to catch hell, having already caught her share." These women, and movement women like Ella Baker, Fanny Lou Hamer, Septima Clark, Diane Nash, and Ruby Doris Smith offered mod-els of courage and commitment.[88]

White students also made a cultural hero of Robert Moses. They admired his Sisyphean spirit, his quiet persistence and his self-effacement. At a November 1964 awards dinner in New York, Jack Newfield empha-sized his "dog-eared copy of Camus' 'Resistance, Rebellion, and Death,'" and compared him to the Biblical Moses, "trying to draw justice from the stone of Mississippi." But Moses detested the acclaim that emphasized his leadership; a firm believer in empowerment instead of leadership, he even changed his name to emphasize his aversion to hierarchy.[89]

The intense experience of Freedom Summer also taught students the pleasures of commitment. White students like Mario Savio felt that they "came alive" in the movement. It was, in fact, possible to get a "freedom high" that came from finally acting in conformity to the beliefs you pro-fessed. Freedom Summer also led to extraordinary bonding among partici-pants, as commitment to a cause often does. Friendships made in the struggle were friendships likely to last, because they replaced the cultural patterns of mere "friendliness" with a more traditional idea of friendship. Students discovered that friendships based on a common commitment to the good were more fulfilling than the usual friendships that entailed only a commitment to feeling good. A common social goal made both the poli-tics and the friendships richer.[90]

White civil rights workers took the values and institutions of the move-ment home with them. According to Michael Harrington, "the great gift which the New Left received from the Negro movement" was "a sense of social outrage. The result," said Harrington, who was not entirely approv-ing, "was an existential, moralistic, and quite emotional critique of the entire society and, in particular, a sense that the self-proclaimed reformers and social changers were hypocrites for maneuvering within the framework of the possible when what the times called for was a nonviolent John Brown." To some extent, as a white SNCC worker suggested in the mid-Sixties, "The Movement is a search for the moral equivalent of blackness." The search combined the hipster bohemianism of the Beats with the political engagement of the civil rights movement, and proved attractive to many college-age white Americans.[91]

Although the civil rights movement had come from the traditions of the African American churches, it had an impact on the mainstream Euro-American churches as well. At the end of the 1950s, *Christianity and Crisis* editor John Bennett suggested that American churches had "tipped too much in favor of [pastoral] identification," and that in the 1960s "we should pray and hope for the tipping of the scales in favor of prophetic challenge and criticism." He also suggested that theological neo-orthodoxy might have inhibited social criticism and social activism, making it too easy for moral man to adjust to an immoral society. In the same way, Gibson Winter, in *The Suburban Captivity of the Churches*, argued for the "social embodiment" of a religion that had been too privatized and secularized.[92]

Martin Luther King and the civil rights movement tipped the scales toward a prophetic and social gospel. Although the churches had long decried racism, traditional social teaching and social organization seemed inadequate in the face of the dramatic changes and challenges in the South. As a result of the religious claims of the civil rights movement, 657 delegates of seventy different organizations met, for example, in January 1963 for a National Conference on Religion and Race. King delivered "A Challenge to the Churches and Synagogues" and the conference issued "An Appeal to the Conscience of the American People." It described racism as "our most serious domestic evil," because "racial discrimination and segregation are an insult to God, the Giver of human dignity and human rights." Because white churches had been complicit with American racism, it was now time to convert the churches to a force for conscience and justice. Later in 1963, the National Council of Churches urged its thirty-one denominations to sponsor "nationwide demonstrations against racial discrimination." The following summer, the National Council of Churches financed the orientation program for Freedom Summer volunteers. For many American Christians, the civil rights movement acted as a catalyst in a pilgrimage from orthodox church teachings to the more basic obligations of Christian love and discipleship.[93]

Conclusion

Martin Luther King Jr. was not the civil rights movement. But, as one of the most important movers of the movement and as its most recognizable spokesman, King articulated personalism in such a way that it became the unspoken philosophy of the civil rights movement. He applied personalism in the Montgomery bus boycott and the subsequent national campaigns of SCLC. In the early 1960s, students who had learned personalism from King (and from Albert Camus) carried on the work in sit-ins and the community organizing of SNCC. Their example caused changes in the South, in national legislation, and in the student movements of the North. By acting as if the truth were true, Martin Luther King and the civil rights movement had made the dignity of persons an essential issue of the 1960s.

In a 1938 "Easy Essay" on "The Race Problem," Peter Maurin had argued that when African Americans evolved a harmonious technique of protest,

> The power of Negro people
> over white people
> will then be the power of example.

Dissolving "the boundaries between ends and means, the self and other, the future and the here-and-now," the civil rights movement offered others an example of personalist protest. Because the civil rights movement was a catalyst for many other social movements of the Sixties, its personalism was often appropriated unconsciously. By its profound example, the civil rights movement passed along personalism without the name.[94]

The successes of the civil rights movement impressed radical pacifists, for example, who began to see the transformative possibilities of nonviolent direct action. In the process, radical pacifism became a political force that linked the civil rights and antiwar movements of the Sixties. In the process, too, as we shall see in the next chapter, personalism found another important expression in postwar America.[95]

LIBERATED PERSONALISM

DURING THE WINTER OF 1955-56, as Allen Ginsberg howled and Martin Luther King Jr. preached, A.J. Muste helped to organize a new advocacy journal called *Liberation*. Muste, Bayard Rustin, Paul Goodman, and David Dellinger were among the editors. The first issue appeared in March 1956. In April, the editors showed their commitment to the civil rights movement with an issue featuring both Martin Luther King's first published essay, "Our Struggle," and Bayard Rustin's "Montgomery Diary." *Liberation* also appreciated the personalism of the Beats: Lawrence Ferlinghetti's "Tentative Description of a Dinner to Promote the Impeachment of President Eisenhower" first appeared in the April 1958 *Liberation;* Gary Snyder's notes on the religious tendencies of the movement were in the June 1959 issue. *Liberation* valued the Beat emphasis on personal authenticity and liberation, and Beat expressions of philosophical anarchism. The editors appreciated the attempt to speak truth to the Social Lie, and to challenge the consciousness of mainstream America. *Liberation* preferred civil disobedience to Beat deviance, but they deeply appreciated the cultural critique of the Beat movement.[1]

From its inception, *Liberation* joined the *Catholic Worker* in providing a civil voice synthesizing religious and libertarian personalism in the interests of personal, political, and cultural transformation. As with the *Catholic Worker*, *Liberation* was not just a magazine; it was a way of life. The editors declared that they would "deal with what they think is humanly important, and the factual test of importance is that they themselves get personally engaged in the events." As members and founders of the Committee for a Sane Nuclear Policy (SANE), the Committee for Nonviolent Action (CNVA), and the War Resisters' League, these radical pacifists countered the passivism of American culture with both civil discourse and civil disobedience. They liberated themselves and others to speak truth to power with the whole weight of their lives.[2]

Their liberation theology (and sociology) also played a part in liberating American women to assume a more public role in antinuclear protest and social activism. Activists connected to *Liberation* and SANE helped to shape the development of Women Strike for Peace in 1961. That "unorganization" allowed women to speak their minds and hearts about nuclear issues and to experience the perils and pleasures of personalist politics.

Between 1955 and 1965, the antinuclear activism of *Liberation* and Women Strike for Peace supplemented the political personalism of the civil rights movement, and created precedents for the social activism of the Sixties. Those precedents were transmitted personally to the younger generation by leaders like Muste, Dellinger, Goodman, Rustin, Staughton Lynd, and Barbara Deming, who were, at least until 1967, among the most important organizers in the peace movement. This chapter tells the story of *Liberation* and the politics of personalism in the anti-nuclear movement.

Person-nel

Contributors to *Liberation* included Dorothy Day, Michael Harrington, Norman Mailer, Lewis Mumford, Kenneth Rexroth, Lawrence Ferlinghetti, Gary Snyder, Daniel Berrigan, E.F. Schumacher, Todd Gitlin, Tom Hayden, Michael Lerner, Robin Morgan, Thomas Merton, Jules Feiffer, Adrienne Rich, Erich Fromm, James Peck, Alex Comfort, George Woodcock, Joan Baez, Charles Cobb, Murray Bookchin, Noam Chomsky, and Nelson Mandela, among many others. But the editorial board came mainly from the War Resisters League, and reflected the league's commitment to nonviolent approaches to peace and justice.[3]

Editor A.J. Muste had been among the civil defense protesters in City Hall Park. Muste was a complex and charismatic figure with philosophical and ethical interests that enriched his work for social justice. His biography shows one way in which the intellectual legacy of the Old Left could be transformed and transmitted to a New Left. In 1955, this man in the prophetic tradition was 70 years old, with experience as a pastor, a labor organizer, a Trotskyist, and a Christian pacifist. A man who lived what he believed, Muste was a leader not because of his power or position, but because he was an "exemplary figure" in a movement that prized the personalist practice of its preachers.[4]

During the 1930s, Muste had helped create the Conference for Progressive Labor Action (a group of industrial unionists whose followers were called Musteites), the Unemployment Leagues, and the Workers Party of the USA (a Trotskyist organization that he served as national secretary). For Muste and for many others in the Thirties, as Daniel Aaron has observed, Marxism seemed "the logical extension of the progressive humanist trend, the continuation and fulfillment of the great Judaeo-Christian tradition."[5]

During a 1936 European vacation, in the church of St. Sulpice in Paris, Muste—like Dorothy Day—had a mystical experience that directed his radicalism back to religion. Although he had been raised in the Dutch Reformed church, and although he had denominational connections to Presbyterianism, the Society of Friends became Muste's "real spiritual home." After the conversion experience, Muste resigned from the party, but he did not resign the social and political ideals that had informed his libertarian socialism. Instead, like the French personalists, he worked to navigate a "third way" between capitalism and communism.[6]

In January 1938, Muste hosted a symposium on personalism coordinated by Catholic Worker Peter Maurin at New York's Labor Temple. Participants included Roger Baldwin of the American Civil Liberties Union, Louis Finkelstein of the Jewish Theological Seminary, Carlton Hayes of Columbia University, and Muste. Baldwin led off the series with a discussion of Emmanuel Mounier's *Personalist Manifesto* (which had been published in English at Maurin's suggestion). Despite their denominational differences, the panelists agreed that "all institutions find their ultimate justification only in the degree they contribute to the personal growth and development of the individual, to the highest of which he is capable." They worried about encroachments of the state and an increasingly mechanistic society. And they hoped that personalist democracy—with participatory political and economic institutions—could reclaim a social focus on the dignity and worth of human beings.[7]

Muste also maintained his radicalism in the Christian pacifist tradition, serving, from 1940 to 1953 as executive secretary of the Fellowship of Reconciliation, which had been founded in 1914 to promote a new "world order based on Love." During World War II, Muste earned, from *Time*, the title of "Number One U.S. Pacifist" for his support of conscientious objectors, his work for incarcerated Japanese Americans, his pleas for the victims of Nazism, and his opposition to Allied obliteration bombing. At a time when American anti-fascism drew many radicals into support of the war, Muste and a few others, including Dwight Macdonald, David Dellinger, Dorothy Day, and Kenneth Rexroth, continued to inveigh against the hypocrisy and violence of the war.[8]

Muste decried the 1945 atomic bombing of Hiroshima and Nagasaki, and he campaigned against the militarism and conscription of the Cold War that followed World War II. "If Dachau was a crime," he argued in 1947, after the first Nuremberg trials, "Hiroshima is a crime." A year later, Muste helped found both the Central Committee for Conscientious Objectors and Peacemakers, a radical pacifist group advocating opposition to the draft, tax resistance and civil disobedience. With Dwight Macdonald, Bayard Rustin, Dave Dellinger, Roy Finch, George Houser, and Jim Peck, Muste served on the executive board of the War Resisters' League. Like many personalists, Muste believed that biography was destiny, and that individuals could, in writing their own lives, right many of the wrongs of American society. But he also understood that biographies were inscribed in communities, and he relied on an exemplary fellowship of persons to embody the new order and become its witness to the world.[9]

Muste opposed the "Christian realism" of such neo-orthodox figures as Reinhold Niebuhr, who synthesized religion and American liberalism in the postwar years. Niebuhr's *Moral Man and Immoral Society* had argued that Christian ethics applied to individuals, but not equally to collectivities like nations or social classes. Niebuhr and other church figures supported nuclear deterrence (which General Omar Bradley called "peace by the accumulation of peril") but many of them opposed the use of nuclear weapons. And they criticized Christian pacifists for their "perfectionism, utopianism, sentimentalism, and political oversimplification."[10]

Muste argued, in reply, that the Bible provided no support for "the notion that there is or can be one law for the individual and another for society." Instead he took the personalist position that ethics should uniformly inform all human decisions. "There is no way to peace," he said. "Peace is the way." And against the idea that it was morally allowable to threaten using weapons which would be immoral to use, Muste argued for the greater consistency of unilateral disarmament. Moreover, Muste denied that pacifists assumed the perfectibility of people or society; he claimed simply that imperfect people could make moral decisions, and that perfection was a worthy, if impractical, goal. Under the influence of Niebuhrian "realism," Muste, like Albert Camus, would work for a "modest utopia" in which people would be "neither victims nor executioners." As C. Wright Mills said later, "We try to be realistic in our utopianism."[11]

From 1950 to 1955, when the Cold War, the Korean War, and the political repression of McCarthyism eviscerated both pacifist and social democratic dissent in America, Muste—like Dorothy Day and the *Catholic Worker*—kept the tradition alive, and tried to formulate a new radicalism rooted in moral values that could transcend the disenchantment of the Cold War consensus. While many American radicals retreated to the "vital center" and "the ideology of liberal consensus," Muste tried to preach and practice a new social theory of personalist politics.[12]

In 1950, as a member of the Church Peace Mission, a group formed to promote conversation between pacifist and nonpacifist Christians, Muste helped draft *The Christian Conscience and War*, a statement which criticized "cultural jingoism and conventional patriotism," and the complicity of the churches with the war-making powers of the state. "War *is* the culture of our age and the culture *is* war," contended the commission, arguing that the Church should "issue a condemnation of war as an instrument of policy."[13]

During the 1950s, Muste dismissed the good intentions of both the superpowers, and advocated a "Third Camp" of neutral nations (like Gandhi's India) to disarm the atomic superpowers and to revolutionize the new (nuclear) world order. To achieve the "Third Camp," he looked to an international coalition of radical pacifists who would work *against* militarism, colonialism, racism, and poverty, and *for* the liberation of persons from the socio-economic and political forces that deprived them of human dignity and self-realization.[14]

In his 1952 essay "Of Holy Disobedience," Muste argued that the "depersonalization" of the modern age was intimately connected to the growth of the "war-making power-state." He thought that, in the name of defense, Americans had left themselves defenseless against a permanent war economy and a permanent war polity. In response, he said, "the human being, the child of God, must assert his humanity and his sonship again. . . . He must understand that this naked human being is the one *real* thing in the face of the mechanics and the mechanized institutions of the age."[15]

In 1955, Muste was part of the thirteen-person committee that composed *Speak Truth to Power: A Quaker Search for an Alternative to Violence*. The pamphlet contended that international relations in the Cold War had reached a point of diminishing and dangerous returns, because they were premised on the use of force and counterforce. The authors suggested that nonviolence offered both a moral and a practical alternative, and offered examples of successful nonviolent campaigns. Finally, they contended "it is practical, and politically relevant, for men and women to move the world toward peace by individually practicing peace themselves, here and now." And they called for a community of conscientious individuals, grounded in faith, to align the politics of time with the politics of eternity, "putting into action the laws of the Kingdom before the Kingdom has really come." *Speak Truth to Power* went through a first printing of 25,000 copies in two months and more than 80,000 copies by the end of the Fifties. The American Friends Service Committee (AFSC) also promoted the pamphlet widely, and estimated that by early 1956, it had been discussed in newspapers with a collective circulation of ten million.[16]

As this suggests, the Quakers were a prominent part of personalist liberation. The Society of Friends embodied a personalist perspective, with their assumption that friendship could serve as a model for other human relationships. They were the only Christian denomination with a tradition of commitment to the inherent equality of the races, and they were the most prominent of the historic peace churches. During the 1950s and 1960s, Quakers were represented in personalist politics by the AFSC. Established by Rufus Jones and thirteen other Friends in 1917, the AFSC performed civilian relief work in World War I, and expanded its pacifist and social justice work afterward with separate sections of foreign service, home service, interracial service, and peace work. During World War II, AFSC administered twenty Civilian Public Service Camps containing 3400 conscientious objectors. Awarded the Nobel Peace Prize in 1947 for postwar relief work in Europe and Japan, the AFSC continued to work for peace in many of the personalist projects of the Fifties and Sixties.[17]

David Dellinger came to his collaboration with A.J. Muste from a different personalist path. Born in 1915, Dellinger attended Yale and Oxford Universities, and Union Theological Seminary. At Yale, he learned something from his coursework, but just as much from his extracurricular activities, including the Social Gospel of Yale's Dwight Hall. Inspired by Saint Francis of Assisi, Dellinger also took to the road to see how the other half lived. "My whole trip was a first experimental step down the road that Francis had followed, rejecting his heritage as the son of a rich Florentine merchant, living the life of the poor." Life as a hobo confirmed Dellinger's sense of structural poverty in a capitalist society and his sense of solidarity with the poor. At Union, he and four other students lived in Harlem, despite the threat of the Seminary president to expel them if they broke Christian fellowship by leaving the residence hall. During the summer of 1940, he moved to Newark, New Jersey, where he helped to establish the Newark Christian Colony, also known as the Newark Ashram, after Gandhi's political/spiritual centers.[18]

Dellinger learned too from his own curriculum of protest and prison. A pacifist and socialist, Dellinger refused to register for the draft in 1940, despite the fact that he qualified for a seminary deferment. Union expelled him and several others, and Reinhold Niebuhr preached a sermon on the resisters' arrogance on the day of their arrest. Dellinger served a year and a day behind bars. In 1943, after getting out of prison and establishing the Peoples' Peace Now Committee, Dellinger was arrested again, and charged, not with refusal to register (which would have constituted double jeopardy) but with refusal to take a physical. Convicted again for essentially the same conscientious crime, he was sentenced to two years.[19]

In prison, Dellinger was one of the organizers of the Danbury prison strike, in which a group of conscientious objectors undertook a hunger strike to protest racial discrimination at the prison. The strike inspired similar actions in other prisons and Civilian Public Service camps, and radicalized American pacifism. Before the war, pacifists preserved their own integrity by passive resistance, noncollaboration, and moral suasion. During the war, however, they increasingly employed pacifism, once seen mainly as a matter of personal morality, as a robust strategy of social change.[20]

Like many pacifists, Dellinger took the atomic bomb as the logical consequence of the American way of life, and as a challenge to personalists. In an editorial for *Direct Action* he argued that "the fight against the swift destruction of human life which takes place in modern warfare cannot be separated from the slow debilitation of human personality which takes place in the families of the rich, the unemployed, and the poor. *The enemy is every institution which denies full social and economic equality to anyone. The enemy is personal indifference to the consequences of acts performed by the institutions of which we are a part.*" The solution, he said, was war, a war for total brotherhood "carried on by methods worthy of the ideals we seek to serve. . . . Every act we perform today must reflect the kind of human relationships we are fighting to establish tomorrow."[21]

After the war and after a brief stay with poet Kenneth Patchen, Dellinger and his family joined the rural communitarian experiment at Glen Gardner, New Jersey, where they lived until 1968. Explaining his participation, Dellinger said that "it seems to me that the current edge of pacifism is the development of communities of sharing, and that those of us who want to attack the causes of war should begin in our lives." In the Sixties, the group named itself Saint Francis Acres, and changed the deed to show God as the owner, with the collective as trustees. The Glen Gardner collective established the Libertarian Press, and published small anarcho-pacifist journals like *Direct Action*, *Alternative*, *Individual Action*, *Cooperative Living*, and *Liberation*. Like the Catholic Worker farms and the Macedonia Cooperative Community in Georgia, Glen Gardner's cooperativism offered anarcho-pacifists an opportunity to practice the politics of personalism. "Best of all, in principle," said Paul Goodman, "is the policy that Dave Dellinger espouses and tries to live by, to live communally and without authority, to work usefully and feel friendly, and so *positively to replace an area of power with peaceful functioning.*"[22]

The community functioned as a support group for personalist protest. Dellinger and his colleagues took part in antinuclear activities, civil rights demonstrations, and other acts of personal witness. They also participated in establishing and sustaining groups like the Committee for Nonviolent Revolution, Peacemakers, the Committee for Nonviolent Action, the War Resisters League, and the Fellowship of Intentional Communities. "During the Fifties," Dellinger recalled, "I was involved in as many activities as at any time during the Sixties, and so were at least a few hundred people whom I knew personally and thousands whom I didn't know." Like many others, Dellinger was essentially a Sixties activist before the Sixties rolled around.[23]

Like Muste and Dellinger, editor Paul Goodman himself embodied an experiment in creative living. His roots in psychological theory and in the politics of anarchism made him a distinctive voice on the *Liberation* board. Born in 1911 in New York City, he decided at age 20 to be a writer in order to avoid choosing a career. After graduate work in literature and philosophy at the University of Chicago, he began in the 1940s to write for such leftist, libertarian, and anarchist periodicals as *Partisan Review*, *Politics*, *Why?*, and *Retort*. He publicly opposed American participation in World War II and declared his own pacifism. After World War II, he lived marginally in New York's intellectual and Bohemian circles, writing fiction, poetry, social criticism and plays. His open bisexuality in a culture of closeted sexual containment also added to his marginality.[24]

Paul Goodman put his faith, not in the Creator—as Martin Luther King Jr. and the Catholic Workers did—but in the creation, deriving his radicalism from the psychobiological imperatives of the individual person. Influenced by Reichian and Gestalt psychology, Goodman rooted his personalism in human instincts, especially sexual instincts, and he looked for society to fulfill people's natural needs, instead of repressing them. Revolting against the repressive institutions of American society, Goodman worked for institutions that would enhance human freedom (which Goodman termed "organismic self-regulation").[25]

As early as 1945, he called for the creation of communitarian groups devoted to mutual aid. Such communities could fulfill human beings through good work, participatory decision-making, and sexual satisfaction. They would also withdraw support from the centralizing, dehumanizing trends of American society. Individuals who lived in such communities would be like "sane men in a madhouse." Like Muste and Dellinger, Goodman's radical politics rejected the economic focus of both liberalism and socialism, and concentrated on personal and cultural questions. Spurning the politics of persuasion, power, and postponement, he called for a here-and-now revolution. Instead of participating in a political system where the direct initiative of the people was, at best, an occasional event, Goodman preferred a politics in which popular initiative was the rule instead of the exception. This was anarchism, pure but not simple, as Goodman spoke in the tradition of Proudhon, Bakunin, and especially Kropotkin. Goodman saw anarchism not as an invitation to chaos or random violence, but as an invitation to self-management and community. Goodman knew, according to George Steiner, "that there are grave problems which can only be treated by exact, modest means, by the scrupulous generosity of the imagination when it is dealing with a single human person or local fabric. Large figures blur their own intent; art and love deal in the singular."[26]

In the tradition of utopian socialists and anarchists, therefore, Goodman was concerned with the character of the "good community," and of alternatives to a society that was neither good nor great. Like George Steiner, Goodman believed that, "if we are to survive, we must devise and articulate the pattern of a world so meaningful to human impulse and creativity that men will *want* to live in it." And, from the time of *Communitas* (1947), Goodman made a series of what he called "utopian essays and practical proposals." Critics claimed that his utopian plans were unrealistic, but Goodman replied that "people think they're *impractical* only because deep down they make sense and so people feel threatened. Really impractical ideas, on the other hand, don't bother people at all."[27]

The 1960 publication of *Growing Up Absurd* made Goodman famous, and led to a decade of activism, including teaching, lectures, and substantial writing. Goodman's tract, claims historian Richard Pells, influenced the politics and culture of the Sixties "more directly than any work save C. Wright Mills' *The Power Elite*." "In its way," suggests Richard King, "*Growing Up Absurd* was to the generation of the early sixties what *Catcher in the Rye* had been to the youth of the fifties. It had the merit of placing certain problems considered formerly to be personal aberrations or special cases in a wider social context, and it suggested that American society had to be worthy of its youth, if it expected its youth to be worthy of it."[28]

Growing Up Absurd addressed itself to national problems of educational competitiveness, youthful disaffection, juvenile delinquency, and the Beat movement. But instead of blaming young people, Goodman indicted the schools and the society they represented. American society, he said, was basically at odds with human nature; its ideals and institutions required role-players who were less than fully human, personnel who were less than persons. Because the schools had been designed to prepare whole persons for the half-lives that awaited them in "the real world," the schools were necessarily depersonalizing and alienating. Goodman's solution combined school reform and social reform.[29]

Goodman saw the schools as part of a utopian project. "Think about the kind of world you want to live and work in," he advised students, quoting Peter Kropotkin. "What do you need to know to help build that world? Demand that your teachers teach you that." Like Thomas Jefferson, Goodman thought that all people should be educated "so much as may enable them to read and understand what is going on in the world, and to keep their part of it going on right; for nothing can keep it right but their own vigilant and distrustful superintendence."[30]

Anarchism also gave Goodman a sense of personal responsibility for the governance (not necessarily the government) of the social order. Anarchism assumed, as did early American republicanism, that people are capable of literal self-government. Historically, however, dependence on Big Government had overshadowed traditions of local initiative and direct action; people had become politically passive. "The fault," said Goodman, "is not with democracy, but that we have failed to have enough of it. . . . If people had the opportunity to initiate community actions, they would be political; they would know that finally the way to accomplish something great is to get together with the like-minded and directly do it."[31]

Personal responsibility for the social order led, in Goodman's life, to personal protest against the nation-state. Looking at the sorry condition of the world and its "national sovereign bellicosity," Goodman looked for a better way, and concluded that "the only possible pacifist conclusion from these facts is the anarchist one, to get rid of the sovereignties. . . . My own bias is to decentralize and localize wherever it is feasible, because this makes for alternatives and more vivid and intimate life. And it is safer."[32]

As an anarcho-pacifist, Goodman consistently opposed the statist policy of conscripting citizens for killing: he was, therefore, an advocate of draft evasion and conscientious objection in World War II, a ban-the-bomb activist who participated in the "Worldwide General Strike for Peace," and an opponent of the Vietnam War and a proponent of draft and tax resistance. In addition, Goodman advocated "covert noncooperation, Schweikism, avoidance, bohemian deviance, privateering, nonallegiance—the antipolitics of the individualist 'opting out' of the repressive system." Goodman claimed that "the only way to make powers tolerable to live with is to squawk and balk till they fear they may lose their control and power . . . because it is too damned dangerous."[33]

In *The Society I Live in Is Mine* (1962), Goodman collected some "angry letters on public morals and politics" which exemplified his personalist response to American culture. Instead of acting as a political spectator, Goodman wrote letters to school boards, to local officials, to newspapers, and even to the President. The letters were, he claimed, "the squawks of a Citizen. The society in which I live is mine, open to my voice and action, or I do not live there at all. The government, the school board, the church, the university, the world of publication and communications, are my agencies as a citizen. To the extent that they are *not* my institutions, at least open to my voice and action, I am entirely in revolutionary opposition to them and I think they should be wiped off the slate." Institutions were irresponsible, Goodman thought, to the extent that they were not responsive to the civic voice. "It is appalling," mourned Goodman, "how few people regard themselves as citizens, as society-makers, in this existential sense. Rather, people seem to take society as a preestablished machinery of institutions and authorities, and take themselves as I don't know what, some kind of individuals 'in' society, whatever that means." But Goodman felt that institutions founded for freedom needed the eternal vigilance of citizens: "We have no right to surrender our inheritance to boors and tyrants. It is entailed to us as citizens." As a citizen, speaking in the civic voice, Paul Goodman and the editors of *Liberation* spoke to those people who saw themselves only as "sitizens."[34]

Like A.J. Muste and David Dellinger, Paul Goodman had a profound effect on young radicals. He became Abbie Hoffman's role model after Hoffman heard Goodman speak at a Catholic Worker meeting. He inspired and supported the Berkeley Free Speech Movement. And, as Richard King wrote in 1972, Goodman's example was as important as his ideas: "It has been Goodman's personal witness to his own ideas, his participation in the life of the society as though it were a genuine community, and his service as a model for a generation of young people which has made it impossible to imagine the current life of the mind in America without him."[35]

Tracts for the Times

The March 1956 premiere issue of *Liberation* included a manifesto called "A Tract for the Times." In it, the editors noted the "decline of independent radicalism and the gradual falling into silence of prophetic and rebellious voices," and they outlined the aims and assumptions that might provide "a post-Soviet, post-H-bomb expression of the needs of today." By providing a space for prophetic and rebellious voices, *Liberation* could, the editors believed, fulfill the moral responsibilities of intellectuals. As public intellectuals, *Liberation*'s leaders hoped to maintain critical and theoretical traditions of American thought in a time when many intellectuals had been hired or silenced by the institutions of American power.[36]

The Bomb was a central feature of *Liberation*'s critique. "From a sociological view," the editors argued, "the H-bomb and what it symbolizes—possible extinction of the race itself—present mankind with a new situation. War is no longer an instrument of policy or a means to any rational end." Both atomic-armed superpowers threatened the survival of civilization. "The H-bomb is not an instrument of peace in the hands of one and of war in the hands of the other. Nor is it a mere accidental excrescence in either of them, but, rather, a logical outgrowth of their basic economic and social orders." As a cogent critic would later say, "The USA and the USSR do not *have* military-industrial complexes. They *are* military industrial complexes."[37]

Liberation's tract embraced a personalist politics. Repudiating Cold War liberalism as a "public ritual lacking roots in private life and behavior," *Liberation* offered an explicit idealist and utopian critique of the "realist" pragmatism of postwar liberalism. It identified statism, centralization, militarism, scientism, poverty, and personal alienation as problems neglected by liberalism. It rejected the *realpolitik* of American diplomacy, arguing with C. Wright Mills that the pseudo-rationality of "defense intellectuals" represented a kind of "crackpot realism." *Liberation* showed that the social construction of reality involved also the social construction of "realism." In the Democratic Party of the 1950s and 1960s, realism meant militant anticommunism, military toughness, missile gaps, missile crises, and a foreign policy of containment and confrontation. Liberal senators like Stuart Symington (D-Mo.) and Henry Jackson (D-Wash.) championed increased military spending and influenced the aims and assumptions of the Kennedy and Johnson administrations. The paradigm of "realism" included its opposite, the "idealism" of critics like Mills and Muste, who, like children, were expected to grow out of their "naive" opinions that realism was not, in fact, very realistic, especially in the long run. Consensus historians like Daniel Boorstin, who defined the American tradition as "pragmatic," permitted idealists to be seen—tautologically—as "un-American."[38]

The *Liberation* crowd rejected all of these liberal assumptions. They feared the bureaucratization of American institutions, because it led to the "depersonalization" of society, substituting roles and functions for the complexities of persons. A strategy focused on the machinery of politics and designed to take control of contemporary institutions was, therefore, insufficient. Instead, *Liberation* envisioned "a more complex and human process in which power as ordinarily conceived plays a minor part," and it considered a cultural politics of decentralization and participation more important than the party politics of the status quo.[39]

Liberation did not find the Old Left any more useful than liberalism in confronting social problems of the Cold War era. The Old Left's doctrinaire Marxism, with its acceptance of the centralized Soviet model, seemed like a heightened version of the liberal corporate order that emerged in the United States after World War II. Labor's role as a partner in the New Deal political coalition and the relative prosperity of American workers made it increasingly unlikely that the proletariat would be agents of social transformation. Losing faith in the "labor metaphysics" of the Old Left and in mass social action, *Liberation* looked to alternative political strategies.[40]

Rejecting contemporary liberalism and the Old Left, *Liberation*'s editors embraced instead the "root traditions" of dissent and civil disobedience in American history. "There is an American tradition," they wrote, " . . . of a nation conceived in liberty and dedicated to the proposition that all men are created equal. It is a tradition which also emphasizes the dignity of man and asserts that government rests upon consent, and institutions are made for man, not man for institutions. Such names as Jefferson, Paine, Thoreau, Emerson, Debs, the Quaker experiment in Pennsylvania, the Utopian community experiments, the Abolition movement, the Underground Railway, are associated with this tradition." They also drew on European anarchists and libertarian socialists like Proudhon, Bakunin, and Kropotkin, and on the Christian pacifist tradition.[41]

"To become significant," the editors declared, "politics must discover its ethical foundations and dynamic." *Liberation* rooted its radicalism in its humanism. Like Dwight Macdonald (referring directly to Marx's *Economic and Philosophical Manuscripts* of 1844), the editors believed that "To be radical is to grasp the matter by the root. Now the root for mankind is man himself." In the "Tract for the Times," Muste and his colleagues contended that "what matters to us is what happens to the individual human being— here and now . . . we will insist on spelling things out in terms of daily consequences, hour to hour, for everyone." The dignity and development of persons would be the root of their radical humanism.[42]

Liberation was not alone. Following Macdonald's lead, many intellectuals of the 1950s redefined politics, extending it to issues formerly considered psychological, sociological, or cultural. Moving from a Marxist focus on economics and the proletariat, they began to concentrate on the culture of the American middle class, and a society that seemed impersonal, bureaucratic, and inhumane. They concerned themselves, therefore, with questions that—outside a personalist framework—look more cultural than political. Like many other critics of the 1950s, they criticized the boredom and anomie of mass society. They criticized the "top-down" trajectory of the hierarchy and centralization that pervaded American life in both the public and private spheres. This cultural critique was an important part of the intellectual life of the 1950s; the age of affluence was also an age of careful criticism.[43]

Liberation's editors believed in the "here and now revolution," a revolution embodied in their personal lives and anticipated in their political activism. Because of their personal focus, the editors grappled seriously with the issue of ends and means. They believed that the processes of politics must be consistent with the goals of political action. They intended to practice what they preached, and so they depended not on the compromises of pluralist politics, not on mass political mobilization, but on participatory democracy, persuasion, nonviolent direct action, and civil disobedience. The exemplary behavior of such activism would, they thought, influence the individual consciences of contemporary Americans, and move them to personal and political revolution. Although political reform was not formally a part of their own political strategy, and although activists like Muste did not support the state with their vote, it is clear from the coalitions they made that they would accept the partial passage of their politics of the unusual by means of politics as usual. They celebrated, for example, the test ban treaty, the Civil Rights Act of 1964, and the Voting Rights Act of 1965.[44]

Because of its interests in changing not just political policy but political culture, the magazine pledged to cover both national and international events *and* "experiments in creative living by individuals, families, and small groups." Convinced that pacifism could be applied in domestic life as well as on the international scene, they hoped that such experiments offered examples of cooperative social organization for American society. This communitarian ethic was shared by more than half of *Liberation*'s readers, who, when polled in 1959, expressed a preference for cooperative communities.[45]

Nonviolent Action

Liberation's editors called for a "synthesis of the ethical and the political" to inspire immediate and direct action. "We mean to speak now," they said, "with the weight of our whole lives." *Liberation*, therefore, supported the Committee for Nonviolent Action (CNVA), when it emerged in 1957 with the Committee for a Sane Nuclear Policy (SANE) to provide complementary approaches to a nuclear test ban and disarmament. Psychologist Erich Fromm, author of *The Sane Society*, suggested the name for SANE. By emphasizing sanity as a criterion for state action, the organizers accomplished a blurring of the personal and political. In a way, the criterion of sanity personalized (or anthropomorphized) the state, subjecting it to the same expectations as everyday personal behavior. SANE and CNVA represented the collaboration of radical personalists and liberals which occurred throughout the 1950s and 1960s. The liberals of SANE emphasized electoral action and citizen lobbying, while CNVA's radicals featured a personal commitment to nonviolent direct action and civil disobedience.[46]

According to the personalists, including Fromm, one element of America's institutionalized insanity was the segregation of morality from policy. The standard operating procedures of bureaucracies accustomed people to policies which, upon critical reflection, seemed incompatible with American values. In some cases, the result was the "bureaucratization of homicide." Lewis Mumford, for example, was amazed at the "detached and depersonalized scientific intelligence" of the Manhattan Project, and astounded by the acquiescence of the American people to atomic bombs. "It is as if the Secretary of Agriculture had authorized the sale of human meat, during the meat shortage, and everyone had accepted cannibalism in daily practice as a clever dodge for reducing the cost of living."[47]

CNVA's founders hoped to create a circle for experimenting with nonviolence, for expressing their political views, and for creating "intra/interpersonal, national, and international social change." While SANE used advertisements and persuasion to change public opinion and ultimately policy, CNVA went "beyond words" in protesting American bomb culture. Led by A.J. Muste, Larry Scott, and Brad Lyttle, and inspired by the civil rights movement, CNVA activists practiced nonviolent direct action at nuclear test sites, bomber and submarine bases, and the Washington headquarters of the Atomic Energy Commission.[48]

Many of the CNVA activists had experience with opposition to militarism. Some were conscientious objectors from World War II. Some were tax resisters, opposed to the compulsory conscription of people and people's resources for war. A.J. Muste, for example, realized that the state's campaigns for national security could proceed only on the basis of internal revenue. In 1948, therefore, he ceased to pay his income taxes, arguing that people could not be compelled "to file returns or pay taxes for war purposes by virtue of the Nuremberg Principles of International Law." Instead he wrote an annual letter to the Internal Revenue Service explaining his position. In 1954, he told the Collector of Internal Revenue that "I do not recognize the right of any earthly government to inquire into my income—or that of other citizens—for the purpose of determining how much they or I 'owe' for the diabolical purpose of atomic and biological war." One year, as "supporting material," Muste enclosed a copy of the Gospels and Thoreau's "Essay on Civil Disobedience." Convicted of failure to pay taxes in 1960, Muste was saved only by his voluntary poverty. As his lawyer told the court, Muste "has no funds. He has voluntarily lived for years at a subsistence level."[49]

Like Muste, other CNVA activists meant to speak with the weight of their whole lives, and so they often lived lives of voluntary simplicity, attempting to avoid complicity with the institutions of militarism in American society. Instead of waiting for conventional political success, they began to "live the revolution now." In CNVA itself they practiced consensus decision-making as a model for the conflict resolution they thought possible on a broader scale.[50]

With SANE, CNVA focused its critique of American militarism on nuclear weapons policy. Immediately after World War II, the government had begun to test nuclear weapons, which the pacifists saw as irrational and immoral. CNVA saw the tests both as a test of the civilian population and as an opportunity to bring statism to public consciousness. In 1957, they called people to civil disobedience at the Nevada Test Site of the Atomic Energy Commission, citing a "moral obligation to cast their whole lives against evil." Quaker activist Larry Scott participated, he said, because "it will confirm that which I feel to be good within myself . . . and the only thing for which I am ultimately responsible to the creator."[51]

Civil disobedience, like conscientious objection, offered activists a distinctly personalist politics. Rooted in religious traditions of noncooperation with unjust laws and political traditions of resistance and revolution against oppressive governments, CNVA's civil disobedience was inspired by the Gandhian protests of the American civil rights movement. It exemplified a challenge to American values in the name of American values. As Paul Goodman said, "the civil disobedience of the Committee for Nonviolent Action is the direct expression of each person's conscience of what it is impossible for him to live with."[52]

In a critical but understanding essay in *Liberation*, Robert Pickus declared that "*the project aided in driving home the fact of personal responsibility*." Many people troubled by nuclear weapons excused "their own passivity and acquiescence in two key phrases: 'I have no choice'—'There is nothing I can do.'" But "the project demonstrated the fact and the possibility of moral choice. By accepting personal responsibility for opposing the government's action, project members provided an occasion for millions of other Americans to recognize *their* responsibility."[53]

In 1958 and 1959, CNVA protested both testing and the American deployment of intercontinental ballistic missiles. The most widely and sympathetically reported CNVA action occurred in 1958, when activists attempted to sail the *Golden Rule* and the *Phoenix of Hiroshima* into the Pacific Ocean bomb-testing area. At Cheyenne, Wyoming, they blocked the gates of Camp Warren in order to confront employees with a clear and conscious decision about their complicity with the missiles. Since the Nuremberg trials had concluded that individuals were responsible for their own actions, A.J. Muste argued that such obstruction was justifiable because it showed people the truth about their work with the war machine. At a similar protest in Omaha, Muste was joined by Karl Meyer, a Catholic Worker personalist from Chicago, who, with Muste and veteran pacifist Ross Anderson, were arrested for trespassing on government land. Although their sentence of a year's probation included the stipulation that they stay away from the missile base, Meyer returned three days after the trial and entered the base again. This time he received six months in a federal penitentiary, where he wrote a pamphlet on *The Nonviolent Revolution*, calling for "poverty, pacifism, prison, and personalism."[54]

The Cheyenne action also inspired the formation of the Student Peace Union in 1959. Karl Meyer, Quaker activists Ken and Ele Calkins, and AFSC's Chicago peace education director Brad Lyttle returned to Chicago attempting to get students to take "personal responsibility for building a just and peaceful world." Within a year, they had twelve chapters in the Midwest and about 120 members. By summer 1962, there were 2,000 members and an annual budget of $22,000.[55]

The confrontations of Cheyenne and Omaha made some activists uncomfortable. Especially after the United States and the Soviet Union both announced a moratorium on testing in 1958, some pacifists dropped out. They thought that nonviolent action, while an excellent expression of individual morality, was politically unproductive. But CNVA continued, as it was conceived, as a complement to liberal political organizations like SANE. In 1960-61, CNVA organized a Walk for Peace from San Francisco to Moscow, and in 1962 they followed with a walk from Quebec to Washington to Guantanamo Bay. When the first march reached Washington, they hoped to speak with President Kennedy, but were met instead by aide Arthur Schlesinger Jr., who told them—in Niebuhrian fashion—that "morality has nothing to do with international relations. These are matters of interest and power." Pacifists, he said, had renounced their responsibility by renouncing military force.[56]

In 1964, on a second walk from Quebec to Guantanamo, marchers were arrested in Macon and Albany, Georgia, for violating local laws prohibiting free speech. During her days in the Albany Jail, *Liberation* editor Barbara Deming had time to consider her commitments to both the peace and civil rights movements. Not surprisingly, Deming took a personalist perspective, combining Christian and radical beliefs. She recognized that Eugene Debs' statement—"While there is a criminal element, I am of it; while there is a soul in prison, I am not free"—was "not a sentimental statement but a statement of fact." In what became almost a mantra for her, she noted that nonviolence "always tries to dramatize the words of St. Paul, 'We are members one of another.'"[57]

In explaining her personalist protest to a friend, she wrote that "we place our hopes in a very particular kind of persuasion"—nonviolent direct action—that the Quakers would call "speaking to that of God in another man." By appealing to the better self of the opponent, practitioners of nonviolence hoped "to force the other person to acknowledge a human relationship and to act accordingly." Exerting the complementary pressures of friendliness and disobedience, they announced their opposition to injustice, while assuring their opponents that "we do not threaten your person. I think it is St. Augustine who says that to love your neighbor means to let him feel: I wish you to be. We try to assert this—in spite of our disagreement with them. And so we disturb their peace of mind, disturb that 'order' in which their minds are used to seeing things."[58]

The hope of nonviolent direct action was to cause oppressors to ask "whether they are willing not so much to *take* any more punishment, which is the question raised by violent struggle, but to deal out any more punishment." By putting their bodies and their persons on the line for the poor and oppressed, the protesters tested the system's capacity for evil. Deming did not expect dramatic conversions as a result of nonviolent direct action. She knew that other people "are not likely to be changed by our actions as much as we ourselves are changed. We tried in Albany, however clumsily, to act out the truth that all men are kin to one another. As the drama ended, it was we ourselves, inevitably, who felt the truth of it most sharply." Reflecting on the love that she and the other peace marchers had come to share, Deming marveled that this "love-for-more-than-one" extended at times even beyond the group of protesters, and prefigured the sympathy and compassion that might befit a beloved community.[59]

During the Sixties, CNVA brought its nonviolent perspectives to the antiwar movement, and, like many personalist organizations, ceased to exist. In 1965, CNVA and the War Resisters League created the Workshop in Nonviolence (WIN), a New York experiment that published the influential magazine *WIN*. In 1967, CNVA sponsored a Spring March on the Pentagon "bearing a message of an affirmation of life and the daily responsibility of each individual to put his truth, his conscience first, without regard for the consequences brought on by an inhuman system." All of these protests stressed "the urgency of personal as well as governmental responsibility for a peaceful world," and they offered both examples and suggestions for citizen action. The same year, the Committee for Nonviolent Action died of success. Realizing that its radical tactics of civil disobedience and nonviolent direct action were an integral part of the mainstream movement, CNVA merged into the War Resisters League. As Paul Goodman recalled, when *Liberation* and CNVA were created in 1956 and 1957, few people thought "that the para-political sometimes para-legal demonstrations of small groups could be of any historical importance. Especially nonviolence—sitting in front of trucks and filling jails—was strictly for the Hindoos." Within ten short years, however, the practices of political personalism had become an accepted strategy for social and political change.[60]

Women Strike for Peace

One of the activists at the City Hall Park civil defense protest in June of 1955 was Orlie Pell, president of the U.S. section of the Women's International League for Peace and Freedom. Although she had been a pacifist for some time, Pell wrote that the Operation Alert protest finally touched her "directly as a person." It forced her to confront her "*innermost* self," and to decide, in the face of the law, that "deep down inside: here I stand—I can do no other."[61]

In 1961, the few activists of CNVA were joined in their antinuclear stand by Orlie Pell and thousands of American women. On November 1, 1961, several thousand women in sixty American communities participated in a Women's Strike for Peace (WSP). Leaving their households and their jobs, they marched with placards proclaiming that "All Children Are Threatened by Fallout," "My Child Wants to Be a Parent Too," "Children Need Milk Strontium Free," and "End the Arms Race—Not the Human Race." In the largest female peace demonstration in American history, the strikers presented petitions to Jacqueline Kennedy and Nina Khrushchev, asking them to "join with us—make the survival of mankind the one great cause of our time."[62]

The size of the strike caught Americans by surprise, even the women who had conceived it. The protest had started six weeks earlier at a cocktail party in the Georgetown home of Dagmar Wilson, an illustrator of children's books. When the conversation turned, "as it always seems to nowadays," to the atom bomb, Wilson found herself frustrated by the lack of opportunities for action. A few days later, Wilson invited two men and a small group of women from the Washington chapter of SANE to her home. She asked them to consider what women could do, as women, to stop the arms race. Among the women were Eleanor Garst, Folly Fodor, Margaret Russell, and Jeanne Bagby, veteran political organizers with connections to both the peace and civil rights movements. Bagby had been part of the Beat scene in New Orleans and had written a well-received article about the Beats for *Liberation*. In March of 1961, her poem "Oh What Farewells" offered *Liberation*'s readers a eulogy for the planet. Just prior to the WSP strike, she had been picketing the White House. Lawrence Scott, a CNVA founder and *Liberation* contributor, suggested a one-day strike. The women decided to send chain letters and make phone calls to friends in other cities urging a demonstration of concern. The message struck a receptive chord. "We are all frightened and that is why we are here," said a Winnetka grandmother of two. "There are some people I'd rather not live with, but I'd rather live with them than die with them."[63]

In the fall of 1961, American conversations turned to the atom bomb because Cold War tensions were at a highpoint. In April, an American invasion of Cuba at the Bay of Pigs had failed. In June, the Vienna summit foundered over the issues of Berlin; in August, the Wall went up. In July President Kennedy called for an increase in military spending, reinforced American troops in Berlin, and increased draft calls. He called for all Americans to build fallout shelters in case of nuclear war. In late August, the Soviet Union ended a three-year moratorium with a series of atomic tests that included the biggest explosion ever, a 50-megaton blast on October 31. On September 15, the United States also resumed testing.

The women of WSP feared the prospect of nuclear war, but they also protested nuclear testing because they knew how radiation affected their bodies, and, more particularly, the bodies of America's children. Jeanne Bagby coordinated WSP's Committee on Radiation Problems, providing data to activists nationwide. While the Atomic Energy Commission justified the tests in abstract terms of weapons modernization and national interest, American mothers were, like the Catholic Workers, more concerned with the flesh and blood of babies. Because radioactive strontium-90 concentrates in teeth and bones, many WSP members sent their children's baby teeth to labs for testing, and then sent the teeth and test results to their Congressional representatives.[64]

Thinking about nuclear war and nuclear testing, they realized that the Defense Department provided no real defense for their families. The President's promotion of fallout shelters suggested that families would have to protect themselves, while the continued atomic testing of the Atomic Energy Commission suggested that Americans would be endangered in the name of their own defense. Women Strike for Peace, recalled Amy Swerdlow, "exposed one of the most important myths of the militarists, that wars are waged by men to protect women and children."[65]

The Tradition of Maternal Pacifism

Although they had no familiarity with the theological and philosophical aspects of personalism, the women of WSP had been thoroughly educated in personalist principles. This education was called "growing up female." A twentieth-century version of the cult of true womanhood, it taught women the virtues of unselfishness, care, concern, protection, and cooperation. It socialized women for "pink collar" professional roles as secretaries, teachers, nurses, domestics, and caregivers, and for the role of wife and mother, which included all the tasks of those separate professions in a single job. American mainstream religions also assigned women a duty of care and collaboration. In the feminization of American religion, there was more emphasis on nurturing than judgment, more emphasis on community than individualism. Although nobody said so in the Fifties, many American women acted as if God had given up on radical individualism in the Garden of Eden.

During the Fifties, the government tried to use the issue of civil defense as a way to enlist women in the cause of the nuclear consensus. Playing on the symbolic connections among postwar fears of sex, liberated women, and atomic energy, civil defense planners and social scientists tried to subsume an evolving family ideology into the statist voice. Women were told that they could serve their country by maintaining traditional gender roles, by raising children within the ideology of liberal consensus, and by preparing their families to survive a nuclear war. In these ways women served not so much as citizens themselves, but as mothers of citizens-to-be and mothers-to-be of citizens. Despite this statist pressure, the personalist question remained, "Will women learn to project beyond a personal circle their deep and sane instinct for the preservation of human life?"[66]

The women of WSP answered in the affirmative. Some of the early WSP members in New York had participated in the civil defense protests sponsored by the Catholic Worker and the War Resisters League. Instead of submitting womanhood to the direction of the state, they defined their own social contract. To do this, the women of WSP spoke what Ruth Rosen calls a "motherist rhetoric" to rally support. They used their children as a metaphor of the future, and contrasted their personal care for their children to the nuclear carelessness of the state. They used the nuclear family to challenge the nuclear state. Although they were not explicitly anti-statist, they made it clear that the state's authority was contingent on its ability to serve human needs. By its rhetoric, Women's Strike for Peace located itself in a long tradition of American reform. As Rosen notes, "motherhood . . . had always justified women's desire to advance their rights, as well as their public efforts to reform society." After the American Revolution, the claims of "republican motherhood" supported education for the women who would be the teachers of future citizens. During the nineteenth century, motherhood offered cultural leverage for women in the prohibition and purity campaigns. During the Progressive Era, women used the metaphor of domestic housekeeping to justify their efforts to get the vote and clean up the nation's cities.[67]

But it is important to note that the organizers called their group, not *Mothers* Strike for Peace, but *Women* Strike for Peace. In a 1963 article on "The New Peace Movement," pacifist Roy Finch noted that the "intriguing" thing about Women Strike for Peace was "that it is the first time in many years (perhaps since the suffragettes) that women have been moved to act as *women*. This is a revolt that has a conscious feminist orientation; the women see themselves and their children as a 'minority' threatened by what men are doing . . . [and] are moved to act in protest against the masculine presumption."[68]

For the women of WSP, mothering was cultural, not biological. It was a defining element of womanhood, but it was not the same thing as womanhood. When America's women went on strike, they posed women's values against men's values, not motherhood against fatherhood, or even motherhood against patriarchy. American women had learned care and concern, compassion and cooperation, and they thought that others (especially male policymakers) could learn as well. Even when they used maternal imagery in their protests, they used motherhood not just as traditionalists, but as personalists. Their protests stressed their conventional role as mothers and nurturers, but in the process, they transformed motherhood from a private and personal role to a public and personalist politics. Rejecting the cult of domesticity and its assumption of separate spheres, the members of WSP saw motherhood "as a social and communal and not just a private activity." They felt that the nuclear policy of the American state had jeopardized their ability to protect their children and to prepare those children for a viable future. And in their protests, they legitimated a civic voice usually silenced in debates on national security and foreign policy.[69]

On peace issues, the women of WSP drew on the precedents of organizations like the Women's International League for Peace and Freedom (WILPF) and the Committee for a Sane Nuclear Policy (SANE), but they rejected the ideological conformity and the hierarchical and bureaucratic structures of earlier organizations. Instead, they invited women of all ideological persuasions to unite behind a position asserting the primacy of "mothers' issues" like the contamination of milk by radioactive fallout.[70]

American women also had the example of their English sisters in the Aldermaston movement. In the late 1950s, women like Jacquetta Hawkes staked out a distinctive role for women in the nuclear age. In her 1958 poem, "Now At Last," Hawkes argued that, because the atomic battlefield was worldwide, "we women must rouse ourselves to resistance/ . . . . If once to live privately was a virtue, it is so no more." Women, she claimed, had been "the continuers, the protectors, the lovers of life." But "now life itself is threatened," and women should "make it known with the wisdom of simplicity/ And the strength of half the world/ That war is no longer heroic or honorable/ But murder, just plain murder."[71]

In America, the wisdom of simplicity offered a civil voice that reverberated with the feminine mystique and a kind of maternal pacifism. Women spoke as creators, as procreators, as mothers, as nurturers, as caretakers; they asked people to listen, not to the rhetoric of politics and foreign policy, but to the "moral force" of women. "As mothers," wrote two WSP leaders, "we are certain that mankind as it now stands is capable of making peace—if the incentive is strong enough. Our work is to strengthen the incentive, just as we do with our children." For many members of WSP, the solution to the politics of war and the wars of politics was "familial society writ large."[72]

The women's strike of November 1, 1961, elicited a response from President Kennedy. "I saw the ladies myself," he said. "I recognized why they were here. . . . I understand what they were attempting to say, therefore, I consider their message was received." President Kennedy acknowledged women's concerns without granting their demands, but he also acted, in the midst of much bluster and toughness, to further their cause. He created the Arms Control and Disarmament Agency (ACDA) in 1961, and committed the agency and the country to the eventual disarmament of all nuclear weapons. In 1963, he told Chester Bowles that, as he was working for a test ban treaty, he was "thinking not so much of our world but of the world that Caroline will live in." The President's June, 1963, American University address echoed Pope John XXIII's *Pacem in Terris*, with its emphasis on peace as a personal and moral concern, not just a political matter. During 1963, Kennedy successfully campaigned for and signed the Limited Test Ban Treaty, which limited the locus but not the number of nuclear tests. "The Test Ban was achieved," reported ACDA Counselor Lawrence Weiler, "because the women of America got concerned about radioactive fallout."[73]

Un-American Activities

For some people, however, WSP's efficacy and inclusiveness looked like invitations to un-Americanism. Especially when Dagmar Wilson and Coretta Scott King led a delegation of fifty-one American women to lobby for disarmament with women from sixteen other nations at the March 1962 Geneva disarmament conference, the organization became suspect to anti-communist zealots. WSP's cooperation with Russian women and its refusal to ban Communists invited surveillance from the Federal Bureau of Investigation, and eventually landed its leaders in front of the House Committee on Un-American Activities (HUAC). The women were only "unsophisticated wives and mothers," critics said. They were too tenderhearted to talk policy. They were dupes of the Communist party.[74]

The House Committee on Un-American Activities practiced McCarthyism before and after McCarthy, using its power to define "the bounds of thinkable thought" in American politics and culture. HUAC's hearings were a form of political theatre in which witnesses either confessed their sins and asked for absolution or subjected themselves to cultural condemnation, including blacklisting. The moral of the play was political conformity. Especially with its attacks on the Left, HUAC narrowed the spectrum of acceptable opinion in the postwar period by its implicit threat of persecution in the future.[75]

From the beginning, WSP's responses to the committee were unorthodox. When HUAC subpoenaed fourteen women associated with the New

York City WSP chapter, almost a hundred women volunteered to testify before the committee. Instead of speaking within the conventional discourse of Americanism, WSP contested the committee's (and the culture's) assumptions about patriotism, contrasting masculine and feminine notions of love of country. WSP's first press release claimed that "with the fate of humanity resting on a push button, the quest for peace has become the highest form of patriotism." Because it threatened the survival of persons and the health of children, the masculine war system, they suggested, was obsolete in the nuclear age.[76]

From December 11 to December 13, 1962, the women of WSP presented the House Un-American Activities Committee with a personalist perspective on nuclear issues. They confronted the statist voice of the committee with a civil voice drawn from the discourses of gender and family. They spoke "the mother tongue" in opposition to the male forms of political discourse that predominated in postwar America. WSP members expressed their compassion for the witnesses by filling the five hundred seats in the hearing room with supportive sisters. They rose in solidarity as each witness was called; they laughed and applauded; they hugged witnesses as they concluded their testimony. On the third day, they all wore white roses tied with ribbons saying "Women Strike for Peace."[77]

While the House members worried about Communist penetration of the peace movement because they feared the subversion of the state, WSP members welcomed the participation of Communists because they feared for the survival of the person. Indeed, the women of WSP prided themselves on the permeability of their "un-organization." Without membership lists, a centralized bureaucracy, and hierarchical leadership, they were almost incomprehensible to the committee members of HUAC. When Dagmar Wilson was asked if she were the leader of WSP, she said "I feel that may be hard to explain to the masculine mind. . . . Nobody controls anybody in Women Strike for Peace. We're all leaders." Amused by the novelty of the feminine voice in civic affairs, the nation's press highlighted "Ladies' Day at the Capitol," and publicized the personalist perspective they offered. Headlines read "Peace Gals Make Redhunters Look Silly" and "Peace Ladies Tangle With Baffled Congress." Because it was so unusual, personalism brought publicity, which had political consequences.[78]

Institutionalizing the Civil Voice of Women

In a 1963 "Letter to WSP," member Barbara Deming applauded the victory of the women who testified before the committee, and interpreted the hearings as a contest between statist and civil voices. While the Women of WSP had spoken from their direct experience as parents, the Congressmen had used the clichés of the Cold War. "It has not dawned on them," wrote Deming, "that the rapidly altering nature of the world about us has drained certain words of all former meaning." The men were "hypnotized by these words. . . whereas the women see the cold fact that we are now willing to lay down our *children's* lives, and are already doing so." Deming hoped that WSP's protests might logically move further in the direction of nonviolent action and unilateral disarmament. "But," she asked prophetically, "if a test ban agreement is reached, and the threat from further fallout is removed, how resolute will our stand against the threat of nuclear slaughter remain?"[79]

WSP expanded its activity in 1962 and 1963, holding its first national conference, sponsoring a trip to Geneva and a pilgrimage to Rome. Over a hundred women attended the first conference of Women Strike for Peace June 9–10, in Ann Arbor, Michigan, the two days preceding the gathering of fifty-nine Students for a Democratic Society at Port Huron. WSP established a national clearing house for information and task forces on radiation, the economics of disarmament, and international outreach. They discussed their relation to civil rights, civil disobedience, and the American presence in Vietnam, but made no policy statements. Like the students of SDS, the women of WSP felt threatened by the Bomb. Both groups emphasized the importance of active citizenship. Both affirmed "the right and . . . the responsibility of the individual in a democratic society to act to influence the course of government." Neither SDS nor Women Strike for Peace would kowtow to the persistent anti-communism of the ideology of liberal consensus. WSP's founding policy statement welcomed women "of all races, creeds, and political persuasions." WSP also renounced the idea of centralized leadership, opting not to elect a national steering or coordinating committee, and leaving policy to the preferences of the local organizations.[80]

In April 1963, WSP organized a pilgrimage to Rome to show their support for Pope John XXIII's encyclical *Pacem in Terris*, and to ask for stronger condemnations of nuclear war and stronger support for nonviolent resistance. The group—called Madre de Pacem in Italian—included women from WSP, the Women's International League for Peace and Freedom, PAX, and the Fellowship of Reconciliation. Among the women who joined the international delegation was Dorothy Day, who spoke to several groups of seminarians in Rome.[81]

Conclusion

Liberation, said Paul Goodman, served as "the annals of people who, like the editors, put their bodies on the line for justice as they see it and try to live in community in a society that has given up on community." In the tradition of American "little magazines," *Liberation* served as a forum for ideas that were unthinkable and unprintable in the mainstream press. Its "Third Camp" neutralism, undogmatic leftism, and practical personalism all stirred the creative energies of American activists. Although circulations were small, little magazines like *Liberation* maintained the circulation of ideas that would ultimately prove influential. *Liberation* offered a social theory of personalist politics that combined some elements of the Old Left with an anarcho-pacifist position in a synthesis that proved increasingly attractive to Americans in the 1960s. Coupled with CNVA, this national *Liberation* movement of the late Fifties and early Sixties offered both ideas and activism that would be appropriated by the New Left and the counter-culture. In the fall of 1960, for example, Al Haber at the University of Michigan noted that "the direct action of the great peace movement has been . . . under adult auspices: the Committee for Nonviolent Action, the War Resisters' League, and the American Friends Service Committee. . . . the new thing is that students are involved."[82]

Like CNVA, Women Strike for Peace was a paradigm of personalism. The protesters appeared, both on the streets and before the committee, out of a sense of personal and civic obligation. Like most women of the Fifties, they had been taught to value the self-in-relation, rather than the rugged individualism of masculine America. They acted in the name of children, whom they defined as victims, both present and potential, of nuclear testing and nuclear war. They demonstrated their belief in the harmony of politics and personal life. Their localized protests and organizations confirmed their faith in the strength of local action, and their use of maternal pacifism clearly showed the relevance of household values to the political world. "Convinced that professional politicians, scientists, and academics were, for the most part, leading the world to extinction, they gloried in their own exclusion from the system." They used their perspective as outsiders to generate a challenge to the statist construction of reality. WSP's success with the committee, and with the passage of the test ban, provided its members with a sense of self-confidence and political efficacy. Success in defending persons succeeded in enlarging persons. Thanks to *Liberation*, CNVA and Women Strike for Peace, when the tribulations of the mid-Sixties came, there would be persons ready to protest.[83]

6

STUDENT PERSONALISM

STUDENTS WERE AMONG THE BEST TEACHERS of the 1960s, not because they knew all the answers, but because they posed some of the most important questions of the decade. The sensibility of Sixties students was deeply rooted in the personalism, anarchism, and pacifism of the Fifties. When students enrolled for lessons on principled dissent and social activism, they turned, not to the Old Left of the postwar period, but to the civil rights movement, the Beat movement, and the ban-the-bomb movement. They also crafted their own idiosyncratic personalism from a synthesis of dissident sociology and psychology, existentialism, and civic republicanism.

In *The Making of a Counterculture*, the best contemporary cultural synthesis of the Sixties, Theodore Roszak noted "the extraordinary personalism that has characterized New Left activism since its beginnings." The New Left had little of the ideological rigidity of its predecessors, he thought, because activists believed that "at whatever cost to the cause or the doctrine, one must care for the uniqueness and dignity of each individual and yield to what his conscience demands in the existential moment."[1]

This emphasis on the primacy of the person can be seen clearly in the establishment of Students for a Democratic Society (SDS), the leading organization of the New Left. The inviolability of the person also inspired many of the campus protests over educational issues that spanned the decade. Although personalism never accounted for all of student activism, personalist perspectives were an important part of the student story in the 1960s. This chapter tells that story. It traces the intellectual and institutional origins of the New Left in Students for a Democratic Society; it examines the campus uprisings of 1964 and 1965 (the Free Speech Movement and the teach-ins); and it explores reforms in higher education in the last half of the Sixties. For the most part, it stays on campus. The off-campus impact of student personalism is explored in subsequent chapters.

The New Left: Students for a Democratic Society

SDS was an offshoot of the Student League for Industrial Democracy (SLID), a socialist organization dating back to 1905. Moribund in the 1950s, it was reconstituted in 1959 and christened Students for a Democratic Society (SDS) in 1960. Although it derived from a tradition of socialist radicalism, it owed more intellectually and tactically to the first student movement of the 1960s, which was not a movement of white middle-class Americans at the nation's elite universities, but the uprising—or more precisely, the sit-down—of African American students in the South.

The Greensboro sit-ins served as a catalyst for the Northern student movement. The fact that committed college students could make a difference inspired young idealists all across the country. Many of the students, like Michigan's Al Haber, framed the sit-ins within a personalist perspective. "The lunch counter," he said, "is of little intrinsic importance. The demand . . . is not for equal rights or constitutional guarantees, or protection of the laws; it is for a personal equality and dignity that has nothing to do with race." In fact, the demand was *both* for legal and constitutional guarantees *and* for personal equality and dignity, and thousands of students responded to the linkage. By the end of 1960, an estimated 5,000–10,000 students picketed Northern chain stores complicit with Southern segregation; between 60,000 and 80,000 participated in other ways. Organizing around the slogan "Called to Be Human," they began to use the person as a criterion for social welfare.[2]

Prominent among the new student leaders were young people also deeply influenced by the Beats. As historian Sara Evans suggests, these activists were nurtured on the folk music and philosophical conversations of campus coffeehouses. Alienated from the fraternity/sorority social life, and resentful of the rules and regulations of the American university, they were ready for a change. Al Haber defined this group as the "beat" group. "The term 'beat,'" he said, "has come to characterize all those who have deviated from the traditional college patterns. They are variously professional students, bohemians, political types, and nonstudents who still seem to be around. They are generally out of sympathy with what is going on in the world. Their reaction is often cynical detachment. [But] the movement has drawn heavily, if not always reliably, on this group."[3]

Such students were elated and inspired by the youthful idealism of the civil rights sit-ins. The first action of SDS's Michigan members was a conference on "Human Rights in the North" at Ann Arbor in the Spring of 1960. In attendance were the Greensboro four; the featured speakers were Michael Harrington and James Farmer, two radicals who had maintained their activist idealism throughout the postwar period. Harrington was a democratic socialist whose radicalism had grown in the Catholic Worker movement. A lapsed Catholic who rediscovered "the existential, and Augustinian, tradition," Harrington had confessed his sins one morning in 1951. "That afternoon," he recalls, "I searched out the Catholic Worker," because it was "as far left as you could go within the Church." He stayed for two years, serving the poor, declaring his conscientious objection to war, and helping to edit the *Catholic Worker*. He left the *Worker* and the church a couple of years later, but he did not renounce the Workers' radicalism. By 1960, Harrington had worked as an organizer for the anti-Stalinist Young Socialist League, and for the civil rights movement. In 1959, he wrote an article for *Commentary* on the persistent poverty he had witnessed in part at the Catholic Worker House; it later became *The Other America*.[4]

James Farmer, the other major speaker at the conference, had helped found the Congress of Racial Equality in the 1940s. He had worked as an organizer for the Student League for Industrial Democracy, and he served as Program Director of the NAACP. Inspired by Tolstoy and the Harlem Renaissance, and schooled in theology at Howard University, Farmer "embodied the Quaker stand in American radicalism, with its emphasis on moral suasion and face-to-face discussion as the way to achieve peace, concord, consensus—the Blessed Community."[5]

Ann Arbor became a center of activism, and one of the most prominent radicals was a young Michigan student named Tom Hayden. Rebelling against the stifling certainties of middle-class life in Royal Oak, Michigan, he identified with *Mad*'s Alfred E. Neuman, movie actor James Dean, and Holden Caulfield, the protagonist of J.D. Salinger's *Catcher in the Rye*. In 1957 Hayden entered the University of Michigan where he was a student of philosophy; he took courses on existentialism from Walter Kaufmann and on political philosophy from Arnold Kaufman; he read Plato and Aristotle, John Dewey and Jacques Maritain, Sartre and Camus, Rainer Maria Rilke, Ignazio Silone, and Norman O. Brown. During the summer of 1960, inspired by the beat-ific vision of Jack Kerouac's *On the Road*, Hayden hitch-hiked to Los Angeles to cover the Democratic National Convention. On the way, he spent time in Berkeley, where, he recalled, "I got radicalized." At the convention in Los Angeles, Hayden interviewed Martin Luther King; "meeting King," he recalled, "transformed me." Inspired to activism, he attended a conference on political action sponsored by Berkeley's radical student group, SLATE, and the convention of the National Student Association, where he was impressed by SNCC activists Charles McDew, Tim Jenkins, and Sandra "Casey" Cason.[6]

In 1960–61 Hayden became the editor of the *Michigan Daily*, where his emerging political sensibility was displayed in a series of September editorials. In explaining the emergence of "this erupting generation," he described a context similar to *Liberation*'s "Tract for the Times." The Cold War, the threat of the Bomb, and a "society which seems directionless, decisionless, amoral" all called a generation to change. Combining the classic liberalism of Jefferson and Mill with Gandhian nonviolence and the existential commitment of Camus, Hayden called for individual commitment to action in support of "a revolution that would reduce complexity to moral simplicity, that would restore emotion to religion, that would in fact give man back his 'roots.'" The shift "from legal action to direct action, from a bureaucratic to an individualistic process" had shown a "new willingness to take up responsibilities of the individual to the democratic order." Criticizing the "myopic realism" of American culture, he quoted Jacques Maritain in calling for commitment to "an ideal more real than reality."[7]

Hayden's politics also showed the influence of the civil rights movement. In February 1961, he visited Fayette County, Tennessee to report on a group of sharecroppers evicted from their land when they tried to vote; in a county with a majority of African Americans, none had been registered to vote in eighty years. In October, he reported on SNCC's McComb County voter registration project in a pamphlet called "Revolution in Mississippi." On October 11, he and Paul Potter, another SDS leader, were pulled from their car in McComb and beaten for their solidarity with the SNCC workers. In December 1961, Hayden participated in a Freedom Ride to test the ICC's ruling desegregating public transportation and facilities; arrested for blocking the sidewalk and obstructing traffic in Albany, Georgia, Hayden celebrated his 22nd birthday in jail. By the summer of 1962, he had already published in *Liberation* and *Dissent*. That writing, and his editorship of the *Michigan Daily*, made him the logical choice to draft SDS's founding document, the Port Huron Statement.[8]

Hayden also married into the civil rights movement. In 1961, Hayden wed Sandra "Casey" Cason, a SNCC worker who embodied a second route to the New Left. Unlike Tom Hayden, who traveled to the Left by way of philosophy and a hunger for experience, Casey Cason came to radical politics via the populist Christian existentialism of the University of Texas YMCA/YWCA. Empowered by her participation in the Christian Faith-and-Life Community (CFLC), Cason embodied the gospel of social solidarity and political protest. During the summer of 1960, she served as a tutor in a parish in East Harlem. She attended the National Student Association (NSA) seminar on civil rights, and the NSA national convention in Minneapolis, where she delivered a dramatic call for nonviolent civil disobedience for civil rights. With other University of Texas activists, she came into contact with NSA's Liberal Study Group, which included Tom Hayden and Al Haber. During the 1960–61 school year, advised by Glenn Smiley of the Fellowship for Reconciliation, Cason and other CFLC members established Students for Direct Action to protest the segregation of Austin's movie theatres.[9]

The Fall 1961 wedding of Casey Cason and Tom Hayden took place at the Christian Faith-and-Life Community in Austin. Joe Mathews performed the ceremony, which included readings from Ecclesiastes and Camus ("I, on the other hand, choose justice in order to remain faithful to the world"). The couple was surrounded by friends who shared their personal and personalist commitments, including many involved in the establishment of SDS. Years later, some people claimed that the idea for the Port Huron Conference was hatched in the late-night political discussions that followed the wedding.[10]

This nascent New Left met in Ann Arbor December 29–31 to shape ideology and institutional structure for the new Students for a Democratic Society. Participants reviewed various programmatic possibilities—civil rights, poverty, university reform, peace, and disarmament—and decided to meet again in June to adopt "a political manifesto of the Left." The manifesto would focus on the concept of democracy and its implications for politics, education, economic structures, international relations, and the arts. What was needed, said Tom Hayden, was "a way to connect knowledge to power and decentralize both so that community or participatory democracy might emerge, to be concerned with the problem of the individual in a time inevitably ridden with bureaucracy, large government, [and] international networks and systems." Three months later, he insisted in a speech on "Student Social Action" that "the time has come for a reassertion of the personal." As SDS itself moved toward face-to-face politics and communitarian commitment, these students hoped to offer a similar vision to the American public.[11]

The Spirit of Port Huron

The Port Huron Conference, the constituting convention for the SDS of the Sixties, took place at Port Huron, Michigan, June 11–15, 1962. In order to examine "The Intellectual Foundations of the Left"—including radical Christianity, the Enlightenment, Marxism and existentialism—SDS had invited Michael Harrington, Donald Slaiman (of the AFL-CIO), Harold Taylor (former president of Sarah Lawrence College and author of *Education and Freedom*), Arnold Kaufman (Michigan philosopher and one of Hayden's teachers), Tim Jenkins (of SNCC), and Roger Hagan (Harvard editor of the newsletter of the anti-nuclear Committee of Correspondence).[12]

The Port Huron Statement, the first manifesto of Students for a Democratic Society, echoed many of the themes of earlier political personalists. The section called "Values"—its most elegant and original contribution—especially articulated these connections. It called for the end of the "depersonalization that reduces human beings to the status of things." In defining "the perimeter of human possibility in this epoch," the statement confessed that "we regard men as infinitely precious and possessed of unfulfilled capacities for reason, freedom, and love." It called on people's "unrealized potential for self-cultivation, self-direction, self-understanding, and creativity." And it suggested that *moral* realignment should precede political realignment. Emphasizing moral over electoral politics, or even political structures, the statement committed the students to a search for transformative social values.[13]

Calling for "human independence" but not "egotistic individualism," the participants at Port Huron emphasized a sense of community as essential to human fulfillment. People needed "personal links" that superseded the loneliness, estrangement, and isolation of modern society's functional relations. The statement even suggested that "politics have the function of bringing people out of isolation and into community, thus being a necessary, though not sufficient, means of finding meaning in personal life."[14]

The idea of "participatory democracy" applied personalist precepts to the processes of political life. "Participatory democracy" assumed the importance of individual human beings, and it invited them to cooperate, in decentralized situations, in naming their political problems and in shaping solutions to them. Like John Dewey, the students of SDS believed that the process of participation was not just good for politics; it was also good for the people who participated, helping them develop their full capacities as persons. They assumed that the private life of the "postwar charter" was not enough for human fulfillment. Clarifying problems and choices, politics should connect people to knowledge and to power so that they could collectively work out their destinies. Participatory democracy complemented the representative institutions of republican government by adding a personalist perspective to democratic theory.[15]

Participatory democracy was one important way in which students tried to harmonize means and ends. As Don McKelvey said in 1963, "We must strive to create—here and now in our everyday functions—a certain mode of relating to people which will serve as a counterweight (for both ourselves and others) to the manipulative, dehumanizing, coercive relations which we so rightly criticize in the society all around us." Participatory democracy led students to create "parallel structures" like Freedom Schools and community unions in order to begin building the new world within the shell of the old. At its best, participatory democracy was not just politics *for* the community, but politics *as* community.[16]

In the section "Agenda for a Generation," SDS's founders described the development of their radicalism: "We are people of this generation, bred in at least modest comfort, housed now in universities, looking uncomfortably to the world we inherit." America's youth had been brought up to believe in the ideals of freedom and equality, and in government of, by, and for the people. Lawrence Wright recalled that he grew up expecting to inherit his father's sense of certainty about American mission. "Since America was on the side of freedom, I wouldn't have to worry about my conscience. Duty would take care of me. When I pledged allegiance to the flag, as I did every school day and every Scout meeting, and every week at Sunday school, I believed in its promise of liberty and justice for all."[17]

"As we grew, however," the SDS students recalled, "our comfort was penetrated by events too troublesome to dismiss. First, the permeating and victimizing fact of human degradation, symbolized by the Southern struggle against racial bigotry, compelled most of us from silence to activism. Second, the enclosing fact of the Cold War, symbolized by the presence of the Bomb, brought awareness that we ourselves, and our friends, and millions of abstract 'others' we knew more directly because of our common peril, might die at any time. We might deliberately ignore, or avoid, or fail to feel all other human problems, but not these two."[18]

Other people in Hayden's generation shared his view of the atomic bomb. Their parents understood the Bomb as the "winning weapon" of World War II, and as the deterrent of World War III. For them, Cold War was better than world war, nuclear testing was better than bombing, and prosperity was better than rationing. But the children of the 1950s had little memory of the "good war," and little appreciation for the nuances of nuclear strategy. They had nuclear nightmares. The younger generation experienced the Bomb as an immediate threat to their lives; school civil defense drills taught children to hide under their desks or to cower in the halls. And "under the desks and crouched in the hallways," recalls Todd Gitlin, "terrors were ignited, existentialists were made." Loud noises and explosions made them think the end had come. Imbued with a precocious "thanatological consciousness," they lived in what Tom Hayden called "the unpredictable meantime."[19]

In both civil rights and civil defense, students experienced the difference between myth and reality, between preaching and practice, as sheer hypocrisy, and as an indictment of American society. As Godfrey Hodgson suggests, the young saw Americans governed, both socially and politically, by a "split-level morality." They questioned the ethical consistency of a society characterized by great affluence and great poverty, by democratic declarations and Negro disfranchisement, and by peaceful promises and nuclear buildup. From a personalist perspective, this hypocrisy—like Kenneth Rexroth's "Social Lie"—was indefensible, so the New Left set out to make American society live up to its ideals.[20]

While some students responded to the fear of the Bomb with fatalism, others reacted with activism. Student SANE was established in 1958, the Student Peace Union in 1959, and Harvard's Tocsin in 1960. At the University of Michigan, Al Haber had started Students for a Democratic Society to "illuminate the connections between issues like the arms race, poverty and racism and the discontents of the students themselves." By February 1962, these groups brought 4,000–8,000 students to a two-day anti-nuclear demonstration at the White House, the largest since the effort to stop the execution of the Rosenbergs in 1953. The student peace movement, therefore, was born *before* the escalation in Vietnam, drawing its inspiration from the anti-nuclear activism of the previous decade. As with the civil rights issue, these organizations and others gave students a first taste of political organizing, of lobbying, of direct action.[21]

While the civil rights struggle and the Bomb were foregrounded in the Port Huron Statement, SDS also focused on the ABCs of apathy, bureaucracy, and college. One of the most important themes of the Port Huron Statement was public apathy. The American democratic system, they said, was "apathetic and manipulated rather than 'of, by, and for the people.'" On college campuses, according to one observer, "Students don't even give a damn about the apathy." And this "apathy toward apathy" bred lives of privatized routines. The students of Port Huron saw apathy as both personal and institutional, and they set out to reform institutions to support people who cared. The Port Huron Statement was intended to combat apathy and the fatalistic "realism" of the "futilitarians" by providing hope for a new politics.[22]

Like Thomas Merton, the students posed empathy and activism against apathy. In his 1966 "Letter to An Innocent Bystander," Thomas Merton contended that the term "innocent bystander" was an oxymoron, and that witnesses to a crime had become accomplices by their inaction. Like Thomas Merton, the New Left of the early 1960s viewed the Eichmann trial as "an extended morality play that made [Eichmann] the epitome of the bureaucratic functionary" apathetic to his own complicity in a monstrous wrong. And the moral of the play was, for them, that in a context of "official wrongdoing and state-sanctioned evil," the individual bears a personal responsibility for resistance to institutionalized evil. While the older generation pointed to the example of Munich to justify the containment policy, the younger generation pointed to Nuremberg to justify their dissent. Their "post-Nuremberg ethic" meant, according to one activist, that "every individual is totally morally responsible for everything he does." Seventeen-year-old Jewish student Bob Ross, for example, joined the sympathy picket lines at the Ann Arbor Woolworth's and Kresge's in 1960 because, he explained, "it was the Jewish thing. If you're silent, you're complicit."[23]

For some members of the New Left, this empathy and engagement was the Christian thing, too. Inspired by the ways in which Martin Luther King applied Christianity to social issues, many students reexamined their own religion and found it more radical than they had believed. "Much of the humanism in the New Left is Christian," explained Dale Brown. "The affirmation that institutions should serve people, not people institutions, is but a restatement of Jesus' teaching about the institution of the Sabbath (Mark 2:27)." Seeing the world through the eyes of the dispossessed had Biblical precedents, for Scriptures too exalted the poor and condemned the rich. Even many students who rejected the established religions of the American Establishment still persisted in a moral mission. Carl Oglesby described his commitments as "Christian atheism," but it could also be called an agnostic liberation theology.[24]

The importance of Nuremberg to the New Left coincided with interest in the theology of the German Protestant and protestant Dietrich Bonhoeffer. During the 1930s, Bonhoeffer acted against apathy by organizing the Confessing Church against the Nazis. An activist in the German resistance, he was imprisoned in 1943, and executed just a month before V-E Day in 1945. With *The Cost of Discipleship* (1937) and the posthumous *Letters and Papers from Prison* (1951), Bonhoeffer argued for the active involvement of religion in the world. "The intention should not be to justify Christianity in the present age, but justify the present age before the Christian message." By his heroic resistance to systematic evil, and his willingness to put his body on the line, Bonhoeffer gave students of the Sixties an example of courage and commitment. And he challenged them to go beyond "cheap grace" to the real cost of discipleship, beyond religious rhetoric to lives lived in conformity to the gospel.[25]

To other students of the New Left, activism was not just a Jewish thing or a Christian thing, but a specifically Quaker thing. The Quaker doctrine of the "inner light" offered inspiration for dissenters, the practice of the Quaker meeting offered a model of consensus decision-making, and the Quaker ideal of the "redemptive community" offered hope for social change through conscientious witness. Casey Hayden had encountered these principles through SNCC; Sharon Jeffrey through a CORE summer workshop; Al Haber and Richard Flacks through connections with conscientious objectors and peace activists in Ann Arbor; and Tom Hayden through the example of Quaker professor and protester Kenneth Boulding. SDS institutionalized these principles with plans for consensus decision-making and a one-year rotation in office.[26]

More than most people now remember, SDS argued that one of the main obstacles to a democratic society was a bureaucratic society. They also observed that apathy flourished in bureaucracies. The Port Huron Statement especially condemned the cumbersome academic bureaucracy which increasingly incorporated "the value standards of business and the administrative mentality." In both the universities and other institutions, bureaucracies reduced persons to their functions and separated people from power. Bureaucracies—and academic empiricism—stifled the search for truth and moral enlightenment: "Our professors and administrators sacrifice controversy to public relations; their curriculums change more slowly than the living events of the world; their skills and silence are purchased by investors in the arms race; passion is called unscholastic. The questions we might want raised—what is really important? can we live in a different and better way? if we wanted to change society, how would we do it?—are not thought to be questions of a 'fruitful, empirical nature,' and thus are brushed aside."[27]

Still the Port Huron Statement contended that American universities could be the seedbed of social change, reminiscent of the university reform connections of the Progressive Era at the beginning of the century. The intellectual freedom of the university offered a powerful place for people dismayed by the intellectual conformity of American culture. Like C. Wright Mills, the members of SDS hoped to redefine "the vocation of the intellectual" and the institutions of higher learning in America. The students imagined a new role for intellectuals: they could be voices for the powerless. By clarifying the social structures of American society, intellectuals could offer analyses that led to social change. As Richard Flacks recalled, "We wanted to find ways to connect intellectual work with the needs and realities of the disadvantaged and oppressed, . . . to combine the analytic and reflective with engaged action, . . . to 'reform' the university so that it could be an arena within which the redefinition of the vocation of the intellectual could occur." Such university reform, the Port Huron students thought, could be substantial, because the universities were part of the problem as well as the solution.[28]

Beyond the university, the students hoped to imitate the personalist protests of civil rights and ban-the-bomb demonstrators by linking a politics of witness to a politics of power. Their first effort was the Economic

Research and Action Project (ERAP), an attempt to organize the people of America's inner cities. As its name suggested, the project combined research and action, connecting intellectual work to the needs and realities of the poor. Working from John Dewey's civic republican premise that "democracy must begin at home, and its home is the neighborly community," ERAP operated according to ideas of participatory democracy and community control, trying to apply SNCC's community organizing methods to the Northern cities. Driven by their personalist commitment to the poor, the SDS workers lived in America's urban slums, creating independent, local people's organizations to raise consciousness, empower impoverished people, solve their everyday problems, and create an interracial movement of the poor. Mobilizing poor people as the civil rights movement had enlisted black voters, ERAP's urban populism would be a first step in a national strategy of decentralized and participatory democracy.[29]

Like the Peace Corps, ERAP offered young people an opportunity to respond to the call of service. In his 1963 "President's Report," Todd Gitlin looked forward to the creation of "a new variety of 'radical vocation,'" in which students could "do real work outside the campus while maintaining educational and programmatic liaison with the campus." SDS started with ten projects in 1964, and had more than 400 volunteers in the cities in the summer of 1965. Almost all of the early SDS leaders entered ERAP projects.[30]

The ERAP volunteers lived like the volunteers of Catholic Worker Houses and SNCC Freedom Houses. Although they did not feed and shelter the poor, the ERAP members lived in voluntary poverty; in Cleveland, individual food expenses were about 30 cents a day. And the members of these small communes tested the limits of democracy in their everyday lives, organizing themselves as well as the poor. At the Cleveland project— an exception to the sexism of the New Left—men even shared household chores. They generally adopted the Quaker rule of decision-by-consensus and searched for personal authenticity in their political organizing. Students created a community center and distributed keys throughout the neighborhood, providing a place for marginalized people to be heard. They measured their success, said Richard Rothstein, "largely in terms of how successfully they give away their own power."[31]

The women of SDS were particularly effective in the ERAP projects, because the issues and relational style of community organizing suited their socialization more than the expectations of the men. Community organizing entailed a focus, not on the workplace, but on the neighborhood and home; it focused more attention on traditional "women's issues." And community organizing entailed a practice of conversation which came more naturally (or culturally) to the young women of SDS, who were able to coordinate the consensus of a neighborhood without imposing their own ideas.[32]

The students learned a great deal in the ERAP projects. But SDS's "cult of the ghetto," as Al Haber styled it, did not last long. Both the difficulties of ERAP organizing and the escalation of the war in Vietnam cut short the community organizing emphasis of SDS. ERAP's organizers confronted the pervasive ideology of American individualism, which taught poor people that they were responsible for their own poverty and deprivation. They faced the learned helplessness of the culture of poverty, and they encountered the opposition of established institutions, which benefitted in some ways from the status quo. Despite their proximate failure, the ERAP projects had some long-term effects. They failed to transform America's cities, but they succeeded in transforming some urban neighborhoods. ERAP's organizers failed to produce a politically effective "interracial movement of the poor," but they inspired the creation of groups like the National Welfare Rights Organization. They did not radicalize the urban underclass as much as they radicalized the suburban middle class who came to serve the poor. They failed to make the poor the vanguard of the New Left, but they succeeded in making the vanguard of the New Left conscious of the perspectives of the poor. "The main thing I've learned," said Casey Hayden in *The New Republic*, "is to see the world from their perspective: from the bottom." ERAP confirmed for American middle-class students the virtues of class analysis. The later New Left, therefore, would be a revolt of the privileged from the perspective of the margins.[33]

The Spirit of the New Left

The students of SDS drew on the precedents of the Fifties, but they also constructed their own personalism out of the materials available to them in college. The Port Huron Statement was written by students who had learned from C. Wright Mills, Erich Fromm, Herbert Marcuse, Albert Camus, and the communitarian anarchists. They adapted the work of these influential teachers to their own needs, creating in the process the eclectic and original spirit of the New Left.[34]

The Port Huron Statement was heavily influenced by the writings of sociologist C. Wright Mills, who taught the students about the structures of society, the role of the intellectual, and the promise of a new politics. In his writing, especially in *The Sociological Imagination*, Mills heralded seismic shifts in the study of sociology that unsettled the prevailing paradigm of functionalism. For several decades, sociologists had elaborated a functionalist paradigm that emphasized cohesion and stability. They saw society as a self-regulating mechanism amenable to scientific intervention. The interacting parts of this metaphorical machine might lose their equilibrium momentarily, but social scientists could identify the problems and tinker with the parts to make them serve the needs of the whole society.[35]

Mills did not believe in the objectivity of social science, or the necessity of "A Balanced View." "I am not a sociological bookkeeper," he said, contending that a balanced view is "usually . . . a vague point of equilibrium between two platitudes." He also rejected the idea of value-free inquiry: "To formulate any problem," he said, "requires that we state the values involved and the threat to those values." Instead, he wanted to return to the origins of sociology, when founders like Comte and Saint-Simon studied the present society in order to influence the society that might be.[36]

Like *Liberation*, Mills argued that activists should "translate personal problems into social issues." In *The Power Elite*, he had identified the political, economic and military powers that structured American society. In *The Causes of World War III*, he castigated the social and political institutions that allowed American generals and scientists to rationally prepare a holocaust of nuclear war. Like Thomas Merton, Mills felt that these people were "not necessarily sadistic; . . . they are efficient, rational, technically clean-cut inhuman acts because they are impersonal." In that book, Mills also delivered a "Pagan Sermon to the Christian Clergy," in which he challenged American churches to consider their complicity in the coming of World War III. As a conscientious critic, Mills told ministers of God that "if you do not alarm anyone morally, you will yourself remain morally asleep. If you do not embody controversy, what you say will inevitably be an acceptance to the drift to the coming human hell." Mills criticized the clergy for their passivism and equivocation, and asked, "Who among you is considering what it means for Christians to kill men and women and children in ever more efficient and impersonal ways?" Finally, he offered the challenge: "As pagans who are waiting for an answer, we merely say: You claim to be Christians. And we ask: What does that mean as a biographical and as a public fact?"[37]

Mills' 1960 "Letter to the New Left" called for a radicalism appropriate to new conditions and framed the possibilities for dissent in the Sixties. Unlike the Old Left, which had organized around the economic issues of the Depression and the anti-fascism of the Thirties and Forties, the New Left would confront "newer discontents like powerlessness, moral disaffection, the purposelessness of middle-class life"—the issues of an affluent society. Avoiding the "labor metaphysic" of the Old Left, the New Left looked for other agents to challenge the alienation, bureaucracy, and cultural hegemony of Cold War America. "In a time of supposed prosperity, moral complacency, and political manipulation," the students said in the Port Huron Statement, "a new left cannot rely on only aching stomachs to be the engine of social reform. The case for change, for alternatives that will involve uncomfortable personal efforts, must be argued as never before."[38]

Mills also provided the promise of a new politics. His analytical framework gave students the conceptual oppositions that would animate the New Left: face-to-face politics versus the politics of a mass society; "person-to-person discussion" versus mediated reality; the participatory democracy of "primary publics" versus the "organized irresponsibility" of bureaucracy; civil society versus the state; grassroots power versus the power elite; decentralization versus the centralization of state and corporation; solidarity with the powerless versus the promises of consumerism; engaged intelligence versus detached specialization; plain speaking versus intellectual jargon. Although it derived from Mills' Marxism, this nonviolent, egalitarian politics was also personalist, and it influenced the development of the New Left throughout the Sixties.[39]

Mills' own life exemplified the public intellectual that the students sought to imitate. Irving Louis Horowitz recalled that Mills "presented himself as someone whose mannerisms excluded manners, civic concerns excluded polite behavior, and personal style excluded conventional dress." With his Harley Davidson motorcycle, his constant smoking, his sexual athleticism, his Texas twang, his plain speech studded with slang and obscenities, and his preternatural energy, he was a Neal Cassady of the academy.[40]

While C. Wright Mills provided a sociological perspective on the plight of modern people, Erich Fromm taught students about the psychology of mass society. Starting with *Escape from Freedom*, Fromm had argued for a "normative human nature." An "atheistic mystic," he emphasized themes of relatedness and transcendence that paralleled personalism. Fromm argued that psychological problems like depersonalization, alienation, neurosis, and spiritual angst had social and political roots. "Man is not a thing," Fromm asserted, and he offered alternatives to a society that "thinged" people. Like other members of the Frankfurt school, Fromm taught young Americans that the subjective side of politics was important. Class consciousness came not just from social position, but from a complex "character structure" formed in family life and interpersonal relations, as well as in the relations of production. He suggested that a politics of consciousness was as important as a politics of bread and butter.[41]

In *The Sane Society*, Fromm investigated "the pathology of normalcy," whereby people adjusted to a system that cut off their full human development. He made it clear that alienation could be seen as a social and political problem. He condemned the mass society which commodified people, where an individual's "value as a person lies in his salability, not his human qualities of love, reason, or his artistic capacities." And, unlike most members of the psychological profession, he advised not individual adjustment to normalcy, but a social adjustment that would make the normal more human.[42]

Fromm surveyed the political possibilities and opted for what he called "humanistic communitarianism." In the tradition of Charles Fourier, Pierre Proudhon, and Peter Kropotkin (and the personalists), he looked for a "third way" between totalitarianism and "supercapitalism." Like the personalists, he contended that a sane society required a combination of political and personal reform. And he argued for reviving "the principle of the Town Meeting into modern industrialized society."[43]

In 1961, Fromm published *Marx's Concept of Man*, which included the first English translation of Marx's *Economic and Philosphical Manuscripts* by a Western scholar. This influential publication presented American radicals with a humanistic Marx concerned with many of the Sixties' social issues: human alienation and fulfillment, social structure and social consciousness. In his introduction to T.B. Bottomore's translation, Fromm located Marx in an Old Testament Messianic tradition that aimed to redeem the world by integrating politics and moral values. Fromm featured Marx's claim that people were alienated from their work, from other people, and from their true selves. Alienated individuals, Fromm thought, lacked a sense of direction and purpose; they lacked a sense of community, and they lacked a sense of vocation that might create a connection between self and community. According to Fromm, Marx's socialism entailed not bureaucratic centralization, but "the eventual disappearance of the state and . . . the establishment of a society of voluntarily cooperating individuals." These were themes that resonated with students in the early Sixties and brought many to the study of Marx.[44]

During the Sixties, Fromm was overshadowed by psychologist and philosopher Herbert Marcuse, who also warned about a system that created "one-dimensional" people. The irrationality of rational society, Marcuse said, reduced persons to a flatness incompatible with fully human life. With a gentle irony, Marcuse called the problem "Happy Consciousness," a state of well-being caused by a combination of material satisfactions and mental manipulation. The state and consumer society had defined "the good life" so that alternative conceptions of goodness were nearly unthinkable. Nor was there any easy escape from this "pacified existence." In a pattern that Marcuse called "repressive tolerance," American society both allowed and absorbed alternative understandings of the society. People were generally free to say what they wanted, but they could be pretty sure that nobody would listen, and nothing would change. Only a revolution in consciousness and a "Great Refusal" could "break this containment and explode the society."[45]

Students of the Sixties practiced "the great refusal" that Marcuse preached, rejecting the consumerism and conformity of consensus culture, and enacting a vision of a society that encouraged multidimensional persons. Their refusal to accept the socialization of their society drew also on Beat precedents, and was reinforced by an existentialist refusal to act as either victims or executioners. Student existentialism was largely an adaptation and Americanization of the philosophy of Albert Camus, as refracted through his novels. "Existentialism," says Doug Rossinow, "gave a name to the feelings of meaninglessness and incoherence that some young white people sought to assuage, and that name was alienation." Growing up absurd, the students now began to confront the absurdities of American life and politics. In *New Left Thought*, Lyman Sargent summarizes the Americanization of existentialism:

1. Existentialists argued that there could not be a certainty about anything. In particular it was impossible to know of any purpose or meaning to life. As Camus says, " . . . all true knowledge is impossible."
2. This belief tended to lead to despair.
3. Despair, though, was not the only answer. Meaning can be *created*.
4. We create our own meaning or purpose through our *actions*.
5. We are individually responsible for the values we create by our actions. (This burden of responsibility could lead to despair, but did not have to.)
6. Men's actions should reject murder in all forms, should assert the value of all men, and should move toward the establishment of world peace and prosperity.

The existentialist emphasis on meaning making, on individual moral action as an avenue to freedom and justice, on the congruence of belief and behavior, on the unity of spirituality (or psychology) and politics, on individual responsibility for social values, and on the dignity of all people intersected with the personalist project. The result was a personally powerful politics of meaning.[46]

Camus rejected the religious foundations of French personalism, but found himself in a parallel universe. "The work of Camus," said Thomas Merton, "is a humanism rooted in man as authentic value; in life, which is to be affirmed in defiance of suffering and death; in love, compassion, and understanding, the solidarity of men in revolt against the absurd, men whose comradeship has a certain purity because it is based on the renunciation of all illusions, all misleading ideals, all deceptive and hypocritical social forms." Suspicious of established religion, Camus wanted people to become "saints without God."[47]

Camus' essay "Neither Victims Nor Executioners" offered a vision of existentialist activism that inspired the early New Left. Originally published in America in a 1947 issue of Dwight Macdonald's *Politics*, this "sacred text" was reprinted and offered as a pamphlet in *Liberation* in 1960, and it was quoted and anthologized throughout the Sixties. In it, Camus outlined a politics of individual moral integrity. Criticizing political movements that justified "actions that no man should ever commit against another man," Camus argued for a politics of social justice that respected all human life. Camus suggested that rebellion was a way of establishing values; people should live their values instead of merely mouthing them, actively creating political communities that fulfilled their personal needs for meaning. This was precisely the ethic of action the New Left lived by: "By social movement, I mean more than petitions and letters of protest," said Paul Potter; "I mean people who are willing to change their lives, who are willing to challenge the system, to take the problem of change seriously."[48]

With its skepticism of established institutions and ideologies, existentialism reinforced anarchist tendencies of the early New Left. Almost all of their adult mentors taught the students a suspicion of the state and centralized systems of control. This anarchist strain of the student Left inoculated them against the "naturalization of the state" so culturally prevalent in American society. While most Americans considered the state both natural and normal, the students saw the state as a part of a status quo that was socially constructed, and that could be, therefore, socially deconstructed. Student anarchism also contributed to the disorganization of the movement, which spread, at times, like wildfire, and was as difficult to channel. But it is hard to overestimate the attraction of disorganization in the Age of the Organization Man. In an age when bureaucracies specialized and divided people functionally and hierarchically, holistic informality was an attraction for many people.

With its emphasis on an ethic of love, the New Left embraced a variation of the communitarian anarchism of Dorothy Day, Kenneth Rexroth, A.J. Muste, David Dellinger, and Staughton Lynd. Sometimes the Sixties are criticized for an apolitical love ethic, but in many cases the love ethic maintained a political edge. When SDS President Carl Oglesby said in November 1965 that "we want to create a world in which love is more possible," he was not only echoing the Catholic Worker, he was arguing—against the American grain of individualist romantic love—that love is socially constituted and influenced, and that institutional and ideological changes could influence the ways that people treated each other. Like SNCC, Oglesby said, SDS would try "to remove from society what threatens and prevents [love]—the inequity that coordinates with injustice to create plain suffering and to make custom of distrust. Poverty. Racism. The assembly line universities of this Pepsi Generation. The ulcerating drive for affluence. And the ideology of anti-communism." A year later, in *New Left Notes*, Greg Calvert restated the agenda for SDS: "While fighting to destroy the power which had created the loveless anti-community, we would ourselves create the community of love—*The Beloved Community.*" Like the Romantic generation, they sought to reduce the societal barriers to genuine love and true community.[49]

The New Left and Liberalism

Although SDS and the early New Left were clearly personalist, they were not *only* personalist or *purely* personalist. Their personalist perspectives co-existed—sometimes uneasily—with other ideological perspectives. And their "prefigurative politics" coexisted with more conventional liberalism as well. Early SDS worked, for example, within the tradition of civic republicanism expressed in the twentieth century by philosopher John Dewey. Like Dewey, the New Left called for a local revival of the idea and practice of citizenship, and of politics as community. They intended to use communities of participatory democracy to stimulate a new national citizenship. SDS did not intend to replace republican institutions: the section on "Alternatives to Helplessness" in the Port Huron Statement referred to plans for political party realignment to create a Democratic Party responsive, not to the conservativism of the solid South, but to the values and goals of movements for peace, civil rights, and labor. Within a month of the Port Huron conference in 1962, Tom Hayden and Al Haber were in Washington, conferring in the White House with Arthur Schlesinger Jr. and meeting with members of Congress who supported disarmament initiatives. That fall, they participated in the congressional campaign of Democratic disarmament candidate Tom Payne. They continued to derive financial support from the United Auto Workers. In 1964, SDS was willing to go "Part of the Way with LBJ" because the Democratic platform was "superior to any passed by a major national party since the first New Deal."[50]

The early New Left hoped to shape liberalism to its personalist goals. Early in the 1960s, many students experienced a synergy of existentialism and liberalism, as they channeled their politics of action into liberal causes. At first, John Kennedy's idealism was an inspiration to many Sixties activists; his call to "get this country moving again" resulted, in part, in "the Movement." Kennedy provided a call for action and a vision of social idealism, including the Peace Corps, which influenced many students. When he finally introduced civil rights legislation, in a speech entitled "A Moral Imperative," he integrated the languages of personalism and liberalism.[51]

But Kennedy's liberalism eventually disappointed the era's activists. His anticommunism and his confrontational Cold War foreign policy, his all-too-deliberate speed on civil rights and poverty legislation, convinced many New Left leaders that liberalism was merely the most human face of a dehumanizing system. Leaders like Todd Gitlin found that even the liberals of the Kennedy Administration were not susceptible to calls for disarmament, because peace had no political constituency. In a meeting with Adam Yarmolinsky, Robert McNamara's special assistant for civil defense, Gitlin realized that *"Men such as this were not going to be persuaded to be sensible.* They were grotesque, these clever and confident men, they were unbudgeable, their language was evasion, their rationality unreasonable, and therefore they were going to have to be dislodged." Like their personalist predecessors, who saw the madness of sanity, young people in the Sixties found it increasingly difficult to place their faith in the rationality of the Bomb, or of the institutions—like the university—that trained these custodians of the Bomb.[52]

The Cuban Missile Crisis was an important turning point for many activists. The Ann Arbor group mounted the first demonstrations against the blockade, and Hayden and Flacks protested in Washington on October 27, the day that President Kennedy activated twenty-four Air Force Reserve squadrons. The crisis, said Hayden, "alienated us from the Kennedys," but not from politics. Hayden and Flacks wrote an article arguing for "massive involvement by peace forces in local Democratic or even independent campaigns by 1964."[53]

The 1963 manifesto of SDS, *America and the New Era*, was written mainly by Richard Flacks and revised at a convention at Pine Hill, New York, where invited speakers included A.J. Muste, James Weinstein (editor of *Studies on the Left*), Stanley Aronowitz and Ray Brown, and Arthur Waskow (of the Peace Research Institute). The document argued that the United States could not pursue an agenda of domestic reform at the same time that it maintained its international interventionism. It would be necessary, therefore, to end the arms race and the Cold War. SDS hoped to use a "new insurgency" of discussion groups, research centers, political protest, direct action, and voter registration "to inspire, catalyze, goad, and irritate the liberal and labor organizations to truly democratic reforms" on unemployment, poverty, and racial discrimination, as a first step towards structural changes that would bring participatory democracy.[54]

The 1964 Democratic convention, however, disillusioned even more members of the New Left and civil rights movements than the Cuban Missile Crisis. The convention's decision to refuse seating to the Mississippi Freedom Democratic Party delegation looked, to activists, either unprincipled or hypocritical. The failure of the mainstream institution most amenable to progressive politics radicalized many students, and caused them to go beyond liberalism. Likewise, the ERAP projects often brought SDSers into conflict with the liberalism of political anti-poverty programs, and alienated young people from potential allies in the Democratic Party. The intense commitments of the young activists made them impatient with leaders and politicians who pleaded for time. At the December 1964 meeting of the SDS National Council Meeting, the group decided not to continue their electoral strategy. At least in SDS, personalist politics parted company with mainstream American political culture.[55]

By 1965, SDS leaders distinguished between humanistic and corporate liberalism, and they argued that corporate liberalism was predominant. "'Corporate liberalism,'" thought Richard Flacks, "meant reforms made by the power elite in the interests of social stability; 'liberalism' meant those groups that favored redistribution and social equality." Within a system of corporate liberalism, liberalism was the language used to hide corporate control. Despite a system of representative democracy, Flacks and other SDS leaders thought that money was better represented than people, especially people without money. They decried corporate liberalism because it focused more on systems than on persons, and because it substituted the functionalist rule of experts for the voice of the people. Having begun the decade with a sense that liberalism could serve the needs of people, they concluded that liberalism served people only when it also served the needs of the nation's corporations.[56]

Free Speech and The Student Movement

In one of his "Easy Essays," Peter Maurin recounted a visit with former Brains Truster Raymond Moley on the campus of Columbia University in the 1930s. "I came here," Maurin said to Moley, "to find out if I could make an impression on the depression by starting a rumpus on the campus." Moley told him, according to Maurin, that "we don't make history on the campus; we only teach it." Maurin worried that

> Bourgeois colleges
> turn out college graduates
> into a changing world
> without ever telling them
> how to keep it from changing
> or how to change it
> so as to make it fit
> for college graduates.

By the 1960s, the times were changing, and students were willing to make a rumpus on the campus. Although the Depression—and the student movements of the Thirties—were history, bourgeois colleges were still in the business of making students safe for business. But the Sixties generation of students was ready to make history.[57]

From its beginning, SDS had seen education as a significant problem of American culture. Although SDS dreamed that the university could catalyze constructive social change, the Free Speech Movement (FSM) at Berkeley first showed how it could be done. During the 1964–65 school year, students at Berkeley mobilized thousands of supporters for a cause that included civil rights advocacy, the practice of active citizenship through participatory democracy, a redefinition of the political to include personal and academic affairs, and an emphasis on the here-and-now community. By the Spring of 1965, when the Johnson Administration rapidly escalated the war in Vietnam, students had prepared a personalist politics that could oppose it.[58]

Institutions like the University of California at Berkeley embodied the postwar ideology of liberal consensus. Universities had been complicit with the Cold War and nuclear weapons, for example, from the beginning. As early as 1945, pacifist Milton Mayer had called the University of Chicago the "institutional daddy" of the atomic bomb, "engaged, up to its ears, in preparing the most stupendous atrocity of the war and the moral disgrace of the nation." MIT and Cal Tech became world-class universities with Department of Defense funds. The University of California supplied several scientists, including J. Robert Oppenheimer and Ernest Lawrence, to the Manhattan Project, and managed both the Los Alamos labs and the Lawrence Livermore Laboratory for the Atomic Energy Commission.[59]

In 1958, in the wake of Sputnik, the American government increased its commitments to education as a weapon in the Cold War. In his 1958 State of the Union address, President Eisenhower called for increased funding for the National Science Foundation and for military research and development, plus a billion dollars (over five years) in scholarships in fields essential to national security. Later that year, he signed the National Defense Education Act, which offered $300 million in low-interest Federal loans to college students, with special inducements to those who might themselves become teachers in the nation's schools. It also provided matching funds to the states for establishing or expanding programs in languages, science, and mathematics.[60]

By the early 1960s, education had further enlisted in the Cold War. In 1961, the president of Michigan State University told a group of parents that "our colleges and universities must be regarded as bastions of our defense, as essential to the preservation of our country and our way of life as supersonic bombers, nuclear powered submarines, and intercontinental bombers." Clark Kerr, president of the University of California at Berkeley, claimed that "intellect has . . . become an instrument of national purpose, a component part of the 'military-industrial complex.'" At Kerr's institution, which he proudly hailed as a "knowledge factory," scientists manufactured knowledge at the Lawrence Radiation Laboratory, where "nine synthetic elements and one-third of all known atomic particles were discovered between 1945 and 1961." The University also operated the Livermore Laboratory, where Edward Teller and other atomic scientists had worked on the hydrogen bomb and other nuclear tests of the 1950s. Moreover, Berkeley's Russian and East European Studies Centers provided analyses of Cold War issues, while its acclaimed sociology department sought new and better techniques for managing social problems.[61]

During the 1964–65 school year, the University of California's total income was $616 million, 54 percent of which came from the federal government. Its research budget was $337 million; $297 million came from the federal government, and $235 million of that appropriation paid for the university's operation of the Los Alamos Scientific Laboratory, the Lawrence Radiation Laboratory, and the Nuclear Medicine and Radiation Biology Laboratory at UCLA. The Lawrence Radiation Laboratory received $140 million during 1964-65, $6 million of which was devoted to the much publicized Project Plowshare, which sought to find peaceful uses for atomic explosions. But 64 percent of the total budget, or $90 million, was spent on nuclear weapons. No educational institution was more involved in American nuclear culture. Within a few years, this government support would raise significant questions about the autonomy of the university. In the wake of Sputnik, too, critics would decry the increasing emphasis of science and research over the humanities and undergraduate teaching.[62]

Despite its own connections to the wider world, the university wanted to protect its students from the pressures of politics. In the fall of 1959, when a student undertook a hunger strike protesting mandatory participation in the Reserve Officers Training Corps (ROTC), the university expelled him. To limit campus conflicts, President Kerr then issued the "Kerr directives," which said that sanctioned student groups "may not be affiliated with any partisan, political, or religious group, nor have as one of its purposes the taking of positions with reference to the off-campus political, religious, economic, international, or other issues of the time." Students, he said in effect, could not act as citizens; their education did not include the practice of democracy.[63]

Berkeley, therefore, was a logical place for a reaction against the utilitarianism and corporate liberalism of the modern multiversity. The uprising began in September of 1964 when the university banned political activity along the Bancroft Strip, a walkway at the main entrance to campus that had served as the traditional locus of political expression at Berkeley. In essence, the university's position was that education and political activity were antithetical. The university's ban seemed to support a culture of specialization in which ethical and political issues could be isolated from questions of technique.[64]

Protesting the ban on political activity and the loss of control of an important symbolic space, students confronted the university. They began with the liberal agenda of free speech, calling for an end to restrictions of political expression. But their liberalism led them quickly to radicalism, as the Free Speech Movement exposed the connections between political expression and other campus issues—parietal hours, pedagogy, and the purposes of the university. In the process, students began to see themselves as political victims and as political actors.[65]

The immediate issue was free speech, but the speech in question was about the issue of civil rights. Throughout 1964, the Berkeley contingent of CORE, the Congress of Racial Equality, had protested discrimination in Berkeley, and thirty to forty Berkeley students had participated in the Mississippi Freedom Summer. By the beginning of classes in 1964, an estimated 10 percent of Berkeley students had participated in some sort of civil rights protest. When these students, and others like them, returned to their campuses, "they were alive in a new way, and other students, who hadn't known how dead their own lives were, found this new life contagious." On October 1, when Berkeley police attempted to arrest Jack Weinberg for passing out CORE literature on Sproul Plaza, students staged a civil rights inspired sit-in, using their bodies to block the police car.[66]

In many ways, the Free Speech Movement was an academic application of the ideals and practices of the Student Nonviolent Coordinating Committee. Inspired by SNCC's courage and commitment in the face of white racism, FSM's students imitated SNCC's democratic leadership practices. They adapted the critical pedagogy of Freedom Schools and the spirit of civil rights personalism in their rallies: "For me," recalled FSM leader Mario Savio, "the civil rights movement was the loving community, people embracing each other, holding each other so that they could withstand the force of the fire hose. So the movement was a means, but it was also an embodiment of the new community."[67]

The sit-in lasted 32 hours. The trapped police car became a podium. Soon, the students connected the specific question of free political expression to wider issues concerning the purposes and practices of higher education. Jack Weinberg, for example, claimed that, in Kerr's "knowledge factory," some "products" [students] were "not coming out to standard specifications, and I feel the university is trying to purge itself of these products so they can once again produce for industry exactly what they specify." Extending his analysis in a January 1965 article, Weinberg argued that "the bureaucratization of the campus is just a reflection of the bureaucratization of American life." In the process of speaking from their own experience, a movement in support of free speech to support the civil rights movement became a movement to reform the university and society. The personal lives and alienations of students had been re-defined as political.[68]

One of the speakers at the sit-in was 21-year-old junior Mario Savio, a philosophy major like Bob Moses and Tom Hayden. A New Yorker who had worked for a Mexican relief agency during the summer of 1963 and in Mississippi during the summer of 1964, Savio had seen the social consequences of structural poverty and racism. And having been suspended by the university for a September free speech protest, Savio was an angry young man unwilling to let liberal rationalizations go unexamined. At the sit-in, he noted that the police "have a job to do. Like Adolph Eichmann. He had a job to do. He fit into the machinery."[69]

Within a week, students had organized the Free Speech Movement, and formed a steering committee representing organizations as diverse as campus Republicans, the University Church Alliance, the Young Socialist Alliance, SNCC, CORE, and Women for Peace. The name "Free Speech Movement" staked a claim on Americanism; like the civil rights movement and SDS, FSM asked Americans to live up to the promises of freedom and democracy in Cold War rhetoric.[70]

At rallies in Sproul Plaza, students sang civil rights songs and union songs from the 1930s. At the rally preceding a sit-in at Sproul Hall on December 2, Joan Baez sang Bob Dylan's "The Times They Are A Changin'" and concluded with the civil rights anthems "Oh Freedom" and "We Shall Overcome." That rally had been called to protest the suspension of Savio and others for the October protest. As in the civil rights sit-ins, the students intended to put their bodies on the line; they would occupy the building and interrupt standard operating procedures until the administration met their demands. The students talked and sang folk songs, watched movies and created courses. Gary Snyder, for example, lectured on American poetry. They held several different religious services and they served food.[71]

At the rally, Savio defined the struggles of African Americans and of students in terms of participatory democracy: "the same rights are at stake in both places—the right to participate as citizens in democratic society and the right to due process of law." At Berkeley, Savio said, paralleling Herbert Marcuse's concept of "repressive tolerance," "students are permitted to talk all they want so long as their speech has no consequences." Savio also framed his ideas within a personalist perspective. In the most quoted excerpt of the speech, he criticized the impersonal depersonalization of the university, noted students' complicity with their own dehumanization, and called for individual commitment to a revolution of the heart. "There is a time," he said, "when the operation of the machine becomes so odious, makes you so sick at heart that you can't take part; you can't even tacitly take part, and you've got to put your bodies upon the levers, upon all the apparatus, and you've got to make it stop. And you've got to indicate to the people who run it, to the people who own it, that unless you're free, the machine will be prevented from working at all." Opposing the organicism of the human body to the mechanism of social institutions, Savio called for the humanization of the university.[72]

The concern for the impersonality and depersonalization of American institutions, including its universities, derived from a personalist ethic. "One of the New Left's most tangled threads," said Jack Newfield, was "the revolt against the IBM card, against urban impersonalization, and the alienation of mass society." In his essay "An End of History," Mario Savio contended that the Free Speech Movement had brought the students "up against what may emerge as the greatest problem of our nation—depersonalized, unresponsive bureaucracy." According to Theodore Roszak, the cultural disaffiliation of the Sixties began with "just this painfully intense experience of *being a person* in a world that despises our personhood, a world whose policy is to grind personhood down into rubble, and then to remold the pieces into obedient, efficient, and, of course, cheerful personnel." Posing freedom against the machine, the students of the Free Speech Movement hoped to escape the "iron cage" of bureaucracy.[73]

America's bureaucracies responded with their standard operating procedures. At Berkeley, the Administration called the police for the initial arrests in September; they promised reform but suspended several students; they spoke of free speech but refused to let Mario Savio speak at an all-college gathering of December 7. The university responded to the Sproul Hall sit-in by calling police to conduct the largest mass arrest in California history: more than 350 police officers took almost twelve hours to book 773 protesters. For students, the police presence confirmed the complicity of the university with the Establishment and radicalized people who watched authorities treat human beings like objects. The arrests also made the faculty more sympathetic to the arguments of the FSM; within a week of the Sproul Hall sit-in, the faculty had voted to support free political expression on campus. By December 18, the Regents also agreed, but by then, the student movement was about much more than free speech: it was about the purpose and value of persons in American society.[74]

The Free Speech Movement dramatically expressed ideas earlier expressed in the personalist idiom. Paul Goodman's *Growing Up Absurd* had claimed that many students were "strangers in their own lives," searching for a deeper meaning to life than American society could provide. They wanted to be persons, not just personnel; they wanted vocations, not just the vocationalism of American education and business. "The 'futures' and 'careers' for which American students now prepare," said Goodman," are for the most part intellectual and moral wastelands." They provided money for people to participate in the "chrome-plated consumer's paradise," but they compromised the principles most dear to the young.[75]

As early as the spring of 1961, Tom Hayden had argued against the impersonalism of American higher education, calling for a university wide conference at Michigan to "work relentlessly at being a face-to-face, rather than a mass society." Mass production lecture classes, with a regimen of memorization and regurgitation, short-circuited the personal aspects of pedagogy. When students carried placards saying, "I am a human being; do not fold, spindle, or mutilate," they criticized the tendency of an industrial society to view persons as interchangeable parts in a machine.[76]

The personalism of student protests also made them sensitive to the scientific objectivism of the universities. They worried that science, and especially behaviorist social science, threatened "dehumanization and manipulation." Like C. Wright Mills, they doubted the neutrality of so-called objective methods, and they objected to the "moral schizophrenia" of an academic ideology that separated knowing and doing, learning and living. "As the student *enragés* keep telling us," noted Professor Kingsley Widmer, "intellectual commitment can no longer be kept separate from moral passion."[77]

The personalism of student protesters also made them resistant to the paternalism of the universities' policies *in loco parentis*. Students who saw themselves as responsible persons had a hard time dealing with institutions that treated them like children. Curfews and visitation rules, alcohol and tobacco policies, dress and dance codes, all were part of broader campus culture that regulated students "for their own good." Women were especially restricted; at Michigan in 1962, nine of fifteen pages in the student handbook contained rules for women. At most colleges and universities, there were curfews for women, who had to sign in and out of their dormitories.[78]

In part, the confrontations over the paternalism of the colleges and universities derived from differing conceptions of human nature and human motivation. Colleges and universities, and the parents they represented, believed that behavior could be molded by following prescribed sequences of courses and experiences. They used the extrinsic rewards of grades to encourage an educational instrumentalism that deferred gratification to the future, when a salary would replace grades as the pay for intellectual work. Students, on the other hand, took a more organic view of persons and personality. They assumed that self-actualization was the natural trajectory of human beings, and they increasingly saw educational structure mainly as a scheme of social control.

Colleges and universities served as a locus for such confrontations because the Baby Boom children had embraced higher education in unprecedented numbers. Both American affluence and the demands of an information society brought almost half of college-age Americans to college during the Sixties, extending adolescence into the early twenties. This boom in college enrollments bespoke parental and peer pressure for the instrumental advantages of a college education; a college degree offered economic advantages and social mobility in the age of affluence. Some students, however, took the introductory paragraphs of college catalogues seriously, and they increasingly interpreted college as a place to develop the whole person. "The university," said Mario Savio in his Sproul Hall speech, "is the place where people begin seriously to question the conditions of their existence and raise the issue of whether they can be committed to the society they have been born into." Students had come to the university, he said, "to learn to question, to grow, to learn—all the standard things that sound like clichés because no one takes them seriously." As the Sixties progressed, more and more students switched to esoteric and "impractical" majors like philosophy and history and English, where they could address these practical questions of human meaning.[79]

More than 10,000 students participated in the Free Speech Movement in its four-month history, because FSM's ideas resonated with a generation of students who had experienced the structures and strictures of college life. And the practice of the Free Speech Movement offered alternatives, both to academic life and political life. The movement's pamphlets and large group-discussions modeled both active learning and active citizenship in a community of scholars. Like the Freedom Schools of 1964, the movement itself was a powerful form of experiential learning, making education come alive. For many students, as for Michael Rossman, the rallies were "the first time I'd heard a really democratic public discussion in America."[80]

In its structure and leadership practice, the Free Speech Movement also offered an example of an institutional alternative. Organizationally, FSM was—like Women Strike for Peace—an "un-organization." Instead of a hierarchical organization with specialized roles, FSM settled on an anarchic democracy that emphasized mass participation in decision-making. For FSM, democracy was both goal and governance, ends and means. The Free Speech Movement was not a membership organization; instead it was a "collective of collectives" able to represent different groups while respecting their autonomy. Attempting to create "a movement in the shape of a community," FSM's leaders scheduled long meetings—often at the campus Presbyterian Center—to hear all points of view and move toward a consensus.[81]

The Free Speech Movement brought the ideas and practices of the civil rights movement to a campus audience, and was the first massive expression of personalist politics by white students in the Sixties. Framing the university experience and students' own lives in a personalist perspective, the FSM created a community in support of educational and social reform. Because the FSM proved successful at mobilizing students to put moral and political pressure on the university, it served as a model for the growing radicalism in the Sixties. By the time that it disbanded in spring of 1965, the Free Speech Movement had created a bridge from the civil rights movement to the antiwar movement, and it brought SDS back to campus organizing. "If Berkeley is any indication," opined a December 1964 SDS publication, "the revolution may come from the universities after all." SDS adopted the slogan "A Free University in a Free Society," and helped arrange a December 1964 national tour of FSM leaders.[82]

Teaching and Teach-ins

The escalation of the war in Vietnam added another dimension to the campus politics of the 1960s, as students and faculty devised teach-ins to discuss issues of war and peace, imperialism and colonialism. The first teach-in took place March 24, 1965, at the University of Michigan. The suffix suggested a connection with the sit-ins of the civil rights movement and of the 1930s labor movement, and defined learning as a political experience. In both cases, people occupied and transformed the spaces of their own lives, bringing social protest into established American institutions. At America's college's and universities, the teach-in offered an alternative to the specialized, departmentalized education of the conventional classroom. Designed to protest the escalation of the war in Vietnam, the teach-in sought to present views not often heard in the mainstream press or the nation's classrooms. It offered engaged, interdisciplinary education on topics not much in evidence in the country's college catalogues.[83]

When the student organizers at Michigan scheduled a nighttime teach-in instead of a work moratorium during class hours, the university administration cooperated, providing classrooms and permitting female students to stay out all night. Women Strike for Peace provided coffee and doughnuts for the all-nighter. The teach-in attracted 3,000 students and concluded with an hour of folk songs.[84]

Although the lectures and discussions focused on Vietnam, the teach-in brought innovations to American higher education. According to Anatol Rapoport, a planner of Michigan's teach-in, "it established a genuine rapport between students and a segment of the faculty," a rapport that had been attenuated in the nation's "mass education institutions." The teach-in also "effected a fusion of scholarly analysis and deep personal concern." Like the Free Speech Movement, teach-ins brought personalist perspectives to campus, and students responded enthusiastically. A Michigan honors student said that the teach-in was the first genuinely educational experience offered by the university in her four years. On that night, said organizer Marc Pilisuk, "people who really cared talked of things that really mattered." On campuses where the fusion of mind and emotion was fairly rare, the catalytic experience of the teach-ins was an education in itself.[85]

In an era of adjustment psychology and functionalist sociology, the teach-in students refused to adapt to an educational system that seemed to ignore them as persons and to train them as mere functionaries. Referring to the students who supported the teach-ins, William Appleman Williams observed that "they are morally committed to the proposition that the American system must treat people as people, and that the system must be changed if that is necessary to achieve that objective. They are deeply angry about the double standard of morality that they constantly experience."[86]

The teach-ins brought institutional and faculty support for a kind of personalist pedagogy that had been going on for years. In small face-to-face groups, students had been educating themselves, reading and discussing the ideas that mattered to them. At the University of Michigan, for example, SDS members set aside Saturday mornings for Al Haber's "seminar model" of politics. Compared with the tedium and format of most college lecture courses, the seminar experience was exhilarating; Richard Flacks described it as "free discussion of generally relevant issues in an atmosphere of equality and authentic search for answers." When the time came, therefore, for teach-ins, some students had the necessary experience.[87]

The Michigan example proved influential; by the summer, teach-ins had occurred at over 120 other educational institutions. The teach-ins showed that higher education could occur productively in places besides classrooms and in formats less structured and hierarchical than the normal student-faculty interactions. Within a year, the discrete single-issue teach-ins would be expanded into alternative institutions of various shapes and sizes. Free universities and experimental colleges continued to challenge the departmental and pedagogical boundaries of university education.

At the same time that they questioned the curriculum and coursework of the academic knowledge factory, students continued to question the complicity of the university with the structures of American society. Many activists understood the university's complicity with the Selective Service System, as student deferments allowed millions of young men to postpone or avoid military service. The connections were especially dramatized in February 1966, when Selective Service Director Lewis Hershey decreed that universities must report the class rank of all male students so that local draft boards could induct students with low grades. SSS also scheduled a national draft examination.[88]

Students opposed university defense contracts and compulsory ROTC programs and they protested campus recruiters for the military services and for companies involved in Vietnam. At the University of Wisconsin in the spring of 1967, a few students picketing Dow Chemical Company recruiters were arrested for disrupting university business, prompting more than 800 students to march and sit-in, wondering what business a university had in the napalm business. In the fall, 300 Wisconsin students obstructed the Dow representatives, and, after talks failed, the university called in riot police, who beat the demonstrators. The event split the university and the state: over 300 faculty, for example, condemned the "animalistic brutality" of the police, while the state legislature passed a resolution 94 to 5 calling for the expulsion of the protesters.[89]

Such confrontations multiplied in the late Sixties. In April 1968, for example, student radicals at Columbia University dramatically challenged the university's involvement with the Institute for Defense Analysis, and its right to expropriate public land for a new gymnasium in Morningside Heights, on the edge of Harlem. The students employed teach-ins, sit-ins, and a strike, but they also took the university into their own hands, holding a dean hostage, blockading a building, and issuing a set of demands. Other students joined them, occupying more buildings and establishing "communes" inside. Although the Columbia strike represented a more secular and confrontational radicalism than the Free Speech Movement, it still maintained some personalist elements. Said Columbia SDS leader Mark Rudd, "This was one of the first times in our experience that 'participatory democracy' had been put into practice. . . . For many it was the first communal experience of their lives—a far cry from the traditional lifestyle of Morningside Heights, that of individuals retiring to their rooms or apartments." As James Miller says, "Here was Al Haber's old seminar model of radicalism and Hayden's moral model of a community of shared risk combined in a few heady days of political adventure." As on other campuses, the university called in the police. On April 30, 2000 police came on campus, clearing the occupied buildings and arresting more than 600 students. In late May, after a student strike and more building occupations, the police again occupied the campus. And, as on other campuses, the police action confirmed for radicals the university's complicity with the structural violence of the powers that be.[90]

Personalizing Education

Between 1964 and 1972, America's colleges and universities became a forum for controversy over the purposes of education in American society.

Students and faculty argued over essential questions: What does education mean? What are the purposes of education? Are those purposes primarily individual or essentially communal? What are the important subjects of education? Which pedagogical practices best enhance students' educational experience? The cultural conversation over the ends and means of education embraced students and faculty and administrators, but it also included politicians, policymakers, and the public as well.

In the Sixties, student demands for academic "relevance" were calls for nothing less than a curricular and pedagogical personalism. When students asked the two essential educational questions—"Why?" and "So what?"—they found that America's educators often lacked satisfactory answers. Revolting against what C. Wright Mills called "the higher ignorance" of specialized higher education, students demanded a curriculum that spoke to contemporary needs. They wanted their "book-learning" integrated with their experiential learning. They wanted universities that served the community in the same way as the Freedom Schools of the South.[91]

By the mid-1960s, students began to realize that the silences of the academic curriculum were as eloquent as the expressed offerings. The fact that few colleges were prepared to teach about Vietnam seemed instructive. Academic ignorance of the experience of African-Americans and women seemed both conscious and unconscionable. Students also demanded a pedagogy that treated them as persons, and they objected to the routines—core requirements, majors, minors, computerized registration, courses, massive lectures, "objective" tests, grades, averages, honors—that reduced them to interchangeable parts.

Students, therefore, established "free universities" to extend their educational range, and to institutionalize the personalist practice of the teach-ins. Like the elementary and secondary "free schools" which also flourished in the late Sixties, and like other counter-institutions of the late Sixties, the free universities were an attempt to build a new society in the shell of the old. The first free university was formed at San Francisco State in the fall of 1965, with 30 faculty participating in student-organized noncredit courses more "relevant" than the standard offerings. In the spring of 1966, there were 21 seminars for 1200 students; by the fall there were 70 seminars. At Berkeley, students established the Free University of Berkeley, which provided a curriculum that integrated politics and education. By 1971, there were 150 free universities in the United States and the curricular focus had expanded from politics to culture. "Prerequisite: Curiosity," said the sign at the University of Man at Kansas State—the curriculum of the free universities was sometimes curious indeed. Stephen Gaskin taught "North American White Witchcraft" and "Magic, Einstein, and God" in Bay area colleges; for physical development, he offered "Meta-P.E." John

Sinclair taught jazz and contemporary poetry at the Artists Workshop's Free University in Detroit.[92]

As students (and faculty) questioned the philosophy and practice of American "hire [and hired] education," colleges and universities began to respond. At Berkeley, for example, the Muscatine Report of March 1966 concluded that "for many students—both undergraduate and graduate—there has not been an adequate connection between their education and what they feel to be their primary concerns as human beings and citizens." The report suggested—in the typically sexist language of the period—that students wanted to be "moral men in a moral society," but that the university taught them instead that their "worth is measured in answers to mass examinations, not in personal assessment of his work and ideas." The report recommended more independent study, more credit for field work, and a Pass-Fail option. It suggested more interdisciplinary programs and more emphasis on teaching. Other colleges and universities offered sub-colleges, field study centers, and storefront colleges.[93]

Most prominent among the academic reforms were revisions in general education and the addition of programs in Black Studies and Women's Studies. Cornell University offered the first official Women's Studies course for credit, in the Spring of 1969. In 1970, San Diego State College offered a complete Women's Studies program; by 1971, almost a hundred colleges offered Women's Studies courses. These new offerings added choices for students, divided the faculty, and multiplied the questions that scholars asked about their disciplines. As a result, the established canon of the disciplines encountered both challenge and change.[94]

The content of old classes changed as well. For example, new "readers" for introductory literature, history, and social science courses included materials that explicitly helped students link their academic studies to understanding of the contemporary world. Often these readers re-constructed histories of difference and dissent that had been subsumed in the curriculum of consensus. As late as 1969, the American Association of University Professors had told faculty members "not to introduce into teaching material controversial matter" from outside the specialist's discipline. Shortly thereafter, the inclusion of controversial material was relatively uncontroversial.[95]

Conclusion

The student protests of the 1960s brought a personalist sensibility to college campuses. Just as the women of WSP had plumbed the public dimensions of motherhood, the students of the 1960s explored the public dimensions of studenthood. Inspired by the education of Freedom Summer, a small number of students began to ask why their colleges could not offer the same kind of catalytic education. Students asked for changes in purpose, curriculum, pedagogy, parietal rules, administration, and institutional affiliation. Hoping to create liberal arts institutions that would really liberate people, they wanted a curriculum focused on freedom and justice. Advocating more substantial freedom than was permitted them as consumers in the cafeteria curriculum of the modern university, they expected teachers to allow them to integrate the personal, the academic, and the political in class sessions and assignments. Sixties students expected colleges to leave students responsible for their own social and sexual behavior, and they looked for an administration focused on the needs of people, not bound by the rules of bureaucracy. Finally, they wanted their institutions to avoid complicity with corporations and government agencies that violated humanistic values.

At the same time, students—especially those associated with Students for a Democratic Society—combined the personalism of the Fifties with existentialism, radical sociology and psychology, and civic republicanism to produce a movement focused on participatory democracy. Working first through established institutions, the students soon learned the intransigence of corporate liberalism, and turned instead to parallel institutions in ERAP and the movement itself. As Howard Zinn suggested, the students of the New Left tried "to create constellations of power outside the state, to pressure it into human actions, to resist its inhumane actions, and to replace it in the carrying on of voluntary activities by people who want to maintain, in small groups, both individuality and cooperation."[96]

While the student movement was an important part of Sixties radicalism, it is important to remember that *most* students moved mainly through the standard labyrinth of courses, examinations, and graduation requirements. For most students, politics was neither an occupation or even a preoccupation. A poll of male seniors conducted during the winter of 1968-69 showed that two-thirds agreed with their parents on most things; three-fourths thought that American higher education was "basically sound"; only 24 percent had smoked marijuana, and only 4 percent offered unqualified support to SDS. If there was a generation gap, it was to some extent a gap *within* the younger generation.[97]

The communal experience of radical politics was an important result of the student movement. "We have the makings of a community," William Appleman Williams told the University of Wisconsin teach-in. At Columbia, one professor observed, "an intense communal life emerged, in which students at last enjoyed a shared commitment and purpose." Like the Catholic Workers, the civil rights marchers, SNCC's volunteers, and the activists of CNVA and WSP, students discovered and rediscovered the pleasures of purposive politics, the ways in which collective action created communities more substantive than the "consumption communities" and "lifestyle enclaves" of mainstream culture.[98]

But the student movements had an impact off campus as well. Student activists taught other people to question authority when authority was questionable. They joined with other personalists, especially the radical pacifists associated with the *Catholic Worker* and *Liberation*, to protest the war that engulfed both Vietnam and the United States. And some students dropped out—and tuned in and turned on—to a new form of experiential education that embodied the communitarian anarchism of their personalist predecessors.

THE VIETNAMIZATION OF
PERSONALISM

WHEN THE UNITED STATES BEGAN TO INCREASE its involvement in
Vietnam in the early 1960s, nobody knew how to organize politically to
end the war. Both liberals and conservatives generally supported the war.
There was no substantial political constituency for any peace except "Peace
Through Strength." The American public generally subscribed to the Cold
War consensus, which prescribed containment as a preventive for a spreading Communist cancer. Besides, military spending created jobs—in government, in industry, and in education—which created income for
consumption. American radicals, who believed in strength through peace,
had mobilized only minuscule movements to oppose World War II and the
Korean War, in part because McCarthyism guaranteed that dissidents
would be equated with Communists.

But, thanks to the activity of the 1950s, there were many people and
groups poised to protest the Vietnam war from personalist perspectives.
These protesters were among the first to offer criticism of the American
presence in Southeast Asia, and they provided leaders for the antiwar movement throughout the decade. Personalist perspectives motivated many of the

different strategies of antiwar activism, including conscientious objection, draft resistance, mass demonstrations, and political organizing. The centrality of nonviolence in a personalist perspective—the emphasis on peaceable ways to peace—guaranteed that the war would become a primary issue for young activists. The personalist presence in the antiwar movement also influenced the framing of the war in moral and cultural terms, as well as in more conventional economic, political, and geopolitical interpretations.[1]

After 1965, however, and especially after 1967, the escalation of the war, the mushroom growth of the antiwar movement, the development of Black Power, the imperatives of the media, and the opposition of the government all complicated the place of personalism in the movement. After mid-decade, antiwar leaders emphasized other criticisms of the Vietnam conflict and shifted strategy and tactics from personalism to mass mobilization and protest. The "here and now revolution" continued, but it was subsumed to the clear and present danger of the war. Personalism still animated many followers of the antiwar movement, and personalist perspectives—though deemphasized—persisted throughout the war at home. But, at the national level, the development of a mass movement seemed to preclude important elements of political personalism. Although personalist perspectives persisted, they were seldom heard in the loud clashes of different perspectives late in the decade.

Vietnam: Personalist Perspectives

By 1965, the Vietnam War attracted the opposition of a wide array of American intellectuals and activists, but—because of their focus on both persons and systems—most personalists had opposed American intervention in Vietnam even before the Gulf of Tonkin incident in August 1964. Early in 1963, Women Strike for Peace described their "special responsibility" to protest the one conflict killing American troops. At the Easter 1963 ban-the-bomb march, a few activists carried signs against U.S. intervention, and A.J. Muste used his speech to decry American involvement in Vietnam. During the August 1963 commemorations of Hiroshima and Nagasaki, the New York Catholic Workers—led by Tom Cornell—protested South Vietnam's discrimination against Buddhists; in Philadelphia, members of the Student Peace Union protested in front of the Federal Building. The War Resisters League sponsored a Vietnam demonstration in October 1963, and the Friends Committee on National Legislation established a Vietnam Information Center in Washington. In April 1964, representatives of the Women's International League for Peace and Freedom lobbied in the nation's capitol. *Liberation* spoke out against the war in July 1964. The personalists of the War Resisters League (WRL), the Fellowship of Reconciliation (FOR), the Committee for Nonviolent Action (CNVA), and the Catholic Worker also demonstrated at the 1964 Democratic National Convention in Atlantic City.[2]

Catholic Worker personalism played an important part in this early antiwar movement. Dorothy Day, who had written about the unfortunate effects of European imperialism in Vietnam as early as 1954, spoke out against the war in the *Catholic Worker*. By 1962, Catholic Workers organized small demonstrations against the war. Workers also established two new organizations, PAX and the Catholic Peace Fellowship, which played an important part in protest against the war. Founded by Eileen Egan, Howard Everngam, and Jim Forest, and sponsored by Dorothy Day, Thomas Merton, and Philip Scharper, PAX was an offshoot of the English PAX, headed by Eric Gill. American PAX established a quarterly, *Peace*, and sponsored both an annual peace Mass, on August 9, and an annual peace conference at Tivoli, the Catholic Worker farm.[3]

While PAX used the just war argument to lobby the church and the government, the Catholic Peace Fellowship (CPF) offered a more activist alternative. The Catholic Peace Fellowship, a Catholic branch of the Fellowship of Reconciliation (FOR), shared FOR's program of peace and civil rights. Among the CPF's founders were Jim Forest, Marty Corbin, Tom Cornell, James Douglass, and Gordon Zahn. During the Sixties, three of its four cochairs—Forest, Corbin, and Cornell—were former managing editors of the *Catholic Worker;* the fourth, Philip Berrigan, had been a contributor to the *Worker* for years. The CPF focused early on conscientious objection, but later came to serve as the keystone of the Catholic resistance.[4]

Both groups cultivated long- and short-term goals. They lobbied the American bishops and the Second Vatican Council, trying to shape the theology and ethics that would frame future wars. James Douglass lived in Rome, where he tried to influence Vatican teachings and the Vatican Council. Dorothy Day traveled to the Eternal City in 1963 with Women Strike for Peace to influence Pope John XXIII. With Gordon Zahn, James Douglass, and Eileen Egan, Day returned to Rome in 1965 to pressure the Council for statements in support of Gospel nonviolence, conscientious objection, and the abolition of nuclear weapons. At an audience with Cardinal Suenens, she had an opportunity "to talk of the dignity of the person which Schema 13 stresses so much, and to talk about our witness for peace coming from the level of the marketplace and the street corner through demonstrations."[5]

Leaders like Jim Forest and Tom Cornell were planners and participants of most of the early antiwar protests. Cornell, who edited the *Catholic Worker* from 1962 to 1964, recalled that "we were in on every single stage, in all of those demonstrations. One or another of us was on every single committee of the mobilization from the time it was conceptualized until it fell apart." Cornell had maintained connections with the War Resisters League, the Fellowship of Reconciliation, and the Committee for Nonviolent Action, and, as the Vietnam protests escalated, he brought the spirit of the Catholic Worker to the protest coalition. Cornell probably burned his draft card more often than anybody else in the movement. Fellowship members extended this witness at the local level. Some tried to influence the church, others focused on political action, still others resisted the draft. They engaged in "beg-ins" to raise money for war victims; they ate "meals of reconciliation," with a menu of rice and tea, and a collection for war victims. In New York, CPF members picketed Cardinal Spellman's offices when he called Vietnam a "war for civilization."[6]

African American personalists protested American participation in Vietnam early on, but muted their opposition because of their support for President Johnson's civil rights initiatives. Martin Luther King's first public protest of the war came during the summer of 1965, when he considered participation in teach-ins and protests. King's dissertation advisor Harold DeWolf, an active member of SANE, encouraged King to speak out, and Coretta Scott King did speak at the June 1965 SANE convention. But moderates like Bayard Rustin advised King not to confuse the antiwar and civil rights movements and not to antagonize the Administration, so he waited two years before committing himself fully to the peace movement. Although King had spoken against the war in sermons at Ebenezer Baptist Church and in a few other places, his most dramatic statement occurred at a meeting of Clergy and Laity Concerned about Vietnam (CALCAV) in April of 1967 at Riverside Church in New York. Because of a "moral commitment to [the] dignity and the worth of human personality," King told the *New York Times*, "I feel that it is necessary to stand up against the war in Vietnam."[7]

Opposing the war and his government, King said, was a "vocation of agony." But "my conscience leaves me no other choice." There was a direct line, he said, between his civil rights activism and his antiwar stance. Because the war sucked resources out of the country, it hurt the poor. Because it selected poor people to fight and die in disproportionate numbers, it further hurt those who needed the most help. "We are called," he said, "to speak for the weak and the voiceless, for victims of our nation and for those it calls enemy, for no document from human hands can make these humans any less our brothers." Linking the war to the nation's core values, King argued that "we as a nation must undergo a radical revolution of values. We must rapidly shift from a 'thing-oriented' society to a 'person-oriented society.' When machines and computers, profit motives and property rights are considered more important than people, the giant triplets of racism, materialism, and militarism are incapable of being conquered."[8]

Outraged that the Federal government would inflict violence on Vietnam at the same time that it tolerated racist violence in Mississippi, Bob Moses—from the Student Nonviolent Coordinating Committee—spoke out much earlier. Moses, who had filed for conscientious objector status in 1960, first announced his opposition to the war in 1964. He spoke at the April 1965 March on Washington, and at the May 1965 Vietnam Day protests in Berkeley "as a member of the Third World." He condemned a policy that sent soldiers to protect the South Vietnamese, but not to protect the civil rights workers of the South.[9]

Women Strike for Peace also framed its protests from a personalist perspective. From 1963 on, WSP protested the loss of American lives in Vietnam. By 1965, the White House was receiving about 1800 messages a week on Vietnam, with antiwar sentiments strongly predominating, especially from women who focused on the immorality of the war. In February 1965, WSP and the Women's International League for Peace and Freedom (WILPF) joined for a "Mother's Lobby" against American involvement. In March, Alice Herz, an 81-year-old Michigan WILPF member, set herself afire in imitation of the Buddhist monks who had immolated themselves to protest the war. The following year, WSP members were the first to protest American use of napalm by blocking shipments. By mid-decade, Women Strike for Peace had adopted the slogan, "Not Our Sons, Not Your Sons, Not Their Sons," emphasizing the importance of soldiers as persons in families. By the end of the Sixties, WSP had over 100,000 members in twenty-five states.[10]

A.J. Muste and the people influenced by *Liberation* were even more important in antiwar protest and organizing. Many of the protests came from Muste's home-away-from-home, 5 Beekman Street in New York City, the address of the Fellowship of Reconciliation, the Committee for Nonviolent Action, the War Resisters League, the Catholic Peace Fellowship, the Student Peace Union, and, after April 1965, the Fifth Avenue Peace Parade Committee. Muste helped to pull these groups together and to coordinate their efforts with the activities of larger liberal groups.[11]

On July 2, 1964, as President Johnson signed the momentous Civil Rights Act, Muste and David Dellinger issued a "Declaration of Conscience" against the war in Vietnam at a demonstration in Lafayette Park across from the White House. In attendance were Daniel and Phillip Berrigan, Joan Baez, and Rabbi Abraham Feinberg. The Declaration had been written by Muste, Dellinger, Rustin, and others in the *Liberation* offices a few weeks earlier. Signers pledged to refuse cooperation with the government in the prosecution of the interventions in Vietnam and the

Dominican Republic, and to encourage the refusal of others. To a great extent, subsequent war protests followed this great refusal.[12]

Personalist opposition to the Vietnam War was rooted in ideas about the preciousness of persons, in pacifism, in American anti-colonialism, in democratic theory, in economic equity, and in religious humanism. The personalist focus on the life and dignity of individual human beings was contradicted by the wholesale slaughter of the war. The weekly bodycount was the ultimate degradation of personal dignity, because the progress of the war was being measured by the destruction of persons. While the Administration cloaked the violation of persons in a metaphorical bodybag of abstractions, personalists asked Americans to empathize with the victims. A 1964 poster of a Vietnamese child disfigured by napalm emphasized the practical and personal consequences of the domino theory. A 1972 photograph of a naked young girl, napalmed and running in terror, also seared American consciences.[13]

Personalists especially decried the "bombing morality" of the war, whereby people at 50,000 feet could destroy others on the ground. This "remote control" of the battlefield seemed especially inhumane. Herbert Marcuse contended that "to the degree to which the agent of destruction is a thing and the person is removed from the victim, guilt and the sense of guilt are reduced. One of the most effective barriers against cruelty and inhumanity has thereby collapsed." More broadly, personalists rejected the rationalization and depersonalization of the war, with its emphasis on quantification and control. The "systems analysis" introduced by Secretary of Defense Robert McNamara and his "Whiz Kids" rationalized the Defense establishment. But the New Left saw the war as the "irrationality of rationality," the technocratic mind gone mad. In a June 1965 meeting, A.J. Muste told McNamara that, because of his "faculty of abstraction," "the monstrosity of [his] work had little or no emotional meaning for him," and he asked McNamara to make room for morality in his decision-making.[14]

The personalist opposition to imperialism was connected to an emphasis on democratic self-determination; both suggested that powerful countries should relinquish control of their colonies, so that people could govern themselves. At the first teach-in at the University of Wisconsin, Professor William Appleman Williams argued that American "reification of the Open Door Policy has resulted in a violation of the moral principle of self-determination." The right of self-determination derived from a sense that persons should be able to make the political decisions that affected them.[15]

Personalists also thought that Americans should be able to make the policy decisions that affected them, but it was hard to imagine an Ameican institution less democratic than the foreign policy establishment. As early as the Gulf of Tonkin (August 1964), SDS claimed that secret policymaking compromised knowledgeable citizen participation in foreign policy decisions. The *New York Times* editorialized in 1965 that emergency procedures of nondemocratic decision-making had been routinized. At the 1965 Vietnam Day rally in Berkeley, Staughton Lynd contended that "people who have been working in the Freedom Democratic Party now have to realize that not only Negroes in Mississippi are unrepresented in the government of the United States; in a situation where Congress has handed over the constitutional power to declare war and peace to the President, all of us are now unrepresented by our government."[16]

Economically, personalists opposed business arrangements in which some people were exploited for the profits and comfort of others. Instead of aiming at economic justice, said Martin Luther King, the United States had chosen to maintain "the privileges and pleasures that come from the immense profits of overseas investment. . . . A true revolution of values [would cause Americans to] look across the seas and see individual capitalists of the West investing huge sums of money in Asia, Africa, and South America, only to take the profits out with no concern for the social betterment of the countries, and say: 'This is not just.'"[17]

The question of means and ends was central to the protests as well. Arthur Waskow contended, at Michigan's first teach-in, that "the new American arrogance says that the ends we seek are so noble, so benign, that any means at all are legitimate to advance them." He argued especially against the arrogant assumption that military means could effect political ends. "We have not yet learned that the political freedom of the Vietnamese people cannot be advanced by a military policy that relies on burning villages with napalm and on torturing the villagers for information."[18]

It is important to remember that the antiwar movement not only opposed the war to protect persons from harm, but it also acted to help persons who had already been harmed. Like the Catholic Worker, antiwar activists tried to ameliorate the immediate suffering. Groups like the Catholic Peace Fellowship raised funds for war victims. The Fellowship for Reconciliation and the American Friends Service Committee sponsored national campaigns to buy medical supplies for use throughout Vietnam. Working from a spirituality called compassion, they tried to heal the wounds of war.[19]

In July 1965, ten members of Women Strike for Peace met with a delegation of Vietnamese women to establish personal contacts in the midst of an impersonal war. The first formal meeting between an American peace group and official Vietnamese representatives, the event personalized the front-page conflict and led to the Committee of Liaison, organized by WSP's Cora Weiss, to maintain contacts between American POWs and their families. Such initiatives in citizen diplomacy, which put persons to work in international relations, continued throughout the decade.[20]

Conscientious Objections

During the Vietnam War, 172,000 young Americans filed conscientious objections with their Selective Service offices. Citing religious and moral reasons for their refusal to fight a war, these objectors offered a personal (and often personalist) protest to the war and the war system. Their objections came from American history and from personalist precedents. Many students admired the early personalist and conscientious objector Henry David Thoreau. More proximately, many of them followed the example of the COs of World War II. The Nuremberg trials were also influential: many conscientious objectors believed that individuals bear a personal responsibility for resistance to institutionalized evil.[21]

The pacifist personalism of the Catholic Worker movement provided many examples of conscientious objection for young people. Karl Meyer was one such example. Born in 1937, Meyer grew up in a pacifist household: his father, a soil conservationist for the National Forest Service, had been a conscientious objector in World War II. Elected to Congress in 1958, William Meyer found himself a one-term representative because of his support for nuclear disarmament. Karl entered the University of Chicago in 1954, but left to live a life of voluntary poverty in New York and Washington, where he met people loosely associated with the Catholic Worker movement. He converted from Protestantism to Catholicism, and from liberalism to radicalism, he said, because of the doctrines in the gospels. In 1955, he filed with the Selective Service as a conscientious objector. At nineteen, he attempted to open a Worker house of hospitality in Washington, but he failed. Moving to New York, he encountered Dorothy Day and Ammon Hennacy, whose autobiography, *The Book of Ammon*, was an important influence. In 1957, he joined the Workers in one of their annual civil defense protests. Returning to Chicago in the fall of 1957, Meyer opened a Catholic Worker house of hospitality at 164 West Oak Street. In April 1959, Meyer joined with Ken Calkins to organize the Student Peace Union at the University of Chicago. By the dawn of the 1960s, the group already had 5,000 members, with 12,000 subscribers to its bulletin.[22]

In addition to personal examples, personalists also provided institutional assistance for conscientious objectors. As early as 1948, the War Resisters League had joined with other peace groups in establishing the Central Committee for Conscientious Objectors. In the early Sixties, the *Catholic Worker* had received three or four letters monthly asking about conscientious objection. By the late Sixties, in their national offices alone, the Catholic Peace Fellowship got 50 to 100 inquiries a week. With other groups, they provided information and draft counseling for thousands of draft-eligible men.[23]

The counseling occurred because the United States Selective Service law provided that young men could be drafted into the military service of their country. In the climate of the 1960s, it also provided a powerful impetus to reflection, as it personalized the ethics of war and the claims of the nation-state. Just as Jim Crow laws made buses and lunch counters a locus for African American political personalism, so the draft forced America's young men to face their personal complicity with the warfare state. The draft gave young men selfish reasons for ethical contemplation and for conscientious objections.

Headed by General Lewis Hershey, the Selective Service operated as if some persons were more equal than others. It provided deferments, for example, to young men enrolled in colleges. According to a 1965 Selective Service memorandum, the student deferment served the purpose of "developing more effective human beings in the national interest." This "channeling" memorandum claimed that the draft served not only to recruit men for the armed forces, but to channel other men into occupations that served the state. At the same time that deferred technicians fought the Cold War in the nation's universities and defense plants, therefore, less skilled human beings were sent to fight the hot war in Vietnam. A Notre Dame survey found that men from poor families were twice as likely to serve in the military, to go to Vietnam, and to see combat. This system of preferment directly contradicted the personalist concern for the poor and marginalized in American society. It was bad enough that they *were* poor and marginalized; it was scandalous that these same people risked their lives at war for the privileged people.[24]

Late in 1965, Selective Service director Lewis Hershey caused an uproar when, citing a need for more military manpower, he ordered a 20 percent reduction in student deferments. Students would need to maintain a "C" grade point average and pass a Selective Service intelligence exam which was heavily weighted by math questions in favor of economics and engineering over the social sciences and the humanities. SDS responded with an antiwar National Vietnam Examination, with questions like "Who said 'I have only one hero—Hitler?'" (The answer was South Vietnam's President Nguyen Cao Ky.)[25]

Sometimes individuals who filed with the Selective Service as conscientious objectors extended their objection to the draft itself. In 1963, Catholic Worker Tom Cornell, for example, became the first person during the Vietnam War to burn his draft card to renounce his personal complicity with the war-making powers of the state. He drew on precedents from 1947, when Dwight Macdonald, A.J. Muste, Bayard Rustin, and David Dellinger had hosted a draft-card burning to protest the possible passage of a peacetime draft.[26]

After mass draft card burnings in May 1964 and August 1965, Congress passed a law making the destruction of a draft card a felony equivalent to draft refusal. In the September 1965 *Catholic Worker*, Cornell responded that "Draft Cards Are for Burning." The Congressional legislation had made the draft card "the symbol *par excellence* of involuntary servitude for the works of death, and . . . it deserved to be burned." In defiance of Congress, Catholic Worker David Miller burned his draft card in October at the first International Days of Protest in New York. Cornell was amazed by the resonance of the act. He knew that part of it was "the whole masculine thing." But even more, he saw the religious symbolism: "There is a kind of civil or state religion which has subsumed large elements of Christianity [and] Judaism. . . . The draft card then becomes a sacrament. And there's nothing worse you can do in sacramental terms than defile a species of the sacrament. And this was a defilement, a blasphemy against the state." About three weeks later, at the suggestion of *New York Times* staffers, the personalist protesters publicized their new symbol. On November 6, in New York's Union Square, A.J. Muste and Dorothy Day introduced five young men—including Tom Cornell—who burnt their draft cards.[27]

Opposition to the draft drew on the claims of individual conscience, but also on anarchist opposition to the compulsions of the state. Like Dorothy Day and the Catholic Workers, the students of the late Sixties rejected the idea that the state could force them to serve its military purposes. At a New York City protest in April 1967, more than 150 men burned their draft cards. As Thomas Powers suggests, this marked "the beginning of an entirely new stage in the opposition to the war. They did not simply protest official policy, but dissociated themselves entirely from the government, and if need be, from the country that sanctioned its policy."[28]

Although personalists led the movement for draft resistance, others followed suit. At its June 1965 convention, Students for a Democratic Society decided to focus, not on public protests but on campus organizing for draft resistance. In October the National Office proposed to encourage young men to seek conscientious objector status, to demonstrate against local draft boards, and to stop colleges from reporting students' class rank. Most liberals and Marxists did not share the pacifist or personalist convictions of the first draft card incendiaries, but some of them also rallied to resistance.[29]

Sometimes soldiers who had already been drafted also objected conscientiously to participation in the war. In 1966, the Fort Hood Three announced that "we will not be a part of this unjust, immoral, and illegal war." A.J. Muste saw it as an ethico-political question: could the government ignore the soldiers' civil right "to think for themselves, to discuss the issues raised by the war in Vietnam, and to refuse to obey orders to commit what they believe to be war crimes?" The government thought so; the Army court-martialed all three and sentenced them to Fort Leavenworth. But GI protests against the war continued.[30]

The conscientious objections of antiwar protesters led to conscientious questioning among the nation's mainstream denominations. Religious figures like Martin Luther King, Robert McAfee Brown, and William Sloane Coffin pressured the nation's churches to reconsider their roles in issues of war and social justice, and many churches reevaluated their position on pacifism and militarism. Even Reinhold Niebuhr and the Christian realists of *Christianity and Crisis* called for an end to the violence. In 1965, a group of American religious leaders—including Richard Neuhaus, Abraham Heschel, and Daniel Berrigan—established Clergy Concerned About Vietnam (soon expanded to Clergy and Laymen Concerned About Vietnam—CAL-CAV) to offer a religious, but not necessarily pacifist, critique of the war. In May 1966, Martin Luther King Jr. agreed to cochair the organization. At a time when most American churches supported the Johnson Administration, CALCAV offered a moderate voice of protest that complemented the conscientious objections of more radical students. Its director, Richard Fernandez, said that it provided a place for people—"as religious people"—to protest the war. By 1969, the group comprised a hundred local chapters and a mailing list of 40,000. Sponsoring demonstrations, vigils, picketing, fasts, publications, and participation in electoral politics, CALCAV put the "protest" back into "Protestant," and deepened understanding of the religious and ethical issues involved in the war. Moderate and mostly middle class, CALCAV maintained a respectable opposition to the war and a link to politicians like Eugene McCarthy and Mark Hatfield who helped to translate conscientious objections into policy proposals.[31]

Protest Demonstrations

Beyond their personal protests against war and conscription, America's political personalists participated in a campaign of mass demonstrations to end the war. While conscientious objection and draft refusal both were acts of witness and example, they also served as acts of political education. Demonstrations extended the tradition of moral witness and political education by applying political pressure; like the civil defense protests of the Fifties, demonstrations could show political leaders that many of their constituents favored peace.

Unfortunately, early in the Sixties, that wasn't very many; there was no organized constituency for peace. If activists were going to effectively oppose the war, they couldn't just mobilize people who agreed with their position. First they had to change people's minds; only then could they begin to think about a political force. While the Sixties were replete with strategies for changing hearts and minds, political personalists generally began with a combination of religion and civic republicanism, in part because of their own convictions, but also because most Americans were familiar with the language, if not with the radical practice of citizenship or vocation.

Demonstrations were an institution in which political mobilization and moral witness came together. At one level, the protests were bids for political power; at another level, they were dramas for the media. But they were also dramas of moral witness, pilgrimages to the shrines of democracy by believers in the slogans of the civil religion. Demonstrations were also a reconstitution of public space by American citizens, just as sit-ins were a reformulation of commercial space by civil rights activists. Formerly, officials acted in public spaces, while citizens watched. Now, citizens redefined public spaces by acting in them while officials pretended not to watch. Similarly, demonstrations exerted a transformative effect on activists, instilling a sense of commitment and efficacy that often traveled back home with them.

The first sizable demonstration against the war took place in December 1964, after the national elections, but before the escalations that brought the war to popular attention. Organized by A.J. Muste and David McReynolds, it brought over a thousand people to Washington Square in New York to hear Muste, Norman Thomas, and A. Philip Randolph call for an end to the war. Later that same month, SDS announced a Vietnam protest march to be held in Washington on Easter weekend, the traditional religious setting for peace protests. After Operation Rolling Thunder raised the spectre of obliteration bombing and after the introduction of American ground troops in March of 1965, the April 17 march was extraordinarily successful, with 20,000 people protesting in the nation's capitol. Speakers like Robert Parris (formerly Robert Moses), I. F. Stone, Staughton Lynd, and a welfare mother from the Cleveland ERAP project reminded the crowd that the war threatened not just the Vietnamese, but Americans searching for social justice. Phil Ochs, Bill Frederick, Joan Baez, Judy Collins, and the Freedom Voices musically reminded marchers of the connections between civil rights and the war. SDS President Paul Potter underlined the systematic character of violence in Vietnam and in America, seeing both as symptoms of "a deeper malaise." He welcomed marchers as antiwar protesters, but also as "participants . . . in a movement to build a more decent society . . . a democratic and humane society in which Vietnams are unthinkable, in which human life and initiative are precious."[32]

Following the precedent of the 1963 March on Washington, the April 1965 march publicized the personalist project. By marching on Washington, protesters dramatized their strength and brought SDS and its personalist politics to the attention of the national media. the *New York Times* offered a major story a month before the march, and the *Nation* and the *New Republic* ran flattering stories afterward.[33]

At the same time, students and faculty began to bring the war home to the nation's campuses with teach-ins. On the weekend of May 21-22, between ten and thirty thousand people attended the Vietnam Day teach-in at the University of California at Berkeley. Students heard from Dr. Benjamin Spock, Norman Thomas, Ernest Gruening, and Norman Mailer. They were challenged to participate in nonviolent civil disobedience by David Dellinger, Staughton Lynd, Mario Savio, and Robert Moses. Vietnam Day also featured performances by Dick Gregory and Paul Krassner, folk songs of Phil Ochs and Malvina Reynolds, and the satire of the improvisational commedy group, the Committee. Like other teach-ins, the Vietnam Day events introduced college students to the nation's preeminent personalists, offered alternative sources of information to supplement the administration's line, and legitimized dissent on the nation's campuses.[34]

In the wake of SDS's ambivalence about anti-war protests, pacifist A.J. Muste called and coordinated—with Robert Parris (Moses) and Eric Weinberger, a CNVA activist and CORE fieldworker—an Assembly of Unrepresented People for a series of demonstrations and discussions to be held on the twentieth anniversary of the atomic bombings of Japan, August 6-9. Sponsored by the Catholic Worker, the War Resisters League, and CNVA, the assembly linked domestic social issues and the war. The delegates hoped to deliver the "Declaration of Conscience"—signed by 6,000 people—to the White House. Written in 1964 by Muste, David Dellinger, Bayard Rustin, and Ralph DiGia, this declaration of human interdependence announced the signers' refusal to cooperate with the government in the prosecution of the war. It called for conscientious citizens to cease their work in war industries, and it declared that "we shall encourage the development of other nonviolent acts, including acts which involve civil disobedience, in order to stop the flow of American soldiers and munitions to Vietnam." And it implied that much of the antiwar activity of the era still came from religious roots.[35]

The assembly claimed to represent the marginalized people of the world, but it also offered a challenge to the American policy elite, questioning whether, in fact, they really represented the American people. On the first day, the 2,000 participants conducted a silent vigil in commemoration of Hiroshima at the White House. The following day they divided into workshops on social issues that could be addressed if the war were stopped: women, Indians, Puerto Rican independence, free universities, the abolition of the House Un-American Activities Committee. On the 9th, some 800 people marched down the Mall and "invaded" the Capitol, trying to present a declaration of peace to the Congress. In the largest mass arrest in Washington's history, 350 people were booked by the police. As President Johnson formally signed the Voting Rights Act of 1965 on August 6, this small but significant minority of Americans were forming the National Coordinating Committee to End the War in Vietnam, with thirty-three separate groups pledged to resist his foreign policy.[36]

In 1966, activists created the "Spring Mobilization Committee to End the War in Vietnam" (MOBE) a coalition of 150 radical and liberal groups with 100,000 members. Because of their involvement with the MOBE, A.J. Muste and David Dellinger were among the most important leaders of the peace movement in 1966–67. As David McReynolds recalls, "Muste played the crucial role of a person *everyone* trusted: both the Communists and the Trotskyists trusted him; SANE trusted him; FOR and WRL trusted him; labor trusted him; religious groups trusted him." Muste's skills in conflict resolution often helped warring activists to find common ground. After Muste died in January 1967, Dellinger and Staughton Lynd maintained the personalist presence in the leadership of the antiwar movement.[37]

By the late 1960s, the peace movement could mobilize great numbers of people for antiwar demonstrations. The 1960 New York civil defense protest attracted 1,000 people; by 1969, the Moratorium marches would attract hundreds of thousands. Demonstrations served both personal and political goals; they supported individuals in their dissent and they demonstrated that dissent to the country at large. At the same time, however, marches de-emphasized the localism and particularism of political personalism. The war made the "here-and-now revolution" into a "there and then revolution," as many demonstrators focused their activity on Washington and on future policy changes. Learning that only national actions generated national media coverage, activists began to replace the local vision of personalism with the broadcast media version of mass protest. The war forced activists to focus on a negative peace, instead of working for the positive peace expressed in "experiments in creative living by individuals, families, and small groups." As many personalists focused on the single issue of Vietnam, they lost sight of the broader personalist project of compassion and care for the poor.

From Protest to Politics

After mid-decade, the escalation of the war and the increasing sense of racial crisis caused many activists to wonder if personalist practice were necessary or sufficient for the ends they supported. For a variety of reasons, a number of people began to question the efficacy of personalism and to pursue alternate strategies, including revolutionary violence and a Marxist-Leninist Party. While personalism seemed a good way to mobilize people, it was not necessarily effective at changing government policy. It unlinked the individual from complicity with evil, but it didn't quickly curtail the evil. Some activists found themselves frustrated that faithful witness made so little difference, that the "here-and-now revolution" seemed so distant.

In general, there were two main responses to the crises of the mid-1960s. Some people who had promoted political personalism decided that, for practical reasons, it was time to move "from protest to politics." Others, including most of the young leaders of SNCC and SDS, decided that, for practical reasons, it was time to move "from protest to resistance." Both responses contained criticisms of political personalism.

Bayard Rustin promoted the first of the two new strategies. In all of his activity for the peace and civil rights movements, Rustin had maintained his faith that the system could deliver at least a semblance of justice. He was heartened by the Civil Rights Act of 1964 and the Voting Rights Act of 1965, and the beginnings of the war on poverty. Deeply influenced by his patron, union leader A. Philip Randolph, Rustin thought that economic issues, and especially the issue of jobs, should be the next step for the movement. Above all, he did not want to alienate the liberal Democrats who might secure future legislative gains.

For Rustin, the Democratic National Convention of 1964 and the April 1965 March on Washington were the breaking points. In Atlantic City, Rustin advocated accepting the proffered compromise. He thought that the intransigence of the Mississippi Freedom Democratic Party would hurt the civil rights movement. Rustin also thought that the decision to allow Communists to participate in the March on Washington would alienate the politicians who were needed for legislative progress on both peace and civil rights. Replaying the argument of the Port Huron convention, the activists had disagreed over the question of Communist participation: the anti-anti-Communists of SDS were willing to allow Communist groups to participate, but radicals like Rustin who were trying to form coalitions with the nation's liberals circulated a document of repudiation which many leaders, including A.J. Muste, signed. After the bombing of North Vietnam began in February, Muste and others gave their full support to the demonstration. The strategic differences caused a split among the editors of *Liberation*, and Bayard Rustin resigned from the editorial board in 1966.[38]

Rustin saw the perfectionism of people like Muste and Dellinger as self-indulgent and politically self-defeating, and he criticized their increasingly confrontational tactics. While he admitted that power corrupts, he also felt that the absence of power corrupts, because it keeps purists from making the progress they purport to want. Antiwar liberals like Rustin, and organizations like SANE and ADA, worked for "*limited* objectives through *limited* means." They expected the antiwar movement to use vigils, fasts, newspaper ads, teach-ins, and orderly demonstrations to persuade the government to accept a negotiated settlement. Rustin wanted the movement to be realistic. To many idealists, however, realism meant offering strategies acceptable to the discredited Democratic Party. Realism meant *realpolitik* in political science, functionalism in sociology, and Christian realism in ethics. It left little room for a personalism that questioned all three.[39]

Most movement leaders were unwilling to make such compromises with the people who were prosecuting the war in Vietnam. They saw that the Gulf of Tonkin resolution authorizing the prosecution of the war had passed in the House 416 to 0 and in the Senate 88 to 2, and they saw little opportunity for meaningful compromise. They were also unwilling to accept the premises of Rustin's dichotomy. They decided that, in the present political context, protest *was* politics. Finally, many activists refused to concede the truth of Rustin's charge that the Sixties radicals lacked an analysis of contemporary America, a vision for the future, or a strategy for getting from one to the other. Indeed, compared with the American political parties, they offered an extravagant banquet of analysis, strategy, and vision. Strategies included the personalist politics of persuasive example, such as conscientious objection and nonviolent civil disobedience; the politics of witness, involving the participation of churches and religious leaders; the coalition politics of protest and political reform; and the resistance politics of "Gandhi and guerilla." All of these strategies involved elements of grassroots democratic process—conversation, publicity, recruiting, and mobilization. In addition, many New Left members participated in conventional party politics, supporting candidates in primaries and voting for the lesser of evils in the elections. Although the New Left espoused some unorthodox strategies—civil disobedience, massive protests, and (at times) violence—they also acted like the orthodox political parties, preparing and publishing platforms, publicizing their ideas with pamphlets, posters, and buttons, creating coalitions, and trying to persuade the public to join their cause. Rhetorically radical, in many ways they were politically as American as apple pie.

Rustin and others overemphasized the Sixties disaffiliation from politics. Liberal peace activists who had voted for Lyndon Johnson as the peace candidate in 1964 looked to the 1966 elections as an opportunity to record their disapproval. In May, SANE and WSP sponsored a gathering of 8,000 in Washington to announce 73,000 "voter pledges" for peace candidates in the 1966 Congressional elections. In a few instances, the Vietnam vote made a difference; in Berkeley, antiwar candidate Robert Scheer won 45 percent of the vote in the Democratic primary. But on the whole, local issues proved more important, and the electorate chose, by default, to continue the policy of liberal internationalism and military escalation. In 1967, activists created Vietnam Summer in which 3,000 volunteers took the war issue into neighborhoods with door-to-door canvassing and electoral planning. Modeled in part on the 1964 Mississippi Freedom Summer, Vietnam Summer hoped to educate people and to help them take their first steps in opposition to the war. In September, the National Conference for a New Politics met to consider the possibility of forcing change within the system.[40]

In 1967 and 1968, thousands of antiwar and countercultural activists got "clean for Gene," and participated in the Presidential primaries. When Senator Eugene McCarthy announced in late November 1967 that he would challenge Lyndon Johnson on a peace platform, thousands of students flocked to New Hampshire to offer their support. It was a "mushroom revolution," claimed columnist Richard Stout: "A lot of little people in a lot of little places were doing a lot of little things." An expression of the grassroots, participatory democracy of the Sixties, the McCarthy campaign renewed the radical hope that "a constituency of conscience" could be found in America. Both the January 1968 Tet offensive and McCarthy's strong 42 percent showing in New Hampshire showed the weaknesses of the President's position. Support for the war shrank, and the number of avowed doves matched the number of hawks for the first time. After Robert Kennedy's announcement that he would run for the Presidency and Lyndon Johnson's announcement that he would not—both in March—it seemed possible that electoral politics could prove responsive to the moral concerns of personalist politics. Kennedy's charisma and his compassion for the poor made him especially attractive to many young activists. The assassinations of Martin Luther King Jr. and Senator Kennedy, and the nominations of Democrat Hubert Humphrey and Republican Richard Nixon dashed those hopes for many. Some people who traveled the road from protest to politics made the return trip.[41]

From Protest to Resistance

As Bayard Rustin counseled a change in strategy from protest to politics, some activists countered with a movement "from protest to resistance." By 1965, the escalation of the war in Vietnam and the outbreak of ghetto riots had raised the stakes for activists. Looking for immediate solutions to these pressing human problems, many New Left activists found the politics of personalism too moralistic, too optimistic, too indecisive, too local, too narrow, too ineffective, too slow. To remedy the militarism of the war and the racism that led to riots, the movement would need to move the federal government. And to many, participatory democracy seemed inadequate to the task. Repudiating Rustin and his complicity with American liberalism, which increasingly seemed responsible for both racial inertia and military escalation, they favored a shift from protest to resistance.

SDS, the New Left, and the antiwar movement all followed shifts in African American activism, particularly in the Student Nonviolent Coordinating Committee. SNCC's shift had begun as early as 1963 and 1964, when some field secretaries argued for strategies more revolutionary than voter registration. Other SNCC workers were radicalized by the 1964 Democratic National Convention, and by a fall 1964 trip to Africa. Especially after the sojourn in Africa, many SNCC workers began to see themselves as part of a worldwide struggle of national and racial liberation. Burdened by the brutal and systematic violence of white racism, they entertained doubts about the power of nonviolence. Many SNCC field workers began to carry guns for self-defense. By 1965, SNCC emphasized racial pride and revolutionary rhetoric more than the personalist ideas of redemptive suffering, moral suasion, love, and integration.[42]

SNCC leaders established links with Malcolm X, whose challenge to the assumptions of civil rights leaders like Martin Luther King undermined faith in white people, liberal institutions, and the efficacy of the moderate movement. King's personalism, his sense that all people were created in the image and likeness of God, allowed him to trust in the goodness of white people, despite substantial evidence to the contrary. King's faith in love's ability to convert the hard-hearted gave him hope that the movement would ultimately succeed. But his hope—the hope of the beloved community—required time, and time was running short. Internally, too, SNCC activists began to wonder if democratic decision-making was compatible with efficacy. The "freedom-high" faction of SNCC wanted to maintain SNCC's commitment to patient, local organizing and decentralized decision-making. But the hardliners were increasingly certain that a militant, disciplined organization was necessary for combatting racism.[43]

Events in Northern cities also affected SNCC's evaluation of personalism. Just five days after President Johnson signed the Voting Rights Act, on August 11 of 1965, thousands of African Americans rioted in the Los Angeles ghetto of Watts. Thirty-four people died and over four thousand were arrested as an army of 14,000 National Guardsmen and 1,600 policemen tried to restore order in the inflamed ghetto. The Watts riot, and the race riots that followed in urban America over the next five years, sent many messages. They showed that King's Southern strategy of personalist protest had not converted African Americans in Northern cities, many of whom responded more to black nationalism and resistance than to personalist precepts. They challenged white liberals to deal with the structural racism of American society, and not just with the legal segregation of the South. Watts signalled that economic justice was as important as the end of legal segregation in assuring the human dignity of people, black and white. The riots taught King and America that, without hope, anger could lead to violence as well as to nonviolence. Unfortunately, the people of America showed the people of Watts that they did not understand the frustrations of African Americans. Middle-class white Americans could see the signs of segregation, and the violence of police dogs and fire hoses, on TV. But, especially given the individualist premises of American life, it was harder to see structural racism, chronic poverty, and the persistent resentment of racial prejudice. A decade after Ralph Ellison's *Invisible Man*, it was still difficult for white people to see African Americans whole.[44]

The resignation of Robert Moses as director of the Council of Federated Organizations (COFO) late in 1964, and his gradual withdrawal from active participation in staff meetings, opened opportunities for SNCC's faction of hardliners. Instead of asking for integration and voting rights, the hardliners began to emphasize "black power." A year after Watts, during the June 1966 Memphis-to-Jackson march, SNCC's chairman Stokely Carmichael began to call for "Black Power," a phrase that complicated the struggle for racial equality. To African Americans, black power resounded with racial pride, community autonomy, self-determination, and self-defense. It meant "parallel institutions," both political and economic, to keep black people protected from the structural racism of white society. To white Americans, it sounded like trouble—black people ungrateful for what had been "given" to them, and unwilling to wait for progress to come rolling in on wheels of inevitability. In a competitive society where power issued from economic and political structures of control, it was hard to imagine anything but zero-sum empowerment. When Carmichael and others began to discard the slogans of the nonviolent civil rights movement, they also began to engender fears and backlash in white Americans. Black Power showed the limitations of both black patience and white liberalism.[45]

The Vietnam War also complicated SNCC's situation, because the war, too, seemed to point to the hypocrisy of the white liberal leadership. The violence of the war, the slaughter of the Vietnamese, the disproportionate casualties of African American soldiers, and the unjust use of resources needed for racial justice all combined to move organizations like SNCC and leaders like Martin Luther King to protest. But when King and other leaders criticized the war, they were attacked in the press. Critics claimed that King should stick to the issue of civil rights. Inspired by his personalist presumptions about the essential unity of the moral universe, King disagreed. "I have always insisted on justice for all the world over," he said, "because justice is indivisible, and injustice anywhere is a threat to justice anywhere. I will not stand by when I see an unjust war taking place and fail to take a stand against it."[46]

To many black activists, the crisis of the mid-Sixties suggested the increasing irrelevance of personalist politics. When SNCC elected a new chairperson in 1966, John Lewis's Christian approach counted *against* him, and Stokely Carmichael was ultimately chosen. By 1969, the Student Nonviolent Coordinating Committee had dropped "nonviolent" from its name. Black Power advocates began to use a rhetoric of revolution that was increasingly appropriated by other Sixties movements. Black Muslims and Black Panthers also brandished the language of colonialism and revolt.[47]

By 1966, many young radicals were disillusioned with liberalism, disappointed by their inability to change the system, and near despair. They had worked long and hard for their ideals, and found the results meager at best. For many, the lack of visible results caused a crisis of confidence. In 1966, Catholic Worker James Forest confessed his despair in a letter to Thomas Merton. "Thanks for the letter," Merton replied, confessing his own crisis. "I can well understand your sense of desperation. . . . You can guess that I don't have magic solutions for bleak moods: if I did I would use them on my own which are habitually pretty bleak too." But Merton did have ways of framing issues that could make sense of contemporary personalist politics.

Merton cautioned Forest against the fetishism of results, the problem-solution sequence of the ideology of liberal consensus. "Do not depend on the hope of results. When you are doing the sort of work you have taken on, essentially an apostolic work, you may have to face the fact that your work will be apparently worthless and even achieve no result at all, if not perhaps results opposite to what you expect." In this situation, Merton said, "you start more and more to concentrate not on the results but the value, the rightness, the truth of the work itself. And there too a great deal has to be gone through, as gradually you struggle less and less for an idea and more and more for specific people. The range tends to narrow down, but it gets much more real." In the end, Merton thought, the personalism of protest could be redemptive, as activists realized not just community between them and the victims of society, but community among themselves as well. "As you yourself mention in passing, it is the reality of personal relationships that saves everything."

Merton saw the frustrations of the rhetoric of idealism. "You are fed up with words and I don't blame you. I am nauseated by them sometimes. I am also, to tell the truth, nauseated with ideals and with causes. This sounds like heresy, but I think you will understand what I mean. It is so easy to get engrossed with ideas and slogans and myths that in the end one is left holding the bag, empty, with no trace of meaning left in it." Merton saw too the enticement to simply pop the empty bag to make a noise: "the temptation is to yell louder than ever in order to make the meaning be there again by magic." But real meaning, he suggested, was heard not in the audible spectrum, but in the recesses of the heart and soul.

Although Merton hoped for a great deal, he was not an optimist. "All that you and I can ever hope for in terms of visible results is that we will have perhaps contributed *something* to a clarification of Christian truth in this society, and as a result a *few* people may have got straight about some things and opened up to the grace of God and made some sense out of their lives, helping a few more to do the same. As for big results, they are not in your hands or mine, but they can happen." This distinction between hope, which depends on faith and looks to the long run, and optimism, which depends on human agency and usually looks for immediate results, was essential to Merton's own activism.

In the final analysis, for Merton, only trust in God justified radical action. "The real hope, then, is not in something we think we can do, but in God who is making something good out of it in some way we cannot see. If we can do His will, we will be helping in this process. But we will not necessarily know all about it beforehand." For Merton and many others in the decade, the spirit of the Sixties was, in part, the Holy Spirit.[48]

Merton's advice reveals the importance of religious faith for many personalists. They did not *know*, and could not know, many things—if God existed, if people were perfectible (or even improvable), if justice was possible, if their actions meant anything or accomplished anything—and yet they acted *as if* the universe bends toward justice. To Merton, that action, and not mere belief in God, was faith. Like Robert Penn Warren, concluding *All the King's Men*, Merton saw people moving "out of history into history and the awful responsibility of time." He knew that it is an awful responsibility to make history without knowing exactly how it will turn out, and yet he expected people to do it every day.

For people without Merton's theology of hope, however, the crisis of confidence could be more consuming and cataclysmic. Without a rooted vision of the future—of human and eschatological possibilities—some radicals blew away in moods of disillusionment, cynicism, and despair. Others, however, looked for more effective political strategies, and "kept the faith," whether or not it was religious faith.

Students for a Democratic Society had always modeled itself on SNCC, and SDS leaders of the mid-Sixties were influenced by SNCC again. Like SNCC, SDS considered domestic initiatives more important than the antiwar effort. When SDS met in convention in June 1965, they decided not to focus on Vietnam, not so much because they misjudged the importance of the antiwar issue, but because they knew that Vietnam policy was just a small part of a impersonalist polity. Instead of mobilizing against the Vietnam War, SDS decided to focus on more fundamental changes like the Economic Research and Action Project that might prevent "the seventh war from now." Even before Watts, they committed themselves to work on issues of race and poverty in America's cities.

SDS leaders spoke at almost all of the antiwar rallies of the late Sixties and SDS chapters remained active on the nation's campuses. But, after the success of April 1965, national SDS generally avoided sponsorship of national antiwar actions. Both domestic and international issues led them to support the movement "from protest to resistance." That shift depended, as in SNCC's case, on assumptions about the audience for protest. Protest made sense if you assumed that politicians listened and learned from it. By 1967, it seemed to many activists that their representatives were deaf. "We have argued and demonstrated to stop this destruction," claimed a call for draft card burning. "We have not succeeded. Murderers do not respond to reason. Powerful resistance is now demanded: radical, illegal, unpleasant, sustained."[49]

Gradually, activists in and out of SDS came to believe that liberalism wasn't the solution to the problem, but the problem itself. Increasingly, there was an understanding of the war's systemic nature. Ban-the-bomb protesters like David Dellinger had come to see the Bomb not as an aberration of a benign American government, but as an essential part of a malevolent system. New Left activists came to see the war not as an aberration of American liberal policy, but as an integral part of the operation of a "military industrial complex." At a November 1965 march sponsored by SANE, SDS president Carl Oglesby listed the men from President Truman to President Johnson who had widened the Vietnam war. "They are not moral monsters," he said. "They are all honorable men. They are all liberals." Himself a liberal, Oglesby argued that there were two liberalisms—"one authentically humanist, the other not so human after all." This corporate liberalism made good men act like moral monsters and it alienated people like Oglesby. "Don't blame me" if I sound anti-American, said Oglesby. "Blame those who mouthed my liberal values and broke my American heart." Calling for a "humanist reformation," Oglesby, like A.J. Muste and Martin Luther King, argued, early on, that the protest over the war in Vietnam was only a part of a larger redefinition of American culture.[50]

As American planes bombed the North and American combat troops streamed into South Vietnam, antiwar activists increasingly cut their intellectual and institutional ties to liberalism. Liberals asked dissidents to work through the system, but most American personalists thought that the system itself structured the depersonalization of peoples. Increasingly, radicals presented a counter-*cultural* critique of the war which expanded the arena of conscientious objection from military service to everyday life. If the patterns of the culture caused the war, then cultural change—in addition to political change—could help end it. A counterculture could be—by its structure and values—an antiwar movement.[51]

SDS realized that ending the war wouldn't create the democratic society, but they also knew that the war provided a case study of the undemocratic society, an organizing issue for a broader campaign of political personalism. As the antiwar movement grew, SDS had to decide whether they should lead or follow it. Eventually, therefore, the broad personalist agenda of the early New Left gave way to a focus on the war in Vietnam and the goals of personalism almost disappeared in the means of protest.

At the same time that SNCC began to frame the urban ghettos as "internal colonies" of industrial capitalism, SDS and antiwar leaders increasingly adopted a Marxist interpretation of the war as a symptom of an imperialist, colonial structure. The Marxist critique offered many advantages to the movement leadership. It provided an integrated explanation for a number of different issues; it satisfied the highly organized Marxist minorities in the movement; and it suggested political strategies that were tried, if not necessarily true.[52]

Like SNCC, SDS also faced internal controversies over its personalist practice. Some members, like Paul Booth, Richard Flacks, Steve Max, and Dickie Magidoff thought that the un-organization was just disorganized. They wanted to create "permanent institutions to embody the movement." They also wanted to be effective in changing society. "SDS has to be more than just an outlet for personal frustrations," said Booth. "It has to have tangible effect on society." He argued for more structure, and for more functional responsibilities, so that SDS could accomplish its goals. Especially as the organization expanded, they argued that SDS needed standard operating procedures to help it serve its members well. The problem of scale, they argued, necessitated a shift from democracy to bureaucracy.[53]

Others, like "prairie populist" Jeff Shero, argued for the anarchistic voluntarism of participatory democracy, insisting that one of the goals of SDS was the development of new forms of democratic practice. Suspicious of elitism and bureaucracy, he argued for decentralized anarchist voluntarism. In the short term, he thought, efficiency might be a virtue. But did it compromise too much? "Explain to me," said a Texas critic of Paul Booth, "how you can change America at the same time you accept her methods." Shero and others thought that free-flowing anarchy *did* institutionalize the movement. They did not see how a movement committed to decentralization could succeed by centralizing itself, or how you could get to participatory democracy except by way of participatory democracy.[54]

Despite the chronic rifts in SDS and the antiwar movement, many activists decided that protest was insufficient to stop the killing in Vietnam and they began to develop resistance strategies. Instead of trying to reason the public out of positions that they hadn't been reasoned into, they decided to give the government more substantial reasons for stopping the war. They obstructed the operation of the draft, both by their own noncooperation and by blocking induction centers. At colleges and universities, they blocked recruiters for the Armed Forces and for companies like Dow Chemical, which manufactured napalm. Hoping to overload the system, they tried to create a situation in which it would be easier for the warmakers to do good.[55]

Although there had been individual and communal acts of resistance from the beginning of the war, the Resistance was a creation of 1967. At Kezar Stadium in San Francisco, former Stanford student body president David Harris announced a shift from a strategy of moral witness to more active obstruction of the war effort. "One's life is one's only political instrument," said David Harris. "We must therefore develop a whole new way of life—a new mentality. And we must do it not by talking about it or leafleting it but by living it." The Resistance, a coalition of more than seventy-five local anti-draft groups, encouraged absolute noncompliance with the draft, suggesting that people ought not to put their bodies on the front lines of the war. Building on the experience of the draft card burners, Resistance leaders suggested that students with deferments, and even conscientious objectors, should burn or turn in their draft cards. More than a thousand men turned in their cards on October 16, one of two Resistance demonstration days that included rallies, interfaith prayer services, marches, teach-ins, workshops, and draft counseling. The Resistance featured collective civil disobedience, which offered "the psychological comfort of fellowship," while emphasizing the moral significance of a sacrifice in opposition to a preferential system of conscription and classification. The point of the Resistance, said Marvin Garson, was "that if you need conscription to have an army, then you will need an army to have conscription. The moral of our play is that you cannot have imperialist war abroad and social peace at home."[56]

Although it often distinguished itself from the merely moral witness of personalist politics, the Resistance followed personalist precedents. Calling for active civil disobedience, the resistance strategy recalled Dwight Macdonald's "negativism," which he saw as the first step in social reconstruction. When Resistance leaders like David Harris called people to "act with the totality of our lives against the machines of the state," they echoed *Liberation*'s "Tract for the Times" and Mario Savio's claim that "when the operations of the machine become so odious . . . you've got to put your body on the gears and upon the wheels, upon the levers, upon all the apparatus, and you've got to make it stop." In many ways, the invitation to resistance was an invitation to the personalist politics that Muste and Dellinger had practiced for years. It extended the ethics of conscientious objection to civil disobedience; it said that people had a moral obligation not just to dissociate from a system of sin, but to keep it from its standard operating procedures. By announcing their intention to preserve their personhood by breaking the law, they offered an important critique of priorities in American culture. By the end of 1967, one person was convicted of draft violations for every 240 inducted.[57]

The shift from protest to resistance collectivized noncooperation in large demonstrations of personal defiance, but it also encouraged small-scale communal groups and conversations. "In Boston and Wisconsin especially, draft-counseling provided a vehicle for the original emphasis of the New Left." Local resistance groups often practiced "deprivatization," in which people "put [their] feelings out there on the table with [their] political actions and opinions." Resistance meetings sometimes resembled group therapy, as activists probed the complex cultural contradictions involved in their dissent, and, ultimately, in themselves. Like the consciousness-raising groups of women's liberation, these meetings allowed people to confirm their own experience and to validate personal acts of conscience.[58]

The Resistance to Lyndon Johnson's war also recalled the Resistance against Hitler. Inspired by the example of partisans like Bonhoeffer and Camus and by the decisions of the Nuremberg trials, some students tried to sabotage the workings of the American system. "When you said the word *resistance*," Bettina Aptheker recalled, "it was with a capital R, and you meant the resistance to fascism in Europe." Some students saw fascism in the Johnson Administration, and began to refer to America as "Amerika." Many also accused the United States of war crimes. Often, in protests, they focused on the bombing and on the B-52s, perhaps because of their connections to atomic bombing. In 1967, when Bertrand Russell convened War Crimes Tribunals in Stockholm and Copenhagen, activists like David Dellinger participated. And when Telford Taylor, U.S. prosecutor at the Nuremberg Trials, said on the Dick Cavett television show that policymakers like Walt Rostow and McGeorge Bundy could be convicted of war crimes, others began to consider the questions of complicity which Nuremberg raised.[59]

At some point, as many students engaged in resistance to the liberal warfare state, they also lost sight of the virtues of the persons who were liberal. They let persistent middle-class apathy overcome their own empathy for the middle class. When they lost sight of the virtues of the opposition, then it was possible to dehumanize and demonize people like Lyndon Johnson. When students chanted "Hey, hey, LBJ, how many kids did you kill today?" they cruelly attacked the President and alienated many supporters. But the chant was a species of personalist politics, of speaking truth to power. It focused attention on the most vulnerable victims of the war, the children and other civilians bombed and napalmed by American forces in Vietnam. It suggested, like the just war theory, that such deaths were unjustifiable. The chant also pointed out that the person of Lyndon Johnson had responsibilities that preceded his position as President. Like the Nuremberg principles, the chant made it clear that individuals are responsible for the actions of the state.

Late in the decade, Daniel and Phillip Berrigan carried resistance to the draft in a new direction. Both of these Catholic Protestants had been inspired by the political personalism of Catholic Workers like Peter Maurin and Dorothy Day and Thomas Merton. By 1967, the Berrigans had decided that the destruction of draft records could be justified in the context of the death and destruction in Vietnam. On October 27, Philip Berrigan and three friends entered a Baltimore draft board office and poured their own blood over the files. In the spirit of "this nation's Judaeo-Christian tradition," they offered their blood in expiation for the sins of their country and begged God's forgiveness for the blasphemy of Vietnam. Awaiting sentencing for their conviction for destroying government records and obstructing the Selective Service, Berrigan and Lewis joined with seven others—including Daniel Berrigan—in Catonsville, Maryland, to burn 1-A draft files with homemade napalm concocted according to a recipe in the Army Special Forces handbook. The first acts of the Catholic ultra-resistance, the draft board raids of the Baltimore Four and the Catonsville Nine sought to obstruct the operation of the Selective Service, and to dramatize, in liturgical fashion, the sacrifice of the innocents in Vietnam and America.[60]

These dramatic activities made the news, but in many ways the real news was the way in which the Berrigans' actions were interwoven with the rest of their lives in a personalist synthesis. Daniel took college teaching jobs on a semester-by-semester basis to maintain the freedom necessary to continue protesting and imprisonment. He refused to pay the phone tax surcharge which had been passed to pay for Vietnam. And he volunteered to work in a cancer hospital to show that peacemakers needed to affirm human life and dignity in other ways than their opposition to war. Philip grew disillusioned with the religious life and left to marry Elizabeth McAlister. Together, they lived at Jonah House, a resistance commune which tried to practice the care and cooperation that they envisioned for international relations. Like the Catholic Workers, members of Jonah House pooled their incomes and lived in voluntary poverty to distance themselves from an American prosperity dependent on American imperialism.[61]

From Resistance to Revolution

Some antiwar activists moved from resistance to revolution. Echoing the call of Black Power, and inspired in part by the riots that convulsed the nation's cities, they began to embrace Marxist interpretations of conflict and social change that excused violent revolution as a means to a nonviolent world. Ignoring the example of Gandhi, who had needed almost a lifetime to overthrow the colonial yoke, they claimed that the experience of five or six years showed that personalist politics was unrealistic and impractical. Protests and petitioning Congress seemed to have "*no* effect on U.S. policy." Consequently, they began to argue for resistance and revolution "by any means necessary" to impede the imperialist project.[62]

SDS was in the vanguard. By 1966, the organization operated largely in conformity to "new working-class theory" which adapted Marxism to describe students as the proletarian agents of "revolution, not reform." Rejecting the revolution of the heart that was the heart of political personalism, SDS National Secretary Greg Calvert told the *New York Times* in May 1967 that "we are working to build a guerilla force in an urban environment; we are actively organizing sedition." Identifying SDS with the legendary guerilla Che Guevara, Calvert scorned organizations like the National Conference for a New Politics that still worked within the system.[63]

At the October 1967 "Confronting the Warmakers" demonstration in Washington, a "Revolutionary Contingent" broke from the nonviolent march to attack the Pentagon. The following year, plans for protests at the Democratic National Convention promised opportunities for revolutionary action. As activists planned for demonstrations at the August 1968 Democratic convention in Chicago, some planned to provoke violence; others began to speak of the inevitability of violent revolution. As Dave Dellinger recalled, "Some of the now disillusioned leaders of the early New Left found it hard to move from protest to resistance without adopting some of the cynicism and *realpolitik* of the society we were resisting." Personalist assumptions about nonviolence and about the consistency of means and ends were sacrificed to feelings of anger and hopes of immediate results. Decoupled from nonviolence and ideas of redemptive sacrifice, personalist existentialism—the willingness to put one's body on the line—began to serve the ends of violence and polarization.[64]

The Chicago convention riots were, as Kirkpatrick Sale suggested, "the symbolic watershed for the end of the resistance period." By 1969, small groups like the Weathermen had formed to wage guerilla warfare against the powers that be. The October 1969 "Days of Rage" in Chicago drew a few hundred people to an orgy of street violence. The paradigm shift that accompanied this violence had significant consequences for the politics of personalism. As SDS increasingly accepted a standard Marxist interpretation of American society, they moved away from the personalist perspectives that had made them a "new" Left. Personalists had presumed that people were responsible for the structures they produced and reproduced. But the Marxist perspective emphasized structures so much that the people almost disappeared. Individuals were practically powerless, except insofar as they contributed as a class to the revolution of structures. Too, as antiwar activists shifted from protest to resistance, and from resistance to revolution, fewer and fewer Americans followed them. Public opinion showed that the movement was making progress, *and* that antiwar protesters remained very unpopular. More and more Americans were reconsidering their positions on Vietnam and many Americans participated in antiwar activities. Rejecting the radical shifts from protest to resistance to revolution, ordinary Americans increasingly accepted moral witness, individual nonviolent resistance, and collective democratic action.[65]

The Persistence of Personalism

Indeed, despite the language of resistance and revolution that seemed to supersede the personalist project, the politics of personalism still persisted in the antiwar movement. Although the media featured the revolutionary rhetoric of movement leaders, the language of personalism still motivated activists at the local level. Leaders trumpeted new directions in the late Sixties, but many local activists marched to their own drummers. As Maurice Isserman and Michael Kazin point out, "Students did not become activists because they joined SDS; they joined SDS because they were already activists." And the anarchic national office provided relatively little guidance for local groups, who shaped their own versions of radicalism.[66]

Indeed, it was often the case that new members of the SDS joined not because of their agreement with Marxism or radical rhetoric, but because of the moral reasoning that still informed much antiwar activity. Many histories of the New Left miss the personalist persistence in the movement because they focus on the careers of the older leaders of the New Left and not on the newer converts to Sixties activism. Writing in 1966, however, Jack Newfield recognized that a large proportion of SDS's membership still preferred more personal presumptions. He acknowledged that the Old Guard, the full-time ERAP organizers, and the "career-orientated liberal intellectuals" of the Eastern campuses constituted an SDS core. But he also noted that newer members tended to be either "patriotic Populists" or "hipster-anarchists."[67]

The patriotic Populists, the newest dimension to SDS, came from Midwestern and Western campuses which lacked the ideological infighting of the coastal enclaves. Idealists without an outlet in the Great Society, they were patriotic people disillusioned by the differences between American rhetoric and reality. "They are taught the Bill of Rights in History One," noted Newfield, "but then they see the Attorney General smear and investigate their own organization because it exercises the freedoms guaranteed by the Bill of Rights. They are taught that America stands for justice and law and order, yet they know that Andy Goodman's murderer is still a sheriff in Mississippi." Like the Old Guard at Port Huron, they felt betrayed by the impersonalism and hypocrisy of America. The anarchist-hipsters were countercultural types suspicious of centralized authority who tried to abolish SDS's leadership posts in favor of rotation and Quaker consensus. They were wary of leaders, a central office, the division of labor, bureaucracy, and formalist democracy. "Spiritual, if not philosophical, anarchists," they helped contribute to "the climate of individual respect and tolerance that permeate[d] SDS." Their "personal ethical code" also promoted SDS's pluralism and decentralism.[68]

Maurice Isserman has also emphasized the important differences between SDS leadership and membership, between the organized New Left and the student movement. He points out that individual chapters of SDS often followed an agenda substantially different than the national leadership. "At the base of SDS," he notes, "anarchist, pacifist, and 'small d' democratic ideas existed alongside the various forms of Maoist orthodoxy being promoted from the top." Isserman also shows that campus chapters often derived more support—in terms of speakers and ideas—from personalist organizations like the Fellowship of Reconciliation, the American Friends Service Committee, the Committee for Nonviolent Action, and the Catholic Worker than from SDS. While many leaders of the Movement went either far left or far out, many of the followers didn't go far from their roots at all. As befitted an "un-organization" like SDS, members sometimes followed their own consciences and preferences more than they followed the leaders. Many students remained interested in reform for religious and ethical reasons, and they responded to leaders who led them back to their convictions. Indeed, many of the conscientious objections of the students were nourished in the campus ministries of the country's campuses. Writing to Staughton Lynd, Tom Bell noted that protest "sessions in the student union are very much like revival services (even including some of the rhetoric at times). We have speeches, a collection for the anti-war office and on-the-spot conversions—signing pledges, plus a lot of personal witnesses." To some extent, SDS began to fracture when its leadership converted from the "second languages" of biblical and republican responsibility to the "foreign languages" of Marxism and Maoism.[69]

Through all the permutations of the antiwar movement, activists tried to keep attention focused on the persons who suffered from the war. Thus, it was a great success when the *Life* issue of June 27, 1969, brought a personalist perspective to the bodycount by showing the names and faces of the young Americans killed in a single week of the war. Over two hundred portraits of death appeared in *Life*; "It was almost unbearable," David Halberstam recalled. "It was an issue to make men and women cry." Because it personalized the victims (who were also executioners) of the war, because "almost nothing else . . . brought the pain home quite so fully," the story "probably had more impact on antiwar feeling than any other piece of print journalism."[70]

At the Moratorium march of November 1969, activists also acknowledged the personalist substructure of the antiwar effort. In a somber and dignified March Against Death, 42,000 people walked in single file, each carrying a candle and the name of a soldier killed in Vietnam. As they passed the White House, they called out the individual names of the dead and placed the namecards in a coffin; the funeral procession lasted forty hours. Such memorials, which were not uncommon in the antiwar protests, laid the groundwork for Maya Lin's personalist Vietnam War Memorial.[71]

Conclusion

Sixties radicals did not accomplish most of their utopian dreams during the decade. The antiwar movement took more than ten years to end the war in Vietnam. But as Maurice Isserman and Michael Kazin point out, "it is striking that while 'nothing' was accomplished by the New Left in its short life, everything was different afterward."[72]

During the 1960s, personalists animated the American antiwar movement. Until 1965, the main organizations protesting the war were the Catholic Worker, the War Resisters League, the Fellowship of Reconciliation, and Women Strike for Peace. After 1965, as the antiwar movement expanded, it depended heavily on A.J. Muste, David Dellinger, Staughton Lynd, and others who worked from the offices of 5 Beekman Street. From the individual moral witness of conscientious objection to the mass marches at the end of the decade, personalist perspectives were prominently featured. Only late in the decade, when some antiwar activists embraced strategies and tactics that violated the principled nonviolence of personalism, did the movement move far from the precedents established in the Catholic Worker movement, the civil rights movement, and the actions of the Committee for Nonviolent Action and Women Strike for Peace.

To a substantial degree, the antiwar movement succeeded—in creating structures for conscientious protest, in motivating people to make a mass movement, in creating a constituency for peace, in teaching the public about Vietnam and American foreign policy, in creating strategies that brought millions of people to oppose the war policy of their own government. It changed churches and moderate political organizations like SANE and Americans for Democratic Action. It changed the Democratic Party. The Movement also succeeded in slowing the escalation of the war, and—eventually—in exerting pressure to end it.

But success in the antiwar movement caused, to some extent, a failure of personalism. The negative peace of the antiwar effort detracted from the positive peace of the personalist polity. The negativism of the antiwar activists prevented the public from looking at the positive program of personalism. Ending the war in Vietnam did not offer a good vision of a society in which it would be easier to be good. It was not a revolution, not here and not now. Still, some people in the 1960s maintained the vision of a more comprehensive communitarian commonwealth, and it is to their story that we now turn.

8

COUNTERCULTURAL PERSONALISM

SOME SIXTIES PEOPLE OBJECTED conscientiously to the instrumental politics of protest, resistance and revolution, and "dropped out" to "live the revolution now." Especially after 1967, they made the political personal by establishing alternative institutions in the hinterlands and the cities of America. "We were setting up a new world," recalled Barry Melton, "that was going to run parallel to the old world but have as little to do with it as possible." In 1965, Herb Caen of the *San Francisco Chronicle* labeled these people "hippies," as if they were apprentice hipsters. The young insurgents called themselves "freaks" or "heads," and they called their "here and now revolution" a counterculture.[1]

Beginning in the Beat and bohemian enclaves of America's cities, the counterculture grew slowly until about 1967. In the early Sixties, these bohemians abandoned cultural expectations of marriage, career, and suburban affluence in favor of a Beat lifestyle of voluntary poverty, sexual freedom, personal expression, and heightened consciousness. Avant-garde art often united the communities, as these hipsters applied Beat perspectives to everyday life. After 1967, the counterculture mushroomed. Increasingly, alienated young people were drawn to the euphoric practices of freedom, while the Vietnam war, urban race riots, and confrontational politics—not to mention the cultural contradictions of everyday life—pushed them away from the spiritual poverty of American society.[2]

Interpretations of this counterculture have been almost as varied as the counterculture itself. The earliest accounts reveal as much about the values of the authors as about the values of the counterculture. With a few notable exceptions, interpretations have focused more on the colorful surfaces of the counterculture than on its heart and head. They reveal a great deal about sex and drugs and rock music, but not so much about the underlying values that led people to embrace these different cultural forms in the Sixties. Remembering the ephemera of the counterculture, they have too often forgotten the ethical core of its constructive criticism. In many of its permutations, the counterculture embodied personalist perspectives. Focusing on the inherent value of persons, and distancing themselves from an authoritarian state and a capitalist economy, people in the counterculture criticized the impersonal institutions of American society, and created communitarian enclaves that prefigured the social and political order they hoped for. Although some counterculturalists acted politically for social and structural change, many "turned on, tuned in, and dropped out" of the cultural mainstream. Dropping out and dropping acid, they dropped in to a variety of experiments with communitarian anarchism and the beloved community.[3]

The counterculture combined a comprehensive cultural critique with an eclectic collection of oppositional cultural institutions. The critique challenged American culture's dominant myths—the work ethic, utilitarian individualism, repressive sexuality, Cartesian rationality, technocratic scientism, denominational religion, industrial capitalism, lifestyle suburbanism, and compulsive consumerism—and offered intellectual and institutional alternatives. In doing so, countercultural critics created an ideological synthesis that Edward Purcell calls "communitarian subjectivism":

> This synthesis reflected three emerging articles of faith. The first was a belief that the human mind gave ultimate meaning to empirical phenomena and that it was capable, by reconceiving and renaming those phenomena, of thereby remaking them. . . . The second was a distinctive belief in human equality, one that proclaimed not merely a universal moral equality but also an individual creative equality. . . . The third element was a faith that communities could draw on the creativity of their members to collectively reconceive and thereby transform their world. . . . The distinctive synthesis of the sixties united collectivism with subjectivism and cohesion with transformation.[4]

The communitarian subjectivism of countercultural personalism was not the same as the personalism of Dorothy Day, Martin Luther King, David Dellinger, Mario Savio, or Tom Hayden, but it complemented their ideas and experience even as it added new elements to create a distinctively energetic fusion.

This chapter explores the personalist dimensions of that multifarious fusion. It begins with humanistic psychology, which offered an interpretation of persons that shaped countercultural assumptions. It explains the countercultural assault on rationality and the contours of an emerging epistemological radicalism. It shows how drugs and sex and rock music served as countercultural critique and practice, and it explains the divergent work ethics of culture and counterculture. Finally, it describes the spread of a personalist Digger ethic from the Summer of Love to national politics, and the diffusion of countercultural ideas in the communitarian personalism of the commune movement.

Personalist Psychology

Like previous personalists, the counterculture concerned itself with the personhood of people. The Catholic Workers cared for America's impoverished people. The Beats worried about persons driven mad. Civil rights activists focused on the "somebodiness" of the country's racial minorities. Women Strike for Peace protested primarily for America's children. All of them worried about the potential destructiveness of nuclear weapons and about a culture more concerned with abstractions than with people. The New Left inherited these concerns about the political and economic oppression of others, and extended them to questions about the cultural foundations of the political economy. The counterculture shared these inherited critical perspectives, but the persons they most hoped to preserve were themselves. Like Romantics, they saw themselves as potential victims of American culture. They thought that American institutions stunted the full development of human personhood, and they developed new forms for human growth and potential.[5]

Although the affluent society provided for people's material needs, the members of the counterculture felt that it also institutionalized alienation. Factories reduced human beings to a series of repetitive motions. With their specialization and division of function, bureaucracies substituted functionaries for people. Population movements in metropolitan America, reinforced by the mobility of dedicated careerists, meant the disintegration of urban neighborhoods and the splendid isolation of the suburban single-family home. Schools and sports reinforced the competitive individualism of the business culture. Judged by their contributions to the development of persons, America's institutions seemed grossly inadequate.[6]

In making judgments about human fulfillment, the counterculture depended on a concept of personhood more psychological than religious, more a rejoinder to the repressions of Freudianism than a response to Judeo-Christian concepts of creation and calling. Humanistic psychology or "client-centered" psychotherapy dated from the postwar period and came to fruition in the early 1960s. In 1954, Gordon Allport, Erich Fromm, Kurt Goldstein, Paul Goodman, Rollo May, Ashley Montagu, Lewis Mumford, David Riesman, Carl Rogers, Paul Tillich, and Abraham Maslow started a committee of correspondence that resulted in the 1961 *Journal of Humanistic Psychology* and the 1962 Association for Humanistic Psychology.[7]

Humanistic psychology's organizing principle was the person, and part of its agenda was to show, in the wake of World War II, the goodness and the possibilities of human nature. At a time when many social critics warned against utopian notions of human perfectibility, these psychologists hoped to demonstrate that people had the capacity for trusting intimacy, for self-government, and for productive participation in democratic politics. Rogers, Maslow, May, Allport, and others emphasized the epistemological importance of personal experience, and the ethical and social importance of personal choice. Countering the scientific objectivism of the Fifties, Rogers contended that people must understand their own needs and experiences, and give other people the space needed to grow as persons. They all suggested that psychological health had a social dimension.[8]

Unlike Freudianism, which focused on people's problems, and behaviorism, which focused on people's overt actions, humanistic psychology focused on people as persons with potential for health, wholeness, and even holiness. Humanistic psychology was "a loose confederation of therapies linked by a common set of assumptions: that it was time to ask what made people healthy, not what made them sick; that it was time to recognize that treating the body was almost as important as treating the mind; that such things as vitalizing transactions really happened." Abraham Maslow's "hierarchy of needs" rooted personal growth in caring community and suggested that as people found their needs met in community, they became increasingly able to serve the community as well. As people fulfilled their basic requirements for food and drink, for clothing and shelter, for love and friendship and self-esteem, they became capable of "self-actualization," which included altruism. The arc of human growth, Maslow thought, tended toward compassion and community.[9]

This humanistic approach to human development offered a lever for social criticism, because it emphasized the social construction of norms and conventions, and promoted the radical idea that institutions should promote the fulfillment of whole persons. Instead of making society the arbiter of mental health, this approach emphasized the arbitrary quality of social expectations. When society did not meet the needs of its citizens, they might need to rebel. If society did not meet the material needs of the poor, then people should exert pressure to change society. If cultural conformity repressed human development, then nonconformity could be a psychologically (and socially) healthy alternative. Abbie Hoffman, who studied psychology with Maslow at Brandeis University, liked Maslow's idea that "you have a need to do good," and claimed that Maslovian theory underlay the optimism of the sixties: "Existential, altruistic, and up-beat, his teachings became my personal code."[10]

For some people, humanistic psychology became a secular counterpart of religious personalism. In 1965, for example, Hoffman discussed Maslow's theory of self-actualization with a group of activists at a Catholic Worker-inspired roundtable; he called his talk "Morality for the Nonreligious." In Hoffman's hands, the "triumph of the therapeutic" meant not the personal promise of peace of mind, but the promise of a politics designed to alter the institutions that conditioned Americans' consciousness. For Hoffman and the counterculture, humanistic psychology led not to adjustment and complacency, but to the reconstruction of society.[11]

In exploring the characteristics of healthy, self-actualized individuals, Maslow himself began to take an interest in "peak experiences." His research suggested that self-actualized people often experienced "transcendent moments of great joy, serenity, beauty, and wonder." He began to explore mysticism and Eastern religions. He was not alone. At Harvard, after a 1960 drug-induced experience of cosmic consciousness, a psychology professor named Timothy Leary began to experiment with psilocybin to see if it could induce peak experiences in predictable ways. Leary hoped that drugs like psilocybin could provide people with what Aldous Huxley called "beatific glimpses . . . of enlightening and liberating grace" that might make it easier for people to be good. Cutting through the game structure of Western life, a drug-induced *satori* could perhaps offer higher consciousness and cosmic communitarianism.[12]

Within the scientific and therapeutic community, drugs like psilocybin were understood in a paradigm in which the therapy went to individuals. They were merely a useful tool for helping individual patients confront subconscious realities. Within the countercultural community, however, drugs were seen as tools for helping people confront destructive social constructions: they served individuals who were expected to serve others. Psychologists like Timothy Leary suggested that individual therapy could lead to social transformation.[13]

The personalism of humanistic psychology inspired the counterculture. Like the Gestalt psychology of Paul Goodman, the psychology of Maslow and Rogers integrated individual and social perspectives, the personal and the political. With its emphasis on self-knowledge, personal transformation, and the social self, it gave the counterculture a lever for cultural criticism and a trajectory for individual and social change. With the social thought of the Catholic Workers, the anarcho-pacifism of the Beats and *Liberation*, the African American Social Gospel of the civil rights movement, and the existential humanism of the New Left, humanistic psychology shaped the Sixties dynamic of politics and personhood.[14]

The Rationality of Irrationality

Humanistic psychology's challenge to conventional definitions of psychological health and wholeness coincided with a broader challenge to the irrationality of rationality in America. Critics claimed that an exaggerated emphasis on rationality in American life created individuals and institutions that were not fully human. The "myth of objective consciousness," as Theodore Roszak called it, had built up America's brains at the expense of its heart and soul. The counterculture reacted against this "demystification of the world," and its adherents often embraced mysteries and mysticisms that spoke to deeper human yearnings. To some extent, the counterculture practiced an epistemological politics, arguing that American ways of knowing conditioned American social and political patterns, and contending that epistemological alternatives offered healthier possibilities for social and political culture. Emphasizing the in-knowing of intuition and spiritualism over the objective knowing of scientific empiricism, this epistemological radicalism emphasized the intrinsic authority of persons more than the positional authority of experts. "The *first* revolution (but not of course the last) is in yr own head," asserted Beat poet Tuli Kupferberg (one of the Fugs). "Dump out *their* irrational goals, desires, morality." Like Kupferberg, the counterculture preached a new mindfulness, a conscientious reconsideration of the rational.[15]

This reconsideration of the rational led many members of the counterculture to a reconsideration of religion. Because institutional religion often rationalized the aims and assumptions of American culture, many members of the counterculture turned to Eastern religions and philosophies for enlightenment. In their own versions of Eastern traditions, they explored the inner world, the subjective self, and spirituality instead of the outer world, the presentation of self, and religiosity. They came to appreciate human "being," instead of the compulsive "doing" of an activist American culture. They often experienced a mystical sense of cosmic belonging that had not been encouraged in a culture that encouraged distancing from and domination of nature.[16]

Many counterculturalists also explored the roots of Christianity, and reinterpreted the religion that they had learned in church. After exploring Eastern religions, and especially Buddhism, Stephen Gaskin realized "that the Sermon on the Mount was tripping instructions for tripping a life trip." He and several hundred others established a commune based on the Acts of the Apostles: "And all that believed were together, and had all things in common; and sold their possessions and goods, and parted them to all men, as every man had need." Sharing possessions, Gaskin and The Farm enacted a communitarian social gospel that seemed faithful to them. "That's the way religion is," Gaskin said. "If religion is compassionate and it excludes nobody and if it doesn't cost money and if it really helps you out in the here and now, that's how you can tell religion—real religion." Real religion, he thought, governed all of life, with a consistency of means and ends. Discovering the latent radicalism of "real religion," some counterculturalists also rediscovered the potent radicalism of Christ. During the late Sixties, Jesus often appeared on posters: "Wanted," they said. "Jesus Christ. Alias: The Messiah, The Son of God, King of Kings, Lord of Lords, Prince of Peace, etc. Notorious leader of underground liberation movement." Wanted for selling food without a license, disturbing the peace of the temple, associating with street people and radicals, and undermining authority, this infamous outlaw was the "typical hippie type—long hair, beard, robe, sandals."[17]

The reconsideration of rationality and religion coincided with a revaluation of nature. Arguing that technocratic culture objectified nature, counterculturalists began look for new, and often personal, relationships with nature. Instead of seeing the creation as a natural resource, members of the counterculture emphasized nature as a personal resource. Countercultural holism also encouraged animist or pantheistic approaches to the creation. By the end of the decade, it also led to Earth Day, celebrated festively in April of 1970.[18]

During the Sixties, drugs reinforced these countercultural critiques of rationality, religion, and nature because they provided an escape from the objective consciousness of the brain and the conditioning of the culture. They seemed to bring to mind the Edenic state of nature before the snake of socialization, and they offered visions of utopia. Aldous Huxley, Timothy Leary, and Allen Ginsberg dared to think that drugs could transform the world. After a psilocybin experiment with Leary early in the Sixties, Allen Ginsberg claimed that "wisdom drugs" were causing people to see "that the Kingdom of God is within them, instead of thinking it's outside, up in the sky and that it can't be here on earth." Leary thought that they were part of "a historical movement that would inevitably change man at the very center of his nature, his consciousness."[19]

Drugs were at the heart of the counterculture's epistemological politics and the production, distribution, and consumption of drugs shaped the psychology, economy, social structure, and cultural consciousness of alternative communities. Drugs countered the work ethic of American culture and offered the pleasures of peak experiences to those who dared to experiment with them. And drugs like marijuana, LSD, and methedrine promised to break down the barricades of repressive consciousness. The consciousness-razing of the drugs opened people to the consciousness-raising possibilities of personalist politics.[20]

Marijuana was the most widespread "wisdom drug," but LSD was more potent. It desocialized people, undermining their social and perceptual conditioning, so that cultural conventions seemed purely arbitrary. At the same time, LSD offered a euphoric experience that intimated the unity of all life. LSD was the countercultural sacrament, the ritual communion for an evolving consciousness and community. It was science in the service of religion. Like the mystical states of religious experience, LSD pointed to the holistic consciousness that would replace the analytical divisions of objective consciousness and the competitive individualism of American capitalism. People who dropped acid returned to "the real world" with an altered sense of reality.[21]

At Harvard, Timothy Leary experimented with LSD and discovered that, with a proper setting, the drug could reveal powers of the mind that remained latent to the culturally conditioned consciousness. But Leary was no mere scientist. Expelled from Harvard in 1963, he took up residence at a New York estate called Millbrook, where he advertised the possibilities of better living through chemistry. In 1966, Leary founded the League for Spiritual Discovery, a semireligious social movement for consciousness-raising and social change. Novelist Ken Kesey also joined the priesthood preaching the virtues of LSD. Kesey first sampled LSD in the late Fifties at a Veterans Administration hospital as part of a scientific study. Soon he was working at the hospital as a psychiatric aide and typing sketches of hospital life. His 1962 novel, *One Flew Over the Cuckoo's Nest*, made him famous, and gave him enough money to play with people and psychedelics. By 1964, Kesey and a group of cultural tricksters (including Neal Cassady) called the Merry Pranksters were using acid to burn the cultural conditioning from their brains. In 1964, they bought a 1939 International Harvester Bus and drove cross-country from California to New York. In the fall of 1965, they began their "acid tests," a liturgy of LSD with strobe lights, costumed communicants, and music by the Grateful Dead. By January of 1966, the acid test became the Trips festival, organized by Kesey, Stewart Brand, and publicist Jerry Mander. It included music, poetry, multimedia presentations on five movie screens, strobe lights, and the phantasmagoria of ten thousand participants—some in costume—who created a synergy of the surreal.[22]

When LSD was criminalized in California in 1966, Haight-Ashbury's Psychedelic Rangers proclaimed "A Prophecy of a Declaration of Independence":

> When in the flow of human events it becomes necessary for the people to cease to recognize the obsolete social patterns which have isolated man from his consciousness and to create with the youthful energies of the world revolutionary communities of harmonious relations to which the two-billion-year-old life process entitles them, a decent respect to the opinions of mankind should declare the causes which impel them to this creation. We hold these experiences to be self-evident, that all is equal, that the creation endows us with certain inalienable rights, that among these are: the freedom of body, the pursuit of joy, and the expansion of consciousness, and that to secure these rights, we the citizens of the Earth declare our love and compassion for all conflicting hate-carrying men and women of the world. We declare the identity of flesh and consciousness; all reason and law must respect and protect this holy identity.[23]

By 1967 thousands of young people all over the country were doing drugs in defiance of mainstream America. Many followed Timothy Leary's advice to "turn on, tune in, and drop out." "Turning on" invited people to come alive, to live their lives to the fullest. Like Thoreau, they wanted "to live deep and suck out the marrow of life"; they lusted for the intensity and spontaneity of the Beats, the peak experiences of humanistic psychology, and the pleasures of sex and intimacy. They wanted more happiness than the standard pursuits of middle-class life allowed. And if drugs would turn you on, then these passionate people would turn on to drugs.

Tuning in meant, among other things, tuning to FM radio, which was relatively new in the Sixties. The FM radio band, as much as any other band of the decade, brought the Sixties generation together. On FM, people heard what AM radio wouldn't play: albums and long tracks, bands too different to make the charts, songs too controversial to pass the AM censors, and music too political for the programming of commercial radio. Tuning in to progressive radio was a part of the Sixties experience. But the tuning devices of the young went beyond their radios. Tuning in also meant tuning in to the ideas that were circulating in the new America. It meant reading fiction like Salinger and Heller and Vonnegut. It meant discussing the social criticism of Goodman and Marcuse and Reich and Roszak. It meant studying the ancient scriptures of Eastern religions, the pseudo-scriptures of Carlos Castaneda, and the newer scripts of the underground press. It meant lectures in the universities and classes in the free universities. It meant movies like "The Graduate," "A Thousand Clowns," "The King of Hearts," "Easy Rider." It meant rap sessions and rock concerts. Tuning in also included the reception of cosmic frequencies by meditation and mystical experiences. Drugs were not the only path to the more ethereal frequencies that transcended the day-to-day experience of American life.[24]

Dropping out was the countercultural metaphor of resistance to a culture that believed in moving up, moving on, and getting ahead. Identifying with the down-and-out, the drop-outs rejected the apparent insanity of mainstream culture by choosing poverty, play, passion, and cooperation. Unlike the sit-in and the teach-in, which occupied the public spaces of mainstream America, the drop-out emptied the public square. Moving down-and-out, as the metaphor suggested, meant a radical disaffiliation with the up-and-coming "progress" of the mainstream. Although there was an element of escapism to this disengagement, this "great refusal" had political implications. Like draft dodgers and deserters, the drop-outs undermined institutions by refusing to perform the roles expected of them. Escaping the culture meant escaping complicity with structural injustice. And freeing themselves from the institutional grasp of the culture seemed a prerequisite to the construction of alternative institutions. Like Yossarian, the main character of Joseph Heller's popular *Catch-22*, they said, in effect, "I'm not running away from my responsibilities. I'm running to them."[25]

Despite the positive effects of drugs for many young protesters, the drug experience heightened mainstream awareness and fear of the counterculture. Despite their own taste for alcohol and tobacco, and for amphetamines and sedatives, most American adults looked with horror on the pharmacological and sociological effects of drugs like marijuana and LSD. After LSD became illegal, hippies increasingly experienced drug raids and arrests that transformed their cultural difference into cultural politics.[26]

The Musical Beat

Young people constructed their counterculture to music, marching to the beat of different drummers and guitarists, who, in turn, marched to the beat of different audience expectations. "We play rock and roll because . . . it's the church music of us kind of folks," said The Farm's Stephen Gaskin. "Rock and roll is one of the mystic arts of communion." Like LSD and marijuana, rock music unified young people. The shared sound offered interpretations of reality that affirmed their personal experience and brought them into community.[27]

Rock was a music that grew at the intersection of the youth culture and the counterculture. Especially after 1955, promoters marketed rock to a booming youth market. But promoters could not control the meanings of rock 'n' roll for its audience. At first, as with folk music, the radicalism of rock was in its associations. Rock's fusion of rhythm and blues, gospel and soul associated it indissolubly with the African American tradition. Rock and roll was musical multiculturalism, with many people's lyrics laid over a foundation of black rhythm and blues. Its covers and crossovers allowed people to feel the beats of different cultures and to extend their own experience. The wide popularity of the Motown and Muscle Shoals sounds, and of African American artists, bespoke an appreciation for difference that had been anathema in the containment culture of the Fifties.[28]

To some extent, rock's radicalism was lyrical and the music carried an implicit association with radical critics of the Fifties and Sixties. Lyrics tended to be culture critical—reinforcing feelings of alienation and the impersonality of the system—and countercultural, promoting the politics of pleasure. Like Beat poetry, they promoted individual freedom and social disaffiliation as solutions to the problem of crafting a good life within the confines of the old society. Unlike folk music, however, rock's main emphasis was not verbal but primitive and preverbal. According to Chester Anderson, rock "engages the entire sensorium, appealing to the intelligence with no interference from the intellect." Like drugs (and with drugs), rock promoted both subjective consciousness and community. Acid rock especially attempted to heighten the drug experience. Using feedback and psychedelic effects, bands like Jefferson Airplane and the Grateful Dead tried to mimic the music of mysticism.[29]

While folk music tended toward the cerebral and the heart, the 4/4 rhythm of rock tended to the kinetic—it was music that made people feel like dancing. Because of the loud amplification and the energy of its rhythms, rock was not generally a music of coffeehouses. Instead, it became a music of auditoriums, dance halls, and the outdoors. "Rock," said John Sinclair, "is the music of RIGHT NOW, every minute, pounding and screaming at your head, twisting inside your belly, pulling you up off your ass to GIVE IT UP and let energy flow through your cells and into the air so you can be FREE again." Unlike folk music, which encouraged the mind to place the body where it counted politically, rock encouraged the countercultural body to blow off the mind and practice the politics of the here and now.[30]

But rock was also the music of home, the stuff that stereos were made for. Played in all the major venues of countercultural life, rock music expressed the ethics of the counterculture. "In its energy, its lyrics, its advocacy of frustrated joys, rock is one long symphony of protest," reported *Time* in 1969. "Although many adults generally find it hard to believe, the revolution it preaches, implicitly or explicitly, is basically moral; it is the proclamation of a new set of values as much as it is the rejection of an old system." But rock lyrics didn't need to be political for rock to be subversive. "Shit," said one hippie, "if the revolution is not about our own lives and getting high and smashing the state and getting in touch with ourselves and each other, then it ain't no revolution."[31]

Music provided a setting for words of protest, but rock festivals provided a setting for the music. At a festival, with thousands of people turned on by the music (and by drugs), words of protest were secondary to worlds of experience. As George Lipsitz suggests, "the ritualized sharing of public space with like-minded 'brothers and sisters' remained at the core of the experience." People danced and took drugs and made love in ways that suggested a cultural community. In some instances, be-ins and rock festivals approximated "peak experiences." More than any other single event of the counterculture, "The Woodstock Music and Art Fair: An Aquarian Exposition," offered a premonition of the counterculture's cooperative commonwealth. A three-day commercial venture, Woodstock invited young people to spend $18 to hear musicians like Jimi Hendrix, Janis Joplin, Joan Baez, Arlo Guthrie, The Grateful Dead, Jefferson Airplane, Creedence Clearwater Revival, Country Joe and the Fish, Ten Years After, Canned Heat, and Crosby, Stills, Nash and Young. Four hundred thousand people accepted the invitation, overwhelming local authorities and creating, for a few days, a culture and a (self-)government of their own. "We're going to need each other to help each other work this out," implored the loudspeakers before the concert. "The one major thing you have to remember tonight is that the man next to you is your brother."[32]

While Woodstock itself was hardly an example of a long-term anarchist alternative—there were shortages of food, water, toilets, medical supplies, and dry clothes—it suggested the numbers attracted to the counterculture. The sense of community that grew in the mud of Max Yasgur's farm seemed a potent possibility. "Woodstock is the great example of how it is going to be in the future," wrote Timothy Leary. "We have the numbers. The loving and peaceful are the majority. The violent and authoritarian are the minority. We are winning. And soon."[33]

To Work and to Love

In the meantime, young people growing up in America confronted cultural expectations of work and love. Parents and other adults told them that they should get an education, get a job, marry, and settle down to raise a family. By the mid-Sixties, however, young people questioned the cultural presumptions and patterns that dictated such a path for persons. In both word and deed, they began to articulate new visions and versions of work and love.

The counterculture, like the New Left, rejected the "labor metaphysic" of the Old Left, but they maintained an interest in work and workers. Counterculturalists challenged the modern work ethic, because work had become impersonal, instrumental, and alienating. They criticized a system based on compulsory work compensated by compulsive consumption. During the course of the twentieth century, America's workers and employers had embraced the "Great Compromise," whereby laborers, in effect, agreed to do meaningless work for high wages that could purchase private satisfactions. This system of deferred gratification was good for the economy because it created an alternating current of production and consumption. In postwar American culture, the work ethic had been complemented by a fun morality. On payday, the payoff was leisure, the socially constructed consumption of "free time" in hobbies, sports, and relaxation. After the work week came the weekend, the paradise of private pleasures. And as compensation for fifty weeks of labor, there was two weeks of vacation.[34]

In mainstream American culture, utilitarian individualism combined with the work ethic to create a culture of competition. Individuals (especially men) in search of social mobility competed with each other for the scarce rewards of alienating work. Sports and education taught people that competition was natural and inevitable. Rewarding the winners, society stigmatized the losers. At the same time, the American work ethic complicated issues of identity for America's young people, who found that, in mainstream America, you are what you do.[35]

This system of alternating work-and-leisure also seemed suspect to many Sixties activists. In their own variation of "the here and now revolution," the hippies asked, "Why wait? Why not take pleasure in the here and now?" The pleasures of American middle-class adulthood seemed tepid to many hippies, who wanted more intensity and passion in their pleasures. Arguing that gratification deferred was too often gratification deterred, the counterculture celebrated the centrality of play, which is not the same as leisure. Immediate and enjoyable, superfluous and unnecessary, playfulness (literally) undermined the dichotomies of the work ethic. For the "Now" generation, the pleasures of the present took precedence over the promises of the future.[36]

This politics of pleasure, which played almost no role in the partisan politics of the decade, pitted the hippie pursuit of happiness against the so-called "Puritan" practices of the mainstream culture. Counterculturalists assumed that genuine affluence could transform an American culture still premised on scarcity by allowing people to work less and live more fully. While mainstream culture assumed that affluence would allow more consumption, however, the counterculture doubted that fulfillment could come from increased consumption. They challenged the materialism that materialized as people spent their wages. Hippies were willing to exchange the American affluence of people who owned much for the Zen affluence of people who wanted little. Rejecting the suburban ideal of a people of plenty, they expected to be fulfilled in lives of voluntary simplicity. In an age of affluence, hippies thought, people didn't need to work for money; they needed to work for community, for personal fulfillment, for reconciliation with the Earth. In recounting the history of the Farm commune, Stephen Gaskin referred to the group's work as "right vocation": "We feel that work is the material expression of love, and that love is not an abstract idea or something for a bumper sticker, but that if you really do love somebody you could find it in your heart to get off your tail for them."[37]

At its best, the countercultural critique of the work ethic resulted in good work. Like earlier antimodern reformers, many counterculturalists turned to the arts and crafts for models of fulfilling labor. Working in the tradition of John Ruskin and William Morris (even when they didn't know it), they counterpoised the personalism of a handicraft society to the impersonality of the manufacturing (and manufactured) world. They emphasized home production of necessities and of the artifacts that made life beautiful. Unlike their parents, who lived in prefabricated housing and gloried in the products of the department store and the supermarket, the young dissidents preferred to craft their own clothes and meals. At its worst, however, the countercultural criticism of work led to the abandonment of both the work ethic and an ethic of service. Like the amiable beatnik Maynard G. Krebs in "The Many Loves of Dobie Gillis," some counterculturalists avoided both work and its intrinsic satisfactions. Living lives of comparative leisure, they found that the conventions of leisure in American society—formed, as they were, as a counterpoint to alienating work—were not sustainably satisfying either. In the long run, "the hippies nonexistent work habits" undermined many of their utopian ideals.[38]

The counterculture also challenged the conventions of American middle-class sexuality—gender difference, deferred gratification, the double standard, monogamous marriage, and (eventually) compulsory heterosexuality. Several social trends set the stage for a reconsideration of the family and sexuality. From the 1920s on, media managers and advertisers increasingly sexualized American culture, integrating images of sex and consumption. Both men and women spent more time in school, and more women were entering the workforce. The Pill premiered in 1960. The sexual revolution of the Sixties was deeply rooted in the sexual evolution of the twentieth century.[39]

The counterculture criticized modern American marriage for restricting both individuals and community. In America, they claimed, monogamous marriage unnecessarily confined the expressive sexuality of individuals.

People with a capacity to love many other persons were restricted to a single life-long mate. Too, the privacy of the nuclear family countered personalist presumptions about the public dimensions of private life. Because it restricted erotic sexual expression to a single person, because it narrowed the care and concern for persons to the nuclear family, monogamous marriage could undercut the possibility of the beloved community. Like Kenneth Rexroth, many counterculturalists hoped for more encompassing love relationships, combining personal friendship (*philia*), sexual love (*eros*), Christian love (*agape*), and universal compassion (*caritas*).[40]

For this reason, the counterculture questioned the conventions of romantic love, the sentimental assumption that "you were made for me," and both of us were made for a life of monogamy and privatized domesticity. Berkeley's Free University, for example, offered a course on "American Romantic Mythology." Exposing "the bullshit of romantic love handed down to American youth by the culture in expectation of their achieving mature and relevant relationships," the course promised discussion of "enlightened alternatives." One of the enlightened alternatives was simply "living together." In these cases, sex was simply a part of a relationship of equal partners and the relationship was defended not so much in terms of free love or pleasure as in terms of honesty, commitment, and family. At colleges, one enlightened alternative was coed housing; one University of Kansas sophomore contended that coed dorms would allow men and women "to meet and interact with one another in a situation relatively free of sexual overtones . . . as human beings, rather than having to play the traditional stereotyped male and female roles."[41]

Many hippies argued that love—and sexual love—could be more deeply felt and widely shared. They saw intercourse as a potential "peak experience," an intense fusion of passion and compassion. Sometimes they combined sex and drugs to make the experience even more intense. Within an ethic of care, too, people might make love with more people than a single mate. Some people experimented with "open marriage," but for all of the talk of sexual revolution, actual practice changed less in the Sixties than in the Seventies. A few communes experimented with sexual freedom and liberation, but most promoted various forms of partnership, with at least serial monogamy.[42]

Members of the counterculture also challenged the gender roles that underlay romantic conventions and the American nuclear family. They contended that the "natural" roles of women and men in the American cult of domesticity were less natural than cultural, and that men and women could both be more fully human if they shared, rather than divided, the attributes of human personality. Countercultural men, especially, embraced a gentle style that separated them from the masculinist militarism of the mainstream culture. Men wore their hair long, and men and women adopted similar styles of dress, leading critics to decry the loss of the sign systems that marked gender differences.

To some extent, the counterculture reflected the efflorescence of family values. Hippies often looked to the family and to spiritual traditions for resources to counter the utilitarian ethos of a business civilization that depersonalized both workers and consumers. Unlike contemporary conservatives, who only want family values in the family, the counterculture wanted to apply these values (care and cooperation, wholeness and personal attention) to the society at large. Indeed, communards often used a language of family to describe their utopian experiments. Conferring the honorific titles of "brother" and "sister" on each other, they tried to create the interpersonal harmony of an extended family in many of their relationships.

The Summer of Love

Many of these perspectives and practices came together in 1967 in the much-vaunted San Francisco "Summer of Love." The Freedom Summer of 1964 focused the ideas and institutions of the radical civil rights movement; the Summer of Love was a second freedom summer, but it demanded freedom, not just for African Americans, but for all Americans who had been caught in the gears of American society. The vortex of the Summer of Love was Haight-Ashbury, a San Francisco neighborhood bordering Golden Gate Park. Because of its low rents, the Haight had become an attraction for many young people. Between 1965 and 1967, they developed a distinctive American subculture in the district, and they advertised it to America. Hippies converted old Victorian homes to residential collectives and the streets to a full-time festival. The Summer of Love was institutionalized in a communitarian collectivism that infused the atmosphere of the street. "Everything was pooled—money, food, drugs, living arrangements," recalled Jay Stevens. "The underlying ethic was that the hippies were all members of an extended family, although the preferred word was *the tribe*." The businesses of Haight Street operated not just for profit, but for the community. The Psychedelic Shop offered books and records and magazines, and functioned as a reading center and meeting place; it eventually expanded to include a meditation room. Dr. David Smith started a Free Clinic that operated continuously; it included a Calm Center to allow drug trippers to return from their pilgrimages.[43]

The hippies of the Haight differentiated themselves from mainstream culture by their drugs and music, but also by their hair and dress and decorum[Like civil rights workers who put their bodies on the line, countercultural activists drew a line with their bodies]When men let their hair grow beyond the regimented haircut, their long hair—sometimes called "the freak flag"—symbolized countercultural identity and defiance of the culture of conformity. African Americans quit straightening their hair and celebrated the kinks of an Afro. Women, too, adopted more "natural" styles, replacing bouffant and flip hairstyles with long tresses or kinky curls. They stopped making up with cosmetics, and they freed themselves from bras and girdles. Countercultural dress also provided a sign of ideological orientation, both in the democracy of denim and in the expressiveness of color. Hippie women shed the skirts and sweaters of American adolescence first for the earth tones of work clothes like jeans and sweatshirts, and later for colorful ethnic and psychedelic costumes. Rejecting the gray flannel suit, men also dressed down, wearing jeans and bell bottoms, tunics and dashikis. Freeing themselves from the fashion world, many wore hand-me-downs and Army surplus which they patched with pride. Men and women adorned themselves with flowers and with crafted beads and colorful baubles. These long-haired hippies in their unconventional dress also acted different. Often, they occupied themselves not with the serious work of school or job, but with childish play. They carried balloons and blew bubbles; they played guitars and sang songs; they chalked sidewalks and painted faces. By appearance and behavior, they declared themselves actors (and sometimes activists) in a new cultural drama.[44]

Residents of the Haight celebrated the community in festivals like the Trips Festival, the Love Pageant Rally, and Now Day. The success of the September 1966 Love Pageant especially inspired planning for an even bigger "gathering of the tribes," scheduled for January 1967. Reminiscent of Peter Maurin, a press release for "The Human Be-in" began by noting that "for ten years a new nation has grown within the robot flesh of the old. Before your living eyes a new free vital soul is reconnecting the living centers of the American body." The press release promised a union of "Berkeley political activists and the love generation." An accompanying article promoted the PowWow and Peace Dance that would signify "the humanization of the American man and woman," a gathering "so that a revolution of form can be filled with a Renaissance of compassion, awareness, and love in the Revelation of the unity of all mankind." "The Human Be-In," it concluded, "is the joyful, face-to-face beginning of the new epoch."[45]

The Diggers were among the people who established this underlying ethic and held the Haight together. Acting within a tradition of personalist service, they highlighted the anarchist politics that characterized the counterculture. The Diggers, for example, were often called the worker-priests of the counterculture. They claimed that "you don't say love you do it," and they did it in the streets, in the road, in the park, and in the neighborhood. They declared "the death of money and the birth of the free," and they invented oppositional institutions that helped people live outside the money economy. Named for the seventeenth-century British rebels who believed literally in the commonwealth of the land, they hoped to create a moneyless economy by recycling society's surplus goods. The Diggers made visible the "invisible complexity" of capitalism in the United States and offered an alternative vision of the cooperative commonwealth. Because capitalism encouraged greed, they considered it "dangerous to the soul . . . dehumanizing . . . hostile to freedom." In a society devoted to the dollar, the Diggers claimed that "moneylust is sickness. It kills perception. Everyone is entitled to make a living, a good living, but everything more than a living is dying." They gleaned food from restaurants and groceries and distributed it free for a year in Golden Gate Park. They collected clothes for a "free store" stocked sometimes with "liberated goods." They gave away marijuana. Their Communications Company—Beat poets Michael McClure and Lenore Kandel, novelist Richard Brautigan, as well as Peter Berg and Emmett Grogan—provided a free news service for the community. They sponsored plays and concerts and potluck meals and listed the price as "$0.00." They talked the Grateful Dead into a free concert in Golden Gate Park. They imagined schemes for free housing, free garages, and an economy of bartering and sharing. Sometimes, like Robin Hood, they tried to convert private property into public property. Like other personalists, they thought that this "service towards a new society in the making" was more political than politics.[46]

The Diggers also practiced a street theater that mocked the everyday dramas of American life. Both Peter Berg and Emmett Grogan had connections to the San Francisco Mime Troupe, and both were inspired by the paradigm dramas of Pop Art and Happenings. The Diggers constructed a twelve-foot "Free Frame of Reference" and invited people to walk through it to remind themselves of the social construction of consciousness and reality. They also considered it a frame for the art of their lives. They butchered a horse at San Quentin, as the people of California executed a human being. They creatively disrupted the social institutions that they described as "hierarchies boxed and frozen for coordinating programmed corpses."[47]

Like the Diggers, the San Francisco Mime Troupe played often in the park near the Haight, with a variety of entertainments. When John Conway of the San Francisco Park Commission saw the troupe, he claimed that they were "out to undermine our society." "Yes, we are!" Ronald Davis assured him. "The society that is hypocritical, that is imperialistic, that supports sham art, that supports sham wars, that censors dialogue, that has the crude audacity to call the opposition 'nervous Nellies,' must be undermined." Both the Diggers and the Mime Troupe were radical existentialists, "anarchists of the deed." They made no petitions or demands of the government because they decried the dependency that asking implied. They did not practice civil disobedience because they rejected the state's authority to make them obey. They did not plan for the future; they lived it. Digger philosophy challenged people to "create the conditions you describe" by practicing self-government, community service, and a form of recreation that could recreate the world.[48]

The mainstream press loved the exoticism and color of the counterculture, the drama presented by its contrasts with straight (and narrow) culture. But mainstream journalism also framed the counterculture so that drugs, dirt, dress, disorder, and sexual deviance became the dominant images of the movement. Because journalism involves only the events of the day, it missed the historical roots of countercultural ideas and practices. When *Time* was planning a cover story on the Hippies, for example, they asked their San Francisco bureau for background on this "controversial, cloud-cuckooland miniculture." The resulting article, along with others in the mainstream press, attracted thousands of curiosity seekers to San Francisco and caused a population explosion in Haight-Ashbury.

By the fall of 1967, the Haight had become so popular that it could not maintain its communitarian voluntarism. The disciplined practice of people like the Diggers gave way to capitalist cooption. And the innocent flower children attracted both drug pushers and petty criminals who succeeded the Summer of Love with a season of danger. Chester Anderson of the Communications Company pointed to the threat:

> Pretty little 16-year-old middle-class chick comes to the Haight to see what it's all about & gets picked up by a 17-year-old street dealer who spends all day shooting her full of speed again & again, then feeds her 3000 mikes [micrograms of acid] & raffles off her temporarily unemployed body for the biggest Haight Street gang bang since the night before last.

As a result of the danger and disorder, the Diggers even declared the "Death of Hippie, devoted son of Mass Media" and buried the corpse in the fall of 1967.[49]

The Politics of (Counter) Culture

The Summer of Love showed the possibilities of the counterculture, but it also showed that substantial changes were needed for those possibilities to be realized. After 1967, countercultural activists followed two major paths to cultural transformation: the revolutionary "magic politics" of the Yippies, and the here and now revolution of rural communes. During the Summer of Love, while millions of young Americans read the Haight hype in the media and thousands traveled to San Francisco to see how the future worked, a few people traveled from San Francisco to proselytize elsewhere. Among these missionaries were Diggers Emmett Grogan and Peter Berg, who brought their theatrics to a gathering of the SDS "Old Guard" in June 1967. Convened to reflect on the state of the New Left, the Michigan conference had been called "Back to the Drawing Boards." Grogan and Berg burst in during a Tom Hayden talk and thoroughly disrupted the meeting. Most of the Old Guard were singularly unimpressed with the Diggers' mad road show. But Abbie Hoffman, an East Village hipster who attended the conference with New York Be-in organizer Jim Fouratt and *Realist* editor Paul Krassner, was inspired.[50]

Hoffman, like many other countercultural activists, had roots in the personalist politics of the preceding decade. As a student at Brandeis University, Hoffman had been a part of the Beat-bohemian scene. Of all the radical speakers he heard at Brandeis, the two that impressed him most were Dorothy Day and Saul Alinsky. In Worcester, where Hoffman worked from 1960 to 1966, he worked closely with a small radical Catholic community coordinated by Father Bernard Gilgun, a Catholic Worker. As program director, he arranged Friday night roundtables at the Phoenix, an ecumenical meeting place that hosted speakers like Dorothy Day, Ammon Hennacy, David McReynolds, Howard Zinn, and Robert Drinan. In 1965, he invited Allen Ginsberg, but got no response. Hoffman was also involved with the civil rights movement, working with the NAACP, helping to start a local chapter of CORE, and organizing for Friends of SNCC in Worcester. In August 1964, Hoffman attended the Democratic National Convention in solidarity with the Mississippi Freedom Democratic Party. In 1965, he and his wife vacationed in Americus, Georgia, and McComb, Mississippi to show Southern civil rights workers that they had Northern support. When he returned, he used his experience as a pharmaceutical salesman to find retail outlets for the manufactured goods of the Poor People's Corporation, an umbrella group for a variety of worker-owned cooperative enterprises.[51]

After the Drawing Boards conference, Hoffman decided that Digger politics was potentially more revolutionary than the politics of SDS, that theatrical activism could dramatize the character of American culture, and that television could bring the American public to a cultural catharsis. In August, Hoffman led a group who dropped dollar bills on the floor of the New York Stock Exchange. With his Digger friends, he contrived a series of such publicity stunts: soot bombs sent to Con Edison, free clothes given away at Macy's, an Army recruiting booth postered with "See Canada Now," 3000 joints of marijuana mailed at random to names in the phone book. Hoffman argued for "revolution for the fun of it." But, as a student of humanistic psychology, he didn't mean just funhouse fun: "when I say fun, I mean an experience so intense that you actualize your full potential. You become LIFE. LIFE IS FUN." Hoffman argued against the utilitarian politics of the New Left and for a prefigurative politics. "Come on out and help build and defend the society you want," he said. "Begin to live your vision." Echoing Peter Maurin, he told movement organizers to "stop trying to organize everybody but yourself."[52]

In the fall of 1967, Hoffman joined Jerry Rubin to apply the Digger ethic at the October March on the Pentagon. Drawing on the ideas of the New York Workshop in Nonviolence and of Allen Ginsberg's "Berkeley Vietnam Days" in the January 1966 *Liberation*, they set out to protest the war by promoting a joyful psychedelic anarcho-pacifism. Instead of sedate parades of earnest citizens, they preferred a politics of spectacle, using flowers, flags, toys, puppets, and props to garner an audience on the other side of the camera. Ginsberg hoped that this "magic politics" would be "a kind of poetry and theater sublime enough to change the national will and open up the consciousness of the populace." Rubin and Hoffman got tremendous publicity for their plan to exorcise the evil demons from the Pentagon, and to levitate the building three hundred feet in the air. By the end of the year, they named themselves Yippies (which they later explained as an acronym for the Youth International Party) and announced that "a cross-fertilization of the hippie and New Left philosophies" would occur at a Festival of Life designed to counter the 1968 Democratic Convention in Chicago.[53]

This politics of the counterculture was peculiar but powerful. Even though the Yippies nominated a candidate (a pig named Pigasus) for President in 1968, the counterculture was not intended to be a mass political movement. It rejected the instrumental politics of the party system. Richard King suggests that its concern was "changing consciousness and as such is nonpolitical." But personalist politics had always challenged the definitions that allowed such distinctions. Countercultural personalists considered consciousness an integral part of any political culture; as "cultural radicals," they knew that ways of seeing were more important in the long run than the more prominent political issues of national campaigns.[54]

This cultural radicalism made the New Left and the counterculture the yin and yang of Sixties radicalism, organically intertwined, two movements of the same Movement. At times, the hippies and the politicos resisted each other: the New Left sometimes saw the counterculture as Romantic and irresponsible escapism, while the counterculture often portrayed New Leftists as neurotics compensating for anger, frustration, and guilt, and obsessed with control and efficacy. Sometimes the hippies and the politicos were the same people. Still the two movements were engaged in a common project. As Edward Morgan suggests, the counterculture carried on "four strains of the democratic vision of the Sixties: an implicit democratic faith in the intuitive wisdom of the people, the liberation and integration of repressed personality, a moral outlook that celebrated the person as sacred, and the quest for community." Together, the oppositional politics of the New Left and the counterculture recovered the complex roots of the word "protest." Conventionally, Americans consider protest negative, a protest against something. But the word is more complex, its "pro" a positive affirmation, as when a person protests their love. While the New Left protested the system, the counterculture pretested an alternative system. According to David Farber, it was "a way of life, a community, an infrastructure, and even an economy, not just a few lifestyle accoutrements like long hair and an occasional toke on an illegal substance."[55]

Communitarian Personalism

Especially after the assassinations and elections of 1968, many young people parted from the path of both conventional and cultural politics. If the revolution could not be made in the voting booth or on the streets, if the powers that be would continue to be, then perhaps the revolution would come from the bottom up. In many cases, the optimism of the counterculture fed on pessimism in the New Left. "I had done the political trip for a while," said one communard, "but I got to the point where I couldn't just advocate social change. I had to live it."[56]

Counterculturalists criticized the New Left of the late Sixties for its sacrifice of means for ends, and created communes to fuse the two. Like the anarchist-hipsters of SDS, they expected political strategy and tactics to prefigure the society of the future. They rejected a revolutionary theory that called for people to do violence (including violence to the principles they hoped to achieve) and that suspended everyday life until after the revolution. Rejecting the revolutionary rhetoric of the New Left, they began to imitate SDS's urban collectives, the SNCC freedom houses, the Catholic Worker houses, and nineteenth-century utopian communities. The medium, they implied, was the message; peaceable living was as important as the peace movement. By the mid-Seventies, several million Americans lived in about 7,000 communes. Most were urban and academic communes, with members often engaged in sustained social action. Reba Place, in Evanston, Illinois, for example, practiced the Christian social gospel. The Kate Richards O'Hare Collective near Cornell University was based on socialist ideals. In Philadelphia, about a dozen communal houses formed a quasi-Quaker social action community called New Life. Boston's Bread and Roses Collective offered a homeplace for women, while the 95th Street Collective in New York served gay men. In 1971, Susan

Gowan, George Lakey, Bill Moyers, and Dick Taylor started the Movement for a New Society, establishing projects and living centers that encouraged a simple lifestyle that could sustain fellowship and moral support and solidarity against oppression.[57]

Others disdained the cities as sores of urban-industrialism and moved back to the land. Stephen Gaskin, a popular teacher in the free universities of the Bay Area, for example, led a group of several hundred heads to Tennessee, where they bought a farm. "I guess farming is about the cleanest way to make a living," Gaskin thought, unconsciously echoing Peter Maurin. "It's just you and the dirt and God." Others agreed that "this country needs in great numbers to become voluntary peasants." Communes like The Farm offered places for personalists to practice what they preached. As the New Left went national in its antiwar organizing, the counterculture went local in the peaceable self-organizing that predecessors like Peter Maurin would have appreciated. While conscientious objectors turned to the civil disobedience of Thoreau for inspiration, counterculturalists embraced the transcendental utopianism of Bronson Alcott. Catholic Worker farms, anarcho-pacifist communities, and Beat pads also contributed to this communitarian ethic of the counterculture.[58]

Between 1965 and 1970, counterculturalists established at least twice as many rural communes as had been established in all of American history. After the breakup of the Boston-based Liberation News Service in the early Seventies, one faction moved to Montague Farm to practice organic agriculture. Gorda Mountain at Big Sur was an open-door, open-land community; Twin Oaks in Virginia was a version of B.F. Skinner's *Walden Two*; Heathcoate in Maryland was a school of living; Drop City, Colorado was a cluster of geodesic domes; The Farm in Tennessee blended Buddhism, Hinduism, and Christianity; Lou Gottlieb's Morning Star Ranch offered a place for the practice of "voluntary primitivism."[59]

Despite the diversity of communal experience (even *within* single communes), all of the communes aimed at what Murray Bookchin called "ecological forms of human association," the creation of communities that served the basic needs of persons more elegantly than the mainstream culture. They tried to ameliorate the alienations of modern life by creating supportive communities. Rejecting technologism and materialism, they embraced hand tools, voluntary simplicity and (sometimes) a subsistence economy. To do this, they drew on anarchist traditions of the face-to-face community and (often) on the mystical and magical traditions of religion.[60]

Celebrating their progress to primitivism, their escape from the specializations of modern American life, many communes settled in out-of-the-way locations that separated them from modern American culture. "It really sets us back in the nineteenth century," said one communard in Grant's

Pass, Oregon. "But, after all, we're more interested in discovering the past than the future." Looking for a usable past, they tried to retain and recover the cultural wisdom of the past. While many in the counterculture suffered from what Kenneth Keniston called "the fallacy of romantic regression," others saw that the past is not just past, but a path to possibilities, a resource for future planning. Against advertisers who colonized the future and who asserted that "the future is now," some countercultural activists revived patterns of the past that seemed fulfilling to human beings.[61]

American Indian cultures offered one important model for these communitarian experiments. While Peter Maurin had modeled his rural communes on the medieval peasantry, the communards of the Sixties or Seventies more often imitated the ideas, institutions, and spirituality of American Indians. Stewart Brand, a Stanford biology student who became interested in the new branch of biology called ecology, proclaimed that "America Needs Indians." Brand created a multimedia show called the "America Needs Indians Sensorium," which was one of the scenes of the Trips Festival. Two years later, he put out a guidebook called *The Whole Earth Catalogue* to provide tools for living in the new America.[62]

Other models were Amish and Mennonite communities, which had practiced communitarian personalism for decades. When Stephen Gaskin and his followers established their farm in Tennessee, they found they had been preceded by Amish settlers from Pennsylvania. "So there's a lot of stuff people accepted about us from the beginning. Once they learned we really weren't scary and we really weren't violent and we really were truthful, they started thinking we were Technicolor Amish." Like the Amish and the Mennonites, countercultural attempts at personal relationships in face-to-face communities often recalled the example of primitive Christianity. The communal spirit of cooperation seemed closer to the spirit of scripture than either the spirit of capitalism or versions of the Protestant work ethic. The participatory democracy of many communes resembled the priesthood of all believers, as did the practice of consensus in leftist religious communities. Although not all communes were intentionally Christian, even some of the secular collectives seemed more radically Christian than the institutions of middle-class life.[63]

Despite the efflorescence of communes and consciousness-raising groups, communal ideas were probably more preached than practiced. "There was no community party of youth culture," David DeLeon notes, "only an unorganized community of affection, a personalist politics of direct, simple, and natural styles of language, dress, hair, and life." Communes seldom lived up to people's imaginative expectations. While they were surely simple, they were also frequently filled with drudgery, drugs, disorder, dullness, and dirt. People who believed in the importance of community and place often showed it by moving to another community in a different place.[64]

Countering the Counterculture

For all of its flakiness, the counterculture threatened conventional American culture. A whole society of hippies would be radically un-American. The mainstream culture responded to this threat in a variety of ways. Politicians, public figures, and parents condemned countercultural practices. Vice President Agnew called for the "positive polarization" of the country, and—as ventriloquist for the "silent majority"—President Nixon construed the apathy of Americans as political opposition to the counterculture and the antiwar movement. Such officious condemnations often convinced counterculturalists that they must be doing something right.[65]

Officials used the law and the police to prosecute people who engaged in alternative cultural practices. In Minneapolis, a city ordinance prohibited more than ten unrelated people living together. State and county officials drafted legislation to prevent rock festivals. Police harassment of hippies was common, with drug raids, health inspections, and arrests for vagrancy and "idleness." Sometimes citizens harassed longhairs with taunts and threats and attacks. Businesses also tried to curtail the counterculture. Even in liberal cities, hippies were, like Negroes a decade earlier, refused service. In Seattle, a group of hippies was hauled off to the police station after a waitress told them, "We don't want or need your business." Retailers signalled their sentiments with the sign "No shirt, no shoes, no service."[66]

More important in the long run, American commercial culture co-opted the counterculture, commodifying dissent and selling it back to the dissenters. Capitalists found that antimaterialism sold very well to selected customers. In Haight-Ashbury, the people the Diggers disdainfully called "the merchants of love" commercialized the counterculture and created "plastic hippies." A Haight Street bar became "The Love Cafe," offering LOVEburgers and LOVEdogs. A jewelry store called "Happiness Unlimited" posted a sign that said "We love you; we hope you love us." The more the counterculture could be construed as a lifestyle apart from politics, the more capitalists could sell the style without the substance. By marketing the outward signs of hippie life—music, psychedelic posters, clothes, beads, and drug paraphernalia—merchandisers found that they could make a profit on the ephemera of prophecy.[67]

Moreover, the counterculture always attracted lots of frivolous and disingenuous people. The alienations of everyday life combined with the lure of freedom and the pursuit of pleasure to subvert the communitarian aspects of the counterculture. "For many of the sixties generation," says

Terry Anderson, "the counterculture was just a lark, a time to smoke weed and get laid, a long party. The hippie lifestyle of dope, free love, music, and values of brotherhood and sharing invited phonies, freeloaders, runaways, drug dealers, smackheads, and various self-appointed preachers and zealots." The communitarian subjectivism of Allen Ginsberg and Gary Snyder often gave way to a simplistic and individualistic "Do your own thing."[68]

To some extent, too, the counterculture's aversion to institutions and authority affected its staying power. Communes tried different strategies for self-government—signup sheets, group meetings, rotating managers— but found that ultimately they depended on the free will of their members. Often the libertarian individualism of "doing your own thing" undermined communitarian voluntarism because people were not willing to sacrifice for the common good. Too, the lack of educational institutions often hurt communal practice. Without a way of desocializing the old and socializing the young, the counterculture's comprehensive cultural critique became a series of lifestyle choices. Young people attracted to the excitement of psychedelics, sexual promiscuity, vagrancy, or communal living might wear the face of the counterculture without being affected by its soul.[69]

Conclusion: The Americanization of Personalism

During the late Sixties and early Seventies, the counterculture created a counter-hegemonic subculture rooted partly in personalist perspectives. Guided by the personalism of humanistic psychology and psychedelia, leaders offered an encompassing criticism of the depersonalized institutions of mainstream culture. More than most earlier utopian experiments, counterculturalists succeeded in establishing working examples of their ideas. But their success was selective, and sustainable only in particular pockets of American culture. Although the counterculture hoped to "personalize" America, the longterm result was the Americanization of personalism, as American values of individualism and consumption subverted many distinctively personalist aspects of the project.

As critique, the counterculture was remarkably successful. By simply asking whether ideas and institutions fulfilled whole persons, critics exposed the shortcomings of American patterns of work, leisure, marriage, family, education, entertainment, science, religion, politics, capitalism and consumption. Looking at life through the prism of personalism, they caused people to think twice about the virtues of the American way of life, and—sometimes—to act on their disquiet. By contesting the cultural practices of middle-class America, the counterculture offered a critique that almost broke the silence of the silent majority.

The counterculture applied its personalist perspectives in a multitude of signs, symbols, institutions, and practices. They dressed and acted differently. They used rock music and drugs to shape the contours of their own "here and now revolution." Suspicious of the instrumentalism of party politics, they practiced a "magic politics" focused on individual transformation as the foundation of social change. Championing community in a culture of individualism, they tried to live in collaborative harmony with each other and with the earth. According to George Lipsitz, "In their affirmations of sexual pleasure, their desire to cross racial barriers, their attempts to neutralize gender as a fixed source of identity, their construction of voluntary affective relationships outside the realm of the biological family, their celebrations of peace and love in a society being consumed by war and hatred, and their revolt against materialism and hierarchy, the counterculture made significant breaks with dominant cultural values in America."[70]

With other personalists, the counterculture helped to redefine American politics, making the personal political and bringing issues like work and love into a national dialogue. It was one thing to be apolitical—and this described the silent majority far better than the counterculture—and another thing to be meta-political. The counterculture was not partisan, not interested in electoral politics or legislative agendas, not pleased by the proliferation of government bureaucracies, not particularly litigious—but they were political in their challenge to the politics of the status quo, including the power to define politics. They understood both power and the powers that be, and they opted for the power of be-ing. Politics, they said, wasn't what you did—it was what you were. They called for "power to the people," but they did not expect the dissolution of government. Instead, in personalist practice, they empowered people to live well with self-government.

Countercultural politics, therefore, was the politics of anarchism—of decentralization, rural romanticism, and libertarianism. Suspicious of the state, of political ideology and party discipline, many members were attracted to ideas of community building and local control. The American party system and the Right-Left continuum of party politics make it almost impossible to see political alternatives that do not fit on the continuum. Anarchism was one such alternative, and, like many of their personalist predecessors, the members of the counterculture were anarchists of the deed.[71]

Countercultural personalism differed from previous personalisms, however, in significant ways. Contesting the societal structures that inhibited their development as full persons, the counterculture called for freedom and liberation. But the context of the late Sixties made that call different from earlier emphases on freedom. "Freedom" is a word with incredible resonance in American culture and activists used it liberally in the 1960s. But the same word had different meanings in different times and places, and the shifting meanings are, in part, an index of the shifting foundations of American activism. In the Catholic Worker movement, freedom existed within a framework of hierarchy and transcendence, as people were free to choose their vocational contribution to the common good. In the civil rights movement, freedom meant the affirmation of oneself as a person within a community contending for justice. Freedom had a collective meaning, as prophets like Martin Luther King called upon a racist culture to "let my people go." In these traditions, and in the language of early SDS, freedom was the word that activists used to mean equality and community. "Freedom now" meant not just a chance to make choices, but a chance to choose a society in which people would be treated equally as persons.[72]

At its best, the counterculture still embodied these traditions of political personalism. But too often, the freedoms of the counterculture—like those trumpeted by middle-class America—were simply freedom from cultural norms and freedom for individual choice and selfishness. Seeing themselves as potential victims of the system, the counterculture often lacked the empathy and compassion that had characterized earlier personalists. In dropping out, the counterculturalists too often dropped away from engagement with the problems of persons who were poor and marginalized. Only the in crowd could afford to drop out; it was a strategy irrelevant to the urban poor, the working class, and racial minorities. Whereas earlier personalists believed that privileged people grew by giving themselves to others, counterculturalists sometimes opted for a kind of self-actualization that could be solipsistic. When concern for the person became concern for the self, then the culture of compassion became the culture of narcissism.[73]

The antinomian desire for direct personal experience can destroy community as well as create it, and when subjectivism broke free of its communitarian boundaries, the result was often an expressive individualism perfectly consonant with the consumer capitalism of American culture. When the counterculture was coopted by American institutions, it was often this libertarian individualism that proved most susceptible to sales. With drugs, for example, the communitarian and quasi-communitarian consciousness-raising of the early Sixties sometimes ended in unconsciousness, and the doors of perception slammed shut on the wider world of personalism. A few people overdosed and died and others found drugs a downer. Still others found that drugs brought them not into community, but into frightful alienation.[74]

Likewise, personalist sexual liberation improved some aspects of American sexual practice, but the sexual revolutions of the counterculture did not always challenge dominant notions of sexuality—the double standard, for example. Consequently, sexual freedom often meant more pressure on women to please men. "We called it the free fuck club," one female remembered. "These guys talked about love, screwed us, and then zoomed off for more cultural revolution." From a personalist perspective, when the intercourse of bodies was not an expression of the intimacy of persons, then making love was just fucking around, or fucking up. Instead of countering the culture, it fit perfectly with the individualist hedonism and sexualization of the culture itself.[75]

With "magic politics," too, the Yippies found that the theater played better than the prefigurative personalism. Although they discovered that television provided access to the hearts and minds of the American public, they also found that, for media coverage, they needed to be outlaws or outrageous. The Digger ethic of personal responsibility and service was subsumed in the Prankster ethic of disruption. While the Yippies got the attention of middle America, they also discovered an inverse relationship between attention and approval. Even as Americans slowly came to oppose the conduct of the war, they opposed the countercultural conduct of the Yippies more. Especially after 1968, the politics of Yippie complicated the course of the New Left and of the counterculture.[76]

For all the hopes and dreams of the counterculture, they couldn't escape human nature or American socialization, which backpacked with them wherever they settled. "Even though we created our own environment at the farm," one communard recalled, "we still carried with us the repressions of the old environment, in our bodies and our minds." They tried to use ideas and institutions to shape human nature so that it would be easier to be good, and, against great odds, they had significant successes. Countercultural outposts persist all across America, both in particular places and in the more general geography of the American mind. Drawing on important traditions of American personalism, they presented both a critique and a collection of countercultural practices to subsequent American personalists.[77]

9

Epilogue

The Sixties and the Seventies were only a day apart, but Sixties personalism did not confine itself to the chronological 1960s, and the "Me Decade" did not immediately supersede the "We Decade." Students, antiwar activists, and counterculturalists all continued their critique of American society. The personalism of the Sixties also affected new movements of the 1970s and 1980s. This final essay simply identifies a few of these continuities, suggesting some ways in which the politics of personalism nurtured people, ideas, and organizational forms for the women's movement, the backyard revolution, the environmental movement, and the antinuclear movement. In general, the humanism of these movements has been more secular than sacred, but they creatively adapted many of the traditions that came from earlier personalists.

Feminist Personalism

More than any other group, the nation's women taught Americans that the personal is political. Like the civil rights and antiwar movements, the women's movement began in the credibility gap between American rhetoric and reality, as personalist perspectives legitimized questions about the legitimacy of inequalities. The contemporary women's movement started in the 1960s, but the most dramatic growth occurred in the Seventies, a rich reverberation of the personalist politics of the Sixties. Extending the analysis of most Sixties personalists (who were often as sexist as their society), feminism asked Americans to consider the personhood of womanhood. Like the early New Left, it grounded its theory in personal experience. Like the counterculture, the women's movement depended on a kind of communitarian subjectivism. Like all personalists, it showed the personal dimensions of political power and the political implications of personal choices. Although the women's movement embraced a wide variety of political perspectives—from liberal to socialist to separatist—most feminists adopted, at least in part, personalist perspectives.[1]

As early as 1963, Betty Friedan had focused her critique of the feminine mystique on its failure to treat women as whole persons. Using the humanistic psychology of Abraham Maslow, Friedan wrote that "our culture does not permit women to accept or gratify their basic need to grow and fulfill their potentialities as human beings." The ideology of femininity prevented women's self-actualization, resulting in the "forfeited self" of modern American womanhood. Influenced by Maslow, Friedan rejected the Freudian notion that women's complaints were neuroses caused by failure to adjust to their natural gender role. Seeing gender roles as cultural, she set out to change the society and its social construction of reality. Because it prevented the full development of persons, she thought, the feminine mystique must be changed.[2]

During the Sixties, many women had been drawn to the New Left and the counterculture because they assumed that household values—which were often women's values—applied to politics. Women had been drawn to the New Left because, "in a sense the new left affirmed 'feminine' qualities in its assertion of morality and its concern for feelings, community, and process." Despite their macho sexuality, the men of the early SDS articulated many of the issues of the day in a language of care, concern, and compassion. The counterculture, too, highlighted domestic values of love and nurturing, feeling and family, in its critique of mainstream culture.[3]

But while the New Left and the counterculture had affirmed many "feminine" qualities, they had not equally affirmed women. While women performed a huge share of the day-to-day work of Sixties movements, they received little credit. SDS had welcomed women, but not as leaders. The Free Speech Movement defined itself mainly in masculine terms. By focusing on male opposition to the draft, the resistance implicitly excluded women from the most radical aspects of the antiwar movement. Similarly, within SNCC, the gender roles of the mainstream culture affected both personal and organizational roles of men and women. Most of the men still assumed that women were for "maternal applause, menial services, and body contact."[4]

Still, although the New Left and the counterculture were caught in the culture's sexism, they also offered women a chance to develop the conceptual and political skills that could be used in a feminist movement. Sixties movements also gave women languages—including the language of personalism—to fight sexism. As early as 1964, Casey Hayden and Mary King used these concepts to critique the gender politics of the new politics. In their historic "Sex and Caste: A Kind of Memo," they acknowledged that they had "learned from the movement to think radically about the personal worth and abilities of people whose roles had gone unchallenged before." They had "talked in the movement about trying to build up a society which would see basic human problems (which are now seen as private troubles) as public problems and would try to shape institutions to shape human needs rather than shaping people to meet the needs of those in power." Now, they said, it was time to shape institutions—including the institutions of SNCC and SDS—to treat women as whole persons.[5]

The December 1965 SDS conference included a women's workshop, which called for "a reassertion of the personal" among women, criticizing the male-dominated, increasingly intellectual style of SDS and the exploitive personal relationships of movement men. Women like Sharon Jeffrey and Carol McEldowney contended that "one of the biggest problems is teaching women to accept ourselves, to accept our limitations, abilities and needs, as WE define them, and not as men define them." Within a few years, women were meeting regularly to articulate their own needs. Their consciousness-raising groups brought the therapeutic practice of humanistic psychology to the political praxis of a social movement, as women created a new sisterhood by sharing their personal stories, and by identifying the social structures that prevented them from becoming fully human persons. According to Jo Freeman, it was "a kind of phenomenological approach to women's liberation. . . . Consciousness-raising exemplified both the frontal assault on sex roles and the personalized approach to politics that soon became hallmarks of the proliferating new feminist groups."[6]

The women's movement succeeded splendidly in making personal issues political. In "A Broom of One's Own," Charlotte Bunch argued that "there is no private domain of a person's life that is not political and there is no political issue that is not ultimately personal. The old barriers have fallen." Abortion, rape, spousal abuse, child abuse, incest, sexual harassment, pornography, health care, and lesbianism all became public policy issues during the 1970s and 1980s. Other issues, like marriage and sexual relations and childbirth and housework became a part of the politics of every-day life. Within a few years, women had created collectives and grassroots organizations like health clinics, bookstores, and newspapers as parallel institutions for the emerging community.[7]

Radical feminists also activated the claim that "the personal is political" by insisting on the application of "household values" to national politics. In *For Her Own Good*, Barbara Ehrenreich and Deirdre English contended that "the human values that women were assigned to preserve [must] expand out of the confines of private life and become the organizing principles of society." Echoing Women Strike for Peace, they argued that "the 'womanly' values of community and caring must rise to the center as the only *human* principles." These cultural feminists criticized masculinist ideas and institutions that had created "a human personality viewed as out of balance and out of touch with much of its essential humanness—man alienated from, and abusive of, his body, his spirituality, his need for intimacy; man denying his own mortality while repressing his connection with nature; man projecting his own cerebral, disconnected self onto women, children, the needy, nature, the cosmos." And they offered, as personalists traditionally have, images and models of more fully human being.[8]

The Backyard Revolution

While the women's movement revived personalism's focus on the person, the "backyard revolution" of the 1970s drew on its localist and communitarian emphases. The national liberation movement predicted by Marxist and Maoist revolutionaries of the late Sixties failed to materialize. But local liberation movements flourished in what Harry Boyte called "the backyard revolution" of the Seventies. More than 20 million people took part in the neighborhood groups created by the new citizen movement. More than 500,000 mutual aid groups came into existence, with membership of more then 15 million. Cooperatives added more than a million members a year during the Seventies. These backyard revolutionaries organized to prevent highways or urban development from ruining their neighborhoods; to lobby for occupational health and workplace reforms; to create cooperative institutions; to agitate for tenants' rights; to protest utility rates and property taxes; to combat bank redlining and capital flight.[9]

The "backyard revolution," said Boyte, "has roots in the sixties protests against institutionalized discrimination, massive bureaucracies, and technocratic values. Like civil rights, its fundamental theme is the rights of citizenship—the demand that democracy be made real in America." The Seventies citizen revolt drew on local communities, churches, and traditions, just as Sixties personalists had drawn on religious and civic republican precedents. It also learned from the women's liberation movement that personal issues often included a political dimension requiring cooperative action for change. Suspicious of big business and big government—both of which treated people as abstractions—the backyard revolutionaries institutionalized participatory democracy and personal politics close to home.[10]

Part of the backyard revolution was the organization of co-operatives. As the Sixties slipped into the Seventies, many activists began to live the revolution, not in the streets, but in the storefronts of America's neighborhoods. Because protest and resistance seemed ineffective against the entrenched institutions of American government, many activists turned their attention from Washington to their own localities. They formed food and housing co-ops, credit unions and insurance co-ops, health care and day care co-ops, and community development corporations. Co-ops constituted an institutional infrastructure for people who had "dropped out" of American life—and into another form of American life. They embodied participatory democracy, giving people an actual voice in the economic institutions of their neighborhoods. As examples of community economics, the co-ops provided goods and services outside the profit nexus and the institutions of competitive capitalism. The co-ops suggested that, if the political was personal, then so was the economic. While communes tried to change the relationships of the household, cooperatives focused on relationships in the market.[11]

"The foundation of the movement," said Craig Cox, was "an almost religious belief in the value of community and personal empowerment." The co-ops embodied the communitarian anarchist idea of mutual aid and offered a nonviolent protest that seemed more productive than street confrontations. Cooperatives provided a model of social change more rooted than the riotous revolution of the streets. According to Cox, co-op leaders expected to change society "individual by individual, neighborhood by neighborhood, through cooperative empowerment. It would be a revolution without guns, without dogma, a revolution that always valued the individual over political parties, people over profit, peace over provocation."[12]

Food co-ops offered, not just cooperative organization, but also an approach to a more nutritious diet. They carried whole grains, dry beans, organic produce, and unrefined sugars that were more "natural" than the plastic foods of the supermarket. Early food co-ops refused to carry "junk foods" and stocked cookbooks like Francis Moore Lappe's *Diet for a Small Planet* that connected the dinner table to issues of agricultural production and distribution. They connected the personal and the political to the palatable.[13]

Like many of the cooperatives, food co-ops encountered practical difficulties that prevented them from realizing all of their goals. In many cases, economics forced diversification to attract a wider clientele, but at a cost of the personal and participatory relationships that accompanied smaller enterprises. Because small co-ops couldn't compete with supermarkets on economies of scale, they often offered workers a negligible wage or some sort of payment in kind. Because they were countercultural, they had a hard time attracting people from the community they were supposed to serve. But co-ops, like other community organizations, offered a way to institutionalize the backyard revolution, even as they prefigured the more comprehensive revolution that never happened. Like the backyard revolution itself, food co-ops stayed mainly in the back pages of the newspapers. Although they challenged the system, they didn't overthrow it. Instead, in the face of the supermarket system, they provided good food, and food for thought.[14]

The Environmental Movement

Like the "backyard revolution," the environmental movement of the 1970s also depended on the idea that people should "think globally, and act locally." In fact, the "NIMBY syndrome"—not-in-my-backyard—of grassroots environmentalists coincided perfectly with the citizen movement's emphasis on local action for state and national policy. Although the mainstream of the environmental movement has been more liberal than radical, there have also been important personalist perspectives. Just as personalists rejected instrumental approaches to people, so many environmentalists resisted the instrumental use of nature, and began to argue for nature's inherent value. Going back to Genesis, religious environmentalists noted that God created the Earth and said that it was good, even before populating the Garden with human beings. Instead of seeing people *and* nature, deep ecologists saw persons *in* nature. At the same time, contemporary environmentalists stressed themes of personal responsibility. Robert Holsworth noted that environmentalism "not only criticizes the ecological consequences of corporate capitalism and bureaucratic socialism, but explicitly endorses the personalist tenet that individuals have to assume responsibility for problems in the world."[15]

The personalist harmonies of private and public, religious and political, were increasingly extended to culture and nature, with the hope that people would be able—both personally and politically—to embrace nature in a communitarian ethic of ecological harmony. The land ethic of Aldo Leopold made this communitarian vision explicit: "a thing is right when it tends to preserve the integrity, beauty, and stability of the biotic community. It is wrong when it tends otherwise." Most variations of radical ecology also assumed the holism of creation.[16]

Bioregionalist variations of radical environmentalism emphasized the decentralist and communitarian visions of personalism. Beginning with former Digger Peter Berg in San Francisco's Planet Drum Foundation, bioregionalism came to public consciousness in the 1970s and 1980s. Reacting against the scale of national and international markets, and the fossil fuels required to supply them, bioregionalists focused on life—human and nonhuman—within particular watersheds. They emphasized life-in-place instead of the mobilities of American life, and, like Catholic Worker Peter Maurin, they asked people to eat what they grew and grow what they ate. Politically, the bioregionalist vision tended toward a communitarian anarchism in which each individual would act as a public person.[17]

Ecofeminist perspectives added a gender dimension to varieties of environmentalism and emphasized the traditionally feminine virtues necessary for a sustainable society. Developed intellectually by Ynestra King of the Institute for Social Ecology in Vermont, it came to prominence in 1980 with a conference on "Women and Life on Earth." Ecofeminist ethics challenged traditional ethics of rights, rules, and utility with ethics of care, love, and trust. An ecofeminist "partnership ethic" emphasized the partnership of humans with each other, and with nonhuman nature. "Constructing nature as a partner," says Carolyn Merchant, "allows for the possibility of a personal or intimate (but not necessarily spiritual) relationship with nature and for feelings of compassion for nonhumans as well as for people who are sexually, racially, or culturally different." Ecofeminist women have been particularly prominent in protests against nuclear power and the disposal of toxic wastes.[18]

Another person who has advanced a kind of personalist environmentalism is Wendell Berry. While bioregionalism and ecofeminism have been more attractive philosophically than practically, Berry is a Kentucky farmer and writer who exemplifies many aspects of recent personalist environmentalism. Born in 1934, Berry was educated at the University of Kentucky and Stanford University, and began teaching in 1959. In 1965, Berry moved to Lanes Landing Farm in Port Royal, Kentucky, where he has farmed ever since. Although he was no hippie, Berry's return to the land was countercultural.[19]

In *The Unsettling of America*, published in 1976, he argued that the ecological crisis was a crisis of character, because people routinely made convenience of "enterprises that they knew to be morally, and even practically, indefensible." The public environmental crises of the Seventies, he said, were "no more than the aggregate of private absurdities." Berry especially attacked the system of specialization that divided and diminished the traditional functions of character: "workmanship, care, conscience, responsibility." Although he understood the importance of the competencies that specialization promoted, he decried the compartmentalization of responsibility that characterized the system. Trained to do one thing well, specialists often overlooked connections to the wider world. That same system of specialization and remote control diminished people and distanced them from nature. "We have given up the understanding," Berry thought, "that we and our country create one another, depend on one another, are literally part of one another." Like Barbara Deming explaining the practice of nonviolence in the jails of the South, Berry believed that "we are all part of one another."[20]

Berry's solution was relatively simple, although immensely difficult. "The only real, practical, hope-giving way to remedy the fragmentation that is the disease of the modern spirit is the small and humble way—a way that a government or agency or organization or institution will never think of, though a *person* may think of it: one must begin in one's own life the private solutions that can only *in turn* become public solutions." Berry knew that environmental bureaucracies and organizations promoted "wise use" or "responsible use" of the land. But he insisted that "the use of the world is finally a personal matter, and the world can be preserved in health only by the forbearance and care of a multitude of persons."[21]

In "The Reactor and the Garden," Berry extended this analysis to antinuclear politics. Describing his participation in a protest against the Marble Hill nuclear plant, about twenty miles from his farm, he recalled that "as a father, as a neighbor, and a citizen, I had begun to look upon the risk of going to jail as trivial in comparison to the risks of living so near a nuclear power plant." He took part, therefore, in a demonstration of nonviolent civil disobedience, trespassing on the property to publicize the trespasses of the company.[22]

Berry believed that, while such protests were necessary, they were not sufficient for solving the complex problems that they identified. Protests could raise consciousness, but they were incomplete actions, because they could only raise consciousness to the level of protest. They did not extricate persons from complicity with the evils—like energy wastefulness—that they were protesting. "Nearly all of us," Berry said, accusing himself, "are sponsoring or helping to cause the ills we would like to cure. . . . The roots of the problems are private and personal, and the roots of the solution will be private or personal too."[23]

Berry advised people, therefore, to quit doing things they knew to be destructive, and to practice a politics of "complete action." For Berry, a complete action was one "which one takes on one's own behalf, which is particular and complex, real not symbolic, which one can both accomplish on one's own and take full responsibility for." A garden, said Berry, was an elegant example of a complete action. Connecting people to nature and disconnecting them from some part of an industrial food system, a garden offered good work in the pursuit of health, and a particular place "to deal with the most urgent question of our time: how much is enough?" Unlike a nuclear plant, which solves one problem by creating others, a garden was "a solution that leads to other solutions. It is a part of the limitless pattern of good sense and good health."[24]

While few Americans were attracted to the disciplined personalism of a Wendell Berry, many were interested in less heroic measures. Books like *Ecology at Home*, *99 Ways to a Simple Lifestyle*, *Muddling Toward Frugality*, *Taking Charge of Our Lives: Living Responsibly in the World*, *Voluntary Simplicity*, *Home Ecology*, and *How to Make the World a Better Place* have proliferated in the past thirty years, spreading the message of personal responsibility and political involvement.[25]

Berry's protest at Marble Hill typified the "backyard" activism against nuclear power in the Seventies. Responding to the energy crisis of 1973–74, President Gerald Ford proposed Project Independence, which included 200 new nuclear power plants by the year 1985. Ralph Nader convened the first Critical Mass conference in 1974 to consider the possibilities for alternate energy sources. Scientists and other experts offered their evaluations of the dangers of nuclear power. But the primary focus of antinuclear activism was local, particular, and personalist.[26]

When Northeast Utilities announced plans for a dual-reactor plant in Montague, Massachusetts, activist Sam Lovejoy took matters into his own hands, wielding a crowbar to fell a weather monitoring tower on the proposed site. Lovejoy was a member of Montague Farm, an organic farming commune that had been founded by former members of Liberation News Service. To Lovejoy and Anna Gyorgy and Harvey Wasserman, other members of the commune, "nuclear power seemed in many ways to be 'the Vietnam war brought home.'" At home, in their own backyard, these local citizens created the Clamshell Alliance to oppose nuclear power and the power structures that promoted it.[27]

Clamshell was the creation of countercultural and communal activists and members of the American Friends Service Committee. It was, according to Barbara Epstein, "the first effort in American history to base a mass movement on nonviolent direct action. It continued the New Left impulse toward a politics of living out one's values and rejected the antiwar movement's machismo and authoritarianism." Adding both feminist and environmentalist perspectives to Sixties personalism, the Alliance combined local affinity groups, consensus decision-making, and nonviolence to protest the nuclear plant. The affinity groups—eight to fifteen people who knew each other—provided support for the nonviolent discipline of the actions, and for the decentralized decision-making. The Clamshell Alliance was the first of many anarchist antinuclear organizations in the Seventies. Rejecting hierarchy, they used consensus process, affinity groups, "spokes" and "spokescouncils" to maximize participation in the project. Anarchist Murray Bookchin of the Institute for Social Ecology attributed these decentralized structures to the anarchist tradition and participated in the Alliance.[28]

The "Clams," as they were called, occupied the Seabrook site three times in 1976 and 1977. More than two thousand people participated in the Spring 1977 occupation and 1400 were arrested. They did not stop the nuclear plant, but they generated a lot of publicity, and a lot of imitators who learned from their example of participatory democracy and prefigurative politics. But the Clams themselves were plagued with problems of leadership, decision-making, and efficacy that continue to confront contemporary personalist radicals.[29]

The Abalone Alliance, created to protest a nuclear plant on the central California coast, introduced modifications of consensus process that solved some of the procedural problems of participatory democracy. Influenced especially by an anarcha-feminist commitment to a movement culture characterized by feminist process and egalitarianism, the Abalone Alliance "strengthened the role of the counterculture within the direct action movement, and it opened the movement to the spirituality that later became one of its most salient aspects."[30]

The Abalone Alliance originated in Mothers for Peace of San Luis Obispo, a local version of Women Strike for Peace. In 1974, when they discovered that there was an earthquake fault line offshore, they began a process of legal protest and educational outreach. They linked up with other activists, including the Philadelphia-based Movement for a New Society, who thought that antinuclear activism might prove the foundation for a widespread protest against corporatism, militarism, and the social structures that supported them. By 1979, after the accident at Three Mile Island, the Alliance had sixty local groups and was able to attract 40,000 people to the largest antinuclear rally in American history.[31]

Small Is Beautiful: Appropriate Technologies

Opposition to nuclear power often entailed support for what Amory Lovins called *Soft Energy Paths*. Instead of the centralized power grids of corporate utilities, Lovins envisioned an energy future that emphasized decentralized, renewable energy sources—like solar and wind power—and simple technologies matched to "end-use needs." These energy paths were a part of a larger movement of smallness called appropriate technology. During the 1970s, this movement for appropriate technology drew on personalist perspectives. The search for economics as if people mattered and for technologies appropriate to the humanity of human beings were both a part of personalism's legacies. Appropriate technology focused on machines for particular purposes, but all together, they were also machines for social transformation.[32]

E.F. Schumacher's *Small Is Beautiful: Economics As If People Mattered* was one of the most widely read books of social criticism in the Seventies. Schumacher, who had spent twenty years as the head of Britain's National Control Board, argued that modern technology and politics conspired in the dehumanization of society. "If technology is felt to be becoming more and more inhuman," he wrote, "we might do well to consider whether it is possible to have something better—technology with a human face." The human-scale decentralism of Schumacher's smallness echoed Peter Maurin's Green Revolution and the anarchism of Sixties personalists like Paul Goodman. Theodore Roszak, in the introduction to *Small Is Beautiful*, placed Schumacher in "the subterranean tradition of organic and decentralist economics whose major spokesmen include Prince Kropotkin, Gustav Landauer, Tolstoy, William Morris, Gandhi, Lewis Mumford, and, most recently, Paul Goodman, Alex Comfort, and Murray Bookchin." This anarchist tradition, he said, focused on the scale of both governmental and economic organization, insisting that neither should stray too far from personal involvement.[33]

While the radical pacifists of the Sixties had preached Gandhi's nonviolence, Schumacher redirected attention to Gandhian economics. As Roszak suggested, "Gandhi's economics started (and finished) with people." So did Schumacher's: "The great majority of economists," he lamented, "are still pursuing the absurd ideal of making their 'science' as scientific and precise as physics, as if there were no qualitative difference between mindless atoms and men made in the image of God." The Mahatma's spinning wheel looked ridiculous to megatechnical eyes; Schumacher saw the wisdom of Gandhi's plan to maintain villages as places of home production, and to keep decision-making in the new India as decentralized as possible.[34]

Schumacher's concept of "Buddhist Economics" was remarkably similar to the personalist thinking of the Catholic Worker. Like them, he called for good work, for "right livelihood," for voluntary simplicity and nonviolence. The Buddhist, Schumacher said, "sees the essence of civilization not in a multiplication of wants but in the purification of human character . . . primarily by a man's work." He decried the gigantic systems that degraded human beings, and he used the principle of subsidiarity from *Quadrogesimo Anno* to justify the decentralization that would maximize freedom and responsibility.[35]

The Whole Earth Catalog was a second scripture for the smallness movement. In explaining its purpose, author Stewart Brand contended that "a realm of intimate, personal power is developing—power of the individual to conduct his own education, find his own inspiration, shape his own environment, and share his adventure with whoever is interested." The catalog advertised hundreds of tools for creating a new society in the shell of the old, from books of philosophy to how-to manuals, from windmills to solar collectors, from cookbooks to carpentry, from birthing to burial. *The Whole Earth Catalog* emphasized local self-reliance and the revival of lost, low technology skills. Launched in 1968 by Stewart Brand—one of the organizers of the 1966 Trips Festival—it grossed $500,000 in 1969, whereupon Brand promptly reduced the price by a dollar.[36]

Hundreds of groups, including the New Alchemy Institute, the Rocky Mountain Institute, the Intermediate Technology Development Group, and the Farallones Institute also organized to protest the status quo by pretesting alternative technologies. The Institute for Local Self-Reliance, created in 1973 to put Paul Goodman's educational ideas into practice, coordinated many of these projects. They experimented with solar and wind power, with transportation technologies, with heating and insulation efficiencies, with aquaculture and permaculture. With its small-scale machines, appropriate technology challenged the machines (both literal and metaphorical) of corporate capitalism, echoing the communitarian anarchism of many political personalists.[37]

In general, appropriate technologists practiced a politics of example, hoping that if they built a better mousetrap, the world would come trooping to the door. Although they understood and criticized the conglomerate of political and economic power that created inappropriate technologies, they made few direct efforts to overturn that power. In California, Governor Jerry Brown created an Office of Appropriate Technology; in national government, the Carter Administration provided funding for alternative energy sources and appropriate technology. But for the most part, like many political personalists, they opted for the here and now revolution of personal and social change on a human scale. Their major successes, however, were neither mechanical nor social; instead, they were intellectual. They challenged many of the main assumptions of the modern technological society. They made Americans think twice about the meaning of basic concepts like efficiency, rationality, productivity, cost, and benefit, and they added new measures of success: human scale, the interconnectedness of things, second law efficiencies, sustainability.[38]

By the end of the 1970s, there was some evidence that personalism had been not just persistent, but pervasive. In *New Rules: Searching for Self-Fulfillment in a World Turned Upside Down*, pollster Daniel Yankelovich suggested that Americans were in the throes of a cultural revolution. The book began with an epigraph from Tom Robbins' countercultural classic *Even Cowgirls Get the Blues*:

"You really don't believe in political solutions, do you?"

"I believe in political solutions to political problems. But man's primary problems aren't political; they're philosophical. Until humans solve their philosophical problems, they're condemned to solve their political problems over and over again. It's a cruel, repetitious bore."

Yankelovich contended that Americans of the 1970s were addressing their philosophical problems and finding conventional ways of thinking inadequate for the fulfillment of human needs. By the mid-Seventies, he said, "a majority of Americans had reached a conclusion compatible to that reached by the intellectual critics of industrial civilization in earlier years, namely, that our civilization is unbalanced, with excessive emphasis on the instrumental, and insufficient concern with the values of community, expressiveness, caring and with the domain of the sacred."[39]

As a consequence, said Yankelovich, Americans turned inward, asking how they might find self-fulfillment in a world of self-interest. Frightened by the "impersonal, manipulative" aspects of American life, they turned to "sacred/expressive" pursuits. In doing so, they asked questions that earlier personalists had posed: "Should people in the workplace be exploited exclusively for instrumental purposes, or do they have intrinsic value as well? Should we value certain aspects of nature and society—a wilderness, a vanishing species, a primitive culture, old automobiles, old buildings—for themselves, apart from any instrumental value?"[40]

Yankelovich interpreted the early Seventies search for self-fulfillment as a denial of an earlier social ethic of self-denial and the Sixties ethic, which sometimes degenerated into self-centered self-indulgence. But Yankelovich saw the pendulum swinging back to a set of "new rules" that valued the self-in-relation. Conceding that many Americans had followed a pop psychology that oversold the self, Yankelovich contended that Americans were beginning to craft an "ethic of commitment" that assumed that selves are constituted in community. "Intuitively," Yankelovich said, "we equate selfhood with caring. When one ceases to care—about the world, the future, friends and family, and when the meaningfulness of experience vanishes, so does an essential part of the self." People with an ethic of commitment, he claimed, were re-searching the transcendent in their lives, practicing a "reverential thinking" that respected all living things—people and plants, animals and wilderness.[41]

Other surveys also suggested a shift to personalist perspectives. A majority of Americans preferred "breaking up big things and getting back to more humanized living" over "developing bigger and more efficient ways of doing things." A majority preferred pleasures from "nonmaterial experiences" than from "more goods and services." More thought that "spending more time getting to know each other as human beings on a person to person basis" was more important than "improving and speeding up our ability to communicate with each other through better technology."[42]

This ethic of commitment required both individual will and institutional support, said Yankelovich. People thinking about extending their household values to politics would need to hear that those values were wanted in public life. Unfortunately, Ronald Reagan became President and used the pulpit of the presidency to preach a return to the old rules of instrumental individualism in a system of corporate control. While Jimmy Carter had supported some elements of the personalist program, Ronald Reagan was generally personable, but not personalist.[43]

The antinuclear protests of the Eighties owed a lot to the militarism of the Reagan administration. The program of "Reagan(at)omics" promised reductions in Federal spending, lower tax rates, a balanced budget, and economic prosperity. The 1981 budget legislation also included an $18 billion increase in military spending, including monies for production of neutron bombs, the B-1 bomber, and a Rapid Deployment Force. Combined with the decreases in tax revenues, the increases in military spending helped the President to eviscerate the social programs which he opposed. Unlike most personalists, he seemed to think that caring for the poor would be too taxing for the American people. Reagan commanded the spotlight in the early Eighties, but upstage, and hoping to upstage him, were several groups of people who had organized to end the arms race as an organizing element of American national behavior. The Seventies environmental protests against nuclear power set the stage for protests against nuclear weapons in the 1980s. Many of the new protesters belonged to traditional peace groups such as the American Friends Service Committee, the Fellowship of Reconciliation, the War Resisters League, Clergy and Laity Concerned, and so on. As early as 1975, the year that the Vietnam War ended, both SANE and Women Strike for Peace had joined Sidney Lens to catalyze a new peace movement focused on nuclear weapons. The February 1976 *Progressive* magazine featured Lens' essay "The Doomsday Strategy," which became the second most-requested reprint in the publication's history. Many of the new activists had participated in the campaign to stop the B-1 bomber, or in the Rocky Flats Action Group, or the Livermore Action Group. Some of them had begun coalitions under the rubric of the Nuclear Weapons Facilities Task Force and Mobilization for Survival; the Mobilization's goals were the abolition of nuclear weapons and the arms race, the end of nuclear power, and the funding of human needs.[44]

Some antinuclear personalists applied the direct action techniques of the Sixties. In September 1980, the Plowshares Eight entered a General Electric plant in King of Prussia, Pennsylvania, and destroyed two warheads. It was, they said, the first nuclear disarmament in thirty-five years. "Without Dorothy [Day]," said defendant Daniel Berrigan, "without that exemplary patience, courage, moral modesty, without this woman pounding at the locked door beyond which the powerful mock the powerless with games of triage, without her, the resistance we offered would have been simply unthinkable."[45]

By the late 1970s, antinuclear activists were looking for a unifying proposal; they found it in 1979 in the call for a nuclear weapons freeze requiring the United States and the Soviet Union to immediately, and verifiably, stop the production, testing, and deployment of nuclear weapons and their delivery systems. Viewing the freeze as a first step in "confining the military to defense as a route to disarmament," freeze proponents hoped to change not just policy, but the political culture of the United States. The freeze mobilized in local communities, where they used a politics of witness and publicity to change public opinion, and, ultimately, to pressure national leaders.[46]

The freeze created "free spaces" in which American citizens empowered each other to speak their civil voice. In these local spaces—churches, schools, universities, community and civic organizations, unions, town meetings, city councils, neighborhood organizations—citizens made nuclear weapons policy a matter of civic conversation. In these conversations, says Robert Holsworth, "their moral and political judgment and their values were mobilized. What had been a debate among national security elites in government, academic, and corporate circles was now up for discussion in every setting an organizer could imagine. The shroud of secrecy had been pulled back, and the assumption that national security policy was made rationally was fundamentally challenged. The seeds for democratizing national security decisionmaking had been planted."[47]

In California, citizens inspired by the Abalone Alliance turned their attention from Diablo Canyon to the diabolical force of nuclear weapons. Starting in 1981, they began a campaign of direct action to close the University of California's Lawrence Livermore National Laboratory and to change national nuclear policy. Creating "a political culture based on nonviolence, feminism, and spirituality," the Livermore Action Group attracted a broad constituency for its diverse actions.[48]

In Richmond, Virginia, the protests were less dramatic but no less personalist. Robert Holsworth's case study of Richmond activists shows how personalism animated the anti-nuclear movement of the 1980s, as people responded to the challenge to exemplify their religious beliefs as a biographical and as a public fact. Many of these activists opposed nuclear weapons not so much for strategic reasons as for religious and moral reasons. During the 1980s, they found ways to witness their faith by creating sustainable collectives of resistance and reconstruction in their local communities. Like their predecessors, the personalists of the Eighties acted from a sense of vocation and citizenship. Faith commitments often brought them into politics, where they acted as if citizens should be actively involved in government and self-government. Indeed, unlike most Americans, who understand citizenship as a variety of consumer choice, the political personalists saw citizenship as a form of moral witness, as exemplary action, and as effective advocacy.[49]

The local peace cultures of the Eighties personalists—often affiliated with Pax Christi or the Fellowship of Reconciliation or other religious groups—campaigned locally for the national changes they wanted. As "pragmatic utopians," they leafleted and wrote letters, they spoke at churches and to civic groups, they taught school classes and their own children, they protested and picketed government buildings, and they boycotted businesses involved in the arms race. A few engaged in civil disobedience and tax resistance. In addition, they made changes in their own lifestyles as they called for changes in government policy. They formed study groups and support groups, planned occasional common meals, and tried parenting for peace and justice.[50]

Some of these activists worked in the tradition of the Catholic Worker and the liberal Protestant Social Gospel, but many also worked from a new evangelical Christian Left. Attributing the evils of American culture to the biblical doctrine of the Fall, they set out to enact redemption in the world. Among the most influential was the Sojourners community, founded in 1975 in Washington, DC. Like the Catholic Workers, the Sojourners moved to an inner city neighborhood and began a ministry to the poor. They simplified their own lives and tried to disconnect themselves from the snares of a consumer society. And, like the Catholic Workers, they propagated their faith in a publication, the magazine *Sojourners*.[51]

While they focused their political organizing on the nuclear freeze, Eighties activists, like their predecessors, had a more comprehensive vision of cultural and economic reorientation in America. For them, nuclearism and militarism were symptoms of deeper ills associated with capitalism, consumerism, and individualism. They resisted a society that seemed to have lost its priorities, and they looked forward to a new world in which people would live simply so that others could live in justice, community, and nonviolence.[52]

Conclusion

The first history of the 1970s was called *It Seemed Like Nothing Happened*, and it did seem that way if you looked at the national level. Although

Watergate captured the public eye, the massive protests of the Sixties had ended. With the erosion of the economy, people spent more time looking for jobs than thinking about good work.

The dramatic demonstrations of the Sixties, however, had only been half of Sixties protest. The other half had been local and personalist, as people tried to demonstrate their values with their lives. That part of Sixties protest survived into the Seventies, and succeeded in carrying the tradition to new issues and constituencies. The women's movement, the environmental movement, the backyard revolution, and the antinuclear movement all refracted personalist perspectives from the Sixties. They continued to make the personal political and to make politics pay attention to personal issues. They continued to emphasize the themes that had begun with the Catholic Worker, the civil rights movement, the Beats, *Liberation,* and Women Strike for Peace.

The personalist movements of the Seventies and Eighties tended to be local and particular, but most of them were also national and cultural. As in the Free Speech Movement, "the issue was not the issue"; the issue, as in the Sixties, was the culture that treated people and nature as commodities. As Barbara Epstein suggests, in accounting for the Abalone Alliance, "the threat that Diablo posed to the environment was the occasion, rather than the impetus, for a movement that was fundamentally about social, communal, and personal transformation." The backyard was, they knew, inextricably connected to the wider world. And so, in their homes and neighborhoods, in church and in the public square, they enacted and enriched the American tradition of personalist politics.[53]

Conclusion

AMERICAN POSTWAR RADICALISM BORE the imprint of political personalism, as the personal became political and vice versa. During the 1950s, when McCarthyism and sectarianism eviscerated the Old Left, several groups of people began to act "as if" persons were precious. The Catholic Workers combined hospitality for the poor with concern for the potential victims of nuclear war. The Beat movement used life and literature to criticize the impersonal conventions of American society from the perspective of communitarian anarchism. Folk musicians brought the most personal concerns of the Old Left into a new era, and provided topical songs for changing times. Martin Luther King Jr. combined his philosophical personalism with African American religion, the social gospel, and Gandhian nonviolence to lead a powerful movement for social change. The Student Nonviolent Coordinating Committee built on King's precedent and added an existential politics of action to their drives for empowerment and enfranchisement. *Liberation* became a forum for political personalism; the Committee for Nonviolent Action tested the personalist strategy of nonviolent direct action in its antinuclear protests. Women Strike for Peace

offered a proto-feminist version of a personalism that was already culturally "feminine." By the early Sixties, therefore, American radicalism had, to
a great extent, been personified by activists with personalist perspectives. It
was this tradition that would shape the distinctive spirit of the Sixties.

During the 1960s, these activists joined with a younger generation to
bring personalist perspectives to the student movement, the antiwar movement, and the counterculture. On campus, students objected to a system of
socialization that prepared them as personnel but not as whole persons.
They protested the universities' complicity with the military-industrial
complex. And they created counter-institutions to embody their own best
hopes for fully human beings. Off campus, students followed personalist
precedents in conscientious objection and resistance to the war in Vietnam.
And both on and off campus, they practiced communitarian anarchism in
the here and now revolution of the counterculture.

From the 1930s to the present, personalism has attempted to create free
spaces for politics between the alternatives of corporate capitalism and
state socialism. Personalism called people to personal responsibility not just
for themselves and their personal acquaintances, but for their fellow men
and women, and for the institutions that in-form (and de-form) people.
Opposing both the national state and the national market, personalism
insisted that people were good enough to govern themselves in socially
harmonious ways, and that they could create institutions that would make
it easier to be good.

In the United States, personalism meant something precise at Boston
University, and, to some extent, in the Catholic Worker movement. For
most American radicals of the postwar period, however, personalism was
more a matter of praxis than a coherent philosophy. In the process of
protesting the social constructions of American life, they created their own
eclectic personalism out of elements of Catholic social thought, the Protestant Social Gospel, African American religion, English Distributism, communitarian anarchism, Gandhian nonviolence, Resistance existentialism,
democratic socialism, civic republicanism, humanistic psychology, proto-
feminism, and their own experience. The result was a movement of extraordinary richness and diversity, with a wide range of political activity.

Personalists believed in a politics of personal responsibility, a politics of
example. They believed that actions spoke louder than words, and that
exemplary behavior could lead other people to their personalist responsibilities. In many ways, their own lives were their most important political
statement.

Sometimes, personalist principles collided with the conventions of
American society, and, at those times, personalist politics inspired a politics
of exhortation. Speaking up and speaking out, personalists tried to speak

truth to power. In their organizations and their publications, they presented their personalist perspectives. But when words were not enough, personalists were often willing to speak with the weight of their whole lives.

Beyond the politics of example and the politics of exhortation, personalists practiced both nonviolent direct action and resistance. Putting your body on the line in these forms of political protest converted a politics of example and exhortation into a politics of witness. By violating the laws, personalists appealed to a higher law. They also dramatized injustice, implicitly appealing to their fellow citizens to change the institutions that depersonalized people.

Both the politics of example and the politics of witness were essentially acts of individuals, no matter how many participated. In many of their actions, however, personalists created counter-institutions to begin to create the new society in the shell of the old. This added a prefigurative politics to the politics of example and witness.

Too, movement leaders organized huge demonstrations in which personalist protests—draft card burning, sit-ins, sit-downs—played a prominent part. These demonstrations served several political purposes—they mobilized and energized the participants, drawing them further into political activity; they publicized issues and perspectives to the mass of American voters who were otherwise dependent on the corporate mass media for information; and they let legislators know that there were constituencies for political and social change.

In all of these efforts, activists hoped that other people would embrace personalist perspectives too. But they had few illusions about the probabilities of mass conversion, and so they depended on coalitions for success. The civil rights movement especially worked with liberals in the Democratic Party to achieve the legislative goals of the movement. The antiwar movement also included people who worked within the system to bring an end to the battles in Southeast Asia. Some personalists even participated in party politics, usually for oppositional candidates like Eugene McCarthy or Robert Kennedy. Although personalists had strong personal (and moral) convictions, many of them engaged in a politics of compromise and coalition.

Still, the primary politics of American personalism was neither Democratic nor Republican, but democratic *and* republican—and anarchist. The participatory democracy of many personalist organizations went far beyond the procedural democracy of conventional American politics. The republicanism of personalism was radical, coming from the root of the word—the Latin "res publica," meaning "the public things." Political personalists assumed, as did American republicans of the late eighteenth century, that the American experiment depended on both virtue and self-government.

In all of their behavior, people should act with an eye to the public good, the common good, the commonwealth.

The anarchism that infused the spirit of the Sixties has generally been ignored or misunderstood. Any number of critics and historians claim that the New Left or the counterculture were apolitical, or politically naive, or politically inept. What this usually means is that the New Left and the counterculture failed to embrace the preferred political position of the critic or historian. To some extent, of course, it is true that the movements of the Sixties were naive and inept. But they were never apolitical, because anarchism is a politics, and practically speaking—if not always theoretically—the spirit of the Sixties was anarchist.

The anarchism of political personalism was communitarian anarchism. It was not anarcho-syndicalism, which looks to labor for leadership. It was not libertarian anarchism, which seeks to maximize the freedom of individuals, and which is consonant with the so-called "free enterprise" system. Instead, it was an interpersonal anarchism that hoped to maximize the freedom of people-in-community. Sixties personalists envisioned a society of human scale, characterized by participatory democracy, by economic sufficiency, by egalitarianism, by good work and good play, by personal intimacy and human growth. They envisioned institutions that would make it easier to be good. Since they did not think that Congress was likely to pass either legislation or a Constitutional amendment to enact this program, they often decided to constitute "the beloved community" themselves.[1]

Critics who assail the political failures of Sixties movements seldom say which political strategies would have been more effective. Would working within the Democratic Party lead to social transformation? Was a third party a real possibility? Did alliances with the established labor movement offer more possibilities for a personalist polity? Did democratic socialism promise to sweep the country? Was community organizing a possible panacea? Were public-interest lobbies a viable solution to the intractable problems of American society? Maybe so, but most of these options required that activists tell it like it wasn't, because these alternatives generally assumed that there were no structural problems in American society, and almost all of them assumed that alienation, anomie, apathy, and spiritual dis-ease were symptoms of private pathology rather than social sickness.

In any event, the spirit of the Sixties moved many activists into personalist politics and communitarian anarchism, where they achieved substantial successes. In many cases, as in the civil rights movement, personalist politics provided an impetus for institutional change, which liberal politicians or institutional leaders carried through. The result was a new America, but not a personalist polity. Still, the list of successes was substantial.

In conjunction with other activists of the Sixties, personalists created political constituencies for justice. Personalist politics influenced the passage of the Civil Rights Act of 1964 and the Voting Rights Act of 1965 and the enfranchisement of African Americans. More importantly, personalist politics influenced the end of legal segregation in the South, reinforced the pride of African Americans in their own persons and cultural traditions, and helped many white Americans to treat African Americans as persons. Political personalists also helped to bring the poor to national attention and to influence the national commitment to preserving human dignity via a war on poverty. Personalists embodied a new spirit of egalitarianism, which resulted in affirmative action and increased opportunities for some members of marginal groups.

Personalists also helped to mobilize constituencies for peace. Early in the Sixties, their ban-the-bomb activity led to the Limited Test Ban Treaty of 1963. Their protests against the Vietnam War made policymakers think twice about escalating the fighting. Their resistance to the draft prompted changes in draft policy and eventually the replacement of the draft by an all-volunteer army. Personalist pressure helped bring an end to America's longest war and created a "Vietnam syndrome" that made foreign intervention more complicated for policymakers.

Sixties personalism influenced a variety of American institutions. Personalist politics changed the Democratic Party so that its conventions are more democratic and more representative of the population of the United States. With its insistence on the consistency of private and public morality, personalist politics made the personal lives of public officials a political matter. And personalist perspectives have influenced American journalism, as New Journalists dropped the myth of objective consciousness for more personal reportage.

Personalist protests dramatized the impersonalism of American higher education and influenced the curriculum and pedagogy of colleges and universities, making education more relevant to human development. Personalist pressures influenced academic interest in the study of previously marginal groups. Personalist perspectives influenced revisions of the academic disciplines, as new canons conformed to the new interest in diverse groups of persons. Student activists influenced educational institutions to treat students as if they were persons, and, with the passage of the 26th Amendment, they got the government to treat them as full citizens.

Personalist politics influenced American religion, converting it from neo-orthodoxy to the Social Gospel and liberation theology. In the Catholic Church, for example, personalist perspectives made their way into the mainstream. The Catholic bishops 1983 pastoral letter, *The Challenge of Peace*, acknowledged the importance of Martin Luther King Jr. and

Dorothy Day in shaping their views on peace issues. And in a 1986 "Pastoral Message" that accompanied their letter on the economy, they laid out six principles as "an overview of the moral vision we are trying to share":

1) Every economic decision and institution must be judged in light of whether it protects or undermines the dignity of the human person.

2) Human dignity can be realized and protected only in a community.

3) All people have a right to participate in the economic life of society.

4) All members of society have a special obligation to the poor and vulnerable.

5) Human rights are the minimum conditions for life in community.

6) Society as a whole, acting through public and private institutions, has the moral responsibility to enhance dignity and protect human rights.

These are the main tenets of a personalism which, preached and practiced, affected the preachers and teachers of the many religious denominations in the United States. Thus, in addition to its influence on American national politics, personalism has been influential in some of America's intermediate institutions.[2]

Personalist politics provided a language and leverage for American women, who have used it well, so that women are increasingly treated as whole persons. The personalist politics of the women's movement brought "private" problems like abortion, rape, spousal abuse, child abuse, incest, sexual harassment, pornography, health care, and lesbianism into American politics. The women's movement also made many Americans aware of the "personal politics" of marriage, sexual relations, childbirth, and housework.

Personalist politics influenced a backlash against the Sixties, including both neoconservativism and the New Right, and the "culture wars" that have resulted from the contested definitions of the good life. The New Right even tried to use the language of personalism in its opposition to abortion. Defining fetuses as persons, the New Right sought to protect them. In their protests against abortion, they often adopted the politics of personal witness and of nonviolent direct action. "The New Right," observed Maurice Isserman and Michael Kazin, "accepted the challenge of 'personal politics,' and responded by organizing its own network of women activists. Phyllis Schlafly's Eagle Forum, the right-to-life movement, and similar groups proved quite adept at stirring, articulating, and channeling fears about the destruction of the male-headed 'traditional family.'"[3]

Finally, personalist politics changed thousands of people who were trying to change the world. "The Movement fell short of social and political liberation," recalled civil rights activist Emma Jones Lapansky, "but it did move us, as black people, a long way toward psychological liberation. Can we call that failure?"[4]

None of these successes was inevitable at the beginning of the 1960s; almost all of them would have been unthinkable without the impetus of the personalist politics of the decade. None of these successes was exclusively personalist, but all of them depended, in part, on personalist perspectives. Still, despite these successes, personalist politics didn't sweep the country. While the anarchists were busy building the new world in the shell of the old, the old world was shelling people with propaganda about the virtues of corporate capitalism, instrumental education, the party system, family values, scientific discoveries, technological marvels, and the American way of life. While personalists succeeded in changing aspects of American institutions, they failed to transform the most powerful structures of American life. The nation-state, the business corporation, the multiversity, the media conglomerate, all remain as entrenched—if not more powerful—as they were in the Fifties.

At the same time, political personalists found that it was not entirely possible to build a new society within the hell of the old, because the new society was necessarily connected to the old, and because the inhabitants of the new society had been socialized in the old. Because the market system still existed, and because people were attuned to the price structure of the market system (which reports prices but not costs, and especially not social or environmental costs), co-ops, for example, found themselves in competition with supermarkets, which had considerable advantages in a system of corporate capitalism.

Too, personalism had plenty of problems of its own. One of them was "the vision thing." Because conventional politics is so short sighted, it generally escapes criticism of its vision. But personalists dared to dream about social transformation and they were called to account for the vision. Unfortunately, personalists put so much emphasis on the means to change that often they weren't very clear about the outcomes. How would local communities, nation-states, and the new world order be governed? How would American society function without materialism and consumerism? How exactly is peace related to economic justice? And how precisely will our present personalist activity get us from here to there?[5]

A second problem was participatory democracy. Participatory democracy represented a return to the American tradition of the town meeting, in which citizens could directly speak their minds, but it could be both contentious and tedious. Sometimes sixties people seemed to spend more time in meetings than in meeting people's needs. The emphasis on consensus often compromised the democracy, as dissidents could effectively block the decisions of the group. Activists in the Clamshell and Abalone Alliances devised modifications of the process that addressed these problems, but they were never widely implemented.[6]

Third, the moral foundation of political personalism was both a strength and a weakness. Many Americans saw the logic of a singular morality and believed that household values could be applied to political institutions. But many others still basically accepted the schizophrenia of Christian realism, which suggested, especially in the area of national security, that moral considerations were secondary to the "vital interests" of the nation-state.[7]

Similarly, the personalist suspicion of the state and the state of American politics sometimes made it difficult for personalists to enter into productive conversations with other political activists. Schooled in nationalism and patriotism, most Americans were uneasy with comprehensive critiques of political culture, and they resisted personalist arguments about the "idolatry" of the nation-state and the corruption of the culture.[8]

A fifth problem was that personalism was personally demanding. Personalists preached personal responsibility, which Americans embraced, but they practiced a kind of personal responsibility that was hard for many Americans to imitate. In the context of a consumer society, it was not simple to embrace voluntary simplicity. In a time-driven society, it wasn't easy to make time for the meetings and moral witness that accompanied political personalism, let alone the time that might be required for jail sentences for civil disobedience. It was also demanding to keep working for transformative social change in a country that preferred its changes packaged in "new, improved" products and political candidates.[9]

Finally, personalists, too, had the full range of human infirmities, including short-sightedness and self-righteousness, sexism and heterosexism, abrasiveness and bullshit, hubris and hypocrisy. To some extent, participatory democracy provided a corrective for such human frailties, but still personalists provided each other with plenty of personal reasons for resentment and internal resistance. Unlike conventional politics, which lets people do politics in the isolation of the voting booth, political personalism put them in proximity, where they could learn to dislike and distrust each other.

During the 1960s, two conceptions of politics competed for the "hearts and minds" of the American people. To a great degree, the war at home was between a personalist and a practical politics. The politics of the liberal consensus offered realism, toughness, practicality, efficiency, expertise, and legislative remedies for social problems. The politics of personalism offered a politics that was idealistic, communitarian, compassionate, prefigurative, impractical, inefficient, democratic, and voluntary. It was no match.

Although it was much moderated by the personalist perspectives, the politics of practicality won. We are now living the legacy of the practical politics of the Sixties, and I'm not sure it's better than the idealist "nonsense" of the political personalists. Practical politics demands organization and mobilization of social groups for political goals, but, in general, as Peter Maurin noted, it demands no reorganization of self or society. Accepting the status quo as a given instead of as a gift, practical politics is, as numerous commentators have said, the art of the possible.

The success of the Sixties, therefore, was the success of Sisyphus. Like Camus' character, condemned to push a rock over and over again to the top of the hill, Sixties activists succeeded in maintaining their commitments despite the apparent futility of their activism. "Though anarchy may never succeed as anarchy," observes David DeLeon, "it is still valuable as a general critique of the failures and myths of official liberal society, providing, in some cases, workable alterations, though not alternatives." Like the American Left more broadly, the personalist politics of the Sixties offered an important critique of American culture, which mainstream institutions adopted when the credibility gap between ideals and reality gaped too wide.[10]

Personalist anarchism offered political and popular advantages because personalists spoke the common languages of religion and civic republicanism. DeLeon suggests that "any radical movement, to be popular in the United States, must draw upon the biblical language of rebirth, liberation, purification, and dignity. Martin Luther King Jr. spoke of 'the blessed community' to be achieved by 'truth force' and 'love force.' It was such appeals to conscience that explained much of the power of King, the antiwar movement of the 1960s, various battles for civil rights, the aura of Robert Kennedy, and support for Cesar Chavez of the United Farm Workers."[11]

American postwar radicalism suffered politically when it gave up the religious and civic language of personalism. Whatever critical and analytical advantages the languages of oppression and imperialism might have had, they had few communicative advantages in the United States. They may have been true, but they didn't sound true to people socialized in a different tradition.

This book has been about the radicalism of tradition. "You know," said Mike Baxter, thinking about the Catholic Worker, "a key to Aristotle's ethics is a sense that you learn by imitating others. That's what tradition is about. Dorothy handed on a tradition to us. She didn't start something incredibly revolutionary and new; deep down she and Peter Maurin and all the others knew that what they were hitting on was very old. They were handing something on, they weren't starting anything. None of us is called to start a community; we're called to join one and be faithful to one.

That's what Dorothy did. She joined one and said, 'Hey, I'm going to take it seriously.'"[12]

The Sixties provide such a tradition for modern Americans, a tradition more important for questions than for answers, more important for assumptions than for conclusions, more important for ideas than for lasting institutions. The task for us is to see where these questions and assumptions and ideas might lead us now. The tradition of political personalism invites us to ask, "What are people for?" and to insist that our institutions operate as if all people mattered.

NOTES

Notes to Introduction

1. Robert Coles, *The Call of Stories: Teaching and the Moral Imagination* (Boston: Houghton Mifflin, 1989), p. 104.
2. Coles, *Call of Stories*, p. 129.

Notes to Chapter 1

1. On the ideology of liberal consensus, see Godfrey Hodgson, *America in Our Time* (New York: Vintage, 1976), pp. 67–98.
2. In one of his "Easy Essays," Peter Maurin wrote:

> According to St. Thomas Aquinas
> man is more
> than an individual
> with individual rights,
> he is a person
> with personal duties
> toward God,
> himself,

and his fellow man.
As a person
man cannot serve God
without serving
the Common Good.

Geoffrey B. Gneuhs, "Peter Maurin's Personalist Democracy," in *A Revolution of the Heart*, ed. Patrick G. Coy (Philadelphia: Temple University Press, 1988), p. 50.

3. Martin Luther King Jr., "A Time to Break Silence," in *I Have a Dream: Writings and Speeches That Changed the World*, ed. James M. Washington (San Francisco: HarperSanFrancisco, 1992), p. 148.

4. In an article titled "Covering the Bomb: The Nuclear Story and the News," Manoff describes the development of these two voices in discussions of nuclear issues:

> The first, tolerant of the White House and War Department news leadership, was responsive to the events of the day and dominated the paper. In its reliance on official sources, in its preoccupation with policy, in its focus on government, it was basically *statist* in orientation. The second, largely reactive to the themes developed by the first, took root in the journalistic interstices— in adjectives, in analysis and editorials, in fugitive paragraphs within statist narrative. In its recourse to moral authority, in its dependence on unmediated expression, in its respect for individual opinion, it was basically a *civil* voice. Although the contrast between the two should not be overdrawn, the former tended to be a journalism of achievement, the latter one of consequences; the former a journalism of causes, the latter of effects; the former a journalism of politics, the latter, of ethics.

Robert Karl Manoff, "Covering the Bomb: The Nuclear Story and the News," *Working Papers for a New Society* (May–June 1983): 20–21.

5. Milton Viorst, *Fire in the Streets: America in the 1960s* (New York: Simon and Schuster, 1979), p. 208.

6. The best discussion of prefigurative politics is Wini Breines' *Community and Organization in the New Left, 1962–1968* (New Brunswick, NJ: Rutgers University Press, 1989).

7. Francis J. Sicius, "Karl Meyer, the Catholic Worker, and Active Personalism," *Records of the American Catholic Historical Society of Philadelphia* 93 (1982): 107.

8. Philip D. Beidler, *Scriptures for a Generation: What We Were Reading in the '60s* (Athens: University of Georgia Press, 1994), p. 5.

9. Paul Deats, "Introduction to Boston Personalism," in *The Boston Personalist Tradition in Philosophy, Social Ethics, and Theology*, ed. Paul Deats and Carol Robb (Macon, GA: Mercer University Press, 1986), p. 6.

10. John Hellman, *Emmanuel Mounier and the New Catholic Left 1930–1950* (Toronto: University of Toronto Press, 1981), p. 5. "Capitalism," claimed *Esprit*'s prospectus, "reduces [people] . . . to a state of servitude irreconcilable with the dignity of man; it orients all classes and the whole personality toward the possession of money; the single desire which chokes the modern soul. Marxism is a rebel son of capitalism from which it has received the faith in the material." Hellman, pp. 42–43.

11. Arthur Sheehan, *Peter Maurin: Gay Believer* (Garden City, NY: Hanover House, 1959), pp. 122–23.
12. Hellman, *Emmanuel Mounier*, pp. 49, 82.
13. Hellman, *Emmanuel Mounier*, pp. 82–83.
14. Hellman, *Emmanuel Mounier*, pp. 39–40, 53.
15. Hellman, *Emmanuel Mounier*, pp. 9, 66.
16. Hellman, *Emmanuel Mounier*, pp. 103, 211–12, 250.
17. Hellman, *Emmanuel Mounier*, pp. 7–8, 85.
18. Hellman, *Emmanuel Mounier*, pp. 207, 252.
19. Sicius, "Karl Meyer, The Catholic Worker, and Active Personalism," p. 107.
20. John H. Lavely, "Personalism," *Encyclopedia of Philosophy*, volume VI, ed. Paul Edwards (New York: Macmillan and Free Press, 1967), p. 108; Deats, "Introduction to Boston Personalism," pp. 2–3.
21. Deats, "Introduction to Boston Personalism," pp. 2, 10–11. "We need not an abstract morality," Bowne claimed, "but the morality of good homes, of good schools, of good farms, of good roads, of good cooking, of good management, of good literature, of good newspapers, of good libraries, of good health, of good politics, of good government, of good citizenship, and of good institutions generally." Harold DeWolf, "Ethical Implications for Criminal Justice," in *The Boston Personalist Tradition*, p. 224.
22. Deats, "Conflict and Reconciliation in Communitarian Social Ethics," in *The Boston Personalist Tradition*, p. 284.
23. Deats, "Conflict and Reconciliation," pp. 284–85.
24. Among the historians who have emphasized these continuities, see Lawrence Lader, *Power on the Left: American Radical Movements Since 1946* (New York: Norton, 1979); Maurice Isserman, *If I Had a Hammer: The Death of the Old Left and the Birth of the New Left* (New York: Basic Books, 1987); Andrew Jamison and Ron Eyerman, *Seeds of the Sixties* (Berkeley: University of California Press, 1994).
25. James Miller, *"Democracy Is in the Streets": From Port Huron to the Siege of Chicago* (New York: Simon and Schuster, 1987), p. 37; Robert S. Ellwood, *The Sixties Spiritual Awakening: American Religion Moving from Modern to Postmodern* (New Brunswick, NJ:1994), p. 9. In the 1950s, for example, an overwhelming majority of Americans inherited their religious identification; by the 1980s, as many as one in three chose their denomination based on ethical stands. Robert Wuthnow, *The Restructuring of American Religion: Society and Faith Since World War II* (Princeton: Princeton University Press, 1988).
26. Dwight Macdonald, "'Here Lies Our Road!' Said Writer to Reader," *Politics* 1 (September 1944): 247–51; Cristina Scatamacchia, *"Politics, Liberation*, and Intellectual Radicalism," (Ph.D. dissertation: University of Missouri, 1990), p. 246; Lyman T. Sargent, *New Left Thought: An Introduction* (Homewood, IL: Dorsey Press, 1972), p. 3.

Notes to Chapter 2

1. Nancy L. Roberts, *Dorothy Day and the Catholic Worker* (Albany: State University of New York Press, 1984), pp. 149–54. Hennacy sometimes called himself

an anarchist, which he defined as someone "who doesn't need a cop to make him behave," but he preferred the term "personalist," because, he thought, you could change the world by changing yourself.

2. Neil H. Katz, "Radical Pacifism and the Contemporary American Peace Movement: The Committee for Nonviolent Action, 1957–1967," (Ph.D. dissertation, University of Maryland, 1974), pp. 19–20.

3. Kay Boyle, "The Triumph of Principles," *Liberation* 5 (June 1960): 5. Jim Forest, *Love Is the Measure: A Biography of Dorothy Day* (New York: Paulist Press, 1986), pp. 138–39; Francis J. Sicius, "Karl Meyer, The Catholic Worker, and Active Personalism," *Records of the American Catholic Historical Society of Philadelphia* 93 (1982): 113.

4. Patricia McNeal, *Harder Than War: Catholic Peacemaking in Twentieth-Century America* (New Brunswick, NJ: Rutgers University Press, 1992), pp. 34–37; George Weigel, *Tranquillitas Ordinis: The Present Failure and Future Promise of American Catholic Thought on War and Peace* (New York: Oxford University Press, 1987), pp. 148–53; Robert Holsworth, *Let Your Life Speak: A Study of Politics, Religion, and Antinuclear Weapons Activism* (Madison: University of Wisconsin Press, 1989), pp. 7–9.

5. Marc Ellis, *Peter Maurin: Prophet in the Twentieth Century* (New York: Paulist Press, 1981), p. 50; Sicius, "Karl Meyer, The Catholic Worker, and Active Personalism," p. 107; Dwight Macdonald, "Dorothy Day," *New Yorker* (October 4 and 11, 1952), reprinted in *Memoirs of a Revolutionist: Essays in Political Criticism* (New York: Farrar, Straus, and Cudahy, 1957), p. 351. For more on the importance of St. Francis of Assisi to the Catholic Worker movement, see Ellis, pp. 69–72. See also Robert Ludlow, "St. Francis and His Revolution," in *A Penny a Copy*, Thomas C. Cornell and James Forest, ed., (New York: Macmillan, 1968), pp. 150–54.

6. For a biographical synthesis, see Anne Klejment, "Dorothy Day and the Catholic Worker Movement," in *American Reform and Reformers*, ed. Randall Miller and Paul Cimbala (Westport, CT: Greenwood, 1996). See Robert Ellsberg's introduction to *By Little and By Little: The Selected Writings of Dorothy Day* (New York: Alfred A. Knopf, 1983), pp. xv–xli.

7. Robert Coles, *A Spectacle Unto the World: The Catholic Worker Movement* (New York: Viking Press, 1973), pp. 21–22; Dorothy Day, *The Long Loneliness* (New York: Harper and Row, 1952), pp. 54–56, 62; William D. Miller, *Dorothy Day: A Biography* (New York: Harper & Row, 1982), pp. 166–69.

8. Berrigan, "Introduction," *The Long Loneliness*, p. xxiii. Michael Harrington reminds us that "Dorothy was very feminine, which was strange for a woman whose first arrest was as a feminist." Rosalie Riegle Troester, ed., *Voices from the Catholic Worker* (Philadelphia: Temple University Press, 1993), p. 74.

9. Day, *The Long Loneliness*, p. 147; Coles, *A Spectacle Unto the World*, pp. 15–16, 32–35; Arthur Sheehan, *Peter Maurin: Gay Believer* (Garden City: Hanover, 1959), pp. 90–92. Day noted that "Gill said that Christ came to make the rich poor and the poor holy." Day, *The Long Loneliness*, p. 245. In a 1934 "Easy Essay," Maurin paraphrased G.K. Chesterton:

The Communists say
that Christianity is a failure
for the very good reason
that Christianity has not been tried.

Day and Maurin intended to try it. Ellis, *Peter Maurin*, p. 82. For more on Day and the Lyrical Left, see Anne Klejment, "The Radical Origins of Catholic Pacifism: Dorothy Day and the Lyrical Left During World War I," in *American Catholic Pacifism: The Influence of Dorothy Day and the Catholic Worker*. ed. Anne Klejment and Nancy L. Roberts (Westport, CT: Praeger, forthcoming). For more on distributism, see Jay P. Corrin, *G.K. Chesterton and Hilaire Belloc: The Battle Against Modernity* (Athens: Ohio University Press, 1981).

10. Sheehan, *Peter Maurin*, pp. 19–28.
11. Sheehan, *Peter Maurin*, pp. 39, 49; Coles, *A Spectacle Unto the World*, pp. 10–12; Ellis, *Peter Maurin*, pp. 26–29.
12. Coles, *A Spectacle Unto the World*, pp. 12–13. Maurin wrote a digest of Kropotkin's *Fields, Factories and Workshops* (London: Hutchinson, 1899), but he had also read *The Conquest of Bread* (London: Chapman and Hall, 1906) and *Mutual Aid: A Factor of Evolution* (New York: Knopf, 1918). Ellis, *Peter Maurin*, p. 177.
13. Ellis, *Peter Maurin*, pp. 87–92, 135, 183; Sheehan, *Peter Maurin*, pp. 122–23.
14. Sheehan, *Peter Maurin*, p. 13; Ellis, *Peter Maurin*, p. 43. Maurin's social models were premodern, but, since he expected them to follow modernism, they were also postmodern. Maurin has been called a reactionary, and the charge is true, as long as you accept the assumption that modernism is eschatologically inevitable and ethically insuperable. "Reactionary" is the term that people who believe in one version of progress use to describe people who have different assumptions about what is good for people.
15. Mary C. Segers, "Equality and Anarchism: The Political and Social Ideas of the Catholic Worker Movement," *Review of Politics* 40 (April 1978): 207; Ellis, *Peter Maurin*, pp. 44, 48, 59; Sheehan, *Peter Maurin*, pp. 88–89. Maurin liked to quote the exchange between Father Vincent McNabb and John Strachey, the leader of the English Communist Party. "I'm a real communist," said the priest, referring to the Dominicans' seven-century tradition of holding property in common. "You are only an amateur."
16. Ellis, *Peter Maurin*, p. 48; Sheehan, *Peter Maurin*, p. 53.
17. Day, *The Long Loneliness*, p. 170.
18. Maurin, "On the Use of Pure Means," *Catholic Worker* (January 1935): 5 and (March 1935): 4. Segers, "Equality and Anarchism," p. 206.
19. Ellis, *Peter Maurin*, pp. 56–57.
20. Coles, *A Spectacle Unto the World*, pp. 12–15. Maurin had served in the French Army in 1898–99, and hated "the slow development of the impersonal human machine demanded by the high command." Sheehan, *Peter Maurin*, pp. 50–51.
21. Ellis, *Peter Maurin*, p. 45. The May 1933 editorial is reprinted in Sheehan, *Peter Maurin*, pp. 93–94.
22. Troester, *Voices from the Catholic Worker*, pp. 92–93.

23. Day, *The Long Loneliness*, pp. 203, 280; Coles, *A Spectacle Unto the World*, p. 58. This position fit also with the Catholicism of the *Catholic Worker*. In 1919, the National Catholic War Council (later the National Catholic Welfare Council) of the Catholic bishops endorsed a program including support for unions, federal employment and unemployment agencies, social insurance for sickness and accidents and old age, producer and consumer cooperatives, labor-management cooperation, and stock and profit sharing plans. During the Depression, the bishops supported most New Deal legislation, and, in the 1940 "The Church and the Social Order," endorsed the limited welfare state and the new industrial unionism of the CIO. Although Peter Maurin and Dorothy Day preferred a more personalist approach than the bishops, they were in the mainstream of Catholic social thought. David J. O'Brien, "Social Teaching, Social Action, Social Gospel," *U.S. Catholic Historian* 5 (1986): 198–99. The Catholic Worker was also instrumental in the organization of the Association of Catholic Trade Unionists (1937), which trained young unionists for labor organizing. Troester, *Voices from the Catholic Worker*, p. 12.

24. Day, *The Long Loneliness*, p. 227. Recalling her own girlhood, Day said that she had "imbibed a 'philosophy of work,' enjoying the creative aspect of it as well as getting satisfaction from a hard and necessary job well done." Day, *The Long Loneliness*, p. 24. During the 1920s, Maurin stopped charging his students for French lessons, offering them as a gift, and taking only whatever honorarium the students offered in return. Sheehan, *Peter Maurin*, p. 83.

25. Ellis, *Peter Maurin*, pp. 47, 62, 75; Sheehan, *Peter Maurin*, p. 95.

26. O'Brien, "Social Teaching, Social Action, Social Gospel," pp. 202–03.

27. O'Brien, "Social Teaching, Social Action, Social Gospel," pp. 214–16; Day, *The Long Loneliness*, p. 150.

28. Roberts, *Dorothy Day and the Catholic Worker*, p. 55.

29. Troester, *Voices from the Catholic Worker*, pp. 62–63.

30. Peter Maurin, *Easy Essays* (West Hamlin, WV: Green Revolution, 1973), pp. 23–24; Forest, "No Longer Alone," p. 141.

31. Sheehan, *Peter Maurin*, p. 96.

32. David DeLeon, *The American as Anarchist: Reflections on Indigenous Radicalism* (Baltimore: Johns Hopkins University Press, 1979), p. 124; Forest, "No Longer Alone," p. 143.

33. Segers, "Equality and Christian Anarchism," p. 203.

34. Sheehan, *Peter Maurin*, pp. 154–61, 166–73, 177–78.

35. Sheehan, *Peter Maurin*, pp. 160–61; Day, *The Long Loneliness*, p. 185; Gandhi, quoted in John J. Ansbro, *Martin Luther King Jr.: The Making of a Mind* (Maryknoll, NY: Orbis, 1982), p. 130.

36. Ellis, *Peter Maurin*, p. 49.

37. James H. Forest, "No Longer Alone: The Catholic Peace Movement," in *American Catholics and Vietnam* (Grand Rapids: William B. Eerdmans, 1968), p. 143. Dorothy Day agreed with William James that "poverty is a worthy religious vocation." See *The Long Loneliness*, pp. 118–19. "Voluntarily embraced, poverty could be liberating," notes Mary Segers; "but involuntarily suffered, poverty could be enslaving and dehumanizing." Segers, "Equality and Anar-

chism," p. 205. Like Thomas Aquinas, Maurin believed that all goods were either necessary, useful, or superfluous. People should keep necessities; they could keep or part with the merely useful; but superfluous goods *belonged* to the poor. Ellis, *Peter Maurin*, p. 141.

38. Day, *The Long Loneliness*, p. 225; Macdonald, "Dorothy Day," p. 367.
39. Walter Brueggeman, *The Prophetic Imagination* (Philadelphia: Fortress Press, 1978), pp. 85–86.
40. Day, *The Long Loneliness*, p. 181. Individual charity was the foundation of the Catholic Worker movement, but a personalist perspective also addressed the systematic nature of poverty. Picketing and leafleting, Day felt, were a part of the spiritual works of mercy, and an integral part of the Catholic Worker movement. Day, *Long Loneliness*, p. 220.
41. Maurin, *Easy Essays*, pp. 37–38; Ellis, *Peter Maurin*, pp. 52–53; Furfey, "Introduction," *A Penny a Copy*, p. xiv; Day, *The Long Loneliness*, p. 185. They preached "personal responsibility, not state responsibility." When faced with a social problem, the personalist response was not "Why don't *they* do something?" It was "What can *I* do?" In an "Easy Essay," Maurin claimed that

> The Communitarian Revolution
> is basically
> a personal revolution.
> It starts with I,
> not with They.
> One I plus one I
> makes two I's
> and two I's make We.
> We is a community,
> while "they" is a crowd.

Sheehan, *Peter Maurin*, pp. 10, 60, 121, 146.
42. Robert Coles, *Dorothy Day: A Radical Devotion* (Reading, MA: Addison Wesley, 1987), p. 96; Day, *The Long Loneliness*, p. 267.
43. Day, *The Long Loneliness*, p. 268; Robert Ludlow, "A Desirable Goal," in *A Penny a Copy*, pp. 136–37. Personalists generally thought that Reinhold Niebuhr emphasized the limitations of human nature too much, and the "divine possibilities" of grace too little.
44. David E. Shi, *The Simple Life: Plain Living and High Thinking in American Culture* (New York: Oxford University Press, 1985), p. 247; Mildred J. Loomis, *Alternative Americas* (New York: Universe Books, 1982), pp. 71–73.
45. Marshal Shatz, *Essentials of Anarchism*, pp. xi–xxix; Sheehan, *Peter Maurin*, p. 136. Maurin also taught his fellows the rudiments of organic agriculture, using Sir Albert Howard's *The Agricultural Testament* as an instructional text. See Ellis, *Peter Maurin*, pp. 93–116.
46. Day, *The Long Loneliness*, p. 195; Segers, "Equality and Christian Anarchism," p. 201, 208–09. The practice of communitarian anarchism was never as elegant as the theory. Dorothy Day was always first among equals. Tom Cornell recalled that Dorothy Day wanted to be an anarchist, but only if she got to be

the anarch. Michael Harrington recalled that they all "had a completely demo-cratic, anarchist discussion, and then Dorothy made up her mind." Too, accord-ing to John Cort, the practice of personalism proved difficult. "The notion was that, according to personalism, or personal responsibility as it was called, you didn't tell anybody to do anything. You just set a good example, and hoped they'd profit from your good example and begin to do good things. But it didn't work too well." Troester, *Voices from the Catholic Worker*, pp. 72–73, 131.

47. Forest, "No Longer Alone," p. 144. For more on Catholic Worker pacifism, see Anne Klejment and Nancy L. Roberts, eds., *American Catholic Pacifism: The Influence of Dorothy Day and the Catholic Worker* (Westport, CT: Praeger, forth-coming)

48. See Gordon Zahn, *Another Part of War: The Camp Simon Story* (Amherst: Uni-versity of Massachusetts Press, 1979) for more on CO camps and CW presence. For almost thirty years, the Catholic Worker was virtually the only Catholic organization providing assistance to conscientious objectors, or objections to the church's complicity in American militarism. Forest, "No Longer Alone," p. 145.

49. Segers, "Equality and Christian Anarchism," 202; Nancy Roberts, *Dorothy Day and the Catholic Worker*, p. 180; Francis Sicius, "Karl Meyer, the Catholic Worker, and Active Personalism," p. 111; Troester, *Voices from the Catholic Worker*, p. 4.

50. Dorothy Day, "We Go On Record," *Catholic Worker* (September 1945) reprinted in *A Penny a Copy*, p. 67

51. Day, *The Long Loneliness*, p. 265; McNeal, *Harder Than War*, pp. x–xii; Roberts, *Dorothy Day and the Catholic Worker*, pp. 52–56; "Graham Okays War for Christians," *Fellowship* 21 (November 1955): 26. Graham admitted that war was a "horrible experience," but argued that "in most wars men are acting as the judicial agents of their governments and are responsible to their governments for their actions."

52. Coles, *A Spectacle Unto the World*, p. 43. For other beatific visions of political personalism, see my Chapter Three, "The Beat of Personalism."

53. The best biography of Merton is Michael Mott's *The Seven Mountains of Thomas Merton* (Boston: Houghton Mifflin, 1984). For the quotation, see "In Acceptance of the PAX Medal, 1963," in Thomas Merton, *The Nonviolent Alternative* ed. Gordon C. Zahn (New York: Farrar Straus Giroux, 1980), p. 257. For an account of Merton's emergence from the snail's shell, and of his famous 1957 "epiphany," see George Woodcock, *Thomas Merton, Monk and Poet: A Critical Study* (New York: Farrar, Straus, Giroux, 1978), pp. 104–107; or Thomas Merton, *Conjectures of a Guilty Bystander* (Garden City, NY: Double-day, 1966), pp. 156–58.

54. I.F. Stone, *The Haunted Fifties, 1953–1963* (Boston: Little, Brown, 1989), p. 120. For provocative interpretations of the religious dimensions of Bomb cul-ture, see Ira Chernus, *Dr. Strangegod: On the Symbolic Meaning of Nuclear Weapons* (Columbia: University of South Carolina Press, 1986), and Ira Cher-nus and Edward Tabor Linenthal, eds., *A Shuddering Dawn: Religious Studies and the Nuclear Age* (Albany: State University of New York Press, 1989).

55. Stephen J. Whitfield, *The Culture of the Cold War* (Baltimore: Johns Hopkins University Press, 1991), pp. 59, 91–92. See also Les K. Adler and Thomas G.

Paterson, "Red Fascism: The Merger of Nazi Germany and Soviet Russia in the American Image of Totalitarianism," *American Historical Review* 75 (1970): 1046–64; and James J. Farrell, "Making (Common) Sense of the Bomb in the First Nuclear War," *American Studies* 36 (Fall 1995): 5–41. For more on the cultural resonance of the Bomb, see also Spencer R. Weart, *Nuclear Fear: A History of Images* (Cambridge: Harvard University Press, 1988), pp. 77–102; and Allan Winkler, *Life Under a Cloud: American Anxiety About the Atom* (New York: Oxford University Press, 1993).

56. Whitfield, *Culture of the Cold War*, pp. 81, 88–89. For an excellent account of postwar religion, see Robert Wuthnow, *The Restructuring of American Religion* (Princeton: Princeton University Press, 1988). For Thomas Merton's response to this popular religion, see *Seeds of Destruction* (New York: Farrar, Straus, and Giroux, 1964), pp. 247–48.

57. Lawrence Wright, *In the New World: Growing Up with America from the Sixties to the Eighties* (New York: Vintage, 1987), p. 55; Whitfield, *Culture of the Cold War*, p. 87.

58. Jean Bethke Elshtain, *Women and War* (New York: Basic Books, 1987), p. 123. For more on Catholics and McCarthyism, see Donald F. Crosby, *God, Church, and Flag: Senator Joseph R. McCarthy and the Catholic Church* (Chapel Hill: University of North Carolina Press, 1978). For an excellent discussion of just war theory, see Michael Walzer, *Just and Unjust Wars: A Moral Argument With Historical Illustrations* (New York: Basic Books, 1977).

59. Weigel, *Tranquillitas Ordinis*, p. 123; Ronald E. Powaski, *Thomas Merton on Nuclear Weapons* (Chicago: Loyola University Press, 1988), pp. 7–11.

60. Mott, *The Seven Mountains of Thomas Merton*, p. 307; Thomas Merton, *A Vow of Conversation* (New York: Farrar Straus & Giroux, 1988), pp. 23, 128. See also pp. 67–68, 92, 103, and the intrusion recounted in "Rain and the Rhinoceros," in *Raids on the Unspeakable* (New York: New Directions, 1966), p. 14. The idea of "political intrusion" comes from a January 1987 lecture by Terence Des Pres at Amherst College.

61. Thomas Merton to Dorothy Day, 20 December 1961, in *Thomas Merton: The Hidden Ground of Love: The Letters of Thomas Merton on Religious Experience and Social Concerns* (New York: Farrar Straus Giroux, 1985), p. 141.

62. Merton, *A Vow of Conversation*, pp. 49–50.

63. Thomas Merton to John Tracy Ellis, 7 December 1961 and 4 February 1962, and Thomas Merton to Dorothy Day, 9 April 1962, in *Thomas Merton: The Hidden Ground of Love*, pp. 145, 175–76. See also Thomas Merton to James Douglass, 26 May 1965; Thomas Merton to Dorothy Day, 22 September 1961, in *Thomas Merton: The Hidden Ground of Love*, pp. 140, 160.

64. Thomas Merton, *A Vow of Conversation*, p. 175. "What society preaches as 'the good life,' said Merton, "is in fact a systematically organized way of death, not only because it is saturated with what psychologists call an unconscious death wish but also because it actually rests on death. It is built on the death of the nonconformist, the alien, the odd-ball, the enemy, the criminal. It is based on war, on imprisonment, on punitive methods which include not only mental and physical torture but, above all, the death penalty." Thomas Merton, *Albert Camus' The Plague* (New York: Seabury Press, 1968), p. 21.

65. Thomas Merton, *Conjectures of a Guilty Bystander*, pp. 81–82; Powaski, *Thomas Merton on Nuclear Weapons*, pp. 81, 85–86; Woodcock, *Thomas Merton*, p. 117.

66. Thomas Merton, *Conjectures of a Guilty Bystander*, pp. 219, 100. Personalist democracy differed from liberal democratic theory, which "began with the individual and the relative nature of values outside the individual." It also differed from Marxist theory, which "subordinated the individual to the process of history made absolute." Ellis, *Peter Maurin*, p. 121.

67. Merton, *Seeds of Destruction*, p. 107.

68. Thomas Merton, *Seeds of Destruction*, pp. 14–15. Merton felt that American racial policy also belied American assertions of concern for persons. He claimed that Americans had "little genuine interest in human liberty and in the human person. What we are interested in, on the contrary, is the unlimited freedom of the corporation. When we call ourselves the 'free world' we mean first of all the world in which *business* is free." William A. Au, *The Cross, the Flag, and the Bomb: American Catholics Debate War and Peace, 1960–1983* (Westport, CT: Greenwood, 1985), pp. 120–21; Merton, *Seeds of Destruction*, pp. 22–23.

69. Merton, "Peace and Revolution: A Footnote from *Ulysses*," in *The Nonviolent Alternative*, pp. 74–75.

70. Mott, *The Seven Mountains of Thomas Merton*, pp. 374–75; Thomas Merton, *Original Child Bomb: Points for Meditation to Be Scratched on the Walls of a Cave* (New York: New Directions, 1962); Thomas Merton, ed., *Breakthrough to Peace: Twelve Views on the Threat of Thermonuclear Extermination* (New York: New Directions, 1962).

71. Thomas Merton to Catherine de Hueck Doherty, 28 December 1957, in *Thomas Merton: The Hidden Ground of Love*, p. 15; Thomas Merton, *A Vow of Conversation*, p. 28. Merton, however, continued to circulate his writings in mimeographed samizdat that reached a small but influential audience. He also published a few articles under pseudonyms like "Benedict Monk" and "Benedict Moore."

72. Thomas Merton, "A Devout Meditation in Honor of Adolf Eichmann," in *Raids on the Unspeakable* (New York: New Directions, 1966), pp. 45–49.

73. Hannah Arendt, *The Life of the Mind, Volume I/ Thinking* (New York: Harcourt Brace Jovanovich, 1971), p. 4; Henry T. Nash, "The Bureaucratization of Homicide," *Bulletin of the Atomic Scientists* 36 (April 1980): 22–27; Lisa Peattie, "Normalizing the Unthinkable," *Bulletin of the Atomic Scientists* 40 (March 1984): 32–36. See also C. Wright Mills, "Culture and Politics," in *The Sixties: Art, Politics, and Media of Our Most Explosive Decade* (New York: Paragon House, 1991), pp. 76–77.

74. Merton, "Devout Meditation," pp. 45–46.

75. Merton, "Devout Meditation," pp. 46–47. For more on the issue of sanity in nuclear discourse, see James J. Farrell, "The Sanity of Madness in Nuclear Discourse, 1945–1965" (Unpublished ms., 1991).

76. Merton's "madness" may have come, in part, from reading *Mad Magazine*, as odd as that may seem. *Mad*, in fact, was one of the topics of the first conversation between Merton and the late love of his life. He also appreciated the black humor of Lenny Bruce and the music of Bob Dylan. Mott, *The Seven Mountains of Thomas Merton*, p. 435, 457, 459.

77. Robert Heyer, ed., *Nuclear Disarmament: Key Statements of Popes, Bishops, Councils, and Churches* (New York: Paulist Press, 1982), pp. 4–7.

78. Nancy Zaroulis and Gerald Sullivan, *Who Spoke Up? American Protest Against the War in Vietnam, 1963–1975* (Garden City, NY: Doubleday, 1984), p. 8.

79. Merton, "In Acceptance of the Pax Medal, 1963," in *The Nonviolent Alternative*, p. 258.

80. James H. Forest, in *Merton, By Those Who Knew Him Best* (San Francisco: Harper & Row, 1984), p. 55.

81. Thomas Merton to Catherine de Hueck Doherty, 12 November 1962, in *Thomas Merton: The Hidden Ground of Love*, p. 20; Au, *The Cross, the Flag, and the Bomb*, p. 116. For Merton's notes on the retreat, see *The Nonviolent Alternative*, pp. 259–60. Gordon Zahn suggests that "one might go so far as to suggest that the 'Great Catholic Peace conspiracy' of the Vietnam years had its real beginning in the quiet setting of Gethsemani." Gordon C. Zahn, "The Spirituality of Peace," in *The Legacy of Thomas Merton*, ed. Brother Patrick Hart (Kalamazoo: Cistercian Publications, 1986), p. 211. For King's retreat plans, see Ansbro, *Martin Luther King Jr.: The Making of a Mind*, p. 308.

82. Dwight Macdonald, "Dorothy Day," p. 350; Daniel Berrigan, *Portraits of Those I Love* (New York: Crossroad, 1982), p. 67. For more on Berrigan, see Chapter Seven.

83. Ellis, *Peter Maurin*, pp. 63, 66–67; Macdonald, "Dorothy Day," p. 368.

84. Day, *The Long Loneliness*, p. 249, 255–56; Macdonald, "Dorothy Day," p. 354. As Macdonald points out, Day considered the crucifixion the supreme example of successful failure.

85. Macdonald, "Dorothy Day," p. 353.

86. Macdonald, "Dorothy Day," p. 366.

Notes to Chapter 3

1. Allen Ginsberg, *Howl and Other Poems* (San Francisco: City Lights, 1956), p. 11. Ginsberg makes the connection explicit, and corrects the location, in Allen Ginsberg, *Howl: Original Draft Facsimile, Transcript and Variant Versions, Fully Annotated by Author, With Contemporaneous Correspondence, Account of First Public Reading, Legal Skirmishes, Precursor Texts and Bibliography*, ed. Barry Miles (New York: Harper & Row, 1986), p. 128.

2. Allen Ginsberg, *Howl and Other Poems*, pp. 9–22. For the history of "Howl," see Ginsberg, *Howl*, ed. Barry Miles.

3. Ann Charters, *The Portable Beat Reader* (New York: Viking, 1992), p. xxvii. Although McClure was a poet, he was not a historian. The Korean War had concluded on July 27, 1953. For a full account of the reading of the six at the Six, see Michael McClure, *Scratching the Beat Surface* (San Francisco: North Point Press, 1982), pp. 11–34. For more on the Beat context, see Charters, pp. 5–6.

4. Allen Ginsberg to Richard Eberhart, 18 May 1956, quoted in Ginsberg, *Howl*, ed. Barry Miles, pp. 151–54. See also Kenneth Rexroth, "San Francisco Letter," *Evergreen Review* 2 (1957): 5–6, 13, reprinted in *World Outside the Window*, (New York: New Directions, 1987), p. 62–63.

5. Rexroth, "San Francisco Letter," pp. 62–63; Jay Stevens, *Storming Heaven: LSD and the American Dream* (New York: Harper & Row, 1987), p. 111; Michael Davidson, *The San Francisco Renaissance: Poetics and Community at Mid-Century* (Cambridge: Cambridge University Press, 1989), pp. 68–69. Writing to his father in 1958, Ginsberg contended that peace would come from "a complete change of values—I'm not talking of moral or political values—those are just ideas—but a change of inward understanding of themselves on the part of masses of individuals." Davidson, p. 29.

6. Charters, *Portable Beat Reader* pp. xix, 3; Allen Ginsberg, "A Version of the Apocalypse," in *The Beat Vision: A Primary Sourcebook*, ed. Arthur and Kit Knight (New York: Paragon House, 1987), pp. 185–91.

7. Linda Hamalian, *A Life of Kenneth Rexroth* (New York: W.W. Norton, 1991), pp. 37–38; Rexroth, "Revolt: True and False," in *World Outside the Window*, p. 75; Davidson, *San Francisco Renaissance*, p. 96. Rexroth converted to Roman Catholicism in his final years.

8. Hamalian, *A Life of Kenneth Rexroth*, pp. xx, 33, 99, 103, 105, 127; Davidson, *San Francisco Renaissance*, p. 26.

9. Hamalian, *A Life of Kenneth Rexroth*, pp. 112–16, 145.

10. Lawrence Ferlinghetti, *Literary San Francisco: A Pictorial History from Its Beginnings to the Present Day* (San Francisco: City Lights and Harper & Row, 1980), p. 169.

11. Hamalian, *A Life of Kenneth Rexroth*, pp. 149, 154, 156, 236; Morgan Gibson, *Kenneth Rexroth* (New York: Twayne, 1972), pp. 69, 93; Davidson, *San Francisco Renaissance*, pp. 26, 38–41; Kenneth Rexroth, "San Francisco's Mature Bohemians," *The Nation* (February 27, 1957): 160. For a good discussion of the personalism of Rexroth's poetry, see Gibson, 86–91.

12. Kenneth Rexroth, "Introduction," in *The New British Poets: An Anthology* (New York: New Directions, 1949), pp. xxiii–xxviii. Alex Comfort, best known in the United States for *The Joy of Sex* (1972) was an anarcho-pacifist English writer. Born in 1920, a conscientious objector in World War II, Comfort was officially blacklisted by the BBC for his denunciations of indiscriminate bombing. A biologist as well as an artist, he believed that people were socially constituted and biologically predisposed toward mutual aid. Influenced by the anarchist Romanticism of Herbert Read, he believed in the transformation of society by way of a change of heart. Although he was not a utopian, he continually emphasized "the unending conflict between the responsible individual and irresponsible society," and he called for the decentralization of human institutions. In *Art and Social Responsibility*, he contended that "revolution is not a single act, it is an unending process based upon individual disobedience." A friend of Bertrand Russell's, Comfort was jailed in 1962 for an antinuclear sitdown in Trafalgar Square. Arthur E. Salmon, *Alex Comfort* (Boston: Twayne, 1978), pp. 21, 23, 28, 29, 35.

13. Hamalian, *A Life of Kenneth Rexroth*, pp. 152–56; Ferlinghetti, *Literary San Francisco*, pp. 153–56.

14. Lawrence Lipton, "Notes Toward an Understanding of Kenneth Rexroth with Special Attention to 'The Homestead Called Damascus,'" *Quarterly Review of*

Literature 9 (1957): 37; Kenneth Rexroth, "The Dragon and the Unicorn," in *The Collected Longer Poems*, pp. 98, 107, 114.

15. Rexroth, "The Dragon and the Unicorn," pp. 140, 153, 160, 211.

16. Rexroth, "The Dragon and the Unicorn," pp. 207, 209.

17. Kenneth Rexroth, "Thou Shalt Not Kill," in *The Collected Shorter Poems of Kenneth Rexroth* (New York: New Directions, 1966), pp. 267–75; Hamalian, *A Life of Kenneth Rexroth*, pp. 231–33; Gibson, *Kenneth Rexroth*, pp. 33, 61. Both Ginsberg and Rexroth insisted that "Howl" had not been influenced by "Thou Shalt Not Kill," despite the similarities in politics and poetic fury. Hamalian, p. 241.

18. Hamalian, *A Life of Kenneth Rexroth*, pp. 149, 154, 156. Davidson, *San Francisco Renaissance*, pp. 19, 34–35, 39; Richard Howard, *Alone With America: Essays on the Art of Poetry in the United States Since 1950* (New York: Atheneum, 1969), p. 146.

19. Ferlinghetti, *Literary San Francisco*, p. 159; Warren French, *The San Francisco Poetry Renaissance, 1955–1960* (Boston: Twayne, 1991), p. 18.

20. Hamalian, *A Life of Kenneth Rexroth*, pp. 225, 234, French, *San Francisco Poetry Renaissance*, p. 15; Davidson, *San Francisco Renaissance*, p. 93; Gibson, *Kenneth Rexroth*, pp. 17, 94.

21. Hamalian, *A Life of Kenneth Rexroth*, pp. 225, 234; French, *San Francisco Poetry Renaissance*, p. 15.

22. Patrick D. Murphy, "Introduction," *Critical Essays on Gary Snyder* (Boston: G.K. Hall, 1991), pp. 6–7; Thomas Parkinson, "The Poetry of Gary Snyder," in *Critical Essays*, pp. 22, 34; Davidson, *San Francisco Renaissance*, pp. 100–101; Dan McLeod, "Gary Snyder," in *The Beats: Literary Bohemians in Postwar America*, ed. Ann Charters (Detroit: Gale Research, 1983), pp. 487–88.

23. Rexroth, "San Francisco Letter," in *World Outside the Window*, pp. 60–62, Lee Bartlett, *William Everson* (Boise: Boise State University, 1985), p. 27. For a meditation on the Catholic Worker experience, see "Maurin House, Oakland," in *A Penny a Copy*, ed. Thomas C. Cornell and James H. Forest (New York: Macmillan, 1968), pp. 138–39.

24. Barry Silesky, *Ferlinghetti: The Artist in His Time* (New York: Warner Books, 1990), pp. 66–69; Hamalian, *A Life of Kenneth Rexroth*, p. 226. City Lights was the first all-paperback bookstore in the world; founded by Peter Martin (son of Italian anarchist Carlo Tresca) and Ferlinghetti, it was meant to pay the rent for the second-floor offices of the little magazine *City Lights*. Both bookstore and journal were named for the Charlie Chaplin film, in which the little tramp personifies the humanist tradition in the city. Ferlinghetti, *Literary San Francisco*, p. 163.

25. Larry Smith, *Lawrence Ferlinghetti: Poet-At-Large* (Carbondale: Southern Illinois University Press, 1983), p. 26; Barry Miles, *Ginsberg: A Biography* (New York: Simon and Schuster, 1989), pp. 227–28, 232–33; Silesky, *Ferlinghetti*, pp. 70–79; Ferlinghetti, *Literary San Francisco*, pp. 180–81. The judge in the case finally ruled that "I do not believe that 'Howl' is without redeeming social importance. The first part of 'Howl' presents a picture of a nightmare world; the second part is an indictment of those elements of modern society destructive of the best qualities in human nature; such elements are predominantly identified as materialism, conformity, and mechanization leading toward war.

The third part presents a picture of an individual who is a specific representation of what the author conceives as a general condition. 'Footnote to Howl' seems to be a declamation that everything in the world is holy, including parts of the body by name. It ends with a plea for holy living. . . . The theme of 'Howl' presents 'unorthodox and controversial ideas.' Coarse and vulgar language is used in treatment and sex acts are mentioned but unless the book is entirely 'lacking in social importance' it cannot be held obscene."

26. Allen Ginsberg, "America," in *Howl and Other Poems* (San Francisco: City Lights Press, 1956), pp. 31–34. "The public was told that it needed goals and that the agenda must be set, and fulfilled, by elites." Walter A. McDougall, *The Heavens and the Earth: A Political History of the Space Age* (New York: Basic Books, 1985), p. 217. For the statist version of national goals, see The President's Commission on National Goals, *Goals for Americans*, (New York: 1960).

27. Miles, *Ginsberg*, p. 184; Allan M. Winkler, *Life Under a Cloud: American Anxiety About the Bomb* (New York: Oxford University Press, 1993), p. 3.

28. Lawrence Ferlinghetti, "I Am Waiting," in *A Coney Island of the Mind* (New York: New Directions, 1958), pp. 49–53; Silesky, *Ferlinghetti*, p. 94.

29. Allen Ginsberg, "Some Metamorphoses of Personal Prosody," in *Naked Poetry: Recent American Poetry in Open Forms* (New York: Macmillan, 1969) pp. 221–222.

30. Lawrence Ferlinghetti, "Tentative Description of a Dinner to Promote the Impeachment of President Eisenhower," *Liberation* 3 (August 1958): 17; collected in *Starting from San Francisco* (New York: New Directions, 1961), pp. 41–44; David P. Szatmary, *Rockin' in Time: A Social History of Rock-and-Roll* (Englewood Cliffs, NJ: Prentice Hall, 1991), p. 148. The poem also caused controversy within the Beat movement. Some felt that it was too political, too committed, that it belied Kenneth Rexroth's 1957 characterization of the anarchist "disengagement" of Beat life. Some felt insulted because Ferlinghetti had criticized "some men [who] sat down in Bohemia and were too busy to come." But Ferlinghetti's reply showed that he had experienced the politics of poetry and he believed in a poetry of politics:

> William Seward Burroughs said, "Only the dead and the junkie don't care— they are inscrutable." I'm neither. Man. And this is where all the tall droopy corn about the Beat Generation and its being "Existentialist" is as phoney as a four-dollar piece of lettuce. Because Jean-Paul Sartre cares and has always hollered that the writer should especially be committed. *Engagement* is one of his favorite dirty words. He would give the horse laugh to the idea of Disengagement and the Art of the Beat Generation [Rexroth's title]. Me too. And that Abominable Snowman of modern poetry, Allen Ginsberg, would probably say the same. Only the dead are disengaged.

Silesky, *Ferlinghetti*, p. 83; Larry Smith, "Lawrence Ferlinghetti," in *The Beats: Literary Bohemians in Postwar America*, ed. Ann Charters (Detroit: Gale Research, 1983), p. 207.

31. Hamalian, *A Life of Kenneth Rexroth*, p. 227.

32. Lawrence Lipton, *The Holy Barbarians* (New York: Julian Messner, 1959), pp. 293–94.

33. John Clellon Holmes, quoted in Stevens, *Storming Heaven*, p. 107; Davidson, *San Francisco Renaissance*, pp. 29–30.

34. Lewis Mumford, "Irrational Elements in Art and Politics," in *In the Name of Sanity* (New York: Harcourt Brace, 1954); Ann Charters, *The Portable Beat Reader*, pp. 3–4; John Hellman, *Emmanuel Mounier and the New Catholic Left 1930–1950* (Toronto: University of Toronto Press, 1981), p. 82; Gibson, *Kenneth Rexroth*, pp. 87–88; Paul Christensen, "Allen Ginsberg," in *The Beats: Literary Bohemians in Postwar America*, ed. Ann Charters (Detroit: Gale Research, 1983), p. 216; George Dardess, "Jack Kerouac," in *The Beats: Literary Bohemians in Postwar America*, ed. Ann Charters (Detroit: Gale Research, 1983), p. 287.

35. Elaine Scarry, *The Body in Pain: The Making and Unmaking of the World* (New York: Oxford University Press, 1985), p. 62. On Ginsberg's "poetics of the body," see Davidson, *San Francisco Renaissance*, pp. 76–85. The exclusive language of this paragraph is intentional; see Barbara Ehrenreich, *The Hearts of Men: American Dreams and the Flight from Commitment* (Garden City, NY: Anchor/Doubleday, 1983).

36. Stephen J. Whitfield, *The Culture of the Cold War* (Baltimore: Johns Hopkins University Press, 1991), p. 43; John D'Emilio and Estelle B. Freedman, *Intimate Matters: A History of Sexuality in America* (New York: Harper & Row, 1988), pp. 275–77, 288–95.

37. Morris Dickstein, *Gates of Eden: American Culture in the Sixties* (New York: Basic Books, 1977), p. 20; John Tytell, "The Beat Generation and the Continuing American Revolution," *American Scholar* 42 (Spring 1973): 309. For more on the connections of the San Francisco Renaissance to sexual politics, see Davidson, *San Francisco Renaissance*, pp. 27, 59, 192. Other important personalists and pacifists, including Bayard Rustin, David McReynolds and Barbara Deming, were also homosexuals.

38. Davidson, *San Francisco Renaissance*, p. 53.

39. Dorothy Day, *The Long Loneliness* (New York: Harper and Row, 1952), p 140; William Miller, *Dorothy Day: A Biography* (San Francisco: Harper and Row, 1982), pp. 484–85; Rosalie Riegle Troester, *Voices from the* Catholic Worker (Philadelphia: Temple University Press, 1993), p. 35. The editor of *Fuck You* was Beat poet Ed Sanders, who combined his poetry with participation in the protests of the Committee for Nonviolent Action. A fierce pacifist, Sanders later founded the Peace Eye Bookstore on New York's Lower East Side, and a rock-and-roll group called the Fugs (with Beat poet Tuli Kupferberg and others). See George F. Butterick, "Ed Sanders," in *The Beats: Literary Bohemians in Postwar America*, ed. Ann Charters (Detroit: Gale Research, 1983), pp. 473–85.

40. Davidson, *San Francisco Renaissance*, pp. 31–32, 36–37.

41. Tom Hayden, *Reunion: A Memoir* (New York: Random House, 1988), p. 19; George Dardess, "Jack Kerouac", pp. 298–99. For another account of the impact of Kerouac and the Beats, see Marilyn Coffey, "Those Beats!" in *The 60s Without Apology*, ed. Sohnya Sayres et. al. (Minneapolis: University of Minnesota Press, 1984), pp. 238–41.

42. Stevens, *Storming Heaven*, p. 120; Kerouac, *The Dharma Bums* (New York: New American Library, 1958), pp. 77–78.

43. Charters, *Portable Beat Reader*, p. 440; Christensen, "Allen Ginsberg," p. 220.
44. French, *San Francisco Poetry Renaissance*, p. xx; George Dardess, "Jack Kerouac," p. 287; Todd Gitlin, *The Sixties: Years of Hope, Days of Rage* (New York: Bantam, 1987), pp. 54; Kingsley Widmer, "The Beat in the Rise of the Populist Culture" in *The Fifties: Fiction, Poetry, Drama*, ed. Warren French (Deland, FL: Everett/Edwards, 1970), p. 159. See also Rexroth, "Disengagement: The Art of the Beat Generation," in *World Outside the Window*, pp. 53–54. On the motif of madness, see Charles DeBenedetti and Charles Chatfield, *An American Ordeal: The Antiwar Movement of the Vietnam War* (Syracuse: Syracuse University Press, 1990), pp. 69–71.
45. Rexroth, "Revolt: True and False," *The Nation* (April 26, 1958); reprinted in *World Outside the Window*, p. 75; Rexroth, "The Students Take Over," *The Nation* (July 2, 1960); reprinted in *World Outside the Window*, p. 116.
46. Christensen, "Allen Ginsberg," pp. 219, 224; Allen Ginsberg, *Allen Verbatim* (New York: McGraw-Hill, 1974), p. 202; Rexroth, "San Francisco Letter," p. 64. "The Beats may be considered the vanguard in a significant shift in post-World War II religious consciousness," claimed Carl Jackson, a shift "marked by rejection of institutional religion, a questioning of Christian values, and an affirmation of the possibility of new religious meaning to be found through mystical experience, hallucinogenic drugs and Asian religions." Carl T. Jackson, "The Counterculture Looks East: Beat Writers and Asian Religion," *American Studies* 29 (1988): 52.
47. Silesky, *Ferlinghetti*, pp. 80, 101; Ferlinghetti, *Literary San Francisco*, p. 188; George Dardess, "Jack Kerouac," p. 287; Gary Snyder, "Note on the Religious Tendencies," *Liberation* 4 (June 1959): 11; reproduced in *The Portable Beat Reader*, pp. 305–06. When asked in 1968 why he wrote about Buddha but not Jesus, Kerouac replied, "I've never written about Jesus? . . . All I *write about* is Jesus." Jackson, "The Counterculture Looks East," p. 58.
48. Snyder, "Note on the Religious Tendencies," p. 306.
49. David R. Pichaske, *A Generation in Motion: Popular Music and Culture in the Sixties* (New York: Schirmer, 1979), p. 96; Jackson, "The Counterculture Looks East," p. 59; Stevens, *Storming Heaven*, p. 112. See also Alan Watts, *Beat Zen, Square Zen, and Zen* (San Francisco: City Lights, 1959).
50. Lipton, *Holy Barbarians*, pp. 149–50; Rexroth, "Disengagement: The Art of the Beat Generation," p. 56. Warren French contends that this emphasis on Beat social theory, such as it was, confuses the spiritual awakening of the Beats with a reformist political movement. But in personalist politics, the two went hand in hand. French, *San Francisco Poetry Renaissance*, p. 90.
51. Silesky, *Ferlinghetti*, p. 121; Theodore Roszak, "This Disease Called Politics," *Liberation* 7 (March 1962): 15–18.
52. Jeff Smith, *Unthinking the Unthinkable: Nuclear Weapons and Western Culture* (Bloomington: Indiana University Press, 1989), p. 137; Stevens, *Storming Heaven*, p. 116–17; Davidson, *San Francisco Renaissance*, pp. 27, 61–62. Such criticism began even before the Beats were a movement; see Mildred Edie Brady, "The New Cult of Sex and Anarchy," Harper's (April 1947): 312–322.
53. Still, Newfield thought that "the Beats' mysticism, anarchy, anti-intellectualism, sexual and drug experimentation, hostility to middle-class values, and ide-

alization of the Negro and of voluntary poverty [note connection to Catholic Workers] all have clear parallels in the New Left." He also noted a similarity of cultural tastes: Bob Dylan, Paul Krassner, Allen Ginsberg, Norman Mailer, Jean Genet, the Beatles, the Fugs, etc. "Both movements," Newfield noted, "represent a rebellion against Puritanism, hypocrisy, repression, and commercialism. Only the Beats were apolitical, self-indulgent, and a bit mad, while the New Left has a moral vision of a new society and is trying to create it with social activism." Newfield, *A Prophetic Minority*, pp. 32–33.

54. Paul O'Neil, "The Only Rebellion Around," *Life* 47 (November 30, 1959): 114–130. *Life* itself was a sign of the society the Beats were rebelling against. O'Neil's dismissive essay was framed by editorials ("Space: An American Necessity"), articles ("Dress-Up Time Across U.S.") and advertisements that promoted the American way of life. The last issue of 1959 was a special two-in-one issue on "The Good Life" that the Beats considered a "Social Lie." *Life* 47 (December 28, 1959): 1–192. See also Wini Breines, "The 'Other' Fifties: Beats and Bad Girls," in *Not June Cleaver: Women and Gender in Postwar America, 1945–1960* (Philadelphia: Temple University Press, 1994), pp. 382–408.

55. Davidson, *San Francisco Renaissance*, p. 24; Gitlin, *Sixties*, p. 54; DeBenedetti and Chatfield, *An American Ordeal*, p. 78.

56. Ferlinghetti, *Literary San Francisco*, pp. 174–76.

57. Sally Banes, *Greenwich Village 1963: Avant-Garde Performance and the Effervescent Body* (Durham: Duke University Press, 1963), pp. 20–22.

58. Eric von Schmidt and Jim Rooney, *Baby, Let Me Follow You Down: The Illustrated History of the Cambridge Folk Years*, 2nd edition (Amherst: University of Massachusetts Press, 1979); "Sibyl With Guitar," *Time* (23 November 1962): 54.

59. Marty Jezer, *Abbie Hoffman: An American Rebel* (New Brunswick, NJ: Rutgers University Press, 1992), pp. 26–27; Rexroth, "The Dragon and the Unicorn," p. 168. "When I started singing," said Joan Baez, "I felt as though we just had so long to live, and I still feel that way. It's looming over your head." "Sibyl With Guitar," *Time* (23 November 1962): 55. See also "Folk Frenzy," *Time* (11 July 1960): 81. For more on the fatuous optimism of the postwar years, see Thomas Hine, *Populuxe* (New York: Alfred A. Knopf, 1986).

60. Bruce Pollock, *When the Music Mattered: Rock in the 1960s* (New York: Holt, Rinehart and Winston, 1983), p. 18.

61. Pete Seeger, *The Incompleat Folksinger* (New York: Simon and Schuster, 1972), pp. 1–17; R. Serge Denisoff, *Great Day Coming: Folk Music and the American Left* (Urbana: University of Illinois Press, 1971), pp. 115–18; Stephen J. Whitfield, *The Culture of the Cold War* (Baltimore: Johns Hopkins University Press, 1991), pp. 201–02; Szatmary, *Rockin' in Time*, pp. 87–89. Guthrie became a hero to the folk-protest culture: he "had been on the road before Kerouac, howling before Ginsberg, and on the left when it was really dangerous to be there." Jerome Rodnitzky, *Minstrels of the Dawn: The Folk Singer as a Cultural Hero* (Chicago: Nelson-Hall, 1976), p. 62. The epigraph to Seeger's *The Incompleat Folksinger* was a quotation from Catholic Worker Ammon Hennacy: "Love without courage and wisdom is sentimentality, as with the ordinary

church member. Courage without love and wisdom is foolhardiness, as with the ordinary soldier. Wisdom without love and courage is cowardice, as with the ordinary intellectual."

62. Denisoff, *Great Day Coming*, pp. 144–50. Seeger was cited for contempt of Congress for refusing to name names for the House Un-American Activities Committee. Seeger, *Incompleat Folksinger*, pp. 468–74.

63. Denisoff, *Great Day Coming*, pp. 166–67; Szatmary, *Rockin' in Time*, p. 87; Elinor Langer, "Notes for Next Time: A Memoir of the 1960s," *Working Papers for a New Society* 1 (Fall 1973); reprinted in R. David Myers, ed., *Toward a History of the New Left: Essays From Within the Movement* (Brooklyn: Carlson Publishing, 1989), pp. 73–74. For more on the campus bohemianism of the late Fifties and early Sixties, see Marty Jezer, *Abbie Hoffman*, pp. 26–29.

64. Gitlin, *Sixties*, p. 74; Jezer, *Abbie Hoffman*, p. 27; "Hoots and Hollers on the Campus," *Newsweek* (27 November 1961): 84.

65. "Sibyl With Guitar," p. 54; Rodnitzky, *Minstrels of the Dawn*, p. xiv. The electrification of Dylan's music at the 1965 Newport Folk Festival was scandalous to folkies. Electrification was modernization, and the cult of folk simplicity demanded consistency of sound and subject.

66. Seeger, *Incompleat Folksinger*, p. 280. Seeger also saw folk music as a protest against the mass productions of Tin Pan Alley and the Hit Parade. "I am against the hit parade," said Seeger in 1956, "because I am against anything that would make a sheep out of a human being." Seeger, p. 169.

67. Szatmary, *Rockin' in Time*, p. 84; Rodnitzky, *Minstrels of the Dawn*, pp. xv, 17; Craig Robert Snow, "Folksinger and Beat Poet: The Prophetic Vision of Bob Dylan," (Ph.D. dissertation: Purdue University, 1978), p. 101; Joseph Wenke, "Bob Dylan," in *The Beats: Literary Bohemians in Postwar America*, ed. Ann Charters (Detroit: Gale Research, 1983), p. 182.

68. Szatmary, *Rockin' in Time*, pp. 87–89; Pollock, *When the Music Mattered*, p. 9; Terry H. Anderson, *The Movement and the Sixties* (New York: Oxford University Press, 1995), p. 89.

69. Catherine Ingram, *In the Footsteps of Gandhi: Conversations With Spiritual Social Activists* (Berkeley: Parallax Press, 1990), pp. 56–57; Joan Baez, *And A Voice to Sing With* (New York: Summit Books, 1987), pp. 40–41, 49–55; von Schmidt and Rooney, *Baby, Let Me Follow You Down*, pp. 14–18, 37–42, 123; Nat Hentoff, "Folk Finds a Voice," *Reporter* (4 January 1962): 39. "I had heard the Quakers argue that the ends did not justify the means," Baez recalls. "Now I was hearing that the means would determine the ends. It made sense to me."

70. Baez, *And A Voice to Sing With*, p. 114; Susan J. Douglas, *Where the Girls Are: Growing Up Female with the Mass Media* (New York: Times Books, 1994), p. 146.

71. Baez, *And a Voice to Sing With*, pp. 117, 130–32; Ingram, *In the Footsteps of Gandhi*, p. 58; Rodnitzky, *Minstrels of the Dawn*, pp. 86–87. Baez claimed that her problem was not with Lyndon Johnson, but with party politics and politicians, whose "allegiance was to the nation state." When she was questioned about her tax refusal, she told the IRS agent, "The way I see it you can either be a good citizen or a good person. If being a good citizen means paying to make

napalm to dump on little children, then I guess I'd rather be a good person and refuse." Baez, p. 121.

72. Pichaske, *Generation in Motion*, pp. 24, 34; Snow, "Folksinger and Beat Poet," p. 130; Robert Shelton, *No Direction Home: The Life and Music of Bob Dylan* (New York: Beech Tree Books, 1986), p. 72; Szatmary, *Rockin' in Time*, pp. 94–95; Wenke, "Bob Dylan," pp. 180–84. Beat poetry also affected such Sixties musicians as Donovan and Phil Ochs. "It seemed," said Ochs, "that protest songs were a natural development from beat poetry, which was very self-analytical."

73. "They Hear America Singing," *Time* (19 July 1963): 53–54; Szatmary, *Rockin' in Time*, p. 96; Arnold Shaw, *The Rock Revolution* (London: Crowell-Collier, 1969), pp. 56–57; Wenke, "Bob Dylan," p. 181.

74. Gross, *Bob Dylan*, p. 62; Douglas, *Where the Girls Are*, p. 147; Rodnitzky, *Minstrels of the Dawn*, pp. 106–110

75. Allen Ginsberg, *Planet News, 1961–1967* (San Francisco: City Lights Books, 1968); Davidson, *San Francisco Renaissance*, p. 29; Szatmary, *Rockin' in Time*, pp. 97–98. Explaining the work of the Freedom Singers, Charles Neblett said that "our real purpose is to carry the story of the student movement to the North. Newspapers and UPI often won't give the real story and SNCC had to find another way to get it out." Bernice Johnson Reagon, "Songs of the Civil Rights Movement 1955–1965: A Study in Culture History," (Ph.D. dissertation: Howard University, 1975), p. 140.

76. Seeger, *The Incompleat Folksinger*, p. 171; Reagon, "Songs of the Civil Rights Movement," p. 97.

77. Reagon, "Songs of the Civil Rights Movement," pp. 79–82, 102, 112–114.

78. Reagon, "Songs of the Civil Rights Movement," p. 132; Seeger, *Incompleat Folksinger*, pp. 111–12; Barbara Deming, *Prisons That Could Not Hold* (San Francisco: Spinsters Ink, 1985), p. 77.

79. Clayborne Carson, *In Struggle: SNCC and the Black Awakening of the 1960s* (Cambridge: Harvard University Press, 1981), pp. 63–64; Seeger, *Incompleat Folksinger*, pp. 232–33; Newfield, *A Prophetic Minority*, pp. 96, 103. On the music of the Albany Movement, see Reagon, "Songs of the Civil Rights Movement," pp. 130–140 and Guy and Candie Carawan, *Sing for Freedom: The Story of the Civil Rights Movement Through Its Songs* (Bethlehem, PA: Sing Out Corporation, 1990), pp. 59–78.

80. Seeger, *Incompleat Folksinger*, pp. 247–48. Seeger also believed in personal witness and action. He said he always heard people asking, "But what can I do? I am just one small person." In "One Man's Hands," Seeger provided the music for a personalist response:

> One man's hands can't build a world of peace
> A woman's hands can't build a world of peace
> But if two by two we work for peace together
> We'll see that day come round
> We'll see that day come round

Seeger, *Incompleat Folksinger*, p. 315. The original words for "One Man's Hands" were from English personalist and anarchist Alex Comfort; Seeger set new words by Kevin Becker to music. Carawan and Carawan, *Sing for Freedom*, p. 81.

81. Seeger, *Incompleat Folksinger*, p. 260; Reagon, "Songs of the Civil Rights Movement," p. 155; Carawan and Carawan, *Sing for Freedom*, p. 175.

82. James Miller, *"Democracy Is in the Streets": From Port Huron to the Siege of Chicago* (New York: Simon and Schuster, 1987), pp. 161, 191; Morris Dickstein, *Gates of Eden: American Culture in the Sixties* (New York: Basic Books, 1977), p. 188. For the music of the March on Washington, see Reagon, "Songs of the Civil Rights Movement," pp. 165–67. Dylan appeared with Pete Seeger in Greenwood, Mississippi in July 1963, and at the SDS national council meeting in December, but he was more attracted to the aesthetics than the ethics of Beat poetry and he soon turned to writing songs that were more imagistic than accusatory.

83. Seeger, *Incompleat Folksinger*, p. 292; Rodnitzky, *Minstrels of the Dawn*, p. 39; Douglas, *Where the Girls Are*, p. 146. "It was all too easy," notes Jerome Rodnitzky, "for folk fans to delude themselves into thinking that they were changing an evil world, when all they were doing was listening to records, strumming guitars, and attending concerts." Rodnitzky, *Minstrels of the Dawn*, p. 25.

84. Denisoff, *Great Day Coming*, pp. 177–78. Denisoff thinks that folk music died of success when it became popular music. Instead, I think that success changed significant aspects of the folk scene, but that the folk perspective persisted, not just in folk, but in the folk-rock and rock music of the later Sixties.

Notes to Chapter 4

1. Clayborne Carson, "Introduction," *The Papers of Martin Luther King Jr.: Volume II: Rediscovering Precious Values* (Berkeley: University of California Press, 1994), p. 11.

2. Keith D. Miller, *Voice of Deliverance: The Language of Martin Luther King Jr. and Its Sources* (New York: Free Press, 1992), pp. 5, 10.

3. John Ansbro, *Martin Luther King Jr.: The Making of a Mind* (Maryknoll, NY: Orbis Books, 1982), p. 16–17, 64–65. Davis understood the progress and personalization of civilization as signs of God's engagement in history. "God has a great plan for the world," he claimed. "His purpose is to achieve a world where all men will live together as brothers, and where every man recognizes the dignity and worth of all human personality." Ansbro, p. 66. King understood African American history in the same way: from 1619 to 1863, black people had been treated as depersonalized cogs in a system of slavery; from the Emancipation Proclamation to 1954, they had been free, but not accepted as persons; the third period of constructive integration after the 1954 Brown vs. Board decision offered possibilities for human dignity. Ansbro, p. 161.

4. Coretta Scott King, *My Life With Martin Luther King Jr.* (New York: Holt, Rinehart and Winston, 1969), p. 88; Ansbro, *Martin Luther King Jr.: The Making of a Mind*, p. 287. See also Paul Deats, "Introduction to Boston Personalism," in *The Boston Personalist Tradition in Philosophy, Social Ethics and Theology*, ed. Paul Deats and Carol Robb (Macon, GA: Mercer University Press, 1986), pp. 1–13. Harold DeWolf directed Martin Luther King's dissertation on love. When King made his life a second dissertation on love, DeWolf was involved again. Despite

threats to his life, he acted as a negotiator between whites and African Americans in St. Augustine, Florida in 1964. He participated in the Mississippi Freedom March of 1966. And he was one of only a few people chosen to deliver a tribute at his student's funeral. Ansbro, *MLK: The Making of a Mind*, pp. 98–99. For the text of the tribute, see "Transcripts of Prayer, Tribute, and Eulogy Delivered at Services for Dr. King," *New York Times* (April 10, 1968): 32.

5. Ansbro, *Martin Luther King Jr.: The Making of a Mind*, pp. 60–61; Carson, "Introduction," pp. 24–25; Kenneth Rexroth, "The Dragon and the Unicorn," p. 178. King's dissertation criticized both Paul Tillich and Henry Nelson Wieman for obscuring the personhood of God.

6. James H. Cone, "The Theology of Martin Luther King, Jr." *Union Seminary Quarterly Review* 40 (January 1986): 23; James H. Cone, *Martin and Malcolm and America* (Maryknoll, NY: Orbis Books, 1991), p. 137; Ansbro, *Martin Luther King Jr.: The Making of a Mind*, p. 22; Warren E. Steinkraus, "Martin Luther King's Contributions to Personalism," *Idealistic Studies* 6 (1976): 21. King's Morehouse professor had explained this depersonalization using Martin Buber: "Instead of an 'I Thou' relationship that allows for mutual personal development, the racist 'I' never chooses to encounter a 'Thou' in the Negro because he has made the 'Thou' invisible, hidden by his own stereotypes. The racist has reduced the Negro to 'the world of It.'" Ansbro, p. 108.

7. Kenneth Smith and Ira Zepp, *Search for the Beloved Community* (Valley Forge: Judson, 1974), pp. 104–107, 111–114.

8. Ansbro, *Martin Luther King Jr.: The Making of a Mind*, pp. 23–24, 31. At Crozer, George Davis had also taught that one of the major shifts in history was "the transition from rank individualism to the solidarity of the social group, which enhances the realization of the personal." Ansbro, p. 66.

9. Miller, *Voice of Deliverance*, pp. 62–63. John Ansbro agrees that "King did not need personalism to provide him with the passion to oppose segregation, but personalism with its emphasis on the value of the person did help formulate the principles for his attack upon this evil." Ansbro, *Martin Luther King Jr.: The Making of a Mind*, pp. 76–77.

10. Cone, *Martin and Malcolm and America*, pp. 121–22; Miller, *Voice of Deliverance*, p. 17–18. "Belief in a personal God and in the dignity and worth of the human person has always been a deeply held conviction in the African American Christian community," says James Cone. "Therefore, it was easy, almost natural, for King to embrace the philosophy of personalism." Cone, *Martin and Malcolm and America*, p. 29. For an eloquent expression of this idea, see King, "Man in a Revolutionary World," quoted in Ansbro, *Martin Luther King Jr.: The Making of a Mind*, p. 22.

11. Cone, *Martin and Malcolm and America*, p. 25. "Whenever whites stripped blacks of their humanity, the church offered dignity." Miller, *Voice of Deliverance*, p. 27.

12. Cone, *Martin and Malcolm and America*, p. 72. For African American men, this could be expressed as the difference between being called "boy" and being a "man." Once when Martin Luther King Jr. was driving with his father, a policeman pulled them over and demanded of "Daddy" King, "Boy, show me your

license." King Sr. replied, pointing to young Martin, "That's a *boy* there. I'm a *man*. I'm Reverend King." Cone, p. 24.

13. Cone, *Martin and Malcolm and America*, pp. 21, 126; Ansbro, *Martin Luther King Jr.: The Making of a Mind*, p. 8.

14. Miller, *Voice of Deliverance*, p. 37; Cone, *Martin & Malcolm & America*, p. 143.

15. Cone, *Martin and Malcolm and America*, pp. 21, 126, 130.

16. Cone, *Martin and Malcolm and America*, p. 21.

17. Miller, *Voice of Deliverance*, pp. 17–28; Cone, *Martin & Malcolm & America*, pp. 21, 126. For the personalist perspective on Divine Providence, see Ansbro, *Martin Luther King Jr.: The Making of a Mind*, pp. 37–60. For King's use of the Exodus theme, see Ansbro, p. 178.

18. Cone, *Martin and Malcolm and America*, p. 144; Miller, *Voice of Deliverance*, p. 22. For King's criticism of the otherworldliness of black religion, see Cone, pp. 148–49. It is important to remember, however, how much a belief in personal immortality can contribute to a person's commitment to social activism. When a person believes, as King did, that God rewards the good, it is easier to be good.

19. Cone, *Martin and Malcolm and America*, pp. 127–28.

20. Cone, *Martin and Malcolm and America*, p. 132.

21. Miller, *Voice of Deliverance*, p. 59; Ansbro, *Martin Luther King Jr.: The Making of a Mind*, pp. 170–71. "All human goodness must be social goodness," said Rauschenbusch. "Man is fundamentally gregarious and his morality consists in being a good member of his community. A man is moral when he is social; he is immoral when he is antisocial." Ansbro, *Martin Luther King Jr.: The Making of a Mind*, p. 167.

22. Cone, *Martin and Malcolm and America*, pp. 29, 34; Miller, *Voice of Deliverance*, pp. 45–49. The Social and Political Action Committee emphasized the importance of voter registration and the work of the NAACP. Ansbro, *Martin Luther King Jr.: The Making of a Mind*, p. 177.

23. Miller, *Voice of Deliverance*, p. 107; Cone, *Martin and Malcolm and America*, p. 30; Ansbro, *Martin Luther King Jr.: The Making of a Mind*, p. 93.

24. Ansbro, *Martin Luther King Jr.: The Making of a Mind*, pp. 157–58, 265; Cone, *Martin and Malcolm and America*, p. 30.

25. Miller, *Voice of Deliverance*, pp. 65–66, 85. See August Meier, "Conservative Militant," in *Martin Luther King Jr.: A Profile*, ed C. Eric Lincoln (New York: Hill and Wang, 1984)), pp. 144–56.

26. Cone, *Martin and Malcolm and America*, pp. 66–67, 281.

27. Sudarshan Kapur, *Raising Up a Prophet: The African American Encounter With Gandhi* (Boston: Beacon Press, 1992), p. 159; Ansbro, *Martin Luther King Jr.: The Making of a Mind*, p. 175.

28. Martin Luther King, Jr., *Stride Toward Freedom: The Montgomery Story* (New York: Harper, 1958), p. 97; Kapur, *Raising Up a Prophet*, pp. 163–64; R. Allen Smith, "Mass Society and the Bomb: The Discourse of Pacifism in the 1950s," *Peace and Change* (October 1993): 355; Mark Silk, *Spiritual Politics: Religion and America Since World War II* (New York: Simon and Schuster, 1988), p. 116. Keith Miller shows that "Gandhi exerted very little direct influence on King";

King learned Gandhian principles from Americans who interpreted the Indian activist for American conditions. Miller, *Voice of Deliverance*, pp. 88–96. The phrase "the Americanization of Gandhi" comes from the title of a chapter in Maurice Isserman's *If I Had a Hammer. . . The Death of the Old Left and the Birth of the New* (New York: Basic Books, 1987), p. 125. Keith Miller explains the process of Americanization: the American Gandhians "paid little or no attention to the communal Gandhi, the cloth-spinning Gandhi, the vegetarian Gandhi, the ascetic Gandhi, the celibate Gandhi, the Hindu Gandhi, and the fast-unto-death Gandhi. Instead they concentrated on the nonviolent Gandhi who orchestrated massive campaigns of civil disobedience." Miller, p. 98.

29. Miller, *Voice of Deliverance*, pp. 53–54; Kapur, *Raising Up a Prophet*, pp. 8, 89–90, 118–23, 134.

30. Robinson, *Abraham Went Out*, p. 117; Kapur, *Raising Up a Prophet*, p. 147.

31. Miller, *Voice of Deliverance*, pp. 92–93. Miller suggests that King's use of the pacifist preachings of the liberal pulpit especially endeared him to white people: "his appeals for nonviolence succeeded in part because he reached a crucial group of Northern, white progressives through anti-war language they already knew and relished."

32. Taylor Branch, *Parting the Waters: America in the King Years 1954–63* (New York: Simon and Schuster, 1988), pp. 176–180; David Garrow, *Bearing the Cross: Martin Luther King Jr. and the Southern Christian Leadership Conference* (New York: Morrow, 1986), p. 116. In 1960, when Adam Clayton Powell threatened to expose Rustin's homosexuality, King dropped him from the SCLC staff. FBI director J. Edgar Hoover also disapproved of Rustin's sexual preferences, and of his past in the Young Communist League. But King did not quit consulting Rustin.

33. Scatamacchia, *"Politics, Liberation*, and Intellectual Radicalism," (Ph.D. dissertation: University of Missouri, 1990), pp. 173–74. Responding to Rustin's civil disobedience, Randolph taught Rustin that "while Thoreau was great, Gandhi was greater, because he organized masses." For a good brief biography of Rustin, see Milton Viorst, *Fire in the Streets: America in the 1960s* (New York: Simon and Schuster, 1979), pp. 199–231; the quotation is on page 207.

34. Scatamacchia, *"Politics, Liberation*, and Intellectual Radicalism," pp. 174–75.

35. Branch, *Parting the Waters*, pp. 168–73. Bayard Rustin is in need of a biography. C. Vann Woodward collected some of his writings in *Down the Line: The Collected Writings of Bayard Rustin* (Chicago: Quadrangle Books, 1971) and Rustin recounted his view of the civil rights movement in *Strategies of Freedom: The Changing Patterns of Black Protest* (New York: Columbia University Press, 1976). For Rustin's contributions to the civil rights movement, see Taylor Branch, *Parting the Waters* and David J. Garrow, *Bearing the Cross*.

36. Arthur Herzog, *The War-Peace Establishment* (New York: Harper and Row, 1965), pp. 240–41. Rustin and Randolph were always more concerned with economic issues than Martin Luther King. Viorst, *Fire in the Streets*, p. 211.

37. Miller, *Voice of Deliverance*, p. 98.

38. Warren E. Steinkraus, "Martin Luther King's Personalism and Nonviolence," *Journal of the History of Ideas* 34 (1973): 106–07.

39. Cone, *Martin and Malcolm and America*, pp. 62–63, 123. Cone notes that King's call for justice based on human dignity preceded the emphasis on love that would later inform his work.

40. Cone, *Martin and Malcolm and America*, pp. 76–77, 124–25.

41. Garrow, *Bearing the Cross*, pp. 66–73. Stephen B. Oates, *Let the Trumpet Sound: The Life of Martin Luther King, Jr.* (New York: New American Library, 1982), pp. 341–42. The importance of "putting your body on the line" confronted King in Montgomery in 1961, when he declined to take part in the Freedom Ride. "Where is your body?" activist students asked. Branch, *Parting the Waters*, p. 466.

42. Ansbro, *Martin Luther King Jr.: The Making of a Mind*, p. 137. For more on the black church sources of King's nonviolence, see Cone, *Martin and Malcolm and America*, pp. 76–79, 128–131.

43. Cone, *Martin and Malcolm and America*, p. 64; King, "Our Struggle," *Liberation* 1 (April 1956): 3–6; Gandhi, quoted in Marian Wright Edelman, *The Measure of Our Success: A Letter to My Children and Yours* (Boston: Beacon, 1992), p. 71. Of course, Gandhi fully expected that the revolution of the person would lead, as it did in the civil rights movement, to a revolution in the world. This was the promise of personalism.

44. Ansbro, *Martin Luther King Jr.: The Making of a Mind*, pp. 135–36.

45. Ansbro, *Martin Luther King Jr.: The Making of a Mind*, pp. 113, 142.

46. Martin Luther King Jr., "The Social Organization of Nonviolence," *Liberation* (October 1959): 6.

47. "How Sane the SANE?" *Time* 71 (21 April 1958): 13–14.

48. Milton S. Katz, *Ban the Bomb: A History of SANE, the Committee for a Sane Nuclear Policy* (New York: Praeger, 1986), pp. 31, 35, 42; Robert A. Divine, *Blowing on the Wind: The Nuclear Test Ban Debate, 1954–1960* (New York: Oxford University Press, 1978), p. 160; Harvard Sitkoff, *The Struggle for Black Equality 1954–1980* (New York: Hill and Wang, 1981), p. 219; Martin Luther King Jr., "Pilgrimage to Nonviolence," *Christian Century* (April 13, 1960): 441; Paul Carter, *Another Part of the Fifties* (New York: Columbia University Press, 1983), p. 286; Frances B. McCrea and Gerald E. Markle, *Minutes to Midnight: Nuclear Weapons Protest in America* (Newbury Park, CA: Sage, 1989), pp. 76–77; Steinkraus, "Martin Luther King's Contributions to Personalism," p. 23.

49. James Miller, *"Democracy Is in the Streets": From Port Huron to the Siege of Chicago* (New York: Simon and Schuster, 1987), p. 34; Bernice Johnson Reagon, *Songs of the Civil Rights Movement 1955–1965: A Study in Culture History* (Ph.D. dissertation: Howard University, 1975), p. 99.

50. Catherine Ingram, *In the Footsteps of Gandhi: Conversations With Spiritual Social Activists* (Berkeley: Parallax Press, 1990), pp. 202–04; Carson, *In Struggle*, pp. 22–23. In retrospect, Nash prefers to call nonviolence by a more positive term, "agapic energy." On Lawson, see Kapur, *Raising Up a Prophet*, pp. 155–56. Lawson, who was one of four African American students attending Vanderbilt University, was expelled from the Divinity School for his involvement, triggering a crisis that called so-called "Christian teaching" into question. See also Silk, *Spiritual Politics*, pp. 108–17.

51. Newfield's careful separation of moral concerns from political and economic action ignores the integrating force of political personalism, which insisted that everyday actions, like an economic boycott, were a form of politics. Jack Newfield, *A Prophetic Minority* (New York: Signet, 1966), p. 44. SCLC volunteers signed Commitment Cards detailing a "ten commandments" for modern times, including: "MEDITATE daily on the teachings and life of Jesus"; "WALK and TALK in the manner of love, for God is love"; "PRAY daily to be used by God in order that all men might be free." Silk, *Spiritual Politics*, p. 114.

52. Miller, *"Democracy Is in the Streets,"* pp. 34–35; Rexroth, "The Students Take Over," in *World Outside the Window: The Selected Essays of Kenneth Rexroth*, ed. Bradford Morrow (New York: New Directions, 1987), pp. 119, 122.

53. Newfield, *A Prophetic Minority*, p. 47. The invitation to the October meeting promised an "action-oriented" agenda focused on the central goal of "individual freedom and personhood." Clayborne Carson, *In Struggle: SNCC and the Black Awakening of the 1960s* (Cambridge: Harvard University Press, 1981), pp. 27–28.

54. Godfrey Hodgson, *America In Our Time* (New York: Vintage, 1976), pp. 188–89; Carson, *In Struggle*, p. 38. Although SNCC saw itself in tension with the established civil rights organizations, few Americans perceived the distinctions. Even in areas of the South served by SNCC, African Americans saw SNCC as an embodiment of the philosophy of Martin Luther King. Carson, p. 164.

55. Carson, *In Struggle*, p. 30; Daniel P. Hinman-Smith, *"Does the Word Freedom Have a Meaning?": The Mississippi Freedom Schools, the Berkeley Free Speech Movement, and the Search for Freedom Through Education* (Ph.D. dissertation: University of North Carolina, 1993), p. 26.

56. Branch, *Parting the Waters*, p. 475. President Kennedy was preparing to meet Soviet Premier Khrushchev in Vienna, and both the Bay of Pigs and the Freedom Rides were undermining his stature. The Kennedys used a national security argument with both the Freedom Riders and the Alabama authorities.

57. Carson, *In Struggle*, p. 37.

58. Carson, *In Struggle*, pp. 46, 114, 140; Eric Burner, *And Gently He Shall Lead Them: Robert Parris Moses and Civil Rights in Mississippi* (New York: New York University Press, 1994), p. 70. Tom Hayden recalls Charles McDew and Bob Zellner quoting Camus on the urgency of action as early as the 1960 NSA Congress: "A man can't cure and know at the same time. So let's cure as quickly as we can. That's the more urgent job." Tom Hayden, *Reunion: A Memoir* (New York: Random House, 1988), p. 39. Although some people see an essential difference between direct action and voter registration, Burner reminds us that "the decision of a Mississippi black to attempt to register was an immediate act of rebellion and self-empowerment. But the disciplines of nonviolence . . . and civil disobedience that King's legions employed were also of that character; they were practices of self-possession and self-transformation. And they too aimed not merely at personal triumph and moral witness against segregation but, in such forms as economic boycott, at a transformation of economic and political institutions. SNCC and SCLC, even in their differences, embody the dual

character of the movement: immediate liberation in empowering personal action and permanent revolution through the redistribution of power." Burner, p. 106.

59. Carson, *In Struggle*, pp. 26, 46–47; Hayden, *Reunion*, p. 56.

60. Burner, *And Gently He Shall Lead Them*, pp. 73, 193. Although it was the motive force, SNCC was not the only organization working to register voters. In fact, after the first summer, SNCC worked as part of the Council of Federated organizations (COFO), which included the NAACP, SCLC, CORE, and the Voter Education Project. Burner, p. 77.

61. Carson, *In Struggle*, pp. 47–55.

62. On the demonstrations as "morality plays" defined by the ethical opposition of nonviolence and violence, see Miller, *Voice of Deliverance*, pp. 99–100.

63. Martin Luther King Jr., "Letter from Birmingham Jail," in *Why We Can't Wait* (New York: 1964), pp. 76–95. On the personalist underpinnings of King's distinction between just and unjust laws, see Ansbro, *Martin Luther King Jr.: The Making of a Mind*, pp. 77–86.

64. For another response to the charge of outside agitation, see Barbara Deming, *Prisons That Could Not Hold* (San Francisco: Spinsters Ink, 1985), p. 29, 30.

65. King, "Letter from Birmingham Jail," p. 80; Bayard Rustin, "The Meaning of Birmingham," in *Seeds of Liberation*, p. 320.

66. Ansbro, *Martin Luther King Jr.: The Making of a Mind*, p. 35. Sunday morning, King said often, was the most segregated time of the week. In Mississippi in the summer of 1964, a black woman was barred from a white church. "But what would Jesus do?" she asked. "Leave Christ out of this," replied a white man. "What does He have to do with it?" Burner, *And Gently He Shall Lead Them*, p. 138.

67. Oates, *Let the Trumpet Sound*, pp. 222, 237–38; Cone, *Martin and Malcolm and America*, pp. 141–42. Paul Goodman complained that Kennedy should have put his own body on the line. Writing of the controversy surrounding James Meredith's admission to the University of Mississippi, he claimed that "Kennedy did not use his moral authority; he did not go to Oxford, take Meredith by the hand, and into the school. If he had then been hit by a bottle—he might well have—there would have been a great change in the Southern liberals. The sane would have ceased cowering." George Steiner, "On Paul Goodman," *Commentary* (August 1963): 163. Steiner had reservations about this approach, but it shows an ability to imagine innovative activity outside the standard operating procedures of political realism.

68. Viorst, *Fire in the Streets*, p. 199.

69. King, quoted in Cone, *Martin and Malcolm and America*, p. 58.

70. At the orientation for the volunteers, Robert Moses framed their purpose in personalist terms: "You have job to do. If each of you can leave behind three people who are stronger than before, this will be 3000 more people we will have to work with next year. This is your job." Burner, *And Gently He Shall Lead Them*, p. 156.

71. Carson, *In Struggle*, pp. 119–21. See also Daniel P. Hinman-Smith, "Does the Word Freedom Have a Meaning?"

72. Hinman-Smith, "Does the Word Freedom Have a Meaning?" pp. 62, 109. The curriculum of the 1965 Freedom Schools reflected changes in emphasis in SNCC. While the 1964 schools emphasized the possibility of change within the system, the 1965 schools showed how the system didn't work. While the 1964 schools used several hundred white teachers and emphasized integration, the 1965 sessions used a higher proportion of black teachers and emphasized racial solidarity. Hinman-Smith, pp. 228–30.

73. Hinman-Smith, "Does the Word Freedom Have a Meaning?" p. 117.

74. Carson, *In Struggle*, p. 121; Burner, *And Gently He Shall Lead Them*, p. 155.

75. Carson, *In Struggle*, p. 117.

76. Carson, *In Struggle*, p. 126.

77. Carson, *In Struggle*, pp. 83–89; Burner, *And Gently He Shall Lead Them*, p. 187. The MFDP delegates were not absolutely uncompromising; they were willing to share the delegation with the regular Democrats, but they were unwilling to accept only token representation.

78. Burner, *And Gently He Shall Lead Them*, pp. 198–99; Anderson, *The Movement*, p. 81. It is too easy to forget the violence of Southern racism. During Freedom Summer alone, six people were murdered, eighty beaten, a thousand arrested; sixty-eight black homes or churches were torched or dynamited. For COFO's account of the violence perpetrated in a three-day period of June 1964, see Burner, pp. 163–64, 168.

79. Burner, *And Gently He Shall Lead Them*, p. 215.

80. Cone, *Martin and Malcolm and America*, pp. 216–17.

81. Richard H. King, "Citizenship and Self-Respect: The Experience of Politics in the Civil Rights Movement," *Journal of American Studies* 22 (April 1988): 7–24.

82. Rexroth, "The Students Take Over," pp. 117, 121.

83. Sara Evans, *Personal Politics: The Roots of Women's Liberation in the Civil Rights Movement and the New Left* (New York: Knopf, 1979), pp. 30–31.

84. Doug Rossinow, "'The Breakthrough to New Life': Christianity and the Emergence of the New Left in Austin, Texas, 1956–1964," *American Quarterly* 46 (September 1994): 309–318; Evans, *Personal Politics*, pp. 33–34.

85. Rossinow, "Christianity and the New Left," pp. 318–31; Evans, *Personal Politics*, p. 35.

86. Doug McAdam, *Freedom Summer* (New York: Oxford University Press, 1988), p. 234; Newfield, *A Prophetic Minority*, p. 69; Dale H. Brown, *The Christian Revolutionary* (Grand Rapids: Eerdmans, 1971), p. 73; Ellen Herman, "Being and Doing: Humanistic Psychology and the Spirit of the Sixties," in *Sights on the Sixties*, ed. Barbara L. Tischler (New Brunswick, NJ: Rutgers University Press, 1992), p. 93.

87. Newfield, *A Prophetic Minority*, p. 69; Hayden, *Reunion*, pp. 39–40.

88. Alice Echols, "'Women Power' and Women's Liberation: Exploring the Relationship Between the Antiwar Movement and the Women's Liberation Movement," in *Give Peace a Chance*, ed. Melvin Small and William D. Hoover (Syracuse: Syracuse University Press, 1992), p. 173; Edward P. Morgan, *The Sixties Experience: Hard Lessons About Modern America* (Philadelphia: Temple University Press, 1991), p. 222; Blanche Linden-Ward and Carol Hurd Green,

American Women in the 1960s: Changing the Future (New York: Twayne, 1993), pp. 36–46.

89. Burner, *And Gently He Shall Lead Them*, pp. 154, 204–05.

90. Hinman-Smith, "Does the Word Freedom Have a Meaning?" p. 265.

91. Harrington, "Introduction," *A Prophetic Minority*, p. 12; Newfield, *A Prophetic Minority*, p. 73; Maurice Isserman and Kazin, "The Success and Failure of the New Radicalism," in *The Rise and Fall of the New Deal Order, 1930–1980*, ed. Steven Fraser and Gary Gerstle (Princeton: Princeton University Press, 1989), p. 218. Eventually they also began to identify with the victim status of African Americans. See, for example, Jerry Farber's "The Student as Nigger," *The Student as Nigger* (New York: Pocket Books, 1969), pp. 90–100.

92. Silk, *Spiritual Politics*, p. 115.

93. Cone, *Martin and Malcolm and America*, pp. 139–42; O'Brien, "Social Teaching, Social Action, Social Gospel," *U.S. Catholic Historian* 5 (1986): 221; Burner, *And Gently He Shall Lead Them*, p. 137; Silk, *Spiritual Politics*, pp. 125–28.

94. Hinman-Smith, "Does the Word Freedom Have a Meaning?" p. 300; Maurin, "The Race Problem," *Catholic Worker*, (May 1938): 8. On Catholic Workers and race, see Arthur Sheehan, *Peter Maurin: Gay Believer* (Garden City, NY: Hanover, 1959), pp. 110–12, 15–17.

95. Charles DeBenedetti and Charles Chatfield, *An American Ordeal: The Antiwar Movement of the Vietnam War* (Syracuse: Syracuse University Press, 1990), p. 23.

Notes to Chapter 5

1. Martin Luther King Jr., "Our Struggle," *Liberation* 1 (April 1956): 3–6; Bayard Rustin, "Montgomery Diary," *Liberation* 1 (April 1956): 7–10; Lawrence Ferlinghetti, "Tentative Description of a Dinner to Promote the Impeachment of President Eisenhower," *Liberation* 3 (August 1958): 17; Gary Snyder, "Note on the Religious Tendencies," *Liberation* 4 (June 1959): 11; reproduced in *The Portable Beat Reader*, pp. 305–06; Charles DeBenedetti and Charles Chatfield, *An American Ordeal: The Antiwar Movement of the Vietnam War* (Syracuse: Syracuse University Press, 1990), p. 77. In fact, Rustin authored both of the Montgomery articles, but King approved the description of "Our Struggle," which was his first publication. David J. Garrow, *Bearing the Cross: Martin Luther King Jr. and the Southern Christian Leadership Conference* (New York: William Morrow, 1986), pp. 73. Rustin was one of King's primary advisors, but he claimed that "during all my work with Martin King, . . . I never made a difficult decision without talking the problem over with A.J. [Muste] first." On the connections between King and Muste and Dellinger, see Jo Ann Ooiman Robinson, *Abraham Went Out: A Biography of A.J. Muste* (Philadelphia: Temple University Press, 1981), pp. 117–18 and David Dellinger, *From Yale to Jail: The Life Story of a Moral Dissenter* (New York: Pantheon, 1993), pp. 262–63.

2. Paul Goodman, "Preface," in *Seeds of Liberation*, ed. Paul Goodman (New York: Braziller, 1965), p. viii. "*Liberation*," claimed Charles DeBenedetti and Charles Chatfield, "signalled a new moment in American radical culture and politics. It

gave radical pacifism a revolutionary wing, and it crystallized many of the differences between radical pacifists and other peace advocates, thereby defining the terrain on which the evolving antiwar movement would fragment between 1955 and 1975." DeBenedetti and Chatfield, *An American Ordeal*, p. 25.

3. David Dellinger, *From Yale to Jail: The Life Story of a Moral Dissenter* (New York: Pantheon, 1993), p. 149; DeBenedetti and Chatfield, *An American Ordeal*, pp 24–25.

4. DeBenedetti and Chatfield, *An American Ordeal*, pp. 20–21. For accounts of Muste's life, see Robinson, *Abraham Went Out* and Nat Hentoff, *Peace Agitator, the Story of A.J. Muste* (New York: Macmillan, 1963).

5. Cristina Scatamacchia, *"Politics, Liberation,* and Intellectual Radicalism," (Ph.D. dissertation: University of Missouri, 1990), pp. 168–70; Daniel Aaron, *Writers on the Left: Episodes on American Literary Communism* (New York: Harcourt Brace, 1961), p. 157.

6. Robinson, *Abraham Went Out*, pp. 24, 63–65.

7. Marc Ellis, *Peter Maurin: Prophet in the Twentieth Century* (New York: Paulist Press, 1981), pp. 117–120.

8. Jo Ann Robinson, "A.J. Muste: Prophet in the Wilderness of the Modern World," in *Peace Heroes in Twentieth-Century America*, ed. Charles DeBenedetti (Bloomington: Indiana University Press, 1986), pp. 148–53; Robinson, *Abraham Went Out*, p. 20; Scatamacchia, *"Politics, Liberation,* and Intellectual Radicalism," p. 51.

9. Paul Boyer, *By the Bomb's Early Light: American Thought and Culture at the Dawn of the Atomic Age* (New York: Pantheon, 1985), p. 219; Robinson, *Abraham Went Out*, pp. 94–96.

10. For Niebuhr's influence on American Cold War culture, see Richard Wightman Fox, *Reinhold Niebuhr: A Biography* (New York: Harper and Row, 1985) and Arthur Herzog, *The War-Peace Establishment* (New York: Harper and Row, 1965), pp. 89–95. Niebuhr suggested that society was immoral, in part, because of its scale. Personalists could agree, but they argued for the communitarian solution of human scale.

11. For Muste's response to Niebuhr, see Robinson, *Abraham Went Out*, pp. 145–50; Hentoff, *Peace Agitator*, pp. 134–39, 180–83, and Boyer, *By the Bomb's Early Light*, pp. 219–20. The much-quoted "there is no way to peace; peace is the way" is paralleled in Dorothy Day's autobiography, where she quotes St. Catherine: "As St. Catherine said, 'All the way to heaven is heaven,' because He [Jesus] had said, 'I am the way.'" Dorothy Day, *The Long Loneliness* (New York: Harper and Row, 1952), p. 247. After Dwight Macdonald translated Camus' essay "Neither Victims Nor Executioners," *Liberation* featured it among its pamphlet reprints. See *Liberation* (December 1961): 22.

12. For more on the "vital center" of the ideology of liberal consensus, see Godfrey Hodgson, *America in Our Time* (New York: Vintage, 1976).

13. Boyer, *By the Bomb's Early Light*, p. 348.

14. Frances B. McCrea and Gerald E. Markle, *Minutes to Midnight: Nuclear Weapons Protest in America* (Newbury Park, CA: Sage, 1989), p. 67; Scatamacchia, *"Politics, Liberation,* and Intellectual Radicalism," pp. 50–52. In the era of

McCarthyism, such activity seemed un-American to many; the American Council of Christian Laymen labeled the Fellowship of Reconciliation a "radical pacifist group using Christian terms to spread Communist propaganda." McCrea and Markle, p. 68.

15. Robinson, *Abraham Went Out*, p. 97. In this, Muste echoed Dwight Macdonald's fears of "bureaucratic collectivism," a concept associated especially with Trotskyists like James Schactman. Scatamacchia, "*Politics, Liberation*, and Intellectual Radicalism," pp. 109–111.

16. *Speak Truth to Power, A Quaker Search for an Alternative to Violence: A Study of International Conflict Prepared for the American Friends Service Committee* (Philadelphia: American Friends Service Committee, 1955); R. Allen Smith, "Mass Society and the Bomb: The Discourse of Pacifism in the 1950s," *Peace and Change* 18 (October 1993): 352. For a completely different interpretation of this document, see Elizabeth Walker Mechling and Jay Mechling, "Hot Pacifism and Cold War: The American Friends Service Committee's Witness for Peace in 1950s America," *Quarterly Journal of Speech* 78 (1992): 173–96.

17. Milton Viorst, *Fire in the Streets: America in the 1960s* (New York: Simon and Schuster, 1979), p. 200; Robert Cooney and Helen Michalowski, *The Power of the People: Active Nonviolence in the United States* (Philadelphia: New Society, 1987), pp. 130–31.

18. Dellinger, *From Yale to Jail*, pp. 49, 61–66. "Like Dorothy Day and others at the New York Catholic Worker who became our close friends, we offered hospitality to anyone who came to our door, sharing whatever food and clothing we had as well as shelter." Like Day and the Catholic Worker, Dellinger wanted to fashion "a way of life that would not accept either the spiritual poverty of the rich or the material poverty of the poor, but would draw on the insights and true riches of both rich and poor." Dellinger, p. 55.

19. Dellinger, *From Yale to Jail*, pp. 63, 73–80.

20. Dellinger, *From Yale to Jail*, pp. 119–27; Scatamacchia, "*Politics, Liberation*, and Intellectual Radicalism," pp. 176–77, 198.

21. Dellinger, *From Yale to Jail*, pp. 141–42.

22. Dellinger, *From Yale to Jail*, pp. 145–50; Scatamacchia, "*Politics, Liberation*, and Intellectual Radicalism," pp. 177–78; Goodman, "Getting into Power," in *Seeds of Liberation*, p. 444. Scatamacchia suggests that these experiments offered "individual salvation" for radicals who had despaired of mass collective action. She does not see them as political. But she and others who see personalism as apolitical forget that politics is just part of civil society, and that people's social patterns shape their expectations of politics. People who live by the rules of competitive capitalism will be little disposed to support social welfare legislation or pacifist foreign policy. Personalist attempts to model alternative social arrangements, therefore, must be seen as an important element of political strategy.

23. Dellinger, *From Yale to Jail*, pp. 150–52.

24. Taylor Stoehr, "Introduction," *Drawing the Line: The Political Essays of Paul Goodman*, ed. Taylor Stoehr (New York: E.P. Dutton, 1977), p. xi.

25. Richard King, *The Party of Eros: Radical Social Thought and the Realm of Freedom* (New York: Delta, 1972), pp. 84–85. In 1951, with Frederick Perls and

Ralph Heffeline, Goodman wrote *Gestalt Therapy*, which emphasized the holism of individual and environment, mind and body, inner self and outer self. It also emphasized a phenomenological approach to life, whereby people probed not for the unconscious origins of their problems, but for an awareness of the person's presence in the present environment. This emphasis, says King, "fitted well with Goodman's voluntarism and emphasis upon political and social initiative."

26. King, *Party of Eros*, pp. 85–87; Joel Kovel, *Against the State of Nuclear Terror* (Boston: South End Press, 1983), p. 97; Langdon Winner, *The Whale and the Reactor: A Search for Limits in an Age of High Technology* (Chicago: University of Chicago Press, 1986) p. 72; George Steiner, "On Paul Goodman," *Commentary* (August 1963): 160.

27. George Steiner, "On Paul Goodman," p. 160; Arthur Herzog, *The War-Peace Establishment* (New York: Harper and Row, 1965), p. 249.

28. Richard Pells, *The Liberal Mind in a Conservative Age: American Intellectuals in the 1940s and 1950s* (New York: Harper and Row, 1985), p. 208; King, *Party of Eros*, p. 106. "The book," says Cristina Scatamacchia, "established a connection between the spiritual condition of the individual and the institutions which shaped and formed that condition. . . . Opposing authoritarianism and centralization, he sought the kind of decentralized, self-governed, communal economy which would become a basic element for the concept of participatory democracy." Scatamacchia, "*Politics, Liberation*, and Intellectual Radicalism," p. 181.

29. Paul Goodman, *Growing Up Absurd: Problems of Youth in the Organized Society* (New York: Vintage, 1960); King, *Party of Eros*, pp. 102–105.

30. Paul Goodman, "The Duty of Professionals," *Liberation* 12 (November 1967): 39; Goodman, *Like a Conquered Province: The Moral Ambiguity of America* (New York: Random House, 1967), pp. 110–111; Jefferson, quoted in Wendell Berry, *The Unsettling of America: Culture and Agriculture* (San Francisco: Sierra Club Books, 1977), p. 144.

31. Stoehr, "Introduction," p. ix; Goodman, *Growing Up Absurd*, p. 107.

32. Goodman, *Like a Conquered Province*, p. 112; Goodman, "Getting into Power," *Liberation* (October 1962); reprinted in *Seeds of Liberation*, p. 434.

33. Kingsley Widmer, *Paul Goodman* (Boston: Twayne, 1980), p. 100; Goodman, *The Society I Live in Is Mine* (New York: Horizon Press, 1962) pp. 159–60.

34. Goodman, *The Society I Live In Is Mine*, pp. viii–ix.

35. Jezer, *Abbie Hoffman*, p. 72; King, *Party of Eros*, p. 115.

36. "A Tract for the Times," *Liberation* 1 (March 1956): 3–6; Scatamacchia, "*Politics, Liberation*, and Intellectual Radicalism," pp. 59–60. Both in its editorial board and its contributors, *Liberation* overlapped *Dissent*, which had begun publication in 1954, but which was not so personalist in its orientation.

37. "A Tract for the Times," pp. 5–6.

38. Lawrence S. Wittner, "How Realistic Is American Diplomacy?" *Reviews in American History* 9 (March 1981): 123; Jean Bethke Elshtain, *Women and War* (New York: Basic Books, 1987), pp. 87–89. For more on the realists, see Arthur Herzog, *The War-Peace Establishment*, pp. 87–99; DeBenedetti and Chatfield, *An American Ordeal*, pp. 18–19, 36–39. For a good summary of lib-

eral and radical approaches to postwar problems, see DeBenedetti and Chatfield, *An American Ordeal*, pp. 25–26. For more on postwar American liberalism, see Richard Pells, *Liberal Mind in a Conservative Age*. On the deradicalization of the New York intellectuals, see Alan M. Wald, *The New York Intellectuals: The Rise and Decline of the Anti-Stalinist Left from the 1930s to the 1980s* (Chapel Hill, NC: University of North Carolina Press, 1987).

39. Scatamacchia, "*Politics, Liberation*, and Intellectual Radicalism," p. 250.

40. Scatamacchia, "*Politics, Liberation*, and Intellectual Radicalism," pp. 15–16.

41. "Tract for the Times," pp. 4–5; Scatamacchia, "*Politics, Liberation*, and Intellectual Radicalism," pp. 192–93.

42. Dwight Macdonald, "Why *Politics*," *Politics* 1 (February 1944): 7; Scatamacchia, "*Politics, Liberation*, and Intellectual Radicalism," p. 43. In his influential essay "The Root is Man," Macdonald contended that radicals "must emphasize the emotions, the moral feelings, the primacy of the individual human being once more, must restore the balance that has been broken by the hypertrophy of science in the last two centuries. The root is man, here and not there, now and not then." In her comparison of the politics of *Politics* and *Liberation*, Cristina Scatamacchia notes that, after the war, Macdonald started thinking in human and personal terms, arriving "at a position of absolute and personalist morality which recalled Ignazio Silone's ideas." Scatamacchia, p. 133.

43. Pells, *Liberal Mind in a Conservative Age*, p. 186.

44. "Tract for the Times," p. 7; Robinson, *Abraham Went Out*, p. 196; Scatamacchia, "*Politics, Liberation*, and Intellectual Radicalism," pp. 57–59. In the long run, this insistence on the harmony of ends and means would allow critics to portray personalists as apolitical people, absent a social theory. But this was both a social theory and a political strategy, even though it was beyond the bounds of thinkable thought for most Americans.

45. "Tract for the Times," p. 4; Roy Finch, "The *Liberation* Poll," *Liberation* 4 (November 1959): 14–17.

46. "Tract for the Times," pp. 4–6; Paul Goodman, "Preface," in *Seeds of Liberation*, pp. viii–ix; DeBenedetti and Chatfield, *An American Ordeal*, pp. 24–26. In responding to criticism of the tract, Dave Dellinger wrote that "The Here-and-Now Revolution begins with one's self. The revolutionist concentrates on carrying out in his own life the principles which characterize the life of both the decent man and the decent society. . . . This is the union of politics and religion, if the terms have any meaning after they have met. The editors of *Liberation* refer to this union as the growing edge of a new society. Francis of Assisi has more meaning than Thomas Aquinas, Dorothy Day than Billy Graham, the conscientious objector than the antiwar orator, Rosa Luxembourg than Stalin, Thoreau than Daniel Webster, Gandhi than Nehru." Dellinger, "The Here-and-Now Revolution," *Liberation* 1 (June 1956): 17. For a history of SANE, see Milton S. Katz, *Ban the Bomb: A History of SANE, the Committee for a Sane Nuclear Policy* (New York: Praeger, 1986).

47. Everett Mendelsohn, "Prophet of Our Discontent: Lewis Mumford Confronts the Bomb," in *Lewis Mumford: Public Intellectual* (New York: Oxford University Press, 1990), ed. Thomas P. Hughes and Agatha C. Hughes, pp. 354–55;

Mumford, "Atom Bomb: Miracle or Catastrophe," *Air Affairs* 2 (July 1948): 328; DeBenedetti and Chatfield, *An American Ordeal*, pp. 71–74.

48. The history of CNVA is best told in Neil H. Katz, "Radical Pacifism and the Contemporary American Peace Movement: The Committee for Nonviolent Action, 1957–1967," (Ph.D. dissertation, University of Maryland, 1974). Quotation is on page 219.

49. Hentoff, *Peace Agitator*, pp. 126–129; Robinson, *Abraham Went Out*, pp. 94–96.

50. Many CNVA activists had been inspired by Peacemakers (established 1948), in which members committed themselves to an "inner revolution" of "nonviolence, communal living, economic co-operation and sharing, production of one's own goods—all coordinated through decentralized disciplined 'cells.' " Katz, "Radical Pacifism," p.12.

51. James Peck, "Trespassing at the Bomb Site," *Liberation* 2 (September 1957): 8–9; Katz, "Radical Pacifism," pp. 40, 47. Some of the participants in the Nevada action were members of the Peninsula Committee for the Abolition of Nuclear Tests, which had been established in 1957 by Roy Kepler, Theodore Roszak, Albert Baez, Ira Sandperl, and Felix Greene among others. Cooney and Michalowski, *The Power of the People*, p. 132.

52. Scatamacchia, *"Politics, Liberation*, and Intellectual Radicalism," p. 193; Goodman, "Getting into Power," in *Seeds of Liberation*, p. 443.

53. Pickus wanted a "marriage of the concerns of the soul with the politics of the time," and criticized the protesters for their political ineffectiveness. As we shall see, they were creating the politics of another time. Robert Pickus, "The Nevada Project: An Appraisal," *Liberation* 2 (September 1957): 3–4. At first, CNVA recommended citizen action in the form of political participation and lobbying of corporations and unions for economic conversion and nonviolent alternatives to the arms race. But eventually, they recommended that citizens examine their own lives and cease supporting the war system through their jobs, their taxes, and their cooperation with the draft. They called on people "to seek livelihoods independent of governmental and industrial bureaucracies to build a society of independent, cooperating communities which do not exploit but cultivate attitudes of social responsibility, brotherhood, freedom, and mutual security." Katz, "Radical Pacifism," pp. 107, 124–25, 148, 206; Francis J. Sicius, "Karl Meyer, The Catholic Worker, and Active Personalism," *Records of the American Catholic Historical Society of Philadelphia* 93 (1982): 118.

54. Albert Bigelow, "Why I Am Sailing Into the Pacific Bomb Test Area," *Liberation* 3 (February 1958): 18–22; Katz, p. 80; Sicius, "Karl Meyer, The Catholic Worker, and Active Personalism," pp. 115–16. For accounts of the voyages of the *Golden Rule* and the *Phoenix*, see Albert Bigelow, *The Voyage of the Golden Rule: An Experiment with Truth* (Garden City, NY: Doubleday, 1958) and Earle Reynolds, *The Forbidden Voyage* (New York: McKay, 1961). See also Bradford Lyttle, "On Nonviolent Obstruction," *Liberation* 3 (November 1958): 10–11.

55. DeBenedetti and Chatfield, *An American Ordeal*, pp. 41, 43.

56. Smith, "Mass Society and the Bomb," 363; Katz, "Radical Pacifism," pp. 170–71. Smith contends that CNVA's civil disobedience assumed antagonism between the individual and society. In fact, it reflected antagonism only

between the individual and the state, and its moral witness included an important communitarian component. Civil disobedience, as practiced in many of the movements of the postwar world, was an act of individual dissent for the common good.

57. Deming, *Prisons That Could Not Hold* (San Francisco: Spinsters Ink, 1985), p. 24.
58. Deming, *Prisons That Could Not Hold*, pp. 57, 61, 72
59. Deming, *Prisons That Could Not Hold*, pp. 78, 120–21, 180–81.
60. Nancy Zaroulis and Gerald Sullivan, *Who Spoke Up? American Protest Against the War in Vietnam* (Garden City, NY: Doubleday, 1984), p. 10; Paul Goodman, "Preface," in *Seeds of Liberation*, p. vii.
61. DeBenedetti and Chatfield, *An American Ordeal*, p. 24.
62. "The Women Protest," *Newsweek* (13 November 1961): 21–22; Midge Decter, "The Peace Ladies," *Harper's* (March 1963): 48–53.
63. "The Women Protest," p. 22; Amy Swerdlow, *Women Strike for Peace: Traditional Motherhood and Radical Politics in the 1960s* (Chicago: University of Chicago Press, 1993), pp. 81–82; Bagby, "Behind the Scene: The Psychological Panorama Underlying the Beat Extravaganza," *Liberation* 4 (May 1959): 11–13; Bagby, "Oh What Farewells," *Liberation* 6 (March 1961): 17–18. In a *Liberation* poll, readers selected Bagby's article as the kind of material they wanted most, rating it even higher than articles by editors Muste and Dellinger.
64. Harriet Hyman Alonso, *Peace Is a Women's Issue: A History of the U.S. Movement for World Peace and Women's Rights* (Syracuse: Syracuse University Press, 1993), p. 207.
65. Amy Swerdlow, "Pure Milk, Not Poison: Women Strike for Peace and the Test Ban Treaty of 1963," in *Rocking the Ship of State: Toward a Feminist Peace Politics*, ed. Adrienne Harris and Ynestra King (Boulder, CO: Westview Press, 1989) p. 234.
66. Elaine Tyler May, "Explosive Issues: Sex, Women, and the Bomb," in *Recasting America: Culture and Politics in the Age of Cold War* (Chicago: University of Chicago Press, 1989), pp. 154–70; May, *Homeward Bound: American Families in the Cold War Era* (New York: Basic Books, 1988), pp. 92–113.
67. Ruth Rosen, "The Day They Buried 'Traditional Womanhood': Women and the Politics of Peace Protest," in *The Legacy: The Vietnam War in the American Imagination*, ed. D. Michael Shafer (Boston: Beacon Press, 1990), " pp. 238–39; Dee Garrison, "'Our Skirts Gave Them Courage': The Civil Defense Protest Movement in New York City, 1955–1961," in *Not June Cleaver: Women and Gender in Postwar America, 1945–1960*, ed. Joanne Meyerowitz (Philadelphia: Temple University Press, 1994), pp. 201–226. See also Marlene Stein Wortman, "Domesticating the Nineteenth-Century American City," *Prospects* 3 (1977): 531–72. Rosen sees this "motherist rhetoric" as biologically based: "until the Vietnam War, in fact, American women . . . had traditionally based their opposition to war—and nuclear weapons—on their biological difference as mothers." I see this differently; I would suggest that they based their opposition to war on their *cultural* difference as women and mothers.
68. Roy Finch, "The New Peace Movement—Part II," *Dissent* 10 (Spring 1963): 140.
69. Jean Bethke Elshtain and Sheila Tobias, ed., *Women, Militarism, and War: Essays in History, Politics, and Social Theory* (Savage, MD: Rowman and Littlefield, 1990), p. 4. Still, despite Finch's use of the term, the women of WSP

were not modern feminists. As Amy Swerdlow recalls, they did not "offer a feminist critique of the bomb and the war. We in WSP, and I include myself, had neither language nor the analytical tools to make a connection between women's secondary status in the family and political powerlessness or between domestic violence and state violence. Swerdlow, "Pure Milk," p. 16.

70. Amy Swerdlow, "Ladies' Day at the Capitol: Women Strike for Peace Versus HUAC," *Feminist Studies* 8 (Fall 1982): 494–95, 509. For the backgrounds of women's peace activism, see Alonso, *Peace Is a Women's Issue*. The decision to found an "un-organization" derived, in part, from a desire to avoid charges of communist complicity that still came in a country freed of McCarthy, but not of McCarthyism. Ironically, Orlie Pell's anti-communism had been a catalyst for Women Strike for Peace, as both WILPF and SANE had capitulated to anti-communist pressures. Alonso, pp. 206–07.

71. Jacquetta Hawkes, "Now At Last," *The New Statesman* 56 (5 July 1958): 10.

72. Dagmar Wilson and Jeanne S. Bagby, " A Reply from WISP," *Liberation* 8 (Summer 1963): 41; Elshtain, *Women and War*, p. 50. There are not many examples of "paternal pacifism." In a 1968 "Statement Against the War in Vietnam," Wendell Berry asked "Why am I against the war? I have two inescapable reasons. The first is that I am a teacher; the second that I am a father." Berry, *The Long-Legged House* (New York: Audobon/Ballantine, 1969), p. 76. Like the women of WSP, Berry has consistently asked for the application of household values to the wider world.

73. Sandra Sedacca, *Up in Arms: A Common Cause Guide to Understanding Nuclear Arms Policy* (Washington: Common Cause, 1984), p. 126; Swerdlow, *Women Strike for Peace*, pp. 93; Swerdlow, "Ladies' Day at the Capitol," pp. 496–97. Kennedy understood the importance of the women's peace movement, granting a January, 1963, interview to the editors of eight women's magazines with a total readership of 33 million. See Robert S. Cramer, "President Kennedy Talks about Women and World Peace," *Parents' Magazine* (November 1963): 57; and Ray Robinson, "President Kennedy Talks about You, Your Children, and Peace," *Good Housekeeping* (November 1963): 73.

74. Swerdlow, *Women Strike for Peace*, p. 101.

75. Jezer, p. 38–39.

76. Swerdlow, *Women Strike for Peace*, pp. 97–100, 104–05.

77. Swerdlow, *Women Strike for Peace*, pp. 108–15; Rosen, "The Day They Buried Traditional Womanhood," pp. 240–41.

78. "The House vs. the Women," *Commonweal* (28 December 1962): 352–53; Swerdlow, *Women Strike for Peace*, pp. 116–118; Rosen, "The Day They Buried Traditional Womanhood," p. 241.

79. Barbara Deming, "Letter to WSP," *Liberation* 8 (April 1963): 18–21.

80. Swerdlow, *Women Strike for Peace*, pp. 88–89. There was at least one point of personal connection between WSP and SDS; Richard Flacks' wife Mickey was already a member of Women Strike for Peace in 1962. James Miller, *"Democracy Is in the Streets": From Port Huron to the Siege of Chicago* (New York: Simon and Schuster, 1987), p. 102.

81. Swerdlow, *Women Strike for Peace*, p. 204; Dorothy Day, *On Pilgrimage: The Sixties* (New York: Curtis Books, 1972), pp. 140, 144.

82. Goodman, "Preface," *Seeds of Liberation*, p. xi; Robert A. Haber, "From Protest to Radicalism: An Appraisal of the Student Movement 1960," *Venture* (Fall 1960), reprinted in Cohen and Hale, *The New Student Left*, p. 36. Other important "little magazines" of the Left in the 1950s were *Dissent*, *I.F. Stone's Weekly*, and the *National Guardian*. On *Liberation's* place in the history of "little magazines," see Scatamacchia, *"Politics, Liberation*, and Intellectual Radicalism," pp. 20–32. As early as 1961, Tom Hayden mentioned *Liberation* in his "Letter to the New (Young) Left," *The Activist* (Winter 1961), reprinted in Cohen and Hale, *The New Student Left*, p. 4.

83. Swerdlow, "Pure Milk," p. 231.

Notes to Chapter 6

1. Theodore Roszak, *The Making of a Counterculture: Reflections on the Technocratic Society and Its Youthful Opposition* (Garden City, NY: Doubleday Anchor Books, 1969), pp. 56–62. The irony of Roszak's statement, of course, is that it occurred at just the time when doctrine and dogma subsumed the gentle personalism of the early New Left and destroyed SDS.

2. Haber, "From Protest to Radicalism: An Appraisal of the Student Movement 1960," *Venture* (Fall 1960), reprinted in Mitchell Cohen and Dennis Hale, *The New Student Left: An Anthology* (Boston: Beacon Press, 1966), p. 38.

3. Sara Evans, *Personal Politics: The Roots of Women's Liberation in the Civil Rights Movement and the New Left* (New York: Knopf, 1979), pp. 106–07; Haber, "From Protest to Radicalism," p. 39.

4. Jack Newfield, *A Prophetic Minority* (New York: Signet, 1966), pp. 95–96; Ellen Herman, "Being and Doing: Humanistic Psychology and the Spirit of the Sixties," *Sights on the Sixties*, ed. Barbara L. Tischler (New Brunswick, NJ: Rutgers University Press, 1992), p. 95; Michael Harrington, *Fragments of the Century: A Social Autobiography* (New York: Saturday Review Press, 1973), pp. 17–25. For Harrington's recollections and criticisms of the Catholic Worker, see Rosalie Riegle Troester, ed., *Voices from the Catholic Worker* (Philadelphia: Temple University Press, 1993), pp. 120–33.

5. James Miller, *"Democracy Is in the Streets": From Port Huron to the Siege of Chicago* (New York: Simon and Schuster, 1987), pp. 36–37. For more on the backgrounds of the Human Rights conference and of student radicalism at the University of Michigan, see Miller, pp. 26–40.

6. Miller, *"Democracy Is in the Streets,"* pp. 42–45, 48; Newfield, *A Prophetic Minority*, pp. 89, 96. Michigan SDS leader Richard Flacks also came to the New Left by way of the Beat movement and the experimental theater. Miller, p. 160.

7. Miller, *"Democracy Is in the Streets,"* pp. 51–52; In "A Letter to the New (Young) Left," Hayden summarized the "liberal realism" of the time: "Man is inherently incapable of building a good society; man's passionate causes are nothing more than dangerous psychic sprees (the issues of this period too complex and sensitive to be colored by emotionalism or moral conviction); ideals have little place in politics—we should instead design effective, responsible programs which will produce the most that is realistically possible." Hayden, "Letter," *The*

Activist (Winter 1961), reprinted in Cohen and Hale, *The New Student Left*, p. 4. In the Port Huron Statement, he again took up the issue of "realism" and "idealism." "Men act," he said, "out of a defeatism that is labeled realistic." They have no utopian visions. "To be idealistic is to be considered apocalyptic, deluded. To have no serious aspirations, on the contrary, is to be 'tough-minded.'" "The Port Huron Statement," in *The Sixties Papers: Documents of a Rebellious Decade*, ed Judith Clavir Albert and Stewart Edward Albert (New York: Praeger, 1984), p. 179.

8. Newfield, *A Prophetic Minority*, p. 88; Miller, *"Democracy Is in the Streets,"* pp. 56–61.

9. Doug Rossinow, "'The Breakthrough to New Life': Christianity and the New Left in Austin, Texas," *American Quarterly* (September 1994): 327. In her NSA address, Cason made the case for civil disobedience in personalist terms. "When an individual human being is not allowed by the legal system and the social mores of his community to *be* a human being," if "he is a human being *now* and the law is unjust *now*," then "a person must at times choose to do the right rather than the legal." Such civil disobedience could "help all of us, Negro and white, realize the possibility of becoming less inhuman humans through commitment and action." Tom Hayden, *Reunion: A Memoir* (New York: Random House, 1988), pp. 40–41.

10. Hayden, *Reunion*, p. 52; Rossinow, "Christianity and the New Left," p. 329. After their wedding, the Haydens moved to Atlanta, she to work with Ella Baker as YWCA liaison to SNCC, he to serve as SDS field secretary in the South. In 1965, she worked for JOIN (Jobs or Income Now) in Uptown Chicago, a part of SDS's ERAP project. According to Jack Newfield, "she personalizes all of the sensitive and lyrical qualities of the movement." Newfield, *A Prophetic Minority*, p. 103.

11. Miller, *"Democracy Is in the Streets,"* pp. 77, 101. The whole sentence is worth quoting: "It [the challenge] is to quit the acquiescence to political fate, cut the confidence in business-as-usual futures, and realize that in a time of mass organization, government by expertise, success through technical specialization, manipulation by the balancing of official secrets with the soft sell, the incomprehensible destruction of the two world wars and the third which may be imminent, and the Cold War which has chilled man's relation to man, the time has come for a re-assertion of the personal." Hayden, *Reunion*, p. 83.

12. Miller, *"Democracy Is in the Streets"*, pp. 110–111. *The Correspondent* brought together disarmament liberals like Kenneth Boulding, Arthur Waskow, and Marcus Raskin with radical pacifists like A.J. Muste. Miller, p. 169.

13. "Port Huron Statement," pp. 180, 187; Miller, *"Democracy Is in the Streets,"* p. 14; Hayden, *Reunion*, p. 75. The language of "infinitely precious" people with "unfulfilled capacities" for good came from Catholic Mary Varela, who cited John XXIII's *Pacem in Terris*. The students knew that they were "countering perhaps the dominant conceptions of man in the twentieth century." But like other personalists, SDS wanted to signal their rejection of Niebuhrian resignation. Hayden, *Reunion*, pp. 94–96. Ellen Herman notes that the Port Huron statement echoed the ideals of humanistic psychology, including "the benevo-

lence of human nature, the ideals of autonomy and growth, the possibilities for comprehensive and conscious self-knowledge, even the use of the word 'potential.'" Herman, "Being and Doing," p. 95.

14. "Port Huron Statement," pp. 180–81.

15. Miller, *"Democracy Is in the Streets,"* p. 94. Miller shows that Hayden took the phrase from one of his philosophy professors, Arnold Kaufman, who contended that "the main justifying function" of participation was "not the extent to which it protects or stabilizes a community, but the contribution it can make to the development of human powers of thought, feeling, and action." For more on the personalist purposes of participatory democracy, see Miller, pp. 144–45.

16. "Port Huron Statement," pp. 180–81; Wini Breines, *Community and Organization in the New Left: 1962–1969* (New Brunswick, NJ: Rutgers University Press, 1989), pp. 53, 58. According to Breines, Staughton Lynd, like McKelvey, saw participatory democracy "as conscientious objection not only to war but to a dehumanizing society." Breines, p. 59.

17. Lawrence Wright, *In the New World: Growing Up with America from the Sixties to the Eighties* (New York: Vintage, 1987), p. 110.

18. "Port Huron Statement," pp. 176–77. Hayden believed that "*moral* realignment had to precede political realignment," and that "politics should flow from experience, not from preconceived dogmas or ideologies." Hayden, *Reunion*, p. 75. For more on the civics class of postwar America, see Frances Fitzgerald, *America Revised: History Schoolbooks in the Twentieth Century* (Boston: Little, Brown, 1979); and Ronald Lora, "Education: Schools as Crucible in Cold War America," in *Reshaping America: Society and Institutions 1945–1960*, ed. Robert H. Bremner and Gary W. Reichard (Columbus: Ohio State University Press, 1982).

19. Elinor Langer, "Notes for Next Time: A Memoir of the 1960s," *Working Papers for a New Society* 1 (Fall 1973): 48–81; reprinted in R. David Myers, ed., *Toward a History of the New Left: Essays From Within the Movement* (Brooklyn: Carlson Publishing, 1989), p. 68; Hayden, *Reunion*, p. 3; Todd Gitlin, *The Sixties: Years of Hope, Days of Rage* (New York: Bantam, 1987), p. 23; Paul Carter, *Another Part of the Fifties* (New York: Columbia University Press, 1983) p. 73.

20. Lyman T. Sargent, *New Left Thought: An Introduction* (Homewood, IL: Dorsey Press, 1972), p. 16; Godfrey Hodgson, *America in Our Time* (New York: Vintage, 1976), pp. 317–20. See also "The Story of Uncle Sam," in Pete Seeger's *The Incompleat Folksinger* (New York: Simon and Schuster, 1972), pp. 213–14. "If we inquire historically into the causes likely to transform *engagés* into *enragés*," noted Hannah Arendt, "it is not injustice that ranks first, but hypocrisy." Keith Melville, *Communes in the Counter Culture: Origins, Theories, Styles of Life* (New York: William Morrow, 1972), p. 91. Even bureaucrats understood this tendency. Chancellor Roger Heyne of Berkeley noted in the *San Francisco Chronicle* of November 13, 1965, that the student generation was "absolutely bugged on the subject of hypocrisy. That is why its angry negations—like those of the prophets—are stronger than its affirmations. This is

why it is surer of what is wrong with where we are as a society, than of where we ought to go. Prophets are not redeemers." Seeger, p. 292.

21. The New Left of the early 1960s was influenced by the ban-the-bomb movement. Mickey Flacks took part in civil defense protests in New York in 1960. SDS members Casey Hayden, Sharon Jeffrey and Mickey Flacks also worked with the Ann Arbor Women Strike for Peace during 1962, the year of the nascent New Left. Hayden and Jeffrey later used WSP's "unorganization" as a model of egalitarian organizing, unlike the hierarchical structures of the New Left. Gitlin, *Sixties*, p. 85; Amy Swerdlow, *Women Strike for Peace* (Chicago: University of Chicago Press, 1993), p. 241; David Westby and Richard Braungart, "Activists and the History of the Future," in *Protest! Student Activism in America*, ed. Julian Foster and Durward Long (New York: William Morrow, 1970), pp. 160, 174.

22. "Port Huron Statement," pp. 177, 183, 186. For Hayden's interpretation of apathy, and his debt to C. Wright Mills, see *Reunion*, pp. 81–82.

23. Thomas Merton, "Letter to An Innocent Bystander," in *Raids on the Unspeakable* (New York: New Directions, 1966), p. 55; Charles DeBenedetti, "On the Significance of Citizen Peace Activism," *Peace and Change* 9 (Summer 1983): 11; Newfield, *A Prophetic Minority*, pp. 92–93; Maurice Isserman and Michael Kazin, "Failure and Success of the New Radicalism," *The Rise and Fall of the New Deal Order, 1930–1980*, ed. Steven Fraser and Gary Gerstle (Princeton: Princeton University Press, 1989), pp. 219–20. For one student's thoughts about Germany and "Amerika," see Wright, *In the New World*, pp. 162–64. For a comparison of American nuclear weapons policy to the German policy of exterminating Jews, see Paul Goodman, *Like a Conquered Province: The Moral Ambiguity of America* (New York: Random House, 1967), p. 7.

24. Dale W. Brown, *The Christian Revolutionary* (Grand Rapids: Eerdmans, 1971), pp. 70–71; Carl Oglesby, "Rescuing Jesus from the Cross," *CoEvolution Quarterly* 39 (Fall 1983): 36.

25. Brown, *Christian Revolutionary*, p. 67; Silk, *Spiritual Politics*, pp. 133–34; Robert Holsworth, *Let Your Life Speak: A Study of Politics, Religion, and Antinuclear Weapons Activism* (Madison: University of Wisconsin Press, 1989), p. 29.

26. Miller, *"Democracy Is in the Streets,"* p. 146. In retrospect, Tom Hayden also saw the agreement on political process as "a rebellion against middle-class careerism." In an organization with "a lot of very strong male egos," the processes of participatory democracy curbed individualist ambition.

27. "Port Huron Statement," pp. 179, 182–85; Norm Fruchter, "Mississippi: Notes on SNCC," *Studies on the Left* 5 (Winter 1965): 77.

28. "Port Huron Statement," pp. 194–96; Breines, *Community and Organization*, pp. 101, 106; Miller, *"Democracy Is in the Streets,"* p. 158. "A new left," said the Port Huron Statement, "must transform modern complexity into issues that can be understood and felt close up by every human being. It must give form to the feelings of helplessness and indifference, so that people may see the political, social, and economic sources of their private troubles and organize to change society." "Port Huron Statement," pp. 195–96.

29. Newfield, *A Prophetic Minority*, pp. 87, 105; Miller, *"Democracy Is in the Streets,"* p. 149.

30. Breines, *Community and Organization*, p. 127. Breines notes that most New Left activists did not desert the campuses for the inner cities, but combined service—in Friends of SNCC, in local community organizing, in literacy programs, etc.—with their studies. Breines, p. 132.

31. Miller, *"Democracy Is in the Streets"*, p. 184–87, 198–99, 204–08; Breines, *Community and Organization*, p. 137.

32. Breines, *Community and Organization*, p. 143.

33. Breines, *Community and Organization*, p. 145; Newfield, *A Prophetic Minority*, p. 134; Nancy Zaroulis and Gerald Sullivan, *Who Spoke Up? American Protest Against the War in Vietnam, 1963–1975* (Garden City, NY: Doubleday, 1984), p. 31; Paul Potter, *A Name for Ourselves* (Boston: Little, Brown, 1971), pp. 136–53.

34. According to Jack Newfield, the sources of the New Left included "elements of anarchism, socialism, pacifism, existentialism, humanism, transcendentalism, bohemianism, Populism, mysticism, and black nationalism." Newfield, *A Prophetic Minority*, p. 16.

35. Hodgson, *America In Our Time*, pp. 76–77; Edward Purcell, "Social Thought," *American Quarterly* 35 (Spring/Summer 1983): pp. 80–100.

36. C. Wright Mills, "Culture and Politics," in *The Sixties: Art, Politics, and Media of Our Most Explosive Decade* (New York: Paragon House, 1991), pp. 81, 83; Melville, *Communes in the Counterculture*, pp. 30–31.

37. C. Wright Mills, *The Causes of World War Three* (New York: Ballantine Books, 1958, 1960), pp. 166–73; Mills "Culture and Politics," pp. 76–77.

38. Newfield, *A Prophetic Minority*, p. 132. The Marxism of the New Left has been over-emphasized. To a great extent, Sixties activists looked back to pre-Marxian socialists like Robert Owen and Etienne Cabet. When they looked to Marx, they looked more to the early manuscripts than to the later *Capital*. And when they looked to Marxists, they looked not to the Communist Party or American socialism, but to Lukacs, Korsch, Gramsci, Luxemburg, and the Frankfurt school. Sargent, *New Left Thought*, p. 2; Breines, *Community and Organization*, p. 16. For more on the relationship of New and Old Lefts, see Breines, pp. 13–17, and Maurice Isserman, *If I Had a Hammer . . . The Death of the Old Left and the Birth of the New Left* (New York: Basic Books, 1987).

39. Breines, *Community and Organization*, p. 56.

40. Irving Louis Horowitz, *C. Wright Mills: An American Utopian* (New York: Free Press, 1983), p. 4.

41. Don Hausdorff, *Erich Fromm* (New York: Twayne, 1972), pp. 48, 51, 61, 104; Andrew Jamison and Ron Eyerman, *Seeds of the Sixties* (Berkeley: University of California Press, 1994), pp. 56–57; Miller, *"Democracy Is in the Streets,"* p. 94.

42. Jamison and Eyerman, *Seeds of the Sixties*, p. 60.

43. Hausdorff, *Erich Fromm*, pp. 89–90; Sargent, *New Left Thought*, pp. 12–15. Cristina Scatamacchia notes that alienation (especially the alienation of artists) had been the "basic theme" of *Partisan Review* as early as the Forties and Fifties. The New Left democratized this theme and applied it more broadly to disenchanted elements of the American population. Cristina Scatamacchia, *"Politics, Liberation, and Intellectual Radicalism,"* (Ph.D. dissertation: University of Missouri, 1990), p. 81.

44. Erich Fromm, *Marx's Concept of Man* (New York: Frederick Ungar, 1961), pp. 47–53, 66, 68.

45. Philip T. Beidler, *Scriptures for a Generation: What We Were Reading in the '60s* (Athens: University of Georgia Press, 1994), pp. 140–42.

46. Sargent, *New Left Thought*, p. 5; Charles DeBenedetti and Charles Chatfield, *An American Ordeal: The Antiwar Movement of the Vietnam War* (Syracuse: Syracuse University Press, 1990), p. 76. The epistemological radicalism of existentialism—the assumption that people made truths instead of discovering *the Truth*—created a synergy with the social constructionism of books like Thomas Kuhn's *Theory of Scientific Revolutions*, suggesting that you could change the world by changing your ideas.

47. Thomas Merton, *Albert Camus' The Plague* (New York: Seabury Press, 1968). Merton's pamphlet was dedicated to Daniel Berrigan.

48. Albert Camus, "Neither Victims Nor Executioners," *Politics* 4 (July–August 1947): 141–47; and *Liberation* 4 (February 1960): 24–43. Sargent, *New Left Thought*, p. 5; Potter, quoted in Brown, *The Christian Revolutionary*, p 78; Rossinow, "Christianity and the New Left," p. 330.

49. Oglesby, quoted in Newfield, *A Prophetic Minority*, p. 19; Calvert, quoted in Breines, *Community and Organization*, pp. 48–49. As a mark of how the movement changed, just five years later, Paul Potter noted that love "is not something we talk about politically; it is not a subject that someone would bring up at an SDS meeting or any other kind of political gathering." Potter, *A Name for Ourselves*, p. 48.

50. Miller, *"Democracy Is in the Streets,"* p. 16, 102, 129, 149, 163, 187, 223. Miller contends that the face-to-face communities of participatory democracy don't fit with programs for national legislation. With his focus on the Sixties, he ignores the long history of the American reform legislation that came from the "free spaces" of such local movements. Even the labor movement, thoroughly nationalized by the 1960s, maintained its locals. Even within the 1960s, he misunderstands the way in which the localism—including the preeminence of "local people"—of SNCC's activity in McComb, Mississippi fit with national agenda of SNCC, SCLC, the NAACP, and white liberal civil rights activists. Miller, pp. 149–50.

51. Rossinow, "Christianity and the New Left," p. 330; Newfield, *A Prophetic Minority*, pp. 27–28. It's important to remember, from the nihilism of the Nineties, how much sense idealism made in the early Sixties. While John Kennedy was offering an idealistic vision of America in the world, John XXIII was transforming the Catholic Church. And if the Catholic Church could change, for God's sake, then virtually anything was possible.

52. Gitlin, *Sixties*, p. 96; Leo Marx, "American Institutions and Ecological Ideals," *Science* 170 (27 November 1970): 948. For a critique of the Kennedy civil rights program, see Tom Hayden, "Just a Matter of Timing?" *Liberation* 7 (October 1962): 24–26.

53. Miller, *"Democracy Is in the Streets,"* pp. 163–64.

54. Miller, *"Democracy Is in the Streets,"* pp. 176–77.

55. Breines, *Community and Organization*, p. 21; Miller, *"Democracy Is in the Streets,"* p. 225.

56. Staughton Lynd, "The New Left," *Annals of the American Academy of Political and Social Science* 382 (March 1969): 69–70. Says Lynd, "Corporate liberalism, then, is understood by the New Left as an ideology that makes reactionary power appear to be liberal." See also Jonathan Eisen and David Steinberg, "The Student Revolt Against Liberalism," *Annals of the American Academy of Political and Social Science* 382 (March 1969): 83–94.

57. Peter Maurin, *Easy Essays* (West Hamlin, WV: The Green Revolution, 1973), pp. 44–45.

58. Bret Eynon, "Community in Motion: The Free Speech Movement, Civil Rights, and the Roots of the New Left," *Oral History Review* 17 (Spring 1989): 39–69. For more comprehensive treatments of the Free Speech Movement and the Berkeley revolts, see Hal Draper, *Berkeley: The New Student Revolt* (New York: Grove Press, 1965); and W.J. Rorabaugh, *Berkeley at War: The 1960s* (New York: Oxford University Press, 1989). For a wonderful account of the connections between Freedom Summer and the Free Speech Movement, see also Daniel P. Hinman-Smith, "'Does the Word Freedom Have a Meaning?': The Mississippi Freedom Schools, the Berkeley Free Speech Movement, and the Search for Freedom Through Education," (Ph.D. dissertation: University of North Carolina, 1993).

59. Paul Boller, "Hiroshima and the American Left: August 1945," *International Social Science Review* 57 (Winter 1982): 24.

60. Walter A. McDougall, . . . *The Heavens and the Earth: A Political History of the Space Age* (New York: Basic Books, 1985), pp. 158–62.

61. David Dickson, *The New Politics of Science* (New York: Pantheon, 1984), p. 120; Gitlin, *Sixties*, pp. 20–21; Hodgson, *America in Our Time*, pp. 288–91. For more on the complicity of the universities, see Kenneth J. Heineman, *Campus Wars: The Peace Movement at American State Universities in the Vietnam Era* (New York: New York University Press, 1993), pp. 13–41; and Miller, *"Democracy Is in the Streets,"* pp. 24–26.

62. Mark Schechner, "The Cold War and the University of California," *Frontier* (August 1966), reprinted in *The California Dream*, ed. Dennis Hale and Jonathan Eisen (New York: Collier Books, 1968), pp. 179–192; Breines, *Community and Organization*, p. 99. UC was not uncharacteristic in its dependence on the government for funds. Of the roughly $2 billion spent on college campuses for research and development in 1965, the Federal government provided $1.6 billion.

63. Miller, *"Democracy Is in the Streets,"* pp. 45–46. For more on Kerr, see Daniel Hinman-Smith "Does the Word Freedom Have a Meaning?" pp. 267–87. According to Hinman-Smith, Kerr believed in "educational liberalism based on pluralism, individual opportunity, and sharp distinctions between scholarship and politics. . . . Freedom, for Clark Kerr, meant entrepreneurial freedom for the faculty; the freedom of the consumer for students; and a bountiful array of services, both material and intellectual for the citizens." Hinman-Smith, p. 258.

64. Hodgson, *America In Our Time*, p. 291; Miller, *"Democracy Is in the Streets,"* p. 93; Hinman-Smith, *Does the Word Freedom Have a Meaning?"*, p. 320. For an excellent account of the liberal corporatism of the university, and of the radicalism

of the students, see Rorabaugh, *Berkeley at War*, pp. 8–19. For a description of the ways in which the neutrality of the university was an illusion, see Hinman-Smith, p. 325. After his arrest, Jack Weinberg explained his position in terms of personalism and citizenship: "We feel that we as human beings first and students second must take our stand on every vital issue which faces this nation, and in particular the vital issues of discrimination, of segregation, of poverty, of unemployment." Hinman-Smith, p. 345.

65. Breines, *Community and Organization*, p. 31. The Bancroft Strip was an emotionally charged symbolic space that symbolized the intersection of the university and the real world. Hinman-Smith, "Does the Word Freedom Have a Meaning?" p. 303.

66. Rorabaugh, *Berkeley at War*, pp. 18–21; Myron B. Bloy Jr., "The Counter Curriculum: A Spiritual Taxonomy of Higher Education," *Commonweal* 91 (3 October 1969): 9. Weinberg had worked with CORE in the South in 1963, and was an activist in Friends of CORE before the Free Speech Movement. Breines, *Community and Organization*, p. 24. He had also been inspired by Allen Ginsberg and the Beats, finding that "just the fact that somebody dared to be different was so incredibly exciting." Hinman-Smith, p. 300. Putting their bodies on the line, the students exemplified the tactics and strategies of political personalism. When acts of individual resistance multiplied, protesters discovered that they could stop the efficient operation of social machines, and begin the questioning that could lead to a crisis of legitimacy. Breines, p. 23.

67. Eynon, "Community in Motion," p. 61. Students joined the Free Speech Movement, not just because they believed in its goals, but because they were attracted to the community of purpose. Mario Savio noted that lonely people were "hungry for some kind of community." "Free speech," he said, "was in some ways a pretext. . . . Around that issue the people could gain the community they formerly lacked." Breines, *Community and Organization*, p. 26.

68. Eynon, "Community in Motion," pp. 56–57, 66. "For the first time," Michael Rossman recalled, "the question became, what about us?"

69. Rorabaugh, *Berkeley at War*, pp. 21–23; Hinman-Smith, "Does the Word Freedom Have a Meaning?", p. 257.

70. Both movements "consciously and unconsciously chose to reinvigorate earlier traditions of American radicalism." Both movements "spoke in a language familiar to Americans, using . . . phrases and ideas buried deep in America's religious and political heritage." Eynon, "Community in Motion," pp. 47, 54, 66.

71. Rorabaugh, *Berkeley at War*, pp. 23–28; Hinman-Smith, "Does the Word Freedom Have a Meaning?" pp. 309, 355–56; Eynon, "Community in Motion," pp. 63–64.

72. Savio, "An End to History," in Cohen and Hale, *The New Student Left*, p. 251; Hodgson, *America in Our Time*, p. 297; Thomas Powers, *Vietnam: The War at Home: Vietnam and the American People, 1964–1968* (Boston: G.K. Hall, 1984), pp. 32–33. The machine metaphor was more apt than Savio probably knew; Clark Kerr preferred thinking of the university as a machine instead of as an organism. Hinman-Smith, "Does the Word Freedom Have a Meaning?", p. 278. An FSM flyer developed this dichotomy: "human nerves and flesh are transmuted under the pressure and stress of the university routine. It is as though we

have become raw material in the strictly organic sense. But the Free Speech Movement has given us a taste of what it means to be part of something organic. Jumping off the conveyers, we become a community of furiously talking, feeling, and thinking human beings." Eynon, "Community in Motion," p. 58. Savio's image of people clogging the machine recalls Charlie Chaplin's "Little Tramp" in *Modern Times*, and it was perhaps no coincidence that students occupying Sproul Hall watched Chaplin films. The image was often echoed in the Sixties. See, for example, A.J. Muste, "Who Has the Spiritual Atom Bomb?" *Liberation* (November 1965), reprinted in *The Essays of A.J. Muste*, pp. 479–502.

73. Newfield, *A Prophetic Minority*, p. 68; Theodore Roszak, *Person/Planet: The Creative Disintegration of Industrial Society* (Garden City, NY: Anchor/Doubleday, 1979), p. xxvii; Hinman-Smith, "Does the Word Freedom Have a Meaning?" pp. 261, 326; Breines, *Community and Organization*, p. 25. C. Wright Mills also objected to the ways in which Americans made young people into "cheerful robots," people "with rationality but without reason." See "Culture and Politics," in *The Sixties*, p. 79. One of the Free Speech Movement's "Christmas carols" emphasized this theme:

> O, come all ye mindless,
> Conceptless and spineless,
> Sell out your integrity to IBM.
> Don't make a commotion,
> [Chancellor] Strong wants a promotion.
> Do not fold or spindle,
> O, do not fold or spindle,
> O, do not fold or spindle,
> Or mutilate.

The Christmas carol recording sold 15,000 copies by January. Hinman-Smith, p. 315.

74. Breines, *Community and Organization*, p. 26.

75. Savio, "An End to History," p. 252; Breines, *Community and Organization*, pp. 9, 100–101. This insight—that the American workplace demanded "socially meaningless work" for socially meaningless consumption—formed the basis of the New Left's new working-class theory. That theory suggested that, because the alienations of the workplace were widespread in America, workers might become agents of radical social change. Breines, pp. 104–110.

76. Miller, *"Democracy Is in the Streets,"* p. 53. Maurice Isserman and Michael Kazin see this as "radical individualism"; but I see it as "radical personalism," which has entirely different implications. Isserman and Kazin, "Failure and Success of the New Radicalism," p. 225.

77. Purcell, "Social Thought," p. 84; Widmer, "Rebellion as Education," *The Nation* (April 28, 1969): 539. The Port Huron Statement argued that "academia includes a radical separation of the student from the material of study. That which is studied, the social reality, is 'objectified' to sterility, dividing the student from life." "Port Huron Statement," p. 184.

78. Hinman-Smith, "Does the Word Freedom Have a Meaning?" p. 333; Beth Bailey, "Sexual Revolution(s)," in *The Sixties: From Memory to History*, ed. David Farber, (Chapel Hill: University of North Carolina Press, 1994), p. 241. "This system of rules," Bailey notes, "in all its inconsistency, arbitrariness, and blindness, helped to preserve the distinction between public and private, the coexistence of overt and covert, that defines mid-century American sexuality." Bailey, p. 242.

79. Savio, "An End to History," p. 251. The booming economy of the Sixties also freed students from many financial constraints.

80. Eynon, "Community in Motion," pp. 41, 55. One student described the first semester as "an essay come alive."

81. Eynon, "Community in Motion," pp. 59–62. The theory was, of course, simpler than the practice, because of the paradoxical place of dissent in an assumption of consensus. Although the theory promised free speech and free decisions, in practice the pressures to conform were intense. Hinman-Smith, "Does the Word Freedom Have a Meaning?" pp. 340, 357.

82. Paul Goodman, "Thoughts on Berkeley," *New York Review of Books* 3 (14 January 1965): 5–6; Hinman-Smith, "Does the Word Freedom Have a Meaning?" pp. 439–41, 463; Miller, *"Democracy Is in the Streets,"* p. 223; Morgan, *Sixties Experience*, p. 117; Breines, *Community and Organization*, p. 97; Hodgson, *America in Our Time*, p. 297.

83. Hinman-Smith, "Does the Word Freedom Have a Meaning?" p. 472. At Washington University in St. Louis, philosopher Bernard Baumrin supported the teach-in by saying that "we are just . . . updating a poorly designed curriculum. We forgot to have courses on Southeast Asian politics in the curriculum this year. The academic community failed in Germany in the 1930s. We are not going to let it happen here." Webster Schott, "The Teach-In: New Forum for Reason," in *Teach-Ins: U.S.A: Reports, Opinions, Documents*, ed. Louis Menashe and Ronald Radosh (New York: Frederick A. Praeger, 1967), p. 25.

84. Anatol Rapoport, "Dialogue or Monologue?" in *Teach-Ins*, pp. 5–7; Marc Pilisuk, "The First Teach-In: An Insight Into Professional Activism," in *Teach-Ins*, p. 11. Zaroulis and Sullivan, *Who Spoke Up?* p. 37; DeBenedetti and Chatfield, *An American Ordeal*, p. 108.

85. Rapoport, "Dialogue or Monologue?" p. 7; Williams, "Our Leaders Are Following the Wrong Rainbow," p. 45; Pilisuk, "First Teach-In," p. 11. See also Breines, *Community and Organization*, pp. 26–27, and Widmer, "Rebellion as Education," 537.

86. Williams, "Pseudo-Debate in the Teach-In: Criticism Contained," in *Teach-Ins: USA*, p. 186.

87. Miller, *"Democracy Is in the Streets,"* p. 158.

88. Morgan, *Sixties Experience*, p. 118.

89. Terry H. Anderson, *The Movement and the Sixties* (New York: Oxford University Press, 1995), pp. 161, 177.

90. Miller, *"Democracy Is in the Streets,"* pp. 290–91.

91. Miller, *"Democracy Is in the Streets,"* p. 81; Widmer, "Rebellion as Education," p. 541; Myron B. Bloy, "The Counter Curriculum: A Spiritual Taxonomy of Higher Eduation," *Commonweal* 91 (March 1969): 10–11.

92. Eisen and Steinberg, "The Student Revolt Against Liberalism," p. 92; Hinman-Smith, "Does the Word Freedom Have a Meaning?" pp. 443–45; Anderson, *The Movement*, p. 274.

93. Hinman-Smith, "Does the Word Freedom Have a Meaning?" pp. 432–34.

94. Judith Hole and Ellen Levine, *Rebirth of Feminism* (New York: Quadrangle, 1971), pp. 322–29.

95. Michael Klein, "Students, Capital, and the Multiversity: Radical Challenges to the Dominant Pattern of American Higher Education from Berkeley to Livingston," in *An American Half Century: Postwar Culture and Politics in the USA*, ed. Michael Klein (London: Pluto Press, 1994), pp. 98–99.

96. Howard Zinn, "Marxism and the New Left," in *Dissent: Explorations in the History of American Radicalism*, ed. Alfred L. Young (DeKalb: Northern Illinois Press, 1968), p. 371.

97. Melville, *Communes in the Counter Culture*, p. 85. Studies consistently showed little generation gap between radical students and their own parents. The parents of protesters were often affluent and well educated, and they were unusually interested in politics. Thirty percent of FSM protesters thought their parents were as radical as they were, and a majority of parents supported their children's activism, even though they had doubts about its practicality. Melville, *Communes in the Counter Culture*, pp. 87–90.

98. Williams, "Our Leaders Are Following the Wrong Rainbow," p. 45; Melville, *Communes in the Counter Culture*, p. 79.

Notes to Chapter 7

1. "It is not accidental," says Wini Breines, "that the new left was an antiwar movement, that saying 'no' to the war in Vietnam was the central issue of the movement, conscientious objectors, conspicuous actors; it was a dramatic demonstration of the dissociation of politics from violence." Wini Breines, *Community and Organization in the New Left: 1962–1969* (New Brunswick, NJ: Rutgers University Press, 1989, p. 56.

2. Charles DeBenedetti and Charles Chatfield, *An American Ordeal: The Anti-War Movement of the Vietnam War* (Syracuse: Syracuse University Press, 1990), p. 87; David McReynolds, "Pacifists and the Vietnam Antiwar Movement," in *Give Peace a Chance*, ed. Melvin Small and William D. Hoover (Syracuse: Syracuse University Press, 1992), p. 57; Nancy Zaroulis and Gerald Sullivan, *Who Spoke Up? American Protest Against the War in Vietnam, 1963–1975* (Garden City, NY: Doubleday, 1984), p. 12, 19. There were also a few liberal protesters and some antiwar organizing in the secular Left. See DeBenedetti and Chatfield, *An American Ordeal*, pp. 84–85, 97–98. Ironically, Ngo Dinh Diem claimed to have been influenced by Mounier's writings in establishing the government of South Vietnam. John Hellman, *Emmanuel Mounier and the New Catholic Left 1930–1950* (Toronto: University of Toronto Press, 1981), p. 251.

3. Mel Piehl, *Breaking Bread: The Catholic Worker Movement and the Origin of Catholic Radicalism in America* (Philadelphia: Temple University Press, 1982),

pp. 230–31; William Miller, *Dorothy Day: A Biography* (San Francisco: Harper and Row, 1982), p. 478–79.

4. Miller, *Dorothy Day*, p. 486; James H. Forest, "No Longer Alone, The Catholic Peace Movement," in *American Catholics and Vietnam*, ed. Thomas E. Quigley (Grand Rapids: William B. Eerdmans, 1968), p. 145.

5. Miller, *Dorothy Day*, pp. 480–81.

6. Rosalie Riegle Troester, *Voices from the Catholic Worker* (Philadelphia: Temple University Press, 1993), pp. 38–40; Forest, "No Longer Alone," pp. 148–49.

7. Zaroulis and Sullivan, *Who Spoke Up?* pp. 69–70; John J. Ansbro, *Martin Luther King Jr.: The Making of a Mind* (Maryknoll, NY: Orbis, 1982), pp. 252–53, 257. King had been inspired to go public, in part, by the photos of Vietnamese children published in the January *Ramparts*. Tom Wells, *The War Within: America's Battle Over Vietnam* (Berkeley: University of California Press, 1994), p. 129.

8. Martin Luther King Jr. "A Time to Break Silence," in *I Have a Dream: Writings and Speeches That Changed the World*, ed. James M. Washington (San Francisco: HarperSanFrancisco), 1992, pp. 136–39, 148.

9. Zaroulis and Sullivan, *Who Spoke Up?* p. 24; Clayborne Carson, *In Struggle: SNCC and the Black Awakening of the 1960s* (Cambridge: Harvard University Press, 1981), p. 184.

10. DeBenedetti and Chatfield, *An American Ordeal*, pp. 106–07; Zaroulis and Sullivan, *Who Spoke Up?*, p. 104; Blanche Linden-Ward and Carol Hurd Green, *American Women in the 1960s: Changing the Future* (New York: Twayne, 1993), p. 163.

11. DeBenedetti and Chatfield, *An American Ordeal*, pp. 21–26, 125.

12. Zaroulis and Sullivan, *Who Spoke Up?* p. 20. To see a copy of the Declaration, see Robert Cooney and Helen Michalowski, ed., *The Power of the People: Active Nonviolence in the United States* (Philadelphia: New Society, 1989), p. 183.

13. Zaroulis and Sullivan, *Who Spoke Up?* p. 104. A few of the antiwar leaders saw effects of the war firsthand. Tom Hayden noted, after a trip to Hanoi with Rennie Davis, that the American military "was doing things that he had never *dreamed* in his childhood that Americans would have anything to do with. Napalm. Phosphorus. Fragmentation bombs. All these things designed by scientists to kill people painfully, to mutilate them, to scar them for life." Personalist witness made such personal witness more likely, and vice versa. James Miller, *"Democracy Is in the Streets": From Port Huron to the Siege of Chicago* (New York: Simon and Schuster, 1987), p. 283. It is a sign of the persistence of personalism that we think of such depictions of war as "naturally" disgusting. But such images did not appear much in World War II or the Korean War, and when they did, they aroused little opposition. See George H. Roeder, *The Censored War: American Visual Experience During World War Two* (New Haven: Yale University Press, 1993).

14. Marcuse, "The Inner Logic of American Policy in Vietnam," in *Teach-Ins: USA: Reports, Opinions, Documents* (New York: Praeger, 1967), p. 66; Jo Ann Ooiman Robinson, *Abraham Went Out: A Biography of A.J. Muste* (Philadelphia: Temple University Press, 1981), p. 199; Lynd, "Nonviolent Alternatives to

American Violence," in *Teach-Ins: USA*, p. 54; Rapoport, "Dialogue or Monologoue (Part 2)," in *Teach-Ins: USA*, p. 180. In November 1965, Carl Oglesby complained that "generals do not hear the screams of the bombed; sugar executives do not see the misery of the cane cutters—for to do so is to be that much *less* the general, that much *less* the executive." Breines, *Community and Organization*, p. 26.

15. William Appleman Williams, "Our Leaders Are Following the Wrong Rainbow," in *Teach-Ins: USA*, p. 52.

16. Miller, *"Democracy Is in the Streets,"* p. 221; Staughton Lynd, "Nonviolent Alternatives to American Violence," in *Teach-Ins: USA*, p. 55.

17. King, "A Time to Break Silence," p. 148.

18. Arthur I. Waskow, "The New American Arrogance," in *Teach-Ins: USA*, pp. 61–62.

19. Forest, "No Longer Alone," pp. 147–48.

20. Zaroulis and Sullivan, *Who Spoke Up?* p. 51. In April 1966, A.J. Muste, Barbara Deming, Bradford Lyttle, Karl Meyer, and two others journeyed to South Vietnam as tourists to attempt the same sort of citizen diplomacy. Zaroulis and Sullivan, p. 81.

21. Charles DeBenedetti, "On the Significance of Citizen Peace Activism," *Peace and Change* 9 (Summer 1983): 11;

22. Francis Sicius, "Karl Meyer, The Catholic Worker, and Active Personalism," *Records of the American Catholic Historical Society of Philadelphia* 93 (1982): 108–114. SDS leader Todd Gitlin worked in William Meyer's reelection campaign in 1960, when Harvard's Tocsin sent volunteers to Vermont. Todd Gitlin, *The Sixties: Years of Hope, Days of Rage* (New York: Bantam, 1987), p. 88.

23. Zaroulis and Sullivan, *Who Spoke Up?* p. 9; Forest, "No Longer Alone," p. 147.

24. Wells, *The War Within*, pp. 125–26; Breines, *Community and Organization*, p. 104; Lawrence M. Baskir and William A. Strauss, *Chance and Circumstance: The Draft, the War and the Vietnam Generation* (New York: Knopf, 1978), p. 9. The channeling memorandum confirmed student intuitions about corporate liberalism: offering the liberal illusion of choice, the corporate state would manipulate citizens and consumers to do what was needed. Staughton Lynd, "The New Left," *Annals of the American Academy of Political and Social Science* 382 (March 1969): 70.

25. Kenneth J. Heineman, *Campus Wars: The Peace Movement at American State Universities in the Vietnam Era* (New York: New York University Press, 1993), p. 134; Baskir and Strauss, *Chance and Circumstance*, pp. 22–23.

26. Patricia McNeal, *Harder Than War: Catholic Peacemaking in the Twentieth Century* (New Brunswick, NJ: Rutgers University Press, 1992), pp. 147–48; Cooney and Michalowski, *Power of the People*, pp. 113–14; Hodgson, *America in Our Time*, p. 275.

27. Cooney and Michalowski, *Power of the People*, p. 186; Zaroulis and Sullivan, *Who Spoke Up?* p. 58. According to Thomas Powers, Miller's act "began a movement of personal, almost existential protest against the war which was to spread quickly and evoke an agonized response from students facing the draft across the country." Thomas Powers, *Vietnam: The War at Home* (Boston: G.K. Hall, 1984), p. 85.

28. Powers, *Vietnam: The War at Home*, p. 189. "To refuse to cooperate with the machine, literally to refuse to fight, and to build instead a community which might serve as an alternative moral and personal standard, was to separate politics from violence and power hierarchies." Breines, *Community and Organization*, p. 56.

29. Zaroulis and Sullivan, *Who Spoke Up?* pp. 58–59; Robinson, *Abraham Went Out*, p. 201. The SDS membership rejected the plan of the national office, but the draft increasingly became an essential element of campus organizing.

30. Robinson, *Abraham Went Out*, pp. 212–14.

31. DeBenedetti and Chatfield, *An American Ordeal*, pp. 144–45; Mitchell K. Hall, "CALCAV and Religious Opposition to the Vietnam War," in *Give Peace a Chance*, pp. 35–52; Wells, *The War Within*, pp. 73–74. For CALCAV's early responses to the war, see Robert McAfee Brown, Abraham J. Heschel, Michael Novak, *Vietnam: Crisis of Conscience* (New York: Association Press, 1967). A year later, CALCAV commissioned a book on "the erosion of moral constraint in Vietnam." See Seymour Melman, *In the Name of America* (Annandale, VA: Turnpike Press, 1968).

32. Zaroulis and Sullivan, *Who Spoke Up?* p. 26; Hayden, *Reunion*, p. 125; James F. Vander Schaaf, "Talking 'Bout Their Generation: Writing the History of the Sixties," *Maryland Historian* 19 (Fall/Winter 1988): 58; Powers, *Vietnam: The War at Home*, pp. 72–81; Edward P. Morgan, *The Sixties Experience: Hard Lessons About Modern America* (Philadelphia: Temple University Press, 1991), pp. 142–43.

33. Fred Powledge, "The New Student Left: Represents Serious Activists in Drive for Changes," *New York Times* (15 March 1965): 1:3; Jack Newfield, "The Peace Opposition," the *Nation* (3 May 1965): 462; Andrew Kopkind, "Rebels with Cause," the *New Republic* (1 May 1965): 5–6.

34. Zaroulis and Sullivan, *Who Spoke Up?*, pp. 43–44; De Benedetti and Chatfield, *An American Ordeal*, p. 109. Spock, Thomas, and Gruening were more liberal than personalist, but Mailer, Moses, Dellinger, and Lynd offered a more radical—and at times personalist—perspective. Representatives of the State Department, the South Vietnamese Embassy, and pro-war faculty all opted not to participate. For a more complete list of speakers, see Robert Randolph, "12,000 at UC Teach-In on Vietnam," in *Teach-Ins*, p. 33.

35. Powers, *Vietnam: The War at Home*, pp. 81–82; Zaroulis and Sullivan, *Who Spoke Up?* p. 20. See also Isidore Ziferstein, "Hiroshima ... Vietnam ... ?" *Liberation* (September 1966): 33–35. Despite a shift of focus from the Bomb to the bombing of Vietnam during the 1960s, antiwar activists had begun to make August 6 a day of peace protests. See David Dellinger, *From Yale to Jail: The Life Story of a Moral Dissenter* (New York: Pantheon, 1993), pp. 209–216. Among the signers of the original Declaration of Conscience were the Berrigan brothers, Julian Bond, Dorothy Day, David Dellinger, Barbara Deming, Ralph DiGia, Lawrence Ferlinghetti, Paul Goodman, Ammon Hennacy, Paul Jacobs, Paul Krassner, John Lewis, Staughton Lynd, Milton Mayer, David McReynolds, A.J. Muste, Jim Peck, Diane Di Prima, A. Philip Randolph, Bayard Rustin, and Ira Sandperl. New signers were asked to return petitions to

the *Catholic Worker*, the Committee for Nonviolent Action, the Student Peace Union, or the War Resisters League. Cooney and Michalowski, *The Power of the People*, p. 183.

36. DeBenedetti and Chatfield, *An American Ordeal*, pp. 120–21; Zaroulis and Sullivan, *Who Spoke Up?* pp. 51–54; Morgan, *Sixties Experience*, p. 145.

37. Irwin Unger, *The Movement: A History of the American New Left, 1959–1972* (New York: Dodd, Mead, 1974), p. 142; Cristina Scatamacchia, *"Politics, Liberation,* and Intellectual Radicalism" (Ph.D. dissertation: University of Missouri, 1990), pp. 231–32; McReynolds, "Pacifists and the Vietnam Antiwar Movement," in *Give Peace a Chance*, p. 61; Zaroulis and Sullivan, *Who Spoke Up?* pp. 81, 97; Wells, *The War Within*, p. 94.

38. Bayard Rustin, "From Protest to Politics: The Future of the Civil Rights Movement," *Commentary* (February 1965): 25–31; Scatamacchia, *"Politics, Liberation,* and Intellectual Radicalism," pp. 207–209.

39. Robinson, *Abraham Went Out*, pp. 135–36; Zaroulis and Sullivan, *Who Spoke Up?*, p. 76.

40. Zaroulis and Sullivan, *Who Spoke Up?* pp. 82–85; Morgan, *Sixties Experience*, p. 151.

41. DeBenedetti and Chatfield, *An American Ordeal*, p. 213. Tet became a symbol of the futility of the war, in part, because of the photograph and videotape showing the murder of one person by another.

42. Daniel P. Hinman-Smith, "'Does the Word Freedom Have a Meaning?' The Mississippi Freedom Schools, the Berkeley Free Speech Movement, and the Search for Freedom Through Education," (Ph.D. dissertation: University of North Carolina, 1993), pp. 223, 254; Newfield, *A Prophetic Minority*, (New York: Signet, 1966), pp. 71–82. While some SNCC staffers, like Jane Stembridge, still emphasized the importance of freedom as a matter of the spirit, most SNCC activists thought differently, and so, apparently, did Hinman-Smith: "By casting freedom as a matter of the spirit, Stembridge . . . was able to downplay the extent to which blacks were physically, politically, and economically unfree, and to avoid a discussion of the possible limitations of both education and faith. Stembridge, along with others who bemoaned the growing separation of means and ends, could not demonstrate that merely loving all people, including oneself, would transform society." Hinman-Smith, p. 186. The key word here is "merely." When critics of personalism used words like "merely," they were forgetting the complexity and comprehensiveness of the "harsh and dreadful love" that animated activists like Dorothy Day. For personalists, love led directly (although not necessarily quickly) to justice. While it was true that "mere" love had not transformed Mississippi in six years, it was also true that more had changed in Mississippi than in any other six years of the twentieth century. And it was no more demonstrable that a movement that deemphasized the spirit could transform society either.

43. Carson, *In Struggle*, p. 161; Eric Burner, *And Gently He Shall Lead Them: Robert Parris Moses and Civil Rights in Mississippi* (New York: New York University Press, 1994), p. 211.

44. James H. Cone, *Martin and Malcolm and America*, (Maryknoll, NY: Orbis, 1991), pp. 221–24.

45. Carson, *In Struggle*, pp. 156–57; Cone, *Martin and Malcolm and America*, pp. 227–232. "Power" became the focus of several movements in the mid-Sixties, as radicals shifted their emphasis from witness to politics, from truth to power. "Black Power," "Student Power," "Power to the People," became the slogans of the new dispensation.

46. Ansbro, *Martin Luther King Jr.: The Making of a Mind*, pp. 254–56, 264.

47. Cone, *Martin and Malcolm and America*, p. 247; Maurice Isserman, "You Don't Need a Weatherman, But a Postman Can Be Helpful," in *Give Peace a Chance*, ed. Melvin Small and William D. Hoover (Syracuse: Syracuse University Press, 1992), pp. 32–33.

48. In a similar spirit, in jail in Albany, Georgia, Barbara Deming noted that "our evidence [of success] can only be 'the evidence of things not seen . . . things hoped for.' Yes, hope will have to satisfy us." Barbara Deming, *Prisons That Could Not Hold* (San Francisco: Spinsters Ink, 1985), p. 90.

49. Wells, *The War Within*, p. 126.

50. David Dellinger, *From Yale to Jail: The Life Story of a Moral Dissenter* (New York; Pantheon, 1993), p. 190; Zaroulis and Sullivan, *Who Spoke Up?* pp. 65–66.

51. See Chapter Eight, "Countercultural Personalism."

52. Paul Buhle, *Marxism in the USA: From 1870 to the Present Day* (London: Verso, 1987), pp. 240–49; Keith Melville, *Communes in the Counter Culture: Origins, Theories, Styles of Life* (New York: William Morrow, 1972), pp. 62–63.

53. Miller, *"Democracy Is in the Streets,"* pp. 246, 253.

54. Miller, *"Democracy Is in the Streets,"* p. 247. In the November 1966 *New Left Notes*, Greg Calvert also expressed his disdain for the "political realism" of SDS's "politicos." While the "realists" disparaged the romanticism and sentimentalism of the organization's anarchists, he said, "the interesting thing about anti-freedom 'politics' is that it defines reality in terms of an existing system which lacks everything that I consider important." Conventional politics seemed exactly the wrong way to the beloved community. Breines, *Community and Organization*, p. 49.

55. Morgan, *Sixties Experience*, pp. 147–48.

56. Dale H. Brown, *The Christian Revolutionary* (Grand Rapids: Eerdmans, 1971), p. 74; Melville, *Communes in the Counterculture*, p. 12; Congressional Quarterly Service, *U.S. Draft Policy and Its Impact* (Washington: Congressional Quarterly, 1968), pp. 12–18; Terry H. Anderson, *The Movement and the Sixties* (New York: Oxford University Press, 1995), p. 180.

57. Congressional Quarterly, *U.S. Draft Policy and Its Impact*, p. 15; Wells, *The War Within*, pp. 126–27. "Committed to a decentralized and personal politics," the Resistance encouraged grass roots support gathered in a political network. Breines, *Community and Organization*, p. 43.

58. DeBenedetti and Chatfield, *An American Ordeal*, p. 234; Craig Cox, *Storefront Revolution: Food Co-ops and the Counterculture* (New Brunswick, NJ: Rutgers University Press, 1994), p. 21; Breines, *Community and Organization*, p. 43.

59. Wells, *The War Within*, p. 125; Dellinger, *From Yale to Jail*, pp. 244, 254.

60. Anne Klejment, "The Berrigans: Revolutionary Christian Nonviolence," in *Peace Heroes in Twentieth Century America*, ed. Charles DeBenedetti (Bloom-

ington: Indiana University Press, 1986), pp. 240–43, 248–49; Troester, *Voices from the Catholic Worker*, pp. 42–48. On the influence of Maurin and Day and Merton, see Daniel Berrigan, *Portraits of Those I Love* (New York: Crossroad, 1982), p. 10.
61. Klejment, "The Berrigans," pp. 245–49.
62. Wells, *The War Within*, p. 126.
63. Wells, *The War Within*, pp. 95–97; Zaroulis and Sullivan, *Who Spoke Up?* p. 118. On "new working class theory," see Wini Breines, *Community and Organization*, pp. 96–115.
64. Miller, *"Democracy Is in the Streets,"* pp. 296, 299.
65. Wells, *The War Within*, pp. 284–85; Morgan, *Sixties Experience*, p. 156.
66. Maurice Isserman and Michael Kazin, "The Failure and Success of the New Radicalism," in *The Rise and Fall of the New Deal Order, 1930–1980*, ed. Steve Fraser and Gary Gerstle (Princeton: Princeton University Press, 1989), p. 222.
67. Newfield, *A Prophetic Minority*, pp. 85–87.
68. Newfield, *A Prophetic Minority*, pp. 86–87; Breines, *Community and Organization*, p. 51.
69. Brown, *Christian Revolutionary*, p. 78; Maurice Isserman, "You Don't Need a Weatherman," pp. 24, 30–31; Wini Breines, *Community and Organization*, pp. xxiv, 35–36, 65. See also David O'Brien, "American Catholic Opposition to the Vietnam War," in *War or Peace?* ed. Thomas A. Shannon (Maryknoll: Orbis, 1980). "When the Maoist-controlled SDS abandoned the group's previous anarchism, its following abandoned it." But the disintegration of SDS was not the end of the Movement, just the end of the centralized phase of it. New Left and countercultural practitioners continued their personalist protests in decentralized forums. David DeLeon, *The American As Anarchist: Reflections on Indigenous Radicalism* (Baltimore: Johns Hopkins University Press, 1979), p. 121.
70. *Life* (29 June 1969); David Halberstam, *The Powers That Be* (New York: Knopf, 1979), pp. 484–85; Wells, *The War Within*, pp. 364–65.
71. Morgan, *Sixties Experience*, pp. 162–63.
72. Isserman and Kazin, "Failure and Success of the New Radicalism," p. 214.

Notes to Chapter 8

1. Terry H. Anderson, *The Movement and the Sixties* (New York: Oxford University, 1995), p. 257.
2. Ann Charters, ed., *The Portable Beat Reader* (New York: Viking, 1992), p. xxix; Timothy Miller, *The Hippies and American Values* (Knoxville: University of Tennessee Press, 1991), pp. 12, 104–08; Marty Jezer, *Abbie Hoffman: An American Rebel* (New Brunswick, NJ: Rutgers University, 1992), pp. 74–75.
3. By the end of the Sixties, a survey found that about a third of college students were interested in communal or collective living and half of them wanted to reside in a rural area, at least for a time. Feeling trapped by the values of American government and society, they were looking for places to dis-cover a new America. Anderson, *The Movement*, p. 270.

4. Edward Purcell, "Social Thought," *American Quarterly* 35 (Spring-Summer 1983): 86–87.
5. Edward P. Morgan, *The Sixties Experience: Hard Lessons About Modern America* (Philadelphia: Temple University Press, 1991), p. 171.
6. Keith Melville, *Communes in the Counterculture: Origins, Theories, Styles of Life* (New York: William Morrow, 1972), p. 27
7. Ellen Herman, "Being and Doing: Humanistic Psychology and the Spirit of the 1960s," in *Sights on the Sixties*, ed. Barbara L. Tischler (New Brunswick, NJ: Rutgers University Press, 1992), p. 89; Jezer, *Abbie Hoffman*, p. 25. In 1961, Carl Rogers published *On Becoming a Person: A Therapist's View of Psychotherapy*. Later in the decade, Rogers founded the Center for Studies of the Person in La Jolla, California.
8. Purcell, "Social Thought," pp. 83–84, 86; Abraham Maslow, *Toward a Psychology of Being*, 2nd ed. (New York: Van Nostrand Reinhold, 1968), pp. 3–4; Herman, "Being and Doing," p. 90; Barbara Myerhoff, "Youth Culture: New Styles of Culture," in *Seasons of Rebellion: Protest and Radicalism in Recent America* (New York: Holt, Rinehart and Winston, 1972), pp. 241–42.
9. Jezer, *Abbie Hoffman*, pp. 22–23. Maslow was emphatic that self-actualization was not selfishness, that self-actualizing people were "altruistic, dedicated, self-transcending, social, etc." Maslow, *Toward a Psychology of Being*, p. vi. "Maslow," says Theodore Roszak, "asked the key question in posing self-actualization as the proper objective of therapy: Why do we set our standard of sanity so cautiously low? Can we imagine no better model than the dutiful consumer, the well-adjusted breadwinner? Why not the saint, the sage, the artist? Why not all that is highest and finest in our species?" Theodore Roszak, *Person/Planet: The Creative Disintegration of Industrial Society* (New York: Anchor/Doubleday, 1979), p. 19.
10. Jay Stevens, *Storming Heaven: LSD and the American Dream* (New York: Harper and Row, 1987), p. 131; Jezer, *Abbie Hoffman*, pp. 22, 24; Herman, "Being and Doing," p. 96. Maslow's daughter served as an assistant for Timothy Leary and Richard Alpert at Harvard and worked with Abbie Hoffman in New York. Maslow himself hated the use of humanistic psychology for political reform.
11. Jezer, *Abbie Hoffman*, p. 50.
12. Jezer, *Abbie Hoffman*, p. 24; Stevens, *Storming Heaven*, pp. 136–42. Leary thought that drugs allowed people to go deeper into personality and the cosmos than the rational mind could delve. They could desocialize people at the same time that they offered alternative visions of fulfilling social life. Stevens, p. 150.
13. In the long run, however, the individualist assumptions of clinical psychology remained, even after the drugs became a tool of a wider community. Drugs that had been meant to transform the consciousness of people who would transform society became simply a trip, a vacation from everyday reality.
14. "The value placed on altered consciousness in the counterculture reflected a belief that social change had to start with self–knowledge. It was difficult to imagine how society could change unless people changed, but it was equally difficult to see how people could become different unless societal structures allowed

them space for reflection and growth. For many young people, the policeman on the corner was less a barrier to social change than the policeman inside their heads." George Lipsitz, "Who'll Stop the Rain?" Youth Culture, Rock 'n' Roll, and Social Crises," in *The Sixties: From Memory to History*, ed. David Farber (Chapel Hill: University of North Carolina Press, 1994), p. 218. Like their hero Yossarian in *Catch-22*, many counterculturalists discovered that "Catch-22 did not exist . . . but it made no difference. What did matter is that everyone thought it existed, and that was much worse, because there was no object or text to ridicule or refute, to accuse, criticize, attack, amend, hate, revile, spit at, rip to shreds, trample upon or burn up." Joseph Heller, *Catch-22*, p. 400.

15. Richard King, *Party of Eros* (Chapel Hill: University of North Carolina Press, 1972), p. 176. "Instead of dualistic, analytical thought, the counterculture was holistic. It perceived reality as interconnected rather than as isolated pieces or categories. It was integrative in that it sought to break down the barriers within the self and between the self and others. It focused on a person as inherently valuable rather than a person as an agent in a world of instrumental or utilitarian reasoning." Morgan, *The Sixties Experience*, p. 171

16. Morgan, *Sixties Experience*, p. 171; Meyerhoff, "Youth Culture," p. 246. In this regard, it is interesting to note the importance of Quakerism—with its own doctrine of the "inner light," and its practices of meditative silence—to the Sixties.

17. Stephen Gaskin et. al., *Hey Beatnik! This Is the Farm Book* (Summertown, TN: The Book Publishing Co., 1974), n.p; Anderson, *The Movement*, pp. 267–68. By the end of the Sixties, former SDS President Paul Potter argued for a revolutionary separatist church. "I have in mind," he said, explaining the term, "some merging of revolutionary religious and revolutionary political ideas; I think of a strong loving band of disciplined . . . people who are enabled by the spiritual solidarity of their community (communion) to explore and survive in the catacombs and caves of Western civilization and still maintain the faith." Paul Potter, *A Name for Ourselves* (Boston: Little, Brown, 1971), p. 185.

18. Roderick Frazier Nash, *The Rights of Nature: A History of Environmental Ethics* (Madison: University of Wisconsin Press, 1989), pp. 166–67; Myerhoff, "Youth Culture," pp. 240–41. See also Ecology Action's "The Unanimous Declaration of Interdependence," in *Sources: An Anthology of Contemporary Materials Useful for Preserving Personal Sanity While Braving the Great Technological Wilderness*, ed. Theodore Roszak (New York: Harper Colophon, 1972), pp. 388–91.

19. Stevens, *Storming Heaven*, pp. 146, 150; Gene Anthony, *Summer of Love: Haight-Ashbury at Its Highest* (Millbrae, CA: Celestial Arts, 1980), p. 54.

20. David Farber, *The Age of Great Dreams: America in the 1960s* (New York: Hill and Wang, 1994), p. 173. "Marijuana," writes Farber, "was a drug particularly suited to the kinds of truths in which young people were interested. The civil rights movement and the student movement both cherished and publicized a vision of a 'beloved community,' a place far different from the atomized world of nuclear families in tract homes cut off from each other by moats of green grass." For many people, marijuana enhanced communitarian connections, as joints were passed between friends. Farber, *Age of Great Dreams*, p. 177. According to Jay Stevens, "Grass opened up a new space for middle class white

kids, an inner space as well as an outer space. It became a ritual—sitting around with your friends, passing a joint from person to person, listening to music, eating, talking, joking, maybe making out—all the senses heightened." Anderson, *The Movement*, p. 259. Sometimes too, of course, marijuana simply made individuals feel good.

21. Stevens, *Storming Heaven*, p. xiv; Morgan, *Sixties Experience*, p. 177; Melville, *Communes in the Counter Culture*, pp. 162–66; Hugh Gardner, *Children of Prosperity: Thirteen Modern Communes* (New York: St. Martin's, 1978), p. 3. "I use psychedelics," explained Stephen Gaskin, "because I find open religious experience to be one step closer to the thing than an open Bible, which was a step closer to the thing than having a Bible of Latin that only the priesthood understood." Gaskin, et al., *Hey Beatnik!* n.p.

22. Stevens, *Storming Heaven*, pp. 226–35, 248–51.

23. Anthony, *Summer of Love*, p. 130.

24. David Pichaske, *A Generation in Motion: Popular Music and Culture in the Sixties* (New York: Schirmer, 1979), p. 150. On the books of the Sixties, see Philip T. Beidler, *Scriptures for a Generation: What We Were Reading in the '60s* (Athens: University of Georgia Press, 1994).

25. Craig Cox, *Storefront Revolution: Food Co-ops and the Counterculture* (New Brunswick, NJ: Rutgers University Press, 1994), p. 3; Joseph Heller, *Catch-22*, p. 440. "Of course freaks never could drop out completely. They drove the roads and had to adhere to highway laws, bought land and had to comply with local ordinances. They paid rent, bills, and had to buy food and other goods. Some worked and paid taxes, others used social services, and some got drafted." Anderson, *The Movement*, p. 255.

26. Farber, *Age of Great Dreams*, pp. 173–74. According to Jay Stevens, within two years of the introduction of the tranquilizer Miltown in 1955, sales had increased from $2.2 million to $150 million. Stevens, *Storming Heaven*, p. 91. Farber also notes that, in the mid–Sixties, American doctors annually wrote 123 million prescriptions for tranquilizers and sedatives, and 24 million for amphetamines. There were about 3,000 deaths a year from overdoses. The hippies were not alone in the quest for a new consciousness.

27. George Lipsitz, "Who'll Stop the Rain?" p. 208; Gaskin et. al., *Hey Beatnik!* n.p. Lipsitz is clear that countercultural music was only one aspect of Sixties music. It is important to remember the music of other subcultures and of other ideological perspectives.

28. For the most part, the multiculturalism remained musical, as the counterculture did not attract America's racial and ethnic minorities. "White youths could not or would not embrace black culture and politics directly; for the most part they preferred to fashion alternative cultures and communities that spoke more to the alienations of middle-class life than they did to the racial and class inequities of American society." Lipsitz, "Who'll Stop the Rain?" pp. 216–18.

29. Timothy Miller, *The Hippies and American Values* (Knoxville: University of Tennessee Press, 1991), pp. 73, 79; Robert A. Rosenstone, "The Times They Are A' Changin'," in *Seasons of Rebellion: Protest and Radicalism in Recent America*, ed. Joseph Boskin and Robert A. Rosenstone (New York: Holt, Rinehart and

Winston, 1972), pp. 325, 331, 333. The words of Sixties songs offer some insight into the worldviews of the counterculture, but single songs—like single advertisements—had little cultural impact. If advertisements collectively create what Michael Schudson calls "capitalist realism," rock songs offered a collective "countercultural realism." See Michael Schudson, *Advertising: The Uneasy Persuasion: Its Dubious Impact on American Society* (New York: Basic Books, 1984), pp. 209–33.

30. Miller, *Hippies and American Values*, p. 74.
31. "The Message of History's Biggest Happening," *Time* 94 (29 August 1969): 32–33; Miller, *Hippies and American Values*, pp. 73, 77.
32. Chester Anderson, quoted in Morgan, *Sixties Experience*, p. 177; Lipsitz, "Who'll Stop the Rain?" pp. 214–15; Anderson, *The Movement*, pp. 277–78.
33. Anderson, *The Movement*, pp. 278–79; Miller, *Hippies and American Values*, pp. 80–81.
34 Miller, *Hippies and American Values*, pp. 112–115.
35. Myerhoff, "Youth Culture," pp. 242–43; Miller, *Hippies and American Values*, pp. 112–15.
36. Melville, *Communes in the Counter Culture*, pp. 95–99; Herman, "Being and Doing," p. 97; Myerhoff, "Youth Culture," pp. 239–40, p. 246. Said Beat poet and Fug Tuli Kupferberg, "Believe me when I say, if you enjoy it, it can still be good, it can still be 'work' (only we'll call it 'play'). Play is as good as work. Work has been defined as something you *dislike* doing. Fuck that. Do the Beatles *work*? Who cares." Anderson, *The Movement*, p. 262.
37. Judson Jerome, *Families of Eden: Communes and the New Anarchism* (New York: Seabury, 1974), pp. 96–97; Gaskin et. al., *Hey Beatnik!* n.p. "If you really want to be spiritual," Gaskin thought, "you don't have to sell your soul for eight hours a day in order to have sixteen hours in which to eat and sleep and get it all back together again. You'd like it that your work be seamless with your life and that what you do for a living doesn't deny everything else you believe in."
38. Potter, *A Name for Ourselves*, p. 163; Jezer, *Abbie Hoffman*, p. 86.
39. Beth Bailey, "Sexual Revolution(s)," in *The 1960s: From Memory to History*, ed. David Farber (Chapel Hill: University of North Carolina Press, 1994), pp. 238–39.
40. Stevens, *Storming Heaven*, p. 197. Monogamous marriage itself was not incompatible with the counterculture, but the mainstream patterns of American monogamy were problematic. Even before the Sixties, some people combined monogamy and communitarianism in communes like the Glen Gardner experiment, which (inter)depended on nuclear families.
41. Melville, *Communes in the Counterculture*, p. 21; Meyerhoff, "Youth Culture," p. 248; Bailey, "Sexual Revolution(s)," pp. 238, 253.
42. Farber, *Age of Great Dreams*, p. 183; Anderson, *The Movement*, p. 271.
43. Morgan, *Sixties Experience*, p. 177; Anthony, *Summer of Love*, pp. 60–61, 70–71.
44. Glenn W. Jones, "Gentle Thursday: An SDS Circus in Austin, Texas, 1966–1969," in *Sights on the Sixties*, ed. Barbara L. Tischler (New Brunswick, NJ: Rutgers University Press, 1992), pp. 75–78.
45. Anthony, *Summer of Love*, pp. 155–56.

46. "Street News for the Tenth of May," (10 May 1967); Jezer, *Abbie Hoffman*, pp. 86–88; Anthony, *Summer of Love*, p. 29; Dale H. Brown, *The Christian Revolutionary*, (Grand Rapids: Eerdmans, 1971), p. 66; Melville, *Communes in the Counterculture*, p. 86.

47. Todd Gitlin, *The Sixties: Years of Hope, Days of Rage* (New York: Bantam, 1987), pp. 222–24; Farber, *Age of Great Dreams*, p. 170; Anthony, *Summer of Love*, p. 31.

48. Anthony, *Summer of Love*, p. 78; Gitlin, *The Sixties*, pp. 223–24.

49. Abe Peck, *Uncovering the Sixties: The Life and Times of the Underground Press* (New York: Pantheon, 1985), p. 47.

50. Gitlin, *Sixties*, pp. 227–31.

51. Jezer, *Abbie Hoffman*, pp. 33–34, 49–61. Hoffman considered Dorothy Day the first hippie. Anne Klejment, "Dorothy Day and the Catholic Worker Movement," in *American Reform and Reformers*, ed. Randall Miller and Paul Cimbala (Westport, CT: Greenwood, 1996), p. 25. Hoffman also heard Paul Goodman speak at a Catholic Worker meeting in New York.

52. Melville, *Communes in the Counter Culture*, p. 69; Herman, "Being and Doing," p. 97,

53. Allen Ginsberg, "Berkeley Vietnam Days," *Liberation* (January 1966): 42–47; Morris Dickstein, *Gates of Eden: American Culture in the Sixties* (New York: Basic Books, 1977), p. 22; Jezer, *Abbie Hoffman*, pp. 112–20. Magic politics, notes Dickstein, "is likely to be scorned by more hard-nosed political types. But . . . it's based on the feeling that certain kinds of political action deform the agent more than they change society, and on a shrewd awareness of the role the media play in altering contemporary opinion." Dickstein, p. 23. In many ways, the story of party politics *since* the Sixties is a story of magic politics, as politicians like Ronald Reagan created a political theater of magical promises.

54. King, *Party of Eros*, pp. 7, 189. But, of course, all politics is cultural. To call personalism cultural radicalism is to pretend that mainstream politics isn't also about consciousness and values. King, p. 189.

55. Melville, *Communes in the Counterculture*, p. 56; Morgan, *Sixties Experience*, p. 173; Anderson, *The Movement*, p. 254; Farber, *Age of Great Dreams*, p. 169; Maurice Isserman and Michael Kazin, "The Failure and Success of the New Radicalism," in *The Rise and Fall of the New Deal Order, 1930–1980*, ed. Steven Fraser and Gary Gerstle (Princeton: Princeton University Press, 1989), p. 227. Keith Melville contends that the New Left and the counterculture shared an agenda, but not priorities. While the New Left focused on power allocation and institutional change, the counterculture focused first on expanded consciousness. The New Left expected cultural changes after the Revolution; the counterculture expected political changes to follow the "here and now revolution." Melville, *Communes in the Counter Culture*, p. 74.

56. Melville, *Communes in the Counter Culture*, pp. 79–83; Anderson, *The Movement*, p. 270.

57. Jerome, *Families of Eden*, p. 15; Anderson, *The Movement*, pp. 273–74; Robert Cooney and Helen Michalowski, ed. *The Power of the People: Active Nonviolence in the United States* (Philadelphia: New Society, 1987), p. 131.

58. Gitlin, *Sixties*, p. 233; Jezer, *Abbie Hoffman*, pp. 85–90; Isserman and Kazin, "Failure and Success of the New Radicalism," p. 227. For a description of a "typical" rural commune, see Jerome, *Families of Eden*, pp. 20–24.

59. Gardner, *Children of Prosperity*, p. 3; Barbara Epstein, *Political Protest and Cultural Revolution: Nonviolent Direct Action in the 1970's and 1980's* (Berkeley: University of California Press, 1991), p. 62; Anderson, *The Movement*, pp. 269–71. Like the previous generation of political personalists, many of these groups propagated the faith in publications. The Canyon Collective in California supported vocations for social change and published *Workforce*. Heathcoate published a newspaper, *The Green Revolution*, and offered workshops on communes and homesteading. The Farm in Tennessee published guidebooks to farming and communal living, as well as cookbooks and spiritual guides. Jerome, *Families of Eden*, p. 9.

60. Melville, *Communes in the Counterculture*, pp. 26–28. For a sense of the variety of communes see Melville, Judson Jerome's *Families of Eden* and John Case and Rosemary C.R. Taylor, *Co-ops, Communes and Collectives: Experiments in Social Change in the 1960s and 1970s* (New York: Pantheon, 1979).

61. Melville, *Communes in the Counter Culture*, p. 158; Richard Fairfield, *Communes USA* (Baltimore: Penguin Books, 1972), p. 242.

62. Stevens, *Storming Heaven*, p. 250. See also Joseph Epes Brown, *The Spiritual Legacy of the American Indian* (Wallingford, PA: Pendle Hill, 1964), reprinted in Roszak, *Sources*, pp. 341–53.

63. Gaskin et al., n.p.; Brown, *The Christian Revolutionary*, p. 76.

64. David DeLeon, *The American as Anarchist*, p. 120.

65. Morgan, *Sixties Experience*, pp. 265–66; Jonathan Schell, *The Time of Illusion* (New York: Vintage, 1975), p. 62. A society of hippies would be un-American, in part, because it would replace American values, but also because it would practice American values. As Barbara Myerhoff notes, the counterculture supported "individualism, but without isolation; responsibility, but for others as well as oneself; autonomy and mastery, but without exploitation of others; equalitarianism, but not for Caucasians only; and democracy, but on a more inclusive scale, involving greater participation of members in the institutions and bureaucracies that affect their lives. . . . 'The American way of life' is being taken with the greatest seriousness by these young people." Myerhoff, "Youth Culture," p. 245.

66. Cox, *Storefront Revolution*, p. 29; Anderson, *The Movement*, pp. 249, 282–85. See also Geoffrey Rips, *The Campaign Against the Underground Press* (San Francisco: City Lights, 1981).

67. Lipsitz, "Who'll Stop the Rain?" p. 224; Charles McCabe, "Love and the Buck," *San Francisco Chronicle* (19 May 1967); John Robert Howard and Mary D. Howard, "The Flowering of the Hippies," in *Seasons of Rebellion: Protest and Radicalism in Recent America*, ed. Joseph Boskin and Robert A. Rosenstone (New York: Holt, Rinehart and Winston, 1972), pp. 270–72. The Diggers detested the "merchants of love," but they celebrated the people who realized "that people are more important than profits," and who created cooperative ventures with a community focus. See "Street News for the Tenth of May: Pub-

lic Acts Are Public Knowledge: Love Is What You Do Not What You Say,"
(May 10, 1967) in *The Digger Archives*.
68. Anderson, *The Movement*, pp. 286–88.
69. Howard and Howard, "The Flowering of the Hippies," pp. 265–66. For a particular example of the problems of voluntarism, see Jerome, *Families of Eden*, pp. 240–50.
70. Lipsitz, "Who'll Stop the Rain?" p. 226. Still, as Lipsitz suggests, "for all of its oppositional intentions, the counterculture did too little to interrogate the axes of power in society—the systematic racism, class domination, sexism, and homophobia that constrained individual choices." The most popular radical critique of American society in the postwar period, it still didn't quite get to the root of the matter.
71. Cox, *Storefront Revolution*, p. 17.
72. Marc Ellis, *Peter Maurin: Prophet in the Twentieth Century* (New York: Paulist Press, 1981), p. 121; James Cone, *Black Theology and Black Power*, (New York: Seabury Press, 1969), p. 42–43; Daniel Yankelovich, *New Rules: Searching for Self-Fulfillment in a World Turned Upside Down* (New York. Bantam, 1981), p. 218. "For biblical religion, freedom meant liberation from the consequences of sin, freedom to do the right, and was almost equivalent to virtue." Robert N. Bellah, "New Religious Consciousness and the Crisis in Modernity," in *The New Religious Consciousness*, ed. Charles Y. Glock and Robert N. Bellah (Berkeley: University of California Press, 1976), p. 336.
73. Lipsitz, "Who'll Stop the Rain?" pp. 222–23. "Freedom is a difficult thing to handle," wrote Richard Fairfield. "Give people freedom and they'll do all the things they thought they never had a chance to do. But that won't last very long. And after that? After that, my friend, it'll be time to make your life meaningful." Anderson, *The Movement*, p. 286. As Anderson says, "Freedom was not free, it took responsibility to make a meaningful life."
74. Anderson, *The Movement*, p. 287.
75. Lipsitz, "Who'll Stop the Rain?" p. 223; Anderson, *The Movement*, p. 286.
76. Gitlin, *Sixties*, pp. 235–37.
77. Anderson, *The Movement*, p. 289.

Notes to Epilogue

1. Robert Holsworth, *Let Your Life Speak: A Study of Politics, Religion, and Antinuclear Weapons Activism* (Madison: University of Wisconsin Press, 1989), p. 185.
2. Marty Jezer, *Abbie Hoffman: An American Rebel* (New Brunswick, NJ: Rutgers University Press, 1992), p. 34; Ellen Herman, "Being and Doing: Humanistic Psychology and the Spirit of the 1960s," in *Sights on the Sixties*, ed. Barbara L. Tischler (New Brunswick, NJ: Rutgers University Press, 1992) p. 98. According to Marty Jezer, Friedan "was the first social activist to grasp the political implications of Maslovian psychology."
3. Sara Evans, *Personal Politics: The Roots of Women's Liberation in the Civil Rights Movement and the New Left* (New York: Knopf, 1979), p. 108.
4. Edward P. Morgan, *The Sixties Experience: Hard Lessons About Modern America* (Philadelphia: Temple University Press, 1991), p. 221. Todd Gitlin's chapter on

"Women: Revolution in the Revolution" is a good brief introduction to these issues. Todd Gitlin, *The Sixties: Years of Hope, Days of Rage* (New York: Bantam, 1987), pp. 362–76. For an account of the hypermasculinity of the Free Speech Movement, see Daniel P. Hinman-Smith, "'Does the Word Freedom Have a Meaning?' The Mississippi Freedom Schools, the Berkeley Free Speech Movement, and the Search for Freedom Through Education" (Ph.D. dissertation: University of North Carolina, 1993), p. 336.

5. Casey Hayden and Mary King, "Sex and Caste: A Kind of Memo," in *The Sixties Papers: Documents of a Rebellious Decade*, ed. Judith Clavir Albert and Stewart Edward Albert (New York: Praeger, 1984), pp. 134, 136; Hayden and King, "Caste and Sex," *Liberation* (April 1966): 35–36; Alice Echols, "Nothing Distant About It: Women's Liberation and Sixties Radicalism," in *The Sixties: From Memory to History*, ed. David Farber (Chapel Hill: University of North Carolina Press, 1994), p. 153.

6. James Miller, *"Democracy Is in the Streets": From Port Huron to the Siege of Chicago* (New York: Simon and Schuster, 1987), p. 257; Evans, *Personal Politics*, p. 214; Jo Freeman, *The Politics of Women's Liberation* (New York: David McKay, 1975), p. 118. See also Pamela Allen, *Free Space: A Perspective on the Small Group in Women's Liberation* (Washington, NJ: Times Change Press, 1970).

7. Evans, *Personal Politics*, p. 212; Holsworth, *Let Your Life Speak*, p. 95; Winifred D. Wandersee, *On the Move: American Women in the 1970s* (Boston: Twayne, 1988), pp. xv–xvi; Maurice Isserman and Michael Kazin, "The Failure and Success of the New Radicalism," in *The Rise and Fall of the New Deal Order, 1930–1980*, ed. Steven Fraser and Gary Gerstle (Princeton: Princeton University Press, 1989), p. 228.

8. Morgan, *Sixties Experience*, pp. 217, 229. For an elaboration of the personalism of feminism, see Sara Ruddick, *Maternal Thinking: Toward a Politics of Peace* (Boston: Beacon Press, 1989).

9. Harry C. Boyte, *The Backyard Revolution: Understanding the New Citizen Movement* (Philadelphia: Temple University Press, 1980).

10. Boyte, *Backyard Revolution*, pp. 4, 18, 197–98.

11. Boyte, *Backyard Revolution*, p. 138; Paul Starr, "The Phantom Community," in *Co-ops, Communes and Collectives: Experiments in Social Change in the 1960s and 1970s*, ed. John Case and Rosemary C.R. Taylor (New York: Pantheon, 1979), pp. 255–56.

12. Craig Cox, *Storefront Revolution: Food Co-ops and the Counterculture* (New Brunswick, NJ: Rutgers University Press, 1992), pp. 4–5, 10.

13. Warren J. Belasco, *Appetite for Change: How the Counterculture Took on the Food Industry, 1966–1988* (New York: Pantheon, 1989), pp. 39–40.

14. Starr, "The Phantom Community," pp. 258–59. See also Daniel Zwerdling, "The Uncertain Revival of Food Cooperatives," in *Co-ops, Communes and Collectives*, pp. 89–111.

15. Daniel Yankelovich, *New Rules: Searching for Self-Fulfillment in a World Turned Upside Down* (New York: Bantam, 1981), p. 226; Holsworth, *Let Your Life Speak*, p. 182.

16. Carolyn Merchant, *Radical Ecology: The Search for a Livable World* (New York: Routledge, 1992), pp. 75–78; Morgan, *Sixties Experience*, p. 247.

17. Merchant, *Radical Ecology*, pp. 217–22; Kirkpatrick Sale, *Dwellers in the Land* (San Francisco: Sierra Club, 1985), pp. 101–04.
18. Merchant, *Radical Ecology*, pp. 185–93; Morgan, *Sixties Experience*, p. 231.
19. Paul Merchant, *Wendell Berry* (Lewiston, Idaho: Confluence Press, 1991), pp. 7–8.
20. Wendell Berry, *The Unsettling of America: Culture and Agriculture* (San Francisco: Sierra Club, 1976), pp. 17, 19, 22.
21. Berry, *The Unsettling of America*, pp. 23, 26.
22. Wendell Berry, "The Reactor and the Garden," in *The Gift of Good Land: Further Essays Cultural and Agricultural* (San Francisco: North Point Press, 1981), p. 164.
23. Berry, "The Reactor and the Garden," pp. 164–65.
24. Berry, "The Reactor and the Garden," pp. 167–70. Like most political personalists, Berry's definition of health is comprehensive. "The concept of health," he notes, "is rooted in the concept of wholeness. To be healthy is to be whole. The world *health* belongs to a family of words, a listing of which will suggest how far the concept of health must carry us: *heal, whole, wholesome, hale, hallow, holy*. . . . It is wrong to think that bodily health is compatible with spiritual confusion or cultural disorder, or with polluted air and water or impoverished soil." Persons, he thought, became whole insofar as they worked in harmony with the Creator and the Creation, including their fellow creatures. "Healing is impossible in loneliness; it is the opposite of loneliness. Conviviality is healing." Berry, *The Unsettling of America*, p. 103.
25. Jacqueline Killeen, *Ecology at Home* (San Francisco: 101 Productions, 1971); Center for Science in the Public Interest, *99 Ways to a Simple Lifestyle* (Garden City, NY: Anchor, 1977); Warren Johnson, *Muddling Toward Frugality* (Boulder: Shambhala, 1978); Duane Elgin, *Voluntary Simplicity: An Ecological Lifestyle That Promotes Personal and Social Renewal* (New York: Bantam Books, 1981); American Friends Service Committee, *Taking Charge of Our Lives: Living Responsibly in the World* (San Francisco: Harper and Row, 1984); Karen Christensen, *Home Ecology: Simple and Practical Ways to Green Your Home* (Golden, CO: Fulcrum, 1990); Jeffrey Hollender, *How to Make the World a Better Place: A Guide to Doing Good* (New York: William Morrow, 1990).
26. Morgan, *Sixties Experience*, p. 244.
27. Barbara Epstein, *Political Protest and Cultural Revolution: Nonviolent Direct Action in the 1970s and 1980s* (Berkeley: University of California Press, 1991), p. 63; Morgan, *Sixties Experience*, pp. 244–45.
28. Epstein, *Political Protest and Cultural Revolution*, pp. 59, 64, 66, 69.
29. Epstein, *Political Protest and Cultural Revolution*, pp. 65–68, 85–91.
30. Epstein, *Political Protest and Cultural Revolution*, pp. 95–96.
31. Epstein, *Political Protest and Cultural Revolution*, pp. 96–97, 100.
32. Morgan, *Sixties Experience*, p. 247.
33. E.F. Schumacher, *Small Is Beautiful: Economics as if People Mattered* (New York: Harper and Row, 1973); Theodore Roszak, "Introduction," pp. 3–4; Boyte, *Backyard Revolution*, p. 142. Roszak agreed about the aesthetics of smallness, but thought that Schumacher might also have added that "'small is free, efficient, creative, enjoyable, enduring'—for such is the anarchist faith." Roszak, p. 4.

34. Roszak, "Introduction," pp. 5, 8–9.
35. Schumacher, *Small Is Beautiful*, pp. 50–54, 230.
36. Morgan, *Sixties Experience*, p. 243
37. Marc Ellis, *Peter Maurin: Prophet in the Twentieth Century* (New York: Paulist Press, 1981), p. 167; Langdon Winner, *The Whale and the Reactor* (Chicago: University of Chicago Press, 1986), p. 72.
38. Langdon Winner, *The Whale and the Reactor*, pp. 62, 79–83. Winner contends that the appropriate technology movement sprang from " a general disillusionment with politics," but it's important to remember that disillusionment with national party politics is not the same as disillusionment with politics itself.
39. Yankelovich, *New Rules*, p. 229.
40. Yankelovich, *New Rules*, p. 5.
41. Yankelovich, *New Rules*, pp. 237, 253.
42. Boyte, *Backyard Revolution*, p. 186.
43. Yankelovich, *New Rules*, pp. 257–58.
44. Pam Solo, *From Protest to Policy: Beyond the Freeze to Common Security* (Cambridge, MA: Ballinger, 1988), pp. 28–34; Robert A. Irwin, *Building a Peace System* (Washington: ExPro Press, 1989), p. 11.
45. Daniel Berrigan, "Introduction," *The Long Loneliness* (New York: Harper and Row, 1952), p. xxiii.
46. Solo, *From Protest to Policy*, pp. 42–45, 61.
47. Solo, *From Protest to Policy*, p. 66. On free spaces, see Sara M. Evans and Harry C. Boyte, *Free Spaces: The Sources of Democratic Change in America* (New York: Harper and Row, 1986). "The great strength of the freeze," claimed James Skelly, "was its initial breakout from the dominant discourse. . . . The energy behind the early freeze movement was a testimony to the fact that it had liberated large numbers of people from their imprisonment in the regime of truth constructed around nuclear weapons. It allowed people who had previously been part of the culture of silence around nuclear weapons to speak, and as such threatened to reinvent a political discourse around foreign and military policy." James Skelly, "Power/Knowledge: The Problems of Peace Research and the Peace Movement," (Paper prepared for presentation at the International Peace Research Association biannual meeting, 1986), pp. 2–6.
48. Epstein, *Political Protest and Cultural Revolution*, p. 127.
49. Holsworth, *Let Your Life Speak*, pp. 80–82.
50. Holsworth, *Let Your Life Speak*, pp. 38, 97–111. Parenting for peace and justice was particularly difficult because, as Holsworth suggests, personalists had to be "willing to raise children who are . . . different from most of the kids growing up in the United States today." It's one thing to choose to be a dissident yourself; it's another thing to make your children misfits. Holsworth, *Let Your Life Speak*, p. 129.
51. Holsworth, *Let Your Life Speak*, p. 22.
52. Holsworth, *Let Your Life Speak*, p. 96.
53. Epstein, *Political Protest and Cultural Revolution*, p. 116.

Notes to Conclusion

1. Judson Jerome, *Families of Eden: Communes and the New Anarchism* (New York: Seabury, 1974), pp. 239–40.
2. O'Brien, "Social Teaching, Social Action, Social Gospel," p. 222; Phillip Berryman, *Our Unfinished Business: The U.S. Catholic Bishops' Letters on Peace and the Economy* (New York: Pantheon, 1989), pp. 18–19. Berryman also suggests that the pastoral letter, especially in its reliance on the principle of subsidiarity, has substantial affinities with anarchism, and he mentions the Catholic Workers and the Berrigans, E.F. Schumacher, and Ivan Ilich. Berryman, pp. 179–80.
3. Clifford E. Bajema, *Abortion and the Politics of Personhood* (Grand Rapids: Baker Book House, 1974), pp. 15–42; Maurice Isserman and Michael Kazin, "The Failure and Success of the New Radicalism," in *The Rise and Fall of the New Deal Order, 1930–1980*, ed. Steven Fraser and Gary Gerstle (Princeton: Princeton University Press, 1989), p. 234.
4. Ellen Herman, "Being and Doing: Humanistic Psychology and the Spirit of the Sixties," in *Sights on the Sixties*, ed. Barbara L. Tischler (New Brunswick, NJ: Rutgers University Press, 1992), p. 94.
5. Robert Holsworth, *Let Your Life Speak: A Study of Politics, Religion, and Antinuclear Activism* (Madison: University of Wisconsin Press, 1989), p. 11. In the midst of the 1996 Presidential campaign, it's hard to say convincingly that conventional politics is much better at describing the route from here to there.
6. Barbara Epstein, *Political Protest and Cultural Revolution: Nonviolent Direct Action in the 1970s and 1980s* (Berkeley: University of California Press, 1991).
7. Holsworth, *Let Your Life Speak*, p. 11.
8. Holsworth, *Let Your Life Speak*, p. 12.
9. Holsworth, *Let Your Life Speak*, pp. 11–12, 147–50. "Living consistently," notes Holsworth, "could require fathers and mothers to examine how they might be in complicity with disturbing trends in the larger culture, to ask themselves about what kind of role models they are, and to consider how the ambitions expressed in their own lives reflect on the ideals they profess to be transmitting to their children." Holsworth, p. 129.
10. David DeLeon, *The American As Anarchist: Reflections on Indigenous Radicalism* (Baltimore: Johns Hopkins University Press, 1979), p. 132.
11. DeLeon, *American as Anarchist*, p. 137.
12. Rosalie Riegle Troester, ed., *Voices from the Catholic Worker* (Philadelphia: Temple University Press, 1993), p. xv.

BIBLIOGRAPHY

PRIMARY SOURCES

Books

Albert, Judith Clavir and Stewart Edward Albert. eds. *The Sixties Papers: Documents of a Rebellious Decade*. New York: Praeger, 1984.
American Friends Service Committee. *Speak Truth to Power*. Philadelphia: AFSC, 1955.
Baez, Joan. *And A Voice to Sing With: A Memoir*. New York: Summit, 1987.
Berrigan, Daniel. *The Trial of the Catonsville Nine*. Boston: Beacon, 1970.
Bloom, Alexander and Wini Breines, eds. *"Takin' It to the Streets": A Sixties Reader*. New York: Oxford University Press, 1995.
Brown, Robert McAfee. *Vietnam: Crisis of Conscience*. New York: Association Press, 1967.
Coffin, William Sloane. *Once to Every Man: A Memoir*. New York: Atheneum, 1977.
Cohen, Mitchell and Dennis Hale. eds. *The New Student Left; An Anthology*. Boston: Beacon, 1966.
Day, Dorothy. *The Long Loneliness*. New York: Harper and Row, 1952.

————. *On Pilgrimage: The Sixties*. New York: Curtis Books, 1972.

Dellinger, David. *More Power Than We Know: The People's Movement Toward Democracy*. Garden City, New York: Doubleday, 1975.

————. *Revolutionary Nonviolence: Essays by Dave Dellinger*. New York: Doubleday, 1971.

Ellsberg, Daniel. *Papers on the War*. New York: Simon and Schuster, 1982.

Everson, William. *The Crooked Lines of God: Poems 1949–1954*. Detroit: University of Detroit Press, 1959.

————. *The Residual Years: Poems 1934–1948*. New York: New Directions, 1968.

Ferber, Michael and Staughton Lynd. *The Resistance*. Boston: Beacon, 1971.

Ferlinghetti, Lawrence. *A Coney Island of the Mind*. New York: New Directions, 1958.

Finn, James. ed. *Protest: Pacifism and Politics*. New York: Random House, 1968.

Fromm, Erich. *Marx's Concept of Man*. New York: Frederick Ungar, 1961.

————. *The Sane Society*. New York: Rinehart, 1955.

Ginsberg, Allen. *Allen Verbatim*. New York: McGraw–Hill, 1974.

————. *Howl and Other Poems*. San Francisco: City Lights, 1956.

————. *Howl: Original Draft Facsimile, Transcript & Variant Versions, Fully Annotated by Author, With Contemporaneous Correspondence, Account of First Public Reading, Legal Skirmishes Precursor Texts & Bibliography*. ed. Barry Miles. New York: Harper & Row, 1986.

Goodman, Paul. *Communitas: Means of Livelihood and Ways of Life*. New York: Random House/Vintage, 1960.

————. *The Community of Scholars*. New York: Random House, 1972.

————. *Growing Up Absurd: Problems of Youth in the Organized System*. New York: Random House, 1960.

————. *Like a Conquered Province: The Moral Ambiguity of America*. New York: Random House, 1967.

————. *The Society I Live In Is Mine*. New York: Horizon Press, 1962.

————. *Utopian Essays and Practical Proposals*. New York: Vintage, 1962.

————, ed. *Seeds of Liberation*. New York: George Braziller, 1965.

Harrington, Michael. *The Other America: Poverty in the United States*. New York: Macmillan, 1962.

Hayden, Tom. *Trial*. New York: Holt, Rinehart and Winston, 1970.

Hayden, Tom and Staughton Lynd. *The Other Side*. New York: New American Library, 1966.

Hennacy, Ammon. *The Book of Ammon*. New York: Catholic Worker Press, 1954.

Hoffman, Abbie (Free). *Revolution for the Hell of It*. New York: Dial Press, 1968.

————. *Soon to Be a Major Motion Picture*. New York: Putnam, 1980.

————. *Steal This Book*. Worcester, Mass: Jack Hoffman Presents, n.d.

————. *Woodstock Nation: A Talk-Rock Album*. New York: Vintage, 1969.

Jacobs, Paul and Saul Landau, eds. *The New Radicals: A Report with Documents*. New York: Vintage, 1966.

Keniston, Kenneth. *The Uncommitted*. New York: Harcourt, Brace and World, 1965.

————. *Young Radicals: Notes on Committed Youth*. New York: Harcourt, 1968.

————. *Youth and Dissent: The Rise of a New Opposition*. New York: Harcourt, 1971.

Kerouac, Jack. *The Dharma Bums*. New York: New American Library, 1958.

————. *On the Road*. New York: Viking Press, 1957.

King, Coretta Scott. *My Life With Martin Luther King, Jr.* New York: Holt, Rinehart and Winston, 1969.

King, Martin Luther, Jr. *I Have a Dream: Writings and Speeches That Changed the World*, ed. James M. Washington. San Francisco: HarperSanFrancisco, 1992.

————. *Stride Toward Freedom: The Montgomery Story*. New York: Harper, 1958.

————. *Why We Can't Wait*. New York: Harper, 1963.

Kropotkin, Peter. *The Conquest of Bread*. London: Chapman and Hall, 1906.

————. *Mutual Aid: A Factor of Evolution*. New York: Knopf, 1918.

Kunen, James Simon. *The Strawberry Statement: Notes of a College Revolutionary*. New York: Random House, 1969.

Leary, Timothy. *Flashbacks: An Autobiography*. Los Angeles, J.P. Tarcher, 1983.

————. *The Politics of Ecstasy*. New York: Putnam, 1968.

Lipton, Lawrence. *The Holy Barbarians*. New York: Julian Messner, 1959.

Lynd, Alice, ed. *We Won't Go: Personal Accounts of the War Objectors*. Boston: Beacon, 1968.

Marcuse, Herbert. *One Dimensional Man: Studies in the Ideology of Advanced Industrial Society*. Boston: Beacon, 1964.

Maurin, Peter. *Easy Essays*. ed. Chuck Smith. West Hamlin, WV: Green Revolution, 1973.

Menashe, Louis and Ronald Rodosh, eds. *Teach-Ins: U.S.A.: Reports, Opinions, Documents*. New York: Praeger, 1967.

Merton, Thomas. *Albert Camus' The Plague*. New York: Seabury, 1968.

————. *Conjectures of a Guilty Bystander*. New York: Doubleday, 1968.

————. *Gandhi on Nonviolence*. New York: New Directions, 1965.

————. *The Nonviolent Alternative*. New York: Farrar, Straus and Giroux, 1971.

————. *Original Child Bomb: Points for Meditation to Be Scratched on the Walls of a Cave*. New York: New Directions, 1962.

————. *Raids on the Unspeakable*. New York: New Directions, 1966.

————. *Seeds of Destruction*. New York: Farrar, Straus and Giroux, 1964.

————. *A Vow of Conversation*. New York: Farrar, Straus and Giroux, 1988.

————, ed. *Breakthrough to Peace: Twelve Views on the Threat of Thermonuclear Extermination*. New York: New Directions, 1962.

————. *The Hidden Ground of Love: The Letters of Thomas Merton on Religious Experience and Social Concerns*, ed. William H. Shannon. New York: Farrar, Straus and Giroux, 1985.

————. *Witness to Freedom: Letters in Time of Crisis*, ed. William H. Shannon. San Diego: Harcourt Brace, 1994.

Mills, C. Wright. *The Causes of World War Three*. New York: Ballantine Books, 1958.

————. *Power, Politics, and People: The Collected Essays of C. Wright Mills*. New York: Oxford University Press, 1963.

————. *The Sociological Imagination*. New York: Grove Press, 1961.

Mumford, Lewis. *In the Name of Sanity*. New York: Harcourt Brace, 1954.

Mungo, Raymond. *Famous Long Ago: My Life and Hard Times with Liberation News Service*. Boston: Beacon, 1970.

——. *Total Loss Farm: A Year in the Life*. New York: Dutton, 1970.

Muste, A.J. *The Essays of A.J. Muste*, ed. Nat Hentoff. Indianapolis: Bobbs Merrill, 1967.

Newfield, Jack. *A Prophetic Minority*. New York: Signet, 1966.

Potter, Paul. *A Name for Ourselves*. Boston: Little, Brown, 1971.

Rader, Dotson. *"I Ain't Marchin' Any More!"* New York: McKay, 1969.

Reich, Charles A. *The Greening of America*. New York: Random House, 1970.

Reynolds, Earle. *The Forbidden Voyage*. New York: McKay, 1961.

Rossman, Michael. *On Learning and Social Change*. New York: Vintage, 1972.

——. *The Wedding Within the War*. Garden City, N.Y.: Doubleday, 1971.

Roszak, Theodore. *The Making of a Counterculture: Reflections on the Technocratic Society and its Youthful Opposition*. Garden City, New York: Doubleday, 1969.

——. *Person/Planet: The Creative Disintegration of Industrial Society*. Garden City, NY: Anchor/Doubleday, 1979.

——. *Sources: An Anthology of Contemporary Materials Useful for Preserving Sanity While Braving the Great Technological Wilderness*. New York: Harper Colophon, 1972.

Rubin, Jerry. *Do It! Scenarios of the Revolution*. New York: Simon & Schuster, 1970.

Rustin, Bayard. *Down the Line: The Collected Writings of Bayard Rustin*. Chicago: Quadrangle Books, 1971.

Sampson, Edward E., et al. *Student Activism and Protest*. San Francisco: Jossey-Bass, 1970.

Schumacher, E.F. *Small Is Beautiful: Economics As If People Mattered*. New York: Harper and Row, 1973.

Slater, Philip. *The Pursuit of Loneliness: American Culture at the Breaking Point*. Boston: Beacon,1970.

Stone, I.F. *The Haunted Fifties, 1953–1963*. Boston: Little, Brown, 1989.

Taylor, Harold. *How to Change Colleges: Notes on Radical Reform*. New York: Holt, Rinehart and Winston, 1971.

——. *Students Without Teachers: The Crisis in the University*. New York: Holt, Rinehart and Winston, 1969.

Teodori, Massimo, ed. *The New Left: A Documentary History*. Indianapolis: Bobbs-Merrill, 1969.

Watts, Alan. *Beat Zen, Square Zen and Zen*. San Francisco: City Lights, 1959.

Yankelovich, Daniel. *The New Morality: A Profile of American Youth in the 70's*. New York: McGraw Hill, 1974.

——. *New Rules: Searching for Self-Fulfillment in a World Turned Upside Down*. New York: Bantam, 1981.

Articles

(Author not cited.) "Graham Okays War for Christians." *Fellowship 21* (November 1955): 26.

Bagby, Jeanne. "Behind the Scene: The Psychological Panorama Underlying the Beat Extravaganza." *Liberation* 4 (May 1959): 11–13.

————. "Oh What Farewells." *Liberation* 6 (March 1961): 17–18.

Bigelow, Albert. "Why I am Sailing Into the Pacific Bomb Test Area." *Liberation* 3 (February 1958): 18–22.

Bloy, Myron B. Jr., "The Counter Curriculum: A Spiritual Taxonomy of Higher Education." *Commonweal* 91 (3 October 1969): 8–12.

Boyle, Kay. "The Triumph of Principles." *Liberation* 5 (June 1960): 10–11.

Cramer, Robert S. "President Kennedy Talks about Women and World Peace." *Parents Magazine* (November 1963): 38, 57, 73.

Davis, Harriet Eager. "What the Bomb Really Blew Up." *Independent Woman* 25 (February 1946): 34–36.

Deming, Barbara. "Letter to WISP." *Liberation* 8 (April 1963): 18–21.

Ferlinghetti, Lawrence. "Tentative Description of a Dinner to Promote the Impeachment of President Eisenhower." *Liberation* 3 (August 1958): 17.

Finch, Roy. "The *Liberation* Poll." *Liberation* 4 (November 1959): 14–17.

————. "The New Peace Movement—Part II." *Dissent* 10 (Spring 1963): 138–48.

Forest, James H. "No Longer Alone: The Catholic Peace Movement." In *American Catholics and Vietnam*, ed. Thomas E. Quigley. Grand Rapids: William B. Eerdmans, 1968.

Fruchter, Norm. "Mississippi: Notes on SNCC." *Studies on the Left* 5 (Winter 1965): 77–79.

Ginsberg, Allen. "Some Metamorphoses of Personal Prosody." In Stephen Berg and Robert Mezey, eds., *Naked Poetry: Recent American Poetry in Open Forms*. New York: Macmillan, 1969.

————. "A Version of the Apocalypse." In Arthur and Kit Knight, eds., *The Beat Vision: A Primary Sourcebook*. New York: Paragon House, 1987.

Goodman, Paul. "The Duty of Professionals." *Liberation* 12 (November 1967): 39.

————. "Getting Into Power." *Liberation* 7 (October 1962): 4–8.

————. "Politics Within Limits." *New York Review of Books* 10 (August 10, 1972): 31–34.

————. "Thoughts on Berkeley." *New York Review of Books* 3 (January 14, 1965): 5–6.

Gorer, Geoffrey. "The Pornography of Death." *Encounter* 5 (October 1955): 49–52.

Haber, Robert A. "From Protest to Radicalism: An Appraisal of the Student Movement 1960." In Mitchell Cohen and Dennis Hale, eds. *The New Student Left*. Boston: Beacon Press, 1967.

Hayden, Casey and Mary King. "Sex and Caste: A Kind of Memo." In Judith Clavir Albert and Stewart Edward Albert, eds., *The Sixties Papers: Documents of a Rebellious Decade*. New York: Praeger, 1984.

Hayden, Tom. "Letter to the New (Young) Left." In Mitchell Cohen and Dennis Hale, eds., *The New Student Left*. Boston: Beacon Press, 1967.

————. "Just a Matter of Timing?" *Liberation* 7 (October 1962): 24–26.

Hawkes, Jacquetta. "Now At Last." *The New Statesman* 56 (July 5, 1958): 10.

King, Martin Luther, Jr. "Letter from Birmingham Jail." In *Why We Can't Wait*. New York: Harper and Row, 1964.

————. "Our Struggle." *Liberation* 1 (April 1956): 3–6.

————. "Pilgrimage to Nonviolence." *Christian Century* 77 (April 13, 1960): 439–41.

———. "The Social Organization of Nonviolence." *Liberation* 4 (October 1959): 5–6.

Kopkind, Andrew. "Rebels with Cause." *The New Republic* (May 1, 1965): 5–6.

Langer, Elinor. "Notes for Next Time: A Memoir of the 1960s." In R. David Meyers, ed., *Toward a History of the New Left: Essays From Within the Movement.* Brooklyn: Carlson Publishing, 1989.

Ludlow, Robert, "St. Francis and His Revolution." In Thomas C. Cornell and James Forest, eds., *A Penny a Copy.* New York: Macmillan, 1968.

Lynd, Staughton. "The New Left." *Annals of the American Academy of Political and Social Science* 382 (March 1969): 69–70.

Lyttle, Bradford. "On Nonviolent Obstruction." *Liberation* 3 (November 1958): 10–11.

Macdonald, Dwight, "Dorothy Day." In *Memoirs of a Revolutionist: Essays in Political Criticism.* New York: Farrar, Straus and Cudahy, 1957.

———. "'Here Lies Our Road!' Said Writer to Reader." *Politics* 1 (September 1944): 247–51.

———. "Why Politics." *Politics* 1 (February 1944): 7.

Marx, Leo. "American Institutions and Ecologial Ideals." *Science* 170 (27 November 1970): 945–52.

Maurin, Peter. "The Race Problem." *Catholic Worker* 6 (May 1938): 1, 8.

McCabe, Charles. "Love and the Buck." *San Francisco Chronicle* (May 19, 1967).

Meitner, Lise. "Your Life in the Atomic Age." *Women's Home Companion* 72 (December 1945): 4, 148.

Merton, Thomas. "Dear Editors." *Liberation* 6 (February 1962): 22.

Mumford, Lewis. "Irrational Elements in Art and Politics." In *In the Name of Sanity.* New York: Harcourt Brace, 1954.

Newfield, Jack. "The Peace Opposition." *The Nation* (May 3, 1965): 462.

Peck, James. "Trespassing at the Bomb Site." *Liberation* 2 (September 1957): 8–9.

Pickus, Robert. "The Nevada Project: An Appraisal." *Liberation* 2 (September 1957): 3–4.

Powledge, Fred. "The New Student Left: Represents Serious Activists in Drive for Changes." *New York Times* (March 15, 1965): 1:3.

Rexroth, Kenneth. "Disengagement: The Art of the Beat Generation." In *World Outside the Window: The Selected Essays of Kenneth Rexroth.* New York: New Directions, 1987.

———. "Revolt: True and False." In *World Outside the Window.* New York: New Directions, 1987.

———. "San Francisco Letter." In *World Outside the Window.* New York: New Directions, 1987.

———. "The Students Take Over." In *World Outside the Window.* New York: New Directions, 1987.

Rossman, Michael, "The Movement and Educational Reform." *American Scholar* 36 (Autumn 1967): 594–600.

Roszak, Theodore. "This Disease Called Politics." *Liberation* 7 (March 1962): 15–18.

Rustin, Bayard. "From Protest to Politics: The Future of the Civil Rights Movement." *Commentary* 39 (February 1965): 25–31.

———. "The Meaning of Birmingham." In Paul Goodman, ed., *Seeds of Liberation*. New York: George Braziller, 1964.

———. "Montgomery Diary." *Liberation* 1 (April 1956): 7–10.

Savio, Mario. " An End to History." In Mitchell Cohen and Dennis Hale. *The New Student Left; An Anthology*. Boston: Beacon Press, 1966.

Schechner, Mark, "The Cold War and the University of California." In Dennis Hale and Jonathan Eisen, eds., *The California Dream*. New York: Collier Books, 1968.

Snyder, Gary. "Note on the Religious Tendencies." *Liberation* 4 (June 1959): 11.

Steiner, George. "On Paul Goodman." *Commentary* 36 (August 1963): 158–63.

Wilson, Dagmar and Jeanne S. Bagby. "A Reply from WISP." *Liberation* 8 (Summer 1963): 41.

Ziferstein, Isidore, "Hiroshima...Vietnam...?" *Liberation* 11 (September 1966): 33–35.

Zinn, Howard. "Marxism and the New Left." In Alfred L. Young, ed., *Dissent: Explorations in the History of American Radicalism*. DeKalb: Northern Illinois University Press, 1968.

SECONDARY SOURCES

Books

Aaron, Daniel. *Writers on the Left: Episodes in American Literary Communism*. New York: Harcourt Brace, 1961.

Alinsky, Saul D. *Rules for Radicals*. New York: Random House, 1971.

Allen, Pamela. *Free Space: A Perspective on the Small Group in Women's Liberation*. New York: Praeger, 1984.

Alonso, Harriet Hyman. *Peace Is a Women's Issue: A History of the U.S. Movement for World Peace and Women's Rights*. Syracuse: Syracuse University Press, 1993.

American Friends Service Committee. *Taking Charge of Our Lives: Living Responsibly in the World*. San Francisco: Harper & Row, 1984.

Anderson, Terry H. *The Movement and The Sixties*. New York: Oxford University Press, 1995.

Ansbro, John J. *Martin Luther King, Jr.: The Making of a Mind*. Maryknoll, NY: Orbis, 1982.

Anthony, Gene. *Summer of Love: Haight-Ashbury at its Highest*. Millbrae, CA: Celestial Arts, 1980.

Arendt, Hannah. *The Life of the Mind, Volume I/Thinking*. New York: Harcourt Brace Jovanovich, 1971.

Au, William A. *The Cross, the Flag, and the Bomb: American Catholics Debate War and Peace, 1960–1983*. Westport, CT: Greenwood, 1985.

Bacciocco, Edward J. *The New Left In America: Reform to Revolution, 1956–1970*. Stanford: Hoover Institution Press, 1974.

Bajema, Clifford E. *Abortion and the Meaning of Personhood*. Grand Rapids: Baker Book House, 1974.

Banes, Sally. *Greenwich Village 1963: Avant-Garde Performance and the Effervescent Body.* Durham, N.C.: Duke University Press, 1993.

Bartlett, Lee. *William Everson.* Boise: Boise State University, 1985.

Baskir, Lawrence M. and William A. Strauss. *Chance and Circumstance: The Draft, The War and the Vietnam Generation.* New York: Knopf, 1978.

Beidler, Philip T. *Scriptures for a Generation: What We Were Reading in the '60s.* Athens: University of Georgia Press, 1994.

Belasco, Warren J. *Appetite for Change: How the Counterculture Took on the Food Industry, 1966–1988.* New York: Pantheon, 1989.

Belfrage, Sally. *Freedom Summer.* Charlottesville: University of Virginia Press, 1990.

Berman, Ronald. *America in the Sixties: An Intellectual History.* New York: Harper and Row, 1970.

Berrigan, Daniel. *Portraits of Those I Love.* New York: Crossroad, 1982.

Berry, Wendell. *The Long-Legged House.* New York: Audobon/ Ballantine, 1969.

Berry, Wendell. *The Unsettling of America: Culture and Agriculture.* San Francisco: Sierra Club, 1976.

Berryman, Phillip. *Our Unfinished Business: The U.S. Catholic Bishops' Letters on Peace and the Economy.* New York: Pantheon, 1989.

Bigelow, Albert. *The Voyage of the Golden Rule: An Experiment With Truth.* Garden City, NY: Doubleday, 1958.

Blanchard, Dallas A. *The Anti-Abortion Movement and the Rise of the Religious Right: From Polite to Fiery Protest.* New York: Twayne, 1994.

Boskin, Joseph and Robert A. Rosenstone. *Seasons of Rebellion: Protest and Radicalism in Recent America.* New York: Holt, Rinehart and Winston, 1972.

Boyte, Harry C. *The Backyard Revolution: Understanding the New Citizen Movement.* Philadelphia: Temple University Press, 1980.

Boyer, Paul. *By the Bomb's Early Light: American Thought and Culture at the Dawn of the Atomic Age.* New York: Pantheon, 1985.

Branch, Taylor. *Parting the Waters: America in the King Years, 1954–1963.* New York: Simon and Schuster, 1988.

Breines, Wini. *Community and Organization in the New Left: 1962–1968.* New Brunswick, NJ: Rutgers University Press, 1989.

Brown, Dale H. *The Christian Revolutionary.* Grand Rapids: Eerdmans, 1971.

Brueggeman, Walter. *The Prophetic Imagination.* Philadelphia: Fortress Press, 1978.

Buhle, Paul. *Marxism in the USA: From 1870 to the Present Day.* London: Verso, 1987.

Burner, Eric. *And Gently He Shall Lead Them: Robert Parris Moses and Civil Rights in Mississippi.* New York: New York University Press, 1994.

Calvert, Gregory and Carol Neiman. *A Disrupted History: The New Left and the New Capitalism.* New York: Random House, 1971.

Capps, Walter H. *The Unfinished War: Vietnam and the American Conscience.* Boston: Beacon, 1982.

Carawan, Guy and Candie Carawan. *Sing for Freedom: The Story of the Civil Rights Movement Through Its Songs.* Bethlehem, Pa: Sing Out, 1990.

Carmichael, Stokely and Charles V. Hamilton. *The Tragedy and Promise of America in the 1970's.* New York: Vintage, 1967.

Carroll, Peter N. *It Seemed Like Nothing Happened: The Tragedy and Promise of America in the 1970's*. New York: Holt, Rinehart, and Winston, 1982.

Carson, Clayborne. *In Struggle: SNCC and the Black Awakening of the 1960's*. Cambridge, Mass.: Harvard University Press, 1981.

Carter, Paul. *Another Part of the Fifties*. New York: Columbia University Press, 1983.

Case, John and Rosemary C.R. Taylor, eds. *Co-ops, Communes & Collectives: Experiments in Social Change in the 1960's and 1970's*. New York: Pantheon, 1979.

Center for Science in the Public Interest. *99 Ways to a Simple Lifestyle*. Garden City, NY: Anchor, 1977.

Chalmers, David. *And the Crooked Places Made Straight: The Struggle for Social Change in the 1960's*. Baltimore: Johns Hopkins University Press, 1991.

Charters, Ann, ed. *The Portable Beat Reader*. New York: Viking, 1992.

Chernus, Ira. *Dr. Strangegod: On the Symbolic Meaning of Nuclear Weapons*. Columbia: University of South Carolina Press, 1986.

Chernus, Ira and Edward Tabor Linenthal, eds., *A Shuddering Dawn: Religious Studies and the Nuclear Age*. Albany: State University of New York Press, 1989.

Christiansen, Karen. *Home Ecology: Simple and Practical Ways to Green Your Home*. Golden, CO: Fulcrum, 1990.

Cluster, Dick, ed. *They Should Have Served that Cup of Coffee*. Boston: South End Press, 1970.

Coles, Robert. *The Call of Stories: Teaching and the Moral Imagination*. Boston: Houghton Mifflin, 1989.

———. *Dorothy Day: A Radical Devotion*. Reading, MA: Addison Wesley, 1987.

———. *A Spectacle to the World: The Catholic Worker Movement*. New York: Viking Press, 1973.

Cone, James. *Black Theology and Black Power*. New York: Seabury Press, 1969.

———. *Martin & Malcolm & America*. Maryknoll, NY: Orbis, 1991.

Congressional Quarterly Service, *U.S. Draft Policy and Its Impact*. Washington: Congressional Quarterly, 1968.

Cooney, Robert and Helen Michalowski, eds. *The Power of the People: Active Nonviolence in the United States*. Philadelphia: New Society, 1989.

Cornell, Thomas C. and James Forest, eds. *A Penny a Copy*. New York: Macmillan, 1968.

Corrin, Jay P. *G.K. Chesterton & Hilaire Belloc: The Battle Against Modernity*. Athens: Ohio Universtiy Press, 1981.

Cox, Craig. *Storefront Revolution: Food Co-ops and the Counterculture*. New Brunswick, NJ: Rutgers University Press, 1994.

Coy, Patrick G., ed. *A Revolution of the Heart: Essays on the Catholic Worker* Philadelphia: Temple University Press, 1988.

Crosby, Donald F. *God, Church, and Flag: Senator Joseph R. McCarthy and the Catholic Church, 1950–1957*. Chapel Hill: University of North Carolina Press, 1978.

Davidson, Michael. *The San Fransisco Renaissance: Poetics and Community at Mid-Century*. Cambridge: Cambridge University Press, 1989.

Deats, Paul and Carol Robb, eds. *The Boston Personalist Tradition in Philosophy, Social Ethics, and Theology*. Macon, GA: Mercer University Press, 1986.

DeBenedetti, Charles. *The Peace Reform in American History*. Bloomington: Indiana University Press, 1980.

———, ed. *Peace Heroes in Twentieth-Century America*. Bloomington: Indiana University Press, 1986.

DeBenedetti, Charles and Charles Chatfield. *An American Ordeal: The Anti-War Movement of the Vietnam War*. Syracuse: Syracuse University Press, 1990.

De Leon, David. *The American as Anarchist: Reflections on Indigenous Radicalism*. Baltimore: Johns Hopkins University Press, 1979.

De Leon, David. *Everything is Changing: Contemporary U.S. Movements in Historical Perspective*. New York: Praeger, 1988.

D'Emilio, John and Estelle B. Freedman. *Intimate Matters: A History of Sexuality in America*. New York: Harper & Row, 1988.

Dellinger, David. *From Yale to Jail: The Life Story of a Moral Dissenter*. New York: Pantheon Books, 1993.

———. *More Power Than We Know: The People's Movement Toward Democracy*. Garden City, N.Y.: Anchor/ Doubleday, 1975.

Deming, Barbara. *Prisons That Could Not Hold*. San Francisco: Spinsters Ink, 1985.

Denisoff, Serge R. *Great Day Coming: Folk Music and the American Left*. Urbana: University of Illinois Press, 1971.

Dickstein, Morris. *Gates of Eden: American Culture in the Sixties*. New York: Basic Books, 1977.

Divine, Robert A. *Blowing on the Wind: The Nuclear Test Ban Debate, 1954–1960*. New York: Oxford University Press, 1978.

Dixon, David. *The New Politics of Science*. New York: Pantheon, 1984.

Douglas, Susan. *Where the Girls Are: Growing Up Female With the Mass Media*. New York: Times Books, 1994.

Echols, Alice. *Daring to Be Bad: Radical Feminism in America, 1967–1975*. Minneapolis: University of Minnesota Press, 1989.

Edsforth, Ronald and Larry Bennett, eds. *Popular Culture and Political Change in Modern America*. Albany: State University of New York Press, 1991.

Ehrenreich, Barbara. *Hearts of Men: American Dreams and the Flight from Commitment*. Garden City, NY: Anchor/Doubleday, 1983.

Elgin, Duane. *Voluntary Simplicity: An Ecological Lifestyle That Promotes Personal and Social Renewal*. New York: Bantam, 1981.

Ellis, Marc. *Peter Maurin: Prophet in the Twentieth Century*. New York: Paulist Press, 1981.

Ellwood, Robert S. *The Sixties Spiritual Awakening: American Religion Moving from Modern to Postmodern*. New Brunswick, NJ: Rutgers University Press, 1994.

Elshtain, Jean Bethke. *Women and War*. New York: Basic Books, 1987.

Elshtain, Jean and Sheila Tobias, eds. *Women, Militarism, and War: Essays in History, Politics, and Social Theory*. Savage, MD: Rowman & Littlefield, 1990.

Epstein, Barbara. *Political Protest and Cultural Revolution: Nonviolent Direct Action in the 1970's and 1980's*. Berkeley: University of California Press, 1991.

Evans, Sara. *Personal Politics: The Roots of Women's Liberation in the Civil Rights Movement and the New Left*. New York: Knopf, 1979.

Evans, Sara M. and Harry C. Boyte *Free Spaces: The Sources of Democratic Change in America*. New York: Harper & Row, 1986.

Fairclough, Adam. *To Redeem the Soul of America: The Southern Christian Leadership Conference and Martin Luther King, Jr.* Athens: University of Georgia Press, 1978.

Fairfield, Richard. *Communes U.S.A.: A Personal Tour*. New York: Penguin, 1972.

Farber, David. *The Age of Great Dreams: America in the 1960s*. New York: Hill and Wang, 1994.

————. *Chicago '68*. Chicago: University of Chicago Press, 1988.

————, ed. *The Sixties: From Memory to History*. Chapel Hill: University of North Carolina Press, 1994.

Farmer, James. *Lay Bare the Heart: An Autobiography of the Civil Rights Movement*. New York: New American Library, 1985.

Ferkiss, Victor. *The Future of Technological Civilization*. New York: G. Braziller, 1974.

Ferlinghetti, Lawrence. *Literary San Francisco: A Pictorial History from Its Beginnings to the Present Day*. San Francisco: City Lights and Harper & Row, 1980.

FitzGerald, Frances. *America Revised: History Schoolbooks in the Twentieth Century*. Boston: Little, Brown, 1979.

Flacks, Richard. *Making History: The American Left and the American Mind*. New York: Columbia University Press, 1988.

Forest, James H. *Love is the Measure: A Biography of Dorothy Day*. New York: Paulist Press, 1986.

————, ed. *Merton, By Those Who Knew Him Best*. San Francisco: Harper and Row, 1984.

Foss, Daniel. *Freak Culture: Life-style and Politics*. New York: Dutton, 1972.

Fox, Richard Wightman. *Reinhold Niebuhr: A Biography*. New York: Harper and Row, 1985.

Fraser, Ronald, et al., eds. *1968: A Student Generation in Revolt*. New York: Macmillan, 1972.

Freeman, Jo. *The Politics of Women's Liberation*. New York: David McKay, 1975.

French, Warren. *The San Francisco Poetry Renaissance, 1955–1960*. Boston: Twayne, 1991.

Gardner, Hugh. *The Children of Prosperity: Thirteen Modern American Communes*. New York: St. Martin's, 1978.

Garrow, David J. *Bearing the Cross: Martin Luther King, Jr. and the Southern Christian Leadership Conference*. New York: William Morrow, 1986.

Gaskin, Stephen and the Farm. *Hey Beatnik! This Is the Farm Book*. Summertown, TN: The Book Publishing Co., 1974.

Gitlin, Todd. *The Sixties: Years of Hope, Days of Rage*. New York: Bantam, 1987.

————. *The Whole World is Watching: Mass Media in the Making and Unmaking of the New Left*. Berkeley: University of California Press, 1980.

Glock, Charles Y. and Robert N. Bellah, eds. *The New Religious Consciousness*. Berkeley: University of California Press, 1976.

Goldstein, Richard. *Reporting the Counterculture*. Boston: Unwin Hyman, 1989.

Goodman, Mitchell, ed. *The Movement Toward a New America: The Beginnings of a Long Revolution*. Philadelphia: Pilgrim Press, 1970.

Graubard, Allen. *Free the Children*. New York: Pantheon, 1972.

Hall, Mitchell K. *Because of Their Faith: CALCAV and Religious Opposition to the Vietnam War.* New York: Columbia University Press, 1990.

Hallin, Daniel C. *The "Uncensored War": The Media and Vietnam.* Berkeley: University of California Press, 1986.

Hamalian, Linda. *A Life of Kenneth Rexroth.* New York: W.W. Norton, 1991.

Hampton Henry, and Steve Fayer. *Voices of Freedom: An Oral History of the Civil Rights Movement from the 1950's through the 1980's.* New York: Bantam, 1990.

Harrington, Michael. *Fragments of a Century: A Social Autobiography.* New York: Saturday Review Press, 1973.

Harris, David. *Dreams Die Hard.* New York: St. Martin's, 1982.

Hausdorff, Don. *Erich Fromm.* New York: Twayne, 1972.

Hayden, Tom. *Reunion: A Memoir.* New York: Random House, 1988.

Hays, Samuel P. *Beauty, Health, and Permanence: Environmental Politics in the United States, 1955–1985.* Cambridge: Cambridge University Press, 1987.

Heath, Jim F. *Decade of Disillusionment: The Kennedy-Johnson Years.* Bloomington: Indiana University Press, 1975.

Heineman, Kenneth J. *Campus Wars: The Peace Movement at American State Universities in the Vietnam Era.* New York: New York University Press, 1993.

Hellman, John. *Emmanuel Mounier and the New Catholic Left 1930–1950.* Toronto: University of Toronto Press, 1981.

Hentoff, Nat. *Peace Agitator: The Story of A.J. Muste.* New York: Macmillan, 1963.

Herzog, Arthur. *The War-Peace Establishment.* New York: Harper & Row, 1965.

Hine, Thomas. *Populuxe.* New York: Alfred A. Knopf, 1986.

Hodgson, Godfrey. *America in Our Time.* New York: Vintage, 1976.

Hole, Judith and Ellen Levine. *Rebirth of Feminism.* New York: Quadrangle, 1971.

Hollender, Jeffrey. *How to Make the World a Better Place: A Guide to Doing Good.* New York: William Morrow, 1990.

Holsworth, Robert. *Let Your Life Speak: A Study of Politics, Religion, And Antinuclear Weapons Activism.* Madison: University of Wisconsin Press, 1989.

Holsworth, Robert, and J. Harry Wray. *American Politics and Everyday Life.* 2nd ed. New York: Macmillan, 1987.

Hopkins, Jerry, ed. *The Hippie Papers: Notes from the Underground Press.* New York: Signet, 1968.

Horowitz, Irving. *The Struggle is the Message: The Organization and Ideology of the Anti-War Movement.* Berkeley: Glendessary Press, 1972.

———. *C. Wright Mills: An American Utopian.* New York: Free Press, 1983.

Howard, Gerald, ed. *The Sixties.* New York: Washington Square Press, 1982.

Howard, Richard. *Alone With America: Essays on the Art of Poetry in the United States Since 1950.* New York: Atheneum, 1969.

Hunt, Lynn, ed. *The New Cultural History.* Berkeley: University of California Press, 1989.

Ingram, Catherine. *In the Footsteps of Gandhi: Conversations With Spiritual Social Activists.* Berkeley: Parallax Press, 1990.

Irwin, Robert A. *Building a Peace System.* Washington: ExPro Press, 1989.

Isserman, Maurice. *If I Had a Hammer...: The Death of the Old Left and the Birth of the New Left.* New York: Basic Books, 1987.

Jamison, Andrew and Ron Eyerman. *Seeds of the Sixties*. Berkeley: University of California Press, 1994.

Jerome, Judson. *Families of Eden: Communes and the New Anarchism*. New York: Seabury, 1974.

Jezer, Marty. *Abbie Hoffman: American Rebel*. New Brunswick, N.J.: Rutgers University Press, 1992.

———. *The Dark Ages: Life in the United States, 1945–1960*. Boston: South End Press, 1982.

Johnson, Warren. *Muddling Toward Frugality*. Boulder: Shambhala, 1978.

Kapur, Sudarshan. *Raising Up a Prophet: The African-American Encounter With Gandhi*. Boston: Beacon, 1992.

Katz, Milton S. *Ban the Bomb: A History of SANE, the Committee for a Sane Nuclear Policy, 1957–1985*. New York: Greenwood, 1986.

Kendrick, Alexander. *The Wound Within: America in the Vietnam Years, 1945–1974*. Boston: Little, Brown, 1974.

Kerman, Cynthia Earl. *Creative Tension: The Life and Thought of Kenneth Boulding*. Ann Arbor: University of Michigan Press, 1974.

Killeen, Jacqueline. *Ecology at Home*. San Francisco: 101 Productions, 1971.

King, Mary. *Freedom Song: A Personal Story of the 1960's Civil Rights Movement*. New York: Morrow, 1987.

King, Richard. *The Party of Eros*. Chapel Hill, NC: University of North Carolina Press, 1972.

Klejment, Anne. *Dorothy Day and the Catholic Worker: A Bibliography and Index*. New York: Garland, 1986.

Klejment, Anne and Nancy L. Roberts. *American Catholic Pacifism*. New York: Praeger, forthcoming.

Kovel, Joel. *Against the State of Nuclear Terror*. Boston: South End Press, 1983.

Kramer, Jane. *Allen Ginsberg in America*. New York: Random House, 1969.

Lader, Lawrence. *Power on the Left: American Radical Movements Since 1946*. New York: Norton, 1979.

Lee, Calvin B.T. *The Campus Scene: 1900–1970*. New York: David McKay, 1970.

Lemann, Nicholas. *The Promised Land: The Great Black Migration and How It Changed America*. New York: Knopf, 1991.

Lens, Sidney. *Unrepentant Radical: An American Activist's Account of Five Turbulent Decades*. Boston: Beacon, 1980.

Lewis, George H., ed. *Side-Saddle on the Golden Calf: Social Structure and Popular Culture in America*. Pacific Palisades, CA: Goodyear, 1972.

Linden-Ward, Blanche and Carol Hurd Green. *American Women in the 1960's: Changing the Future*. New York: Twayne, 1993.

Loomis, Mildred J. *Alternative America*. New York: Universe Books, 1982.

Lora, Ronald, ed. *America in the 60's: Cultural Authorities in Transition*. New York: Wiley, 1974.

Lyttle, Bradford. *The Chicago Anti-Vietnam War Movement*. Chicago: Midwest Pacifist Center, 1988.

Matusow, Allen J. *The Unraveling of America: A History of Liberalism in the 1960's*. New York: Harper and Row, 1984.

May, Elaine Tyler. *Homeward Bound: American Families in the Cold War Era*. New York: Basic Books, 1988.

McAdam, Doug. *Freedom Summer*. New York: Oxford University Press, 1988.

McClure, Michael. *Scratching the Beat Surface*. San Francisco: North Point Press, 1982.

McCrea, Frances B. and Gerald E. Markle. *Minutes to Midnight: Nuclear Weapons Protest in America*. Newbury Park, CA: Sage, 1989.

McDougall, Walter A. . . . *The Heavens and the Earth: a Political History of the Space Age*. New York: Basic Books, 1985.

McGill, William J. *The Year of the Monkey: Revolt on the Campus, 1968–69*. New York: McGraw-Hill, 1982.

McLaughlin, Corinne and Gordon Davidson. *Builders of the Dawn: Community Lifestyles in a Changing World*. Walpole, N.H.: Stillpoint, 1985.

McNeal, Patricia. *Harder Than War: Catholic Peacemaking in Twentieth-Century America*. New Brunswick, NJ: Rutgers University Press, 1992.

McQuaid, Kim. *The Anxious Years: America in the Vietnam– Watergate Era*. New York: Basic Books, 1989.

Meconis, Charles. *With Clumsy Grace: The American Catholic Left, 1961–1977*. New York: Seabury, 1979.

Melville, Keith. *Communes in the Counter Culture: Origins, Theories, Styles of Life*. New York: William Morrow, 1972.

Merchant, Carolyn. *Radical Ecology: The Search for a Livable World*. New York: Routledge, 1992.

Merchant, Paul. *Wendell Berry*. Lewiston, Idaho: Confluence Press, 1991.

Meyerowitz, Joanne, ed. *Not June Cleaver: Women and Gender in Postwar America, 1945–1960*. Philadelphia: Temple University Press, 1994.

Miles, Barry. *Ginsberg: A Biography*. New York: Simon and Schuster, 1989.

Miles, Michael W. *The Radical Probe: The Logic of Student Rebellion*. New York: Atheneum, 1971.

Miller, Douglas and Marion Nowack. *The Fifties: The Way We Really Were*. Garden City, NY: Doubleday, 1977.

Miller, James. *"Democracy Is in the Streets": From Port Huron to the Siege of Chicago*. New York: Simon and Schuster, 1987.

Miller, Keith D. *Voice of Deliverance: The Language of Martin Luther King, Jr. and Its Sources*. New York: Free Press, 1992.

Miller, Timothy. *The Hippies and American Values*. Knoxville: University of Tennessee Press, 1991.

Miller, William. *Dorothy Day: A Biography*. San Francisco: Harper and Row, 1982.

Miller, William Lee. *Piety Along the Potomac: Notes on Politics and Morals in the Fifties*. Boston: Houghton Mifflin, 1964.

Mills, Kay. *This Little Light of Mine: The Life of Fannie Lou Hamer*. New York: Dutton, 1993.

Mills, Nicholas. *Like a Holy Crusade: Mississippi 1964: The Turning of the Civil Rights Movement in America*. Chicago: Ivan Dee, 1992.

Morgan, Edward P. *The Sixties Experience: Hard Lessons About Modern America*. Philadelphia: Temple University Press, 1991.

Morris, Aldon D. *The Origins of the Civil Rights Movement: Black Communities Organizing for Change.* New York: Vintage, 1970.

Mott, Michael. *The Seven Mountains of Thomas Merton.* Boston: Houghton Mifflin, 1984.

Oates, Stephen B. *Let the Trumpet Sound: The Life of Martin Luther King, Jr.* New York: Mentor, 1982.

O'Neill, William L. *Coming Apart: An Informal History of America in the 1960's.* New York: Quadrangle, 1971.

O'Rourke, William. *The Harrisburg 7 and the New Catholic Left.* New York: Crowell, 1972.

Peck, Abe. *Uncovering the Sixties: The Life and Times of the Underground Press.* New York: Pantheon, 1985.

Pells, Richard. *The Liberal Mind in a Conservative Age: American Intellectuals in the 1940's & 1950's.* New York: Harper & Row, 1985.

Perry, Charles. *The Haight-Ashbury: A History.* New York: Random House, 1984.

Pichaske, David. *A Generation in Motion: Popular Music and Culture in the Sixties.* New York: Schirmer, 1979.

Piehl, Mel. *Breaking Bread: The Catholic Worker and the Origin of Catholic Radicalism in America.* Philadelphia: Temple University Press, 1982.

Pollock, Bruce. *When the Music Mattered: Rock in the 1960's.* New York: Holt, Rinehart and Winston, 1983.

Powaski, Ronald E. *Thomas Merton on Nuclear Weapons.* Chicago: Loyola University Press, 1988.

Powers, Thomas. *The War at Home: Vietnam and the American People, 1964–1968.* Boston: G.K. Hall, 1984.

Price, Jerome. *The Antinuclear Movement.* Boston: Twayne, 1982.

Rips, Geoffrey. *The Campaign Against the Underground Press.* San Francisco: City Lights, 1981.

Roberts, Nancy L. *Dorothy Day and the Catholic Worker* New York: State University of New York Press, 1984.

Robinson, Jo Ann. *Abraham Went Out: A Biography of A.J. Muste.* Philadelphia: Temple University Press, 1981.

Rodnitzky, Jerome. *Minstrels of the Dawn: The Folk-Singer as a Cultural Hero.* Chicago: Nelson-Hall, 1976.

Roeder, George H. *The Censored War: American Visual Experience During World War Two.* New Haven: Yale University Press, 1993.

Rorabaugh, W.J. *Berkeley at War: the 1960s.* New York: Oxford University Press, 1989.

Rossman, Michael. *New Age Blues: On the Politics of Consciousness.* New York: E.P. Dutton, 1979.

Ruddick, Sara. *Maternal Thinking: Toward a Politics for Peace.* New York: Ballantine Books, 1989.

Rustin, Bayard. *Strategies of Freedom: The Changing Patterns of Black Protest.* New York: Columbia University Press, 1976.

Sale, Kirkpatrick. *Dwellers in the Land.* San Francisco: Sierra Club, 1985.

———. *SDS.* New York: Vintage, 1974.

Salmon, Arthur E. *Alex Comfort*. Boston: Twayne, 1978.

Sargent, Lyman T. *New Left Thought: An Introduction*. Homewood, IL: Dorsey Press, 1972.

Sayres, Sohnya, Anders Stephanson, Stanley Aronowitz, and Frederic Jameson, eds. *The 60's Without Apology*. Minneapolis: University of Minnesota Press, 1984.

Scarry, Elaine. *The Body in Pain: The Making and Unmaking of the World*. New York: Oxford University Press, 1985.

Schell, Jonathan. *The Time of Illusion*. New York: Knopf, 1976.

Sedacca, Sandra. *Up in Arms: A Common Cause Guide to Understanding Nuclear Arms Policy*. Washington: Common Cause, 1984.

Seeger, Pete. *The Incomplete Folksinger*. New York: Simon and Schuster, 1972.

Shannon, Thomas A., ed. *War or Peace?* Maryknoll, NY: Orbis, 1980.

Shaw, Arnold. *The Rock Revolution*. London: Crowell-Collier, 1969.

Sheehan, Arthur. *Peter Maurin: Gay Believer*. Garden City, NY: Hanover House, 1959.

Shelton, Robert. *No Direction Home: The Life and Music of Bob Dylan*. New York: Beech Tree Books, 1986.

Shi, David E. *The Simple Life: Plain Living and High Thinking in American Culture*. New York: Oxford University Press, 1985.

Silesky, Barry. *Ferlinghetti: The Artist in His Time*. New York: Warner Books, 1990.

Silk, Mark. *Spiritual Politics: Religion and America Since World War II*. New York: Simon and Schuster, 1988.

Sitkoff, Harvard. *The Struggle for Black Equality, 1954–1980*. New York: Hill and Wang, 1981.

Small, Melvin and William D. Hoover, eds. *Give Peace a Chance: Exploring the Vietnam Anti-war Movement*. Syracuse, N.Y.: Syracuse University Press, 1992.

Smith, David and John Luce. *Love Needs Care: A History of San Francisco's Haight-Ashbury Free Medical Clinic and Its Pioneer Role in Treating Drug-Abuse Problems*. Boston: Little, Brown, 1971.

Smith, Jeff. *Unthinking the Unthinkable: Nuclear Weapons and Western Culture*. Bloomington: Indiana University Press, 1989.

Smith, Larry. *Lawrence Ferlinghetti: Poet-At-Large*. Carbondale: Southern Illinois University Press, 1983.

Smith, Kenneth and Ira Zepp. *Search for the Beloved Community*. Valley Forge: Judson, 1974.

Solo, Pam. *From Protest to Policy: Beyond the Freeze to Common Security*. Cambridge, MA: Ballinger, 1988.

Stevens, Jay. *Storming Heaven: LSD and the American Dream*. New York: Harper & Row, 1987.

Stoper, Emily. *The Student Non-Violent Coordinating Committee: The Growth of Radicalism in a Civil Rights Organization*. Brooklyn: Carlson, 1989.

Swerdlow, Amy. *Women Strike for Peace*. Chicago: University of Chicago Press, 1993.

Szatmary, David P. *Rockin' in Time: A Social History of Rock-and-Roll*. Englewood Cliffs, NJ: Prentice Hall, 1991.

Tipton, Steven M. *Getting Saved from the Sixties: Moral Meaning in Conversion and Cultural Change*. Berkeley: University of California Press, 1982.

Tischler, Barbara L., ed. *Sights on the Sixties*. New Brunswick, N.J.: Rutgers University Press, 1992.

Troester, Rosalie Riegle, ed. *Voices from the Catholic Worker*. Philadelphia: Temple University Press, 1993.

Unger, Irwin. *The Movement: A History of the American New Left, 1959–1972*. New York: Dodd, Mead, 1974.

Useem, Michael. *Conscription, Protest, and Social Conflict: The Life and Death of a Draft Resistance Movement*. New York: Wiley, 1973.

Vickers, George R. *The Formation of the New Left: The Early Years*. Lexington, Mass.: Lexington Books, 1975.

Viorst, Milton. *Fire in the Streets: America in the 1960s*. New York: Simon and Schuster, 1980.

Wald, Alan M. *The New York Intellectuals: The Rise and Decline of the Anti-Stalinist Left from the 1930s to the 1980s*. Chapel Hill: University of North Carolina Press, 1987.

Wandersee, Winifred D. *On the Move: American Women in the 1970s*. Boston: Twayne, 1988.

Walzer, Michael. *Just and Unjust Wars: A Moral Argument With Historical Illustrations*. New York: Basic Books, 1977.

Weart, Spencer R. *Nuclear Fear: A History of Images*. Cambridge: Harvard University Press, 1988.

Weigel, George. *Tranquillitas Ordinis: The Present Failure and Future Promise of American Catholic Thought on War and Peace*. New York: Oxford University Press, 1987.

Wells, Tom. *The War Within: America's Battle over Vietnam*. Berkeley: University of California Press, 1994.

Whalen, Jack and Richard Flacks. *Beyond the Barricades: The Sixties Generation Grows Up*. Philadelphia: Temple University Press, 1989.

Whitfield, Stephen J. *The Culture of the Cold War*. Baltimore: Johns Hopkins University Press, 1991.

Widmer, Kingsley. *Paul Goodman*. Boston: Twayne, 1980

Winkler, Allan M. *Life Under a Cloud: American Anxiety About the Atom*. New York: Oxford University Press, 1993.

Winner, Langdon. *The Whale and the Reactor*. Chicago: University of Chicago Press, 1986.

Wittner, Lawrence S. *Rebels Against War: The American Peace Movement, 1933–1983*. Philadelphia: Temple University Press, 1984.

Wofford, Harris. *Of Kennedys and Kings: Making Sense of the Sixties*. New York: Farrar, Straus and Giroux, 1980.

Woodcock, George. *Thomas Merton, Monk and Poet: A Critical Study*. New York: Farrar, Straus, Giroux, 1978.

Wright, Lawrence. *In the New World: Growing Up with America from the Sixties to the Eighties*. New York: Vintage, 1987.

Wuthnow, Robert. *The Restructuring of American Religion: Society and Faith Since World War II*. Princeton: Princeton University Press, 1988.

Yankelovich, Daniel. *New Rules: Searching for Self-Fulfillment in a World Turned Upside Down*. New York: Bantam, 1981.

Yinger, J. Milton. *Countercultures: The Promise and the Peril of a World Turned Upside Down*. New York: Free Press, 1982.

Zahn, Gordon. *Another Part of War: The Camp Simon Story*. Amherst: University of Massachusetts Press, 1979.

Zaroulis, Nancy, and Gerald Sullivan. *Who Spoke Up? American Protest Against the War in Vietnam, 1963–1975*. Garden City, NJ: Doubleday, 1984.

Zinn, Howard. *SNCC: The New Abolitionists*. Boston: Beacon, 1965.

Articles

Adler, Les K. and Thomas G. Paterson, "Red Fascism: The Merger of Nazi Germany and Soviet Russia in the American Image of Totalitarianism." *American Historical Review* 75 (1970): 1046–64.

Bailey, Beth. "Sexual Revolution(s)." In David Farber, ed., *The Sixties: From Memory to History*. Chapel Hill: University of North Carolina Press, 1994.

Berrigan, Daniel. "Introduction." In Dorothy Day, *The Long Loneliness: The Autobiography of Dorothy Day*. New York: Harper & Row, 1952.

Berry, Wendell. "The Reactor and the Garden," In *The Gift of Good Land: Further Essays* Culture and Agriculture. San Francisco: North Point Press, 1981.

———. "A Statement Against the War in Vietnam." In *The Long-Legged House*. New York: Audobon/Ballantine, 1969.

Boller, Paul, "Hiroshima and the American Left: August 1945." *International Social Science Review* 57 (Winter 1982): 13–28.

Bolton, Charles D. "Alienation and Action: A Study of Peace Group Members." *American Journal of Sociology* 78 (November 1972): 537–61.

Boyer, Paul. "From Activism to Apathy: The American People and Nuclear Weapons, 1963–1980." *Journal of American History* 70 (March 1984): 821–44.

Breines, Wini. "The 'Other Fifties': Beats and Bad Girls." In Joanne Meyerowitz, ed., *Not June Cleaver: Women and Gender in Postwar America, 1945–1960*. Philadelphia: Temple University Press, 1994.

Christenson, Paul. "Allen Ginsberg." In Ann Charters, ed. *The Beats: Literary Bohemians in Postwar America*. Detroit: Gale Research, 1983.

Cole, Audrey S. "The Catholic Worker Farm: Tivoli, New York 1964–1978." *The Hudson Valley Regional Review* 8 (March 1991): 25–42.

Cone, James H. "The Theology of Martin Luther King, Jr." *Union Seminary Quarterly Review* 40 (January 1986): 21–39.

Deats, Paul. "Introduction to Boston Personalism." In Paul Deats and Carol Robb, eds., *The Boston Personalist Tradition in Philosophy, Social Ethics, and Theology*. Macon, GA: Mercer University Press, 1986.

———. "Conflict and Reconciliaton in Communitarian Social Ethics." In Paul Deats and Carol Robb, eds., *The Boston Personalist Tradition in Philosophy, Social Ethics, and Theology*. Macon, GA: Mercer University Press, 1986.

DeBenedetti, Charles. "On the Significance of Citizen Peace Activism: America, 1961–1975." *Peace and Change* 9 (Summer 1983): 6–20.

Des Pres, Terence. "Orwell and the O'Brienists." In *Writing Into the World: Essays 1973–1987.* New York: Viking, 1991.

DeWolf, Harold. "Ethical Implications for Criminal Justice." In Paul Deats and Carol Robb, eds., *The Boston Personalist Tradition in Philosophy, Social Ethics, and Theology.* Macon, GA: Mercer University Press, 1986.

Echols, Alice. "Nothing Distant About It: Women's Liberation and Sixties Radicalism." In David Farber, ed., *The Sixties: From Memory to History.* Chapel Hill: University of North Carolina Press, 1994.

———. "'Women Power' and Women's Liberation: Exploring the Relationship Between the Antiwar Movement and Women's Liberation." In Melvin Small and William D. Hoover, eds., *Give Peace a Chance: Exploring the Vietnam Anti-War Movement.* Syracuse: Syracuse University Press, 1992.

Eynon, Bret, "Community in Motion: The Free Speech Movement, Civil Rights, and the Roots of the New Left." *Oral History Review* 17 (Spring 1989): 39–69.

Fairclough, Adam. "Martin Luther King, Jr., and the War in Vietnam." *Phylon* 45 (March 1984): 19–39.

Farber, David. "The Counterculture and the Antiwar Movement." In Melvin Small and William D. Hoover, eds., *Give Peace a Chance.* Syracuse: Syracuse University Press, 1992.

Farrell, James J. "American Atomic Culture." *American Quarterly* 43 (March 1991): 157–64.

———. "Making (Common) Sense of the Bomb in the First Nuclear War," *American Studies* 36 (Fall 1995): 5–41.

Garrison, Dee. "'Our Skirts Gave Them Courage': The Civil Defense Protest Movement in New York City, 1955–1961." In Joanne Meyerowitz, ed., *Not June Cleaver: Women and Gender in Postwar America, 1945–1960.* Philadelphia: Temple University Press, 1994.

Herman, Ellen. "Being and Doing: Humanistic Psychology and the Spirit of the 1960s." In Barbara L. Tischler, ed., *Sights on the Sixties.* New Brunswick, NJ: Rutgers University Press, 1992.

Howard, John Robert and Mary D. "The Flowering of the Hippies." In Joseph Boskin and Robert A. Rosenstone, eds., *Seasons of Rebellion: Protest and Radicalism in Recent America.* New York: Holt, Rinehart and Winston, 1972.

Isserman, Maurice. "You Don't Need a Weatherman But a Postman Can Be Helpful: Thoughts on the History of SDS and the Antiwar Movement." In Melvin Small and William D. Hoover, eds., *Give Peace a Chance.* Syracuse: Syracuse University Press, 1992.

Isserman, Maurice and Michael Kazin. "The Success and Failure of the New Radicalism." In Steven Fraser and Gary Gerstle, eds., *The Rise and Fall of the New Deal Order, 1930–1980.* Princeton: Princeton University Press, 1989.

Jackson, Carl T. "The Counterculture Looks East: Beat Writers and Asian Religion." *American Studies* 29 (1988): 51–70.

Katz, Milton S., and Neil H. Katz. "Pragmatists and Visionaries in the Post-World War II American Peace Movement: SANE and CVNA." In Solomon Wank, ed., *Doves and Diplomats: Foreign Offices and Peace Movements in Europe and America in the Twentieth Century.* Westport, CT: Greenwood, 1978.

King, Richard H. "Citizenship and Self-Respect: The Experience of Politics in the Civil Rights Movement." *Journal of American Studies* 22 (April 1988): 7–24.

Klein, Michael, "Students, Capital and the Multiversity: Radical Challenges to the Dominant Pattern of American Higher Education from Berkeley to Livingston." In Michael Klein, ed., *An American Half Century: Postwar Culture and Politics in the USA*. London: Pluto Press, 1994.

Klejment, Anne. "Dorothy Day and the Catholic Worker Movement." In Randall Miller and Paul Cimbala, eds., *American Reform and Reformers*. Westport, CT: Greenwood, 1996.

————. "The Radical Origins of Catholic Pacifism: Dorothy Day and the Lyrical Left During World War I." In Anne Klejment and Nancy L. Roberts, eds., *American Catholic Pacifism: The Influence of Dorothy Day and the Catholic Worker*. Westport, CT: Praeger, forthcoming.

————. "War Resistance and Property Destruction." In Patrick Coy, ed., *A Revolution of the Heart: Essays on the Catholic Worker*. Philadelphia: Temple University Press, 1988.

Klejment, Anne and Nancy L. Roberts. "The Catholic Worker and the Vietnam War." In Anne Klejment and Nancy L. Roberts, eds., *American Catholic Pacifism*. New York: Praeger, forthcoming.

Lavely, John H. "Personalism." In Paul Edwards, ed., *The Encyclopedia of Philosophy*, Volume VI. New York: Macmillan and Free Press, 1967.

Lipsitz, George. "Who'll Stop the Rain? Youth Culture, Rock 'n' Roll, and Social Crises." In David Farber, ed., *The Sixties: From Memory to History*. Chapel Hill: University of North Carolina Press, 1994.

McReynolds, David. "Pacifists and the Vietnam Antiwar Movement." In Melvin Small and William D. Hoover, eds., *Give Peace a Chance*. Syracuse: Syracuse University Press, 1992.

Manoff, Robert Karl. "Covering the Bomb: The Nuclear Story and the News." *Working Papers for a New Society* (May-June 1983): 19–27.

May, Elaine Tyler. "Explosive Issues: Sex, Women, and the Bomb." In Lary May, ed., *Recasting America: Culture and Politics in the Age of Cold War*. Chicago: University of Chicago Press, 1989.

Mendelsohn, Everett. "Prophet of Our Discontent: Lewis Mumford Confronts the Bomb." In Thomas P. Hughes and Agatha C. Hughes, eds., *Lewis Mumford: Public Intellectual*. New York: Oxford University Press, 1990.

Murphy, Patrick D. "Introduction." *Critical Essays on Gary Snyder*. Boston: G.K. Hall, 1991.

Myerhoff, Barbara. "Youth Culture: New Styles of Humanism." In Joseph Boskin and Robert A. Rosenstone, eds., *Seasons of Rebellion: Protest and Radicalism in Recent America*. New York: Holt, Rinehart and Winston, 1972.

Nash, Henry T. "The Bureaucratiziation of Homicide." *Bulletin of the Atomic Scientists* 40 (March 1984): 32–36.

O'Brien, David J. "Social Teaching, Social Action, Social Gospel." *U.S. Catholic Historian* 5 (1986): 195–224.

Oglesby, Carl. "Rescuing Jesus from the Cross." *CoEvolution Quarterly* No. 39 (Fall 1983): 36.

Parkinson, Thomas. "The Poetry of Gary Snyder." *Critical Essays on Gary Snyder.* Boston: G.K. Hall, 1991.

Purcell, Edward. "Social Thought." *American Quarterly* 35 (Spring–Summer 1983): 80–100.

Robinson, Jo Ann. "A.J. Muste: Prophet in the Wilderness of the Modern World." In Charles DeBenedetti, ed., *Peace Heroes in Twentieth-Century America.* Bloomington: Indiana University Press, 1986.

Rosen, Ruth. "The Day They Buried 'Traditional Womanhood': Women and the Politics of Peace Protest." In D. Michael Shafer, ed., *The Legacy: The Vietnam War in the American Imagination.* Boston: Beacon Press, 1990.

Rosenstone, Robert A. "The Times They Are A'Changin'." In Joseph Boskin and Robert A. Rosenstone, eds., *Seasons of Rebellion: Protest and Radicalism in Recent America.* New York: Holt, Rinehart and Winston, 1972.

Rossinow, Doug. "'The Break-through to New Life': Christianity and the Emergence of the New Left in Austin, Texas, 1956–1964." *American Quarterly* 46 (September 1994): 309–318.

Schuman, Howard. "Two Sources of Antiwar Sentiment in America." *American Journal of Sociology* 78 (Nov. 1972): 513–36.

Segers, Mary C. "Equality and Christian Anarchism: The Political and Social Ideas of the Catholic Worker Movement." *Review of Politics* 40 (April 1978): 196–230.

Sherry, Michael. "War and Weapons: The New Cultural History." *Diplomatic History* 41 (Summer 1990): 433–46.

Sicius, Francis, J. "Karl Meyer, The Catholic Worker, and Active Personalism." *Records of the American Catholic Historical Society of Philadelphia* 93 (1982): 107–123.

Smith, Larry. "Lawrence Ferlinghetti." In Ann Charters, ed., *The Beats: Literary Bohemians in Postwar America.* Detroit: Gale Research, 1983.

Smith, R. Allen. "Mass Society and the Bomb: The Discourse of Pacifism in the 1950s." *Peace and Change* 18 (October 1993): 347–72.

Starr, Paul. "The Phantom Community." In John Case and Rosemary C.R. Taylor, eds., *Co-ops, Communes & Collectives: Experiments in Social Change in the 1960s and 1970s.* New York: Pantheon, 1979.

Steinkraus, Warren E. "Martin Luther King's Contributions to Personalism." *Idealistic Studies* 6 (1976): 20–32.

———. "Martin Luther King's Personalism and Nonviolence." *Journal of the History of Ideas* 34 (January–March 1973): 97–111.

Swerdlow, Amy. "Ladies' Day at the Capitol: Women Strike for Peace Versus HUAC." *Feminist Studies* 8 (Fall 1982): 493–520.

Tytell, John. "The Beat Generation and the Continuing American Revolution." *American Scholar* 42 (Spring 1973): 308–317.

VanderSchaff, James F. "Talking 'Bout Their Generation: Writing the History of the Sixties." *Maryland Historian* 19 (Fall/Winter 1988): 49–62.

Wagstaff, Thomas. "*Liberation.*" In Joseph R. Conlin, ed., *The American Radical Press, 1880–1960.* Westport, CT: Greenwood, 1974.

Widmer, Kingsley. "The Beat in the Rise of the Populist Culture." In Warren French, ed., *The Fifties: Fiction, Poetry, Drama.* Deland, FL: Everett/Edwards, 1970.

——. "Rebellion as Education." *The Nation* 208 (April 28, 1969): 537–41.

Wittner, Lawrence S. "How Realistic Is American Diplomacy?" *Reviews in American History* 9 (March 1981): 118–23.

Wortman, Marlene Stein. "Domesticating the Nineteenth Century American City." *Prospects* 3 (1977): 531–72.

Zahn, Gordon C. "The Spirituality of Peace." In Patrick Hart, ed. *The Legacy of Thomas Merton.* Kalamazoo: Cistercian Publications, 1986.

UNPUBLISHED MANUSCRIPTS

Farrell, James J. "The Madness of Sanity and the Sanity of Madness in the Nuclear Age." (Paper Presented at the convention of the Mid-America American Studies Association, 1992).

Hinman-Smith, David P. "Does the World Freedom Have a Meaning?: The Misissippi Freedom Schools, the Berkeley Free Speech Movement, and the Search for Freedom Through Education." Ph.D. dissertation: University of North Carolina, 1993.

Katz, Neil H. "Radical Pacifism and the Contemporary American Peace Movement: The Committee for Nonviolent Action, 1957–1967." Ph.D. dissertation, University of Maryland, 1974.

Reagon, Bernice Johnson. "Songs of the Civil Rights Movement 1955–1965: A Study in Culture History." Ph.D. dissertation: Howard University, 1975.

Scatamacchia, Cristina. *"Politics, Liberation,* and Radical Politics." Ph.D. dissertation: University of Missouri, 1990.

Skelly, James. "Power/Knowledge: The Problems of Peace Research and the Peace Movement." Paper prepared for presentation at the International Peace Research Association biannual meeting, 1986.

Snow, Craig Robert. "Folksinger and Beat Poet: The Prophetic Vision of Bob Dylan." Ph.D. dissertation: Purdue University, 1987.

Thorne, Barrie. "Resisting the Draft: An Ethnography of the Draft Resistance Movement." Ph.D. dissertation: Brandeis University, 1971.

Index

Here and now revolution 7, 8, 123, 172, 203, 215, 221, 229, 244, 252
Hershey, Lewis 165, 179
Highlander Folk School 77, 92, 102
Hippies 203, 212, 215–219, 221, 223, 227
Hiroshima 21, 37, 38, 41, 44, 114, 126, 172, 183
Hoffman, Abbie 9, 16, 121, 207, 222, 223
Holmes, John Clellon 63, 66, 67
Hoover, J. Edgar 22, 62
House Committee on Un-American Activities 133, 134
Household values 8, 88, 136, 234, 236, 246, 258
Human Be-In 219
Humanistic psychology 6, 16, 205–208, 211, 223, 228, 234, 235, 252
    self-actualization 206, 207, 230, 234
Humphrey, Hubert 70, 187
Huxley, Aldous 207, 209
Hypocrisy 8, 75, 101, 104, 106, 114, 144, 189, 199, 258 947

Ideology of liberal consensus 6, 70, 115, 131, 135, 152, 157, 171, 190, 258
Imperialism 164, 173, 176, 177, 193, 194, 196, 197, 259
In loco parentis 162
Individualism 7, 8, 10, 12, 13, 19, 23, 26, 28, 29, 36, 69, 130, 136, 142, 148, 204, 205, 210, 215, 228–230, 246, 248
Industrial Workers of the World 26, 28, 32, 59, 71
Institute for Local Self-Reliance 244
Institute for Social Ecology 239, 242
Intermediate Technology Development Group 244

Jazz 53, 58, 70, 71, 73, 168
Jefferson Airplane 213, 214
Jefferson, Thomas 123, 140
Jeffrey, Sharon 146, 235
Jenkins, Tim 140, 142

Jews 18, 45, 145
Johnson, Lyndon 50, 74, 104, 157, 174, 175, 184, 186–188, 192, 195, 196
Johnson, Mordecai 89
Jonah House 196
Jones, Rufus 116
Joplin, Janis 214
Just war 37, 41, 42, 173, 196
Justice 6, 7, 9, 18, 19, 29, 31, 37, 39, 41, 47, 65, 73, 82, 83, 84–89, 92, 94, 97, 99–101, 104, 105, 108, 109, 112, 116, 135, 141, 143, 152, 153, 169, 177, 181, 182, 185, 189–191, 199, 230, 248, 255, 257

Kandel, Lenore 220
Kaufman, Arnold 139, 142
Kaufmann, Walter 139
Keniston, Kenneth 226
Kennedy, Jacqueline 129
Kennedy, John F. 64, 74, 99–101, 122, 127, 130, 133, 154, 155
Kennedy, Robert F. 98, 187, 253, 259
Kent State 17
Kerouac, Jack 53, 59, 65–68, 75, 79, 139
Kerr, Clark 158, 159
Kesey, Ken 210
King, Martin Luther, Jr. 5, 6, 9, 13–15, 18, 48, 50, 53, 70, 74, 75, 80–95, 97, 98, 99–102, 104–107, 109–111, 118, 140, 145, 174, 177, 181, 187–189, 192, 205, 230, 251, 255, 259
    "Letter from Birmingham Jail" 100, 101
King, Coretta Scott 95, 133, 174
King, Mary 235
King, Ynestra 239
Krassner, Paul 183, 222
Kropotkin, Peter 24–26, 35, 54, 55, 119, 120, 123, 151, 243
Kupferberg, Tuli 208

Labor 9, 28, 37, 105, 122, 154, 155, 164, 184, 215, 254
Labor metaphysic 123, 149, 215
Land ethic 238

INDEX